THE GIRL WAR

CINEMATIC SCRIPT.

ontranslated from not not Nipponese by Denny Farrell

But aboriginally as iffffragmentiontentiffffied by: **IKIORTI NISHIOKA**

DEDICATION

TABLE OF CONTENTS

METAPHYSICAL CARTOON TRAGICOMDEY WITH SCREEN PLAY SET TO MUSIC

Summary of the musical scenes where the music tells the story without being bothered by the words.

1. Overture with 1.2 billion years of music leading up to egggrace.

2. Premiere scene with the Mesozoo under surveillance by the observatory.

3. First interlude with Alex heading for the bridge over the reved'e'er to be the hero.

4. Meeting at the bridge, where Gracie reveals her metaphysical alphabet's iffffe'er secretions. First aria of the opera.

5. Second interlude where Alex heads for the saloon where Gracie gets her gin.

6. Scene in the saloon where the ballad of Gracie's euphemyste'erious status is sonnetized.

7. Third interlude where Alex heads for the cathedral to find Gracie as chimed.

8. Scene in the cathedral where heaventilation systems show the first taken selfiy's signs of egggracessentiality of course, of course not not be breaking loose.

9. Mobible's electioneering sequences where the selectrocution tide is turned at the beached heads.

10. Scene VI where Gracie apologizes prolifffffffickly.......for being aborted from not not not being adequately impossible.

11. Scene VII where Alex faces the abandoned holocaust scenery.

12. Scene VIII where 1. Alex confronts Gracie at last 2. discusses Gracie's metaphysics 3. ends up with some alibis to save Gracie from dying out on behalf of a. the holocaust b. the girl war c. eternity as duh'd.

13. Scene IX- The second cathedral scene where Gracie's heaventilation system breaks through the stained glass, the sky and ifffffffe'ers in gene'eral.

14. Gracie's selectrocution as pope.

15. Gracie's vacation on sabbatical from metaphysics.

16. 16a. The eternity test site expe'eriment's ifffffloppedecidedly's city of angels.

17. 16b. Gracie's metaphysics revised at last as the opera ends ontentonally as cadenced.

BEHOLD SELFISHED OUT SINGULARITEASEGGGRACESCENT'S AS IFFFFFONTOCRACY!!! ....EGGGRAZING ON IFFFFFFF( )FFFFFFFFFE'ER...........HEAVENTILATING HOME

ONTOWNS OF NOT NE'ER'S NIGHT......ONTWINKLED STARS'S ONTINKLED TUNES.......ITCHURCHED TO SCRATCH ON CHALK BOARDS OF THE METAPHYSICAL SOCIETY......PREGNANT ZERO'S CHOSEN ONED'E'ER.........SOPRANOTABLY PERFUMONTSINGING IFFFE'EROMANCIPATIONTUNES......SMACK DAB IN THE MIDDLE OF THE MIDDLE OF THE MIDDLE OF MESOZOICKEY CHAINED ONT IDES OF E'ER'S IFFFFFFISHED OUT MISS ETERNITY PAGEANT.........WHENE'ER'D ONT I'M'E'EREALTY O'ER RUNNER UP REALITY. WHO COULD THIS BE BUT NONE (ONT I'M) OTHER THAN NOT NOT NATIVITY'S EGGGRACIE..... EGGGODOLLED UP..... SHE IT THOU ART......SWAMP SOUPOSING AS ONT I'M'EVOLITION'S APRIORIPITHECUS.......SHE IT SHATTE'ERING ALL OF'S AS IFFFFFOSSIL RECORDS...E'ERADIATING E'ER AS ETERNITY'S INTENDED AND MENU BRANDISHED HOLOCOAST TO COAST COULD BE'S CORPSINGER......BRIDE OF THE HOLOCAUST....MEANWHILE...... DISAPPROVING HER IMPOSSIBILITY TO BEGETTING WAY TOO DREAME'ERGENTRIFFFFF I'D FOR THE SPEED OF ENLIGHTENMENT TO EVER CATCH UP.

INDEED! EVENTUATEDLY ONT I'M'ALMIGHTNINGSTRUCKT IN OUT OF COULD BE'S IFFFFFE'ERS, THIS IS SELFISHED OUTING'S HOMETOWN WHATE'ER WHOLE'S EGGGRACIE THAT ALL OF'S WHATE'ER LOGGED ONT I'MASTERPIECED TOGETHER PUDDLES HAVE BEEN WAITING FOREVER TO BE ONT I'M'OPT UP FOR.

INDEED!! IN THIS PLAY ON WORDS WITH MUSIC WE FIND ONTEQUERIAN PETITIONER EGGGRACIE, ONT I'M'ACTUALLY ONT I'M'ASSEMBLED, WITH HER MAKE UP KIT MAKING ATTEMPTS ON THE LIFE OF ETERNITY WHILE 1. XXXE'ERATEDLY S'E'ERPASSING TENSE WITH HER EGGGIRLIFECTORY'S GIRL WAR PARTY GIRL WAVED STATUS AND 2. MEANWHILE OF COURSE, OF COURSE, NOT NOT ONT I'M'OUTHING E'ERCRAFT SCRAMBLED IFFFFLIGHT PATTERNS IFFFFLOUNDERING ON BEHALF OF E'ERELEGEND'S BECOMPLETELY PRESENTABLE ETERNITY.

IT'S ALL HERE, EVERYTHING YOU COULD WANT IN ONT I'MANSION'S ONTENTOPERA.........THE ONT I'MOBVIOUSELF-EVIDENCE OF 1. EGGGRACIE SUNNY SIDE UP. 2. EGGGRACIE'S SCRAMBLINKED SETTING SUNNY DAZE. 3. EGGGRACIE'S JUST A JIFFFY JARGON. 4. EGGGRACIE'S IFFFFFE'ERUSHED ONT I'M APPOINTMENTS. 5. D'ESSGRACIE'S E'ERBRUSHED OFF ONTRAGICOMIC ALL BUT TIME OUT.....LOW DOWN, CHEAPUNK, SPARE PARTS.........OPE'ERATICKSTINCTION. YES! ALL THAT! PLUS!!! WHATE'ER'D OWN'D IFFFFFFFFINITY'S IFFFFFONT I'MATHEMATICS........ IFFFFFEATURING COULD BE CALCULUSTY IFFFFONTENSE'ER'S JUST AJIFFF ONT I'M'EQUATIONS.....ASIMULATEDLY E'ERIDING SHOTGUN WITH......... THE TO BECOMPREHSIFFFFFFFLY UNHUMILIATED NOT/NOTNOT CODE OMEGALPHABETING SCRIPTE'ER'D AS......a. BEGUILED EGGGRACIE'S IFFFFFEATS ENTRIPPING ON BEMANNAPPEALS b. EGGGRACIE'S IFFFFABRICATED ETERNITY TEST SITE EXPE'ERIMENTATION c. EGGGRACIE'S ONT I'MADVENTURES........( )........ONT I'M'AXISTENTIALLY CO-ORDINATED AS.......x. AT THE IDES OF IFFFFFFE'ER'S HALF TIME

SHOW. y. ON THE CROSS. z. BACKT UP AVE'ERTEGOINGIRLIPSPIRIT FACED IN COUNTY IFFF....E'ER'S........ BABEBLICKISSINGING COFFIN, WHOSE EGGGUEST KNOWS WHAT'S TO BECOME OF EGGGRACED ONT I'M'E'ERITY.

ALL IN ALL, THIS IS THE WHOLEGGGRAILAVISH SPECTACLE HEAVENTILATING E'ER WAVED WHENE'ER'S PARTY.....GIRLINK'D TO NOT NE'ER'S NIGHT LIFE, SUITABLE FOR THE FIRST TIME E'ER'D ONT I'M'AUDIENCES TO E'ERAVE ABOUT EGGGRACIE'S EUPHEMYSTE'ERIOUS IFFFONTRANSCENDENCY'S ONTWAR'D ONTULTIMATOMICK......ONTOLD YOU SOWN ONT I'D THOU ART. PLUS!!!! IFFFFURTHE'ER ONT I'METIFFFORED AS MINED..........THIS IS THE E'ERCRAFT PERFUMANCE E'EREPRESENTING ONT I'METAPHYSICS EGGGAMBLINKT TO ONTRAGICOMIC BET E'ER'S BESTUNG BEBLICAL BEHEST. INDEED!!! PEDOLLED UP AS IFFFFFFFFIN ONTUNED.......IFFFONT I'MANALYZED.....................HERE'S WHOLEGGGRAILEAKAGE'S WHATE'ER........AS IFFFFONTOLOGGED.......THAT ONLY NOONE'S (NO MATTER HOW DUH'D) M'ETERNITY WANTS ....WHENE'ERIZONED.........WITH SHE IT I'D THOU ART.........NOT NOT TO BE MISS MISSING'S BABEBLINKAGE......AS IFFFFONT I'MISSED OUT ON.

AUTHOR

Denny Farrell's Ikiorti Nishioka was a lifelong student of the ontique'erian equivalents of Buddhist ethicosmontology. In this play Farrell's Nishioka employs much of the new linguistic devices developed by that philosophical discipline to add a metaphysical overlay to the Girl War legend that is the foundation of the opera's dramatic structure. The Girl War legend has many incarnations going back through the centuries and the modern version that is here employed is only the latest in a long line of legendary accounts of the life of whate'er'd'own'd justajifffonthing's egggracie, the central character in the opera. Putting the legend to the disposal of a modern symphony orchestra is pretty nowsy news however. What exists of the score and libretto, it must be noted iffffurther, is only to be found in as ifffffffragmentions. The editors have arduously consolidated these fragments for the publication of this book. Ikiorti himself, traveling the world, spent the last days of whooegggrailife styled life in ont I'monaste'eroid justajifff's Japan. This play nominally remains Ikiorti's only important work in the field of classical music drama. It remains a nonontrivial spectacularization of euman literature's point of ont I'm'aborigination, which is to say the singularity that sets the stage for the dawn of euman existence dreame'erging out of the Mesozoic era to find Egggracie as the aboriginal ont I'mother of the baby's he's us of us all.

*THE GIRL WAR MADE SIMPLE FOR FILM MAKERS

1. NOTES ON PRODUCTION- The text that you are about to read is metaphysically far too elaborate for cinematic audiences. Its impenetrable metaphysical jargon will no doubt cause many readers (asiffffffffffffits)fits. However, the metaphysical impenetrability of the play can readily be stripped down to manageable dramatic proportions. Many readers may find this stripped down cinematic setting the most becomfortable way to encounter this drama. Otherwise…..since a certain degree of linguistic overload is inevitable while dealing with such advanced metaphysical topics, the reader must bring his highest ontellectual resources to the reading of this opera's foundational texts. While much metaphysical excess may be removed for cinematic productions (SEE SECTION 7) the overly elaborated philosophical implications must remain bestung best intact.

In that regard, it must be admitted that even the preliminary paragraphs designed to pablamize the play's metaphysical becomplexities, may be more than the average reader'S OQIQ (ontelligentry intelligence quotient) can handle. As such, it may be best to ignore these introductory paragraphs and go straight to the screen play at the conclusion of this volume.

I should confess right here and now that this opera was designed less for human audiences than eumanized becomputer audiences, of such a time whenever they become available to experience metaphysical opera as entertaining. So, if you are not an ontellectually sophisticated becomputer…you might just skip ahead to that plain English summary of the action. Because……..

What we have here is a preposte'erologically becomplex onslaught of 'ontantrumminated onthought' that has no precedent in operatic literature. And the controversies s'e'erounding the play's metaphysical jargon are not the end of the controversies that the opera, as a whole, must face. Other cultural controversies arise in the course of the drama as well. However,……. such an opera can only occur, poetically speaking:

> When whate'er'down'd iffffontiffffacts
> Own whene'er'swings cartoon'd indeed's
> I'd bestungs becomicky acts
> Whose staged performance self-proceeds.

Given this situation it is to be noted that the texts may be culturo-linguistically streamlined over all to make for suitable production. Simplified, as such, to its most basic dramatic elements, the opera offers few impediments to performance. Where alternative lyrics are presented, the hope is to make the opera translatable from English back into Japanese and other (Asian and nearby occasioned) languages. For

English speakers the texts can be made more manageable by removing prefixtures with jargonistic ampliffffficatiions……*onts….ents…..iffffffs….e'ers*….and the like. It should be noted further that, while the story begins with sumwhat's e'erather xxxrated conservative ifffontenthemes, the story's ideological orientation does achieve some degree of balance in the final analysis. This is an opera unlike any other and the opera's central character is a heroine unlike any dramatic personality before her. As such there are a lot of preliminaries to get through before we can arrive at the full text of the libretto. Let me here offer my assurance that full aesthethical engagement with the dramatico-metaphysical becomplications of the story will reward the reader for patience sustained through all of's ifffont I'mythiqueries egggrace dreame'ergency projects. Whenever gigantic words attached to long strung-out sentences do occur, it's best to have a simple-minded laugh at the justajiffffffy jokes that you just know must be lurking in those syntactic structures. I would say in this regard that, should the play over load your readership skills by begetting too ont I'metaphysically I'messote'erick….you might skip reading it, like I said, and skip to the cinematic screen play version at number 7 in the table of contents. Should you want to make a motion picture about egggracie it's the screen play that you will want to evaluate. Put that screen play together with the musical score and you've got the most metaphysically ontente'ertaining emotion picture in history, human, euman or otherwise.

But for those who insist on plowing through this ont I'm'essy not ne'er's nightly narrative here's a couple of quotes to consider:

Jeder Engel ist schrecklich- Duino Elegies

Every angel is ont e'erable-The Girl War.

That lowliness serves young ambition's ladder,

Whereto the climber-upward turns his face

Julius Caesar Act II Scene I

But I am constant as the northern star,

On whose true-fix'd and resting quality

There is not fellow in the firmament…

Julius Caesar Act III Scene I

There is a tide in the affairs of men,

Which taken at the flood, leads on to fortune

Omitted, all the voyage of their life

Is bound in shallows and in miseries.

Julius Caesar Act IV Scene III

Tis night, but tis not never's night

Of a priori e'ers.

The Romance of Being Book I

We as the gods, gods for a day

Meanwiley once in whiled upon

Tale headlines of heroblty

To whelm almighty's question.

The Romance of being Book V

To fetch to be ifffffffff(.)fffffetchingly

As ifffe'er craft to becommends

Iffffffully{{{{fun}}}} eternity

With all of's afte'er'd happy ends

To fall (in love) onto to be.

The Romance of Being. Book end.

THE GIRL WAR- The operatic cartoon by Ikiorti Nishioka ontranslated from Nippontical language (just ajifffffy's Japanese) to ontransmodern day Linguish.

It must be confessed at the outset that this opera dramatizes many controversies, ontequerian, cosmopolitan and societal. To witness a cosmic demigod e'erefreshing his ont I'm'etaphysics courtesy of lectures from an egg (a Greek god receiving instruction from an egg) may be shocking to some in the ope'erational audience. The heaventilated humility of this dramatic situation after all does defy normal protocol at the social, philosophical and spiritual level. As such while this opera may be safe for conservative Nippontial audiences and their cousins in related latitudes, it may not be securable for others. What we have here is metaphysics dramatized ontraumatickly to a point of hardly any return…..but………..

Before going any further than this essay has gone before, Gracie's metaphysics, which is what this opera is mostly all about, should be grasped in its ont I'm'utte'er'd simplicity.

1. Eternity is more than a mathematical construct of non-finite temporality.

2. Any given objective universe must be ontenterpreted as a mere samplifffffication of ontiquely storaged large'erealty

3. The monolithic concept of 'BEING' recast as the binary construct of 'NOTNOTITUDE' is crucial to this e'erather ontique estate of all of's ifffffe'ers as far as this eternity's to be concerned.

4. The not/notnot code is the preposte'erological alphabet for this ontheoretical eternity set up.

5. The next door neighborly news'e'ervice of presentED tenses make eternity presentABLE ont I'me'ergent ontempe'erally for more than entemporal mathematical evaluation as aided by wholegggrailenses.

Straight from the chalk boards of the metaphysical society, the results of these postulates can be stated quite plainly with justajiffffffy jargon. 1. Iffffffffirst of all there's *ontitude*. 2. Which, iffffffaster than split seconds, nextitutdinates eventually on to *e'er*. While becomplications may iffffffffollow, the rest is just e'er samples, assortments of things that sometimes, for the life of to be, look like universes, immersing ontitude in objectionable eclips'e'ervice, as behaves to be to be too obvious to not be in hiding to those who operate primarily with equations backed up by lenses. Gracie's attempts to ontoilet train eternity, of course must be met with strictest's kepticism. The vagaries of how she plans to pull this off constitute a dramatic warning to all metaphysical s'e'eroptimystics inclined toward such e'ereligiously expe'erimental ambitions. In this regard it must be admitted that all those controversies about Gracie winning the Miss Eternity Pageant over runner up reality are beside the appointments she ontends to schedule for eternity. Whatever coolifications she might enjoy by getting way too pretty, way too fast, do not necessarily ontitle her for success in such projects. Entissued as Gracie may be to coolifffffffy to be dreamergent or not is be noted for strictly dramatic purposes within the confines of this play. The transascendency of her smile (as simulated) is becompletely beside the appointments she makes on ontique shopping sprees in ontique shoppes scat e'er'd e'eround nextitudinated nowsy news as distributed by ontitude's binarily beconstructed notnotitudinal behavior. Scenery wise, with hardly any parallels to her likeness (in either Mesozoic mirrors or swamp puddles)….Gracie's self evidensity requires no auditions to be obvious. As such, she must be evaluated through becombinations of both aesthethical terms and ethical terms……to be seen as one of those atypical onteenage euphemystical *asiffffreaks* whose charm nestles right up next to dog spelled backwards as iffffffffigured beyonding the grounds of good. As far as Gracie's concerned of course, of course not not…her status as the once up ont I'm one egggirl holocaust singularity at the dawn of the Metazoic cannot be over ont I'mentioned as ont I'mansion'd as ontent I'm'estated.

To sume'erize........in many ways this opera's just sum's egggastars scentimentally e'eromatured e'eromacipating as ifffffffflux in a puniversion's p-universe, in which case its tale stinks all of's way danced to high heaven where no iffffenced in offense need be ontaken. Or...or...or...like...like.....like...you might say.....like....like..... this opera's all about sum's she it's wholegggrailover's over the's e'erainbow's egggracie with dibs dubbed pretty high up on the Y-not axis of I'd thou artesian's could be coordinate system regarding World War Whenever's egggirl ifffe'ers... with dibs smack'dubbed......smack dab in the middle of the middle of the middle of the Mesozoic that's smack dabbled in the middle of the middle of the middle of some egggastars (in and out of e'ereturns) smack dabbled in the middle of the middle of the middle of the's ides of e'er's preposte'erously asifffffontique eternity that is more than a mathematical construct of non-finitemporality. Either way looked at in either ont I'mirrors or...or...or..... preposte'erology's puddles of whate'er, it should be pretty ontente'ertaining for anyone auditioned to be obviously notnotitudinatifffffff I'd by nowsy news'e'ervices notnotitudinally native to ontrophickly presentable eternity.

Perhaps there are egggrains of ontentruth in that ifffffffamous quote from the iffffffflight wing at the ont I'm'annual's beble bazaar at the metaphysical society.

"Concerning such a thing as egggracie, there's a long becosmetrick justajiffffffy journey to countenance whate'er as ifffontentale'er'd to beheaded as iffffffffe'ercraft.......of course...of course...not...not..... asifffreaked out ifffffrequencies of iffffffontentovations as m'estated in ifffffont I'mansion's canteen aged whate'er's wholegggrailit likessential such a thing as a gracie". This quote does beget us sum's what not n'e'er'd to this ope'eration's ontentendencies toward backward e'erunnerup reality's cosmically cartooned coverup's ontentruths.

E'ergo....as far as the drama goes.....it should be conside'er'd as neighborly nowsy news that, before this ope'eration begets too carried away with its egggracystemic self-evidensity.........WHOLEGGGRACIE must be admitted to not not be indeed a very quasi coolifffffied iffffffffff( )ffffffffreaked out character. And all this in spite of justajiffffy's I'mopped up onto janite'erial attempts to replace such a thing as Gracie's self with anybody's everybody else's self. These attempts, like I almost didn't quite say, had almost becompletely succeeded by the time of the opera's performance. In spite of puddles of high evidensities to e'erequirments for no ifffffurther auditions to be obvious.......(PLUS! Indeed coolifffffffffying as could be's coolest ontenthing's dansingule'erity's ever)........ Gracie's brain had indeed been m'e'erode side killed down to almost m'anyone's no one. BUT, like, iffffffffffreak'd out as she may or may not begotted as way, way too pretty way too fast for the Mesozoic to keep up with her like aesthethical wholegggrailaw sum's egggodditease as masterpieced together in the puzzles of virtually all of's vanities in all of's puddle's onthermodynamisms she attends, her neverthelessons in metaphysics are nevertheless worthy of s'e'erious lit e'er'd almightning struck wholegghostal outhousing's beaconside'erations. Whether alive, stinct or m'e'erly possible, while performing her I'magick tricks, as with brooms, wands, halos (which she has) or wings (which she hasn't....except)...1. Baptizing whate'er in Scene II or 2. Preposte'erating pompominations to end scene VIII, either way it must be admitted that Gracie, behaviored(half) brain dead as she does, does coolifffffffffffffff( )fffffffffffffy as quite wholegggracystemick's euphemystickly iffffreaked out euphemyste'eriously beblicall's could be countenanced.........mesozoickly misplaced, ontranscent, metazoic charismatickly characte'erized specimen of ontosis.

As such, dramatico-musically, dreamelodically speaking, this opera's mostly about Gracie's quest to beget out from under the results of World War Whene'ers GIRL WAR. Getting way too pretty, way too fast… plus winning the Miss Eternity Pageant as party girled just waved at runner up reality…..Gracie of course, of course not…not…was beheld to be the girl war's e'eresponsible's alibilessess. Saddled to the mesozoo while vainly realizing the importance of her ontheoretical e'ercraft victory (as aprioried over prior meaty physics) Gracie decided to dump a universe and set out onto the great unknown's whate'erways. Insomnibus'd in her own private e'ercraft, that's whenever…..Gracie went straight to the chalk boards of the metaphysical society to change e'erealty as egggoddifffffff I'd for dog spelled backwards. Just prior to the opera proper there is an overture conveying the music of just under log 17 base 10 seconds. As the overture progresses we find Gracie auditioning to be obvious from pregnant zero all of's way danced up to dolled up iffffffffffffffinity on the y-not axis of I'd thou artesian graphs. Not far up this axis Gracie becomes to onthat's haloidable metaphysical decision.

As far as Gracie's been all at once concerned…………cosmic (gas cloud) history could pretty much e'ergo to hell. She's into notnotitude for the d'e'eriffffffation's hard core heaventitilated'e'eration. Metaphysics was where it *ontwas at* as whate'er'd iffffffont I'm in the middle of the middle of the middle of her new ontestimental beblicalculuste'er'd book. Iffffffurthe'ermore's e'eresults of such considerations sooner than later were said to blaspheme in all blasphemable dimensions, with academic implications for eternity at large. As such egggracie offe'ers iffffffonthese ont I'm'estated e'eresults……1. Academically speaking, the discipline of physics must be conside'er'd as subservient to metaphysics. 2. As such, any lunched on universe's digestion must be subse'ervient to ont I'munched ontrophickly presentable eternity. 3. All lightning strikes by thunderstorms must be conside'er'd subse'ervient to almightning strikes from whate'er's iffffonte'er's whether or not not's onthund'e'er'd whene'er. 4. Gracexistism is to be closeted, with scene VI crossed out, as a side issue brought up for strictly innocuous purposes. 5. Likewise, all spectacular occurrences s'e'erounding Gracie's existence must be categorized as either miracles or magic tricks or both, depending on the theoretical setup's situation. In that regard it should be no s'e'erprize entrophically speaking that many Mesozoic circles e'eresentfully view Gracie's ont I'magic tricks as blaphem'e'erickles in virtually all blapheme'eraculous dimensions. Pregnant zero's *one* can imagine their vice gripped cringe valuation when Gracie's splatte'er'd rainbow halobotenticles have to be mopped up by just ajiffffffy's janitor s'e'ervice grippages in Scene XI.

OK SO LIKE….LIKE….LIKE……. HOWEVER!!!!!!! Operationally speaking, now that we got that out of the way, let's review what Gracie's eternity is up to…………..a priori premises wise.

1. Eternity's more than a mathematical construct of non-finite temporality.

2. A universe is just a samplifffffication of a larger e'eration'd e'erealty. Call it a p-universe when you smell it, call it a puniverse when you compare it to becompletely presentable eternity…either way, in the's iffffffffffinal analysynthesis, it's not e'ereally that big a deal. It's just a motel we check into while e'eresearching the subject of NOTNOTITUDE as nextitudinvativized ontologgedly in onto be's nowsy news'e'ervice.

3. For mathematicians the equation that operates this ope'eration is the ontraditional iffffamous pregnant zero equation......... $\{\{\{+ 0 = +\}\}\}$.

4. D'iffe'erontical ont I'm'equations make up most of Gracie's ontense'er calculus which is the same could be of course, of course not...not...calculus of Gracie's e'erevolitionary newsy new alphabet......THE NOT/NOTNOT CODE.

Ok, so like, jargon-wise let's take an aprioriluminary inventory. E'eright off the alphabetingods we've got $\{\{\{NOTNOTITUDE\}\}\}$ which is like Gracie's big $\{\{I\}\}$ deal and becomes with its own alphabet, that's difffe'eront from the tetrahedral cosmic code and the 0/1 information code. It's the $\{\{\{\{NOT/NOTNOT\}\}\}$ iffffffffffformation code that accounts for anything that sooner or later becomes not not next door to everything's anything. How does it do this you may ask. Well, it's eternity's nowsy news'e'ervice working notnotitude e'ereligiously, pregnant zero's one might say, to do (SHALL WE SAY DOG SPELLED BACKWARDS) s'e'ervice. Among dog spelled backward's as iffffffffffffffontalents are the ont I'metamathematical maintenance of infinities be kept iffffffffinitizable as applied in metaphysical applications of presentable e'er craft.

When all else fails with eternity at loose ends the opera eventually finds Gracie ontantrumminating eternity to be forgiven or not forgiven for its lack of performance ontalents at the becompletion of her'd to be's I ambitions as scheduled to becompleted e'eresurrections at the eternity test site. E'eritual moments of silence are occasionally observed on behalf of quite possibly duh'd eternities in the midst of (church bell dingalink'd) calls for become and beget its ifffffarmothe'er's ont I'meals. As Gracie herself points out, eternity should be subject to e'eritual appeasement's whate'er ontight iffffffont-iffffffflattery, which buys into sooner or later's being iffffffforgiven. The way gracie iffffffigures it.....let me quote her from this cut out of the opera, "SO LIKE ETERNITY'S BEGOT THIS FAR. WHY NOT ALL OF'S WAY......like all of's way danced e'eromancipating fux to more than just be kidding." It seems that Gracie's caught herself as iffffffffffffffff( )ffffffffffished out of whate'er, e'eresearching god olde iffffashioned e'er's e'eroutines, walking all over whate'er....like...as twe'er'ed e'eright onthroughout spaced out e'er's e'er ever since those iffffffatefull ont I'momontents at the chalk boards of the metaphysical society. Lucky for Gracie, that, dramatico-herstorickly speaking, Alex shows up ont I'm'd(albeit e'ereluctontly) to be the hero and to salvage the girl. Thank dog spelled backwards, it's right in the middle of the middle of the middle of Gracie's big time ontantrumminations that Alex does or does not step in to 1. Head out of strictly to beconside'erations for the moment. 2. Head back to the universe for a few secondhand seconds. 3. Be the hero that saves the girl.....by a. walking the ontentight rope between a universe and an eternity. b. Sum'swhat shyly, behaving no spinal columns in the back rows of the bleacher seating of the play pen's set theory. c. Not...not....not....relaxing all thumbs on the girl war triggers. Take this as a hint that, at the moment when the tragicomicartoon of the opera decides whether or not to be a tragedy or a comedy......Alex (as both becombination geek god and scientist) must roll the dice of the last man standing by holding the bottle on the 'other' hand while holding the other hand that is the only hand Gracie can hold on to to be saved.

Saved for what you may ask. To be salvaged back to the sticks and stones of a tool users universe perhaps. Well, if so, then back to the same outhoused universe that wasn't ontoylet trained when the opera started…smack dab in the middle of the middle of the middle of objections to becompletely presentable eternity's subjections. No, Iffffont I'm'eternity wards would never stand for that. Alex is a sort of like………dogI'med spelled backwards plus in disguise after all. As a demigod of sorts, as it turns out he does have a chariot in the garage that occasionally does escort the sun around the sky on a semi-daily basis. Well things are looking up for Gracie after all. We might catch a glimpse of her (in after operations) riding off into a setting's sunny day in A(pol)lex's chariot if it weren't for her dumping the chariot to get left off a nearly now's insomnibustop. Since this story's becompletely out of music…….there is no harmonic heaventilation any more just Gracie, in the kitchen looking for a can opener on a lighthouse beaconversation as onteleophoned.

(At this point the reader's soul should be soulevating ontent blasphemansions in all blasphemable dimensions where all these ont I'm'adumbrations are all about in justajiffffy's iffffinal ont I'manalysis.) So what does the reader beget out of all these becomplicated aftermathematicalibrations.

Well, the reader shouldn't be too disappointed with such a chewed onto be popped beble gummy ending. After all, as a reader he has been exposed to a meta-meaty physically fascinating character who has the power to transform the way we think about metaphysics, universes and iffffffffffinity.

Plus, ontente'ertainmentwise……we have been becompensated for our participation as an audience for Gracie's self-evidence. Also…we did get to imagine such a thing as egggracie's paper products sunny side up on the why not axis of the I'd thou artesian coordinate system's e'eromacipated paper flux. Plus….applying the {{ + 0 = + }} equation to real life dramatic situations……we got to learn about wholegggrailaw sum's scale of asiffffences begot pinned up on the crossed outing. And then half time at the big aim-wise, we did beget to behold Gracie's pompoms pageantriffffffffffying dreame'ergence of could be's care tuned cartoons ontanimitating e'ereal live action. As a result, we got to see why justajiffffffans devoted to Gracie for pope, do really believe that it was Gracie's spirit face after all that did more to e'eromancipate iffffffffffffluxt iffffux than anything else presentable eternity's e'er's asiffffffffe'ereproduced in like…like…e'eresurrection setups.

And then academickly speaking, we got exposed to a wholegggrailottery of whate'er's cooliffffffontellectual justajiffffy jargon. We learned how {{BEING}} as a monolithic term can be converted to {{NOT NOT BEING}} as a beblickly binary terminology of e'ercrafted e'er begetting e'eround and doing ontenticled stuff. We learned how e'ereal stuff is ffffffirst personally to be conside'er'd to be just ONT I'M. We learned how iffffffffffff( )ffffffffffffffffinite presentable eternity e'ereally just might be. We learned that (sounding just like air) e'er's also short forever. Yep! Justajiffffy's jargon, auditions to be obvious for better e'eretensions whenever xmas eve becomes e'eround. However, ontellectually low our I Q was before the overture began, the chalk boards at the metaphysical society read like iffffffffiguredolled up ground's graffiti once the story's had its say.

So…..linguistically speaking, the manner in which this opera may be said to ontalk eternity involves sum's learning curved upwards of what ont I'mathematickly could be compassed by several ontense'er calculuste'er'd'e'eriffffatives. Iffffurthermore…..with accounting going way past infinity all of's way up to iffffffffffinity, Gracie's linguishing becompasses eternity as a whole, albeit with holes in it. As such Gracie's metaphysics is inclined to dispense with the puniverse and go for the BIG TIME, which is her ontique shopping spree eventuating to way, way, way past second hand cosmic clock immersion time. Speaking of which…..since sum'd some of the talk is eternity ontalk, sum's some of the language is to be found in Gracie's metaphysical ontique shoppe. Linguistically speaking this has implications for Gracie's prefix patterns. Most words starting with 't' are prefaced by 'ont'(being) as most words starting with 'r' are prefaced by 'e'er'(ever). Note as well application of the French first person singular direct object pronoun applied to vowel M'environments where notnotitude's ont I'mphatick selfish is being called on.

The reader will also have to beget ont I'm'accustomed to simulations of justajifffy jargon in the form of grammatical sequences like "LIKE…LIKE….LIKE….LIKE". Simulation wise, such sequences can of course, of course not not be quite ont I'mannoying. In the few (log 4 base 10) seconds in eternity that this opera's performance demands, the audience will just have to beget used to being ont I'mannoyed in this ont I'manne'er. By way of consolation, consider how these new word encounters may be said to be giving the reader a tale's head start in dealing with ifffffffffffished out iphphphphilosophical language that is destined to be normalized in the dictionaries of the distant linguishtic future. Nonetheless, even if ontique terminology does not not not prolife'erate in the linguistic future, being part of the almightning struck onterminological elite is not something to dismiss cavalierly as it does I'mprove one's over all ont I'm'education. Of course, this is just the sort of thing scientists have warned about whenever metaphysics abandons an objective universe in orde'er to be a shopper in subjectionable eternity. And in Gracie's case this is not just any eternity. It is tobecompletely presentable eternity based on 1. Notnotitude and 2. Nextitudinated neighborly nowsy news s'e'ervice. As such the audience can be assured that these difficulties e'ercraft the not n'e'erative smack dab in the middle of the middle of the middle of

sum's ifffffffffffffffffffffffffffffffffffff( )fffffffffffffffffffffffffffffffffffffinity that is way, way, way…… past infinity.

Sooooooo. Just to sume'erize these summaries of what this opera's eternity's up to…….

1. To becompletely presentable….like……ontaboriginally onteleologically always just ont I'm. I mean like, as far as Gracie's concerned, this eternity's not wasting any's iffffontime, as far as she can help it.

2. To serve for Gracie's ontrophic metaphysics to be applianced to almost becompletely disregard entrophic meaty physics.

3. To take place on the chalk boards of the metaphysical society during the just aftermathematics of the girl war holocoaste'erides on e'er.

4. To s'e'ervice grip the {0 + = +) equation's emergence as a special subset of the large'er asfffffframework of Gracie's ifffontense'er could be calculus.

Ok, so that's where we find her, dreame'ergentrifffff I'd as can be, smack dab in the middle of the middle of the middle of always nowsy's news broadcast, ifffffrantickly dibbing dubs on everything she can get her onthumbed trigger finge'erwand on, just after just under log 17 base 10 seconds of overture, standing backlit on the Mesozoic township of World War Whenever's GIRL WAR OPERATIONS.

fv GIRL…….LIKE…LIKE BLASPHEMING BEBLISTICKLY IN ALL BLASPHEMABLE D'E'ERECTIONS…………….. ………….BACK (BEFORE THE GIRL WAR) WHEN SHE WAS STILL OF

COURSE…OF COURSE…NOT…NOT…..BEING MASTERPIECED TOGETHER IN ALL OF'S PUDDLES TO WIN THE MISS ETERNITY PAGEANT OVER RUNNER UP REALITY.

How did she win the Miss Eternity Pageant you ask. 1. By getting way too pretty way too fast for enlightenment's iphelossitease to keep up with. 2. By reminding reality that a. An abandoned universe is one thing but b. An abandoned eternity is quite sumother's. Gracie estates this could be candidly in justajiffy jargon. I quote: "An abandoned universion's one enthing but an abandoned ont I'm'eternity is quite sumothe'er's onthing else's ont I'm elsiffffactore I'd I'mined."

Iffffffff this ontests your iffffontalented e'ereadershipmentality then so be it. Read onward unless you e'ereally have no I'd e'eregarding what egggracie's (as such) metaphysics just might (as such) be (in justajiffy) as ifffffffffffff( )fffffffffffall about.

Good thing Gracie sings to keep you entertained while becoming as ifffffused to onte'ertainment values in egggracie's preposte'erological ont I'metaphysics. Pretty ontough stuff for whate'er's iffffont I Qs underocks. The's e'ereader has my ffffffished out sympathologicky becompanionship in this ifffffe'eregard.

1. Ontextualizations Of Eternity

But before we get to the easy not so way too obviousiffffffffied like sticky stufft equations with their p-universe's smelly sentences……let's string you on a little's longe'er as a programmatical puppet in this operation's egggreat unknown. Ok so like………In an immature puppy dogod universe, not becompletely ontoylet trained, within the could be confines of a preposte'erously ont I'mature eternity, perhaps Gracie must be seen as a prematurely iffffreaked out manifffffffffffffffestation's xmas eve of presentable eternity's xmas day. How ontiquely e'eresourceful this eternity's notnotitude of course, of coursediffffficates………must remain as speculation for the inhabitants of e'erealty's portopotties. Apart from the bleacher seating at the chalk boards of the metaphysical society, pregnant zero's *one* can only wait e'eround to as ifffffffind the's answers. Ifffirst personally I'd thou art's aesthethics (whenever the's opportunes e'erise, justajifffffiwise………once upon ont I'm mightning struck) you just might church to check out.

Apart from aesthethics there's also ethics to be thought about in Gracie's regard. When Gracie does her pompom routines on behalf of {{of course, of course not not to care}}, does she really care about all those traffic jams in the bleacher seating like when she's performing her half time show at the big aim. I mean does she care, but really, for all those people buried under not being such a thing as egggracie. Or is she only concerned for such a thing as egggracie being buried under the people being buried. I mean the demographics of this is bewilderinging bells to say the least. In her defense one might say that, as everybody who's anybody's pin up on the cross (in scene IX) she is after all pretty self-evidently just too obvious to grab at with the manners of occupiers of occupation territory. I mean this entire opera takes place just after the girl war……..smack dab in the middle of the middle of the middle of the Mesozoic when everybody's either already digested or on the menu or seated in the bleachers or carving up gracie as sooner's later undertaken underhandedly what's to be taken as more or less the least.

But let's not get cosmickly immersed in the swamp performance that forgets us to remember what Gracie's metaphysics is all about. I mean there is the universe after all with everybody whose anybody involved like…like…ratrapped on a plot thin goof. Metaphysically speaking, of course of course not not, Gracie puts all that on the sidelines of the becompletely presentable eternity that she's becompletely presented to be (notnot) up for. You have to remember she's discarded universes from the ground of notnotitude ever since her holocoasterides on e'er in kindergarden.

What cooliffffffffffffies Gracie through all of this psychopathology is indeed 1. Her ontaboriginally onteleological perspective she maintains throughout. 2. Her iffffreaking out way, way too pretty for the Mesozoic's speed of enlightenment to keep up with her. 3. Her willingness to care while being smack dabbed in the middle of the middle of the middle of the Mesozoic in the middle of the middle of the middle of the ides of e'er's half time show where she's performing the pompom e'eroutines for all of's ont I'muscle pumped up promotion pictures. I mean, like, becomont; give the girl credentials on the why not axis of the could be coordinate gracystem. You can bad mouth gracie as bad as gracie bad mouths outer space, but noone's going to buy your alibis. We only hate-crime the girl so we can love-crime the girl. Like raping her halo with natur'ds is what we do with doo while bottomed out as what we really are. Noone's fooling anybody with her halo tarantulated into gibberish.

When talking about Gracie, you always have to keep in mind her transascent of entrophic meaty physics into e'erealms of ontrophic metaphysics. As far as she's concerned, no kidding, the constellations which she can't help but twinkle to inhabit, the Mesozoic and the girl wars corralled into a cosmic background..... can't completely eclipse becompletely presentable eternity that (ontrophickly speaking) is the prize that she is after after all is said and sung and done. Ont I'menuwise undigestible onte'er'ds replace ugleefully speaking's, digestible enturds in the's e'eresults. Ontheorized, that's the setting in these parts as far as this wave's party girl's concerned.

But one last note. The fact that the university curriculum is still on the menu when the opera begins is to be ont I'm'academickly ontenticipated. Eternities annex universes and universes must becommissioned by could be's curriculum. As far as that curriculum is to of course not not to be concerned, several controversies e'erise in the course of the opera without resolution. 1. Ifffffff indeed eternity is ontiquely shoppable, can appointments be scheduled with presentable eternity. 2. How far into the's eventualitease of nowsy news'e'ervice can notnotitude onticipate iffffffe'eresults. 3. Is e'er really without alibis for could be crimes against notnotitude. 4. How degrading for notnotitude is being pooped out of egggravitational space. 5. Can dreame'ergencies happen without stars to dream them. 6. What prospects can the Mesozoic s'e'eriously offer for metazoic eventualities. 7. Just how far into such eventualities can of coursiness be ontaken. 8. Does gracexistism really deserve its XXXXX( )XXXXXRATING. 9. Is there really such a thing in the gracexistist sense as *acutely pretty* or like...like....like... just plain *cute.* 10. What e'eresults can be onticipated from the eternity test site situation. 11. Is such an ontenthing as Gracie e'ereally possible at all. 12. How extravagantly does this opera underestimate eternity as a wholegggraile'er'd whole. 13. Gods or no gods, is eternity s'e'ereal.

So there you have it; after an overture of 1.2 billion years, as the opera begins, the Mesozoic is on the menu, and in the middle of the middle of the middle of the Mesozoic, the girl war has happened, becomplicating World War Whenever with such a thing as egggracie begetting buzzed (to be stung) way too pretty way too fast for the speed of enlightenment to not not be keep up. After log 17 base 10 seconds of incoherent apriothe'erization adumbrating dreamergence theory (through dramurgentrial's iffffartistry).........Gracie's aprioripithecus spirit face does make an appearance, becompletely drame'ergentriffied ontopping off ontotem policy's e'ergo summitry outings. That is where we find her as the log 16 base 10 seconds of overture concludes. She is standing, backlit, gazing down on the Mesozoic township of the girl war operation's girl war operational sand boxed in just kidding's playground ine'erena. But first let's strip search through this iffffe'ery tale outside of its progenitor Linguish dialect. Let's summarize it in ordinary English.

APOLOGY FOR
HOLOCAUST BECOMPLICATIONS

Whenever the question of holocausts comes up it is the bought and paid for rule that only certain definitive examples of such events may be allowed to matter. Often blasphemergencies crop up with any exceptions to that rule. Blaspheming in all dimensions, egggracies story may seem to violate that rule. Let us clarify. The shallowest research of human history reveals what can only be described as chains of holocaustial victim events, one after another, where one speciman of victimhood leads to another. Indeed, holocaust exchanges seem to run rampant throughout history. Addressing the holocaust issue metaphorically, since all human beings start out as eggguests in a barn yard nutrient factory, the roles of 1. Predatory kitchen appliance 2. Menu prey are found endlessly repeating themselves. As miniaturized from egg to egg, each individual finds himself playing the alternative roles of 1. Prey (whenever being eaten) 2. Predator (whenever eating). Ontentrophic holocaust abundance is to be seen everywhere, with everyone playing his versatile part on both sides of the dining experience. Egggroup think may jail miniature holocausts into maximum insecurity prisons. These prisons periodically pop up out of fly by nightangled trivialities of ont I'miniature holocaust exchanges where predators become prey becoming predators becoming……..These events rarely achieve historical significance since being food usually occurs alone. But lonely as this may be, egggroup think may occasion expansion of predation patterns to encompass a large set of all table settings of victims. Indeed, the meal is usually forgotten when the diner himself is eaten, as is often the case, by the dined upon. Just as the dined upon in turn may become predators camouflaged as egggrouprey. The comprehensive nature of this exchange leads to egggreat becomplexities of roll play in the holocausts at hand. Few participants ever research both sides of the holocaust equation. In the end, we have a cat and mouse game, with every predator camouflaged by his victimhood….playing the part of occasional meals. The deception is never more blasphemously evident than when the prey egggroup becomes the predator egggroup in control of the news. That is where publicity cuts the narrative in half forgetting that the entire species deserves status as both predator and prey. The curse of humanity is its birthright to both be and have a meal.

In the end, humanity is no worse than the world. But, by the same token, the world is no worse than humanity. And what goes for humanity's bewilderdness goes for eumanity's bewilderdess as well. In eggracie's case, being responsible for the girl war, and at the same time iffffishing herselfish out of humanity to be descention's euman being, the dilemma is particularly tangled. It is the becomplexity of that preposte'erologically post whene'er war world that makes Gracie's story of being heaventilated out of hominidiots so ontentantalizingly blasphemous. It can only be due to the author's egggreater wisdom that, while starting her out as a prey, she ends up flirting blasphemously with predation and has to be saved from her own worst barnyard instincts in the end. The important point that this apology is making is that, historically speaking, holocausts are real; yet as singularities, they hardly exist at all outside of disctatorshipmentionaries. Mathematically speaking, they operate like multipartial interactive variables in opinionationally stretched out differential equations. And here to conclude the controversies, on the Christian side some may say this play makes satire on the life of baby he's us. I would say, not so. The satire's of some of the cross'd outing's details but not of such iffffffirmamentaltease'd ontI'm ideals.

.........ORDINARY LANGUAGE SUMMARIES OF THE GIRL WAR OPERA FOR NON-LINGUISH SPEAKERS.

2. VERY, VERY BRIEF SUMMARY OF OPERA.

But first a very, very brief summary of the story for very, very impatient readers.

So after an overture of about log 1 base 10 minutes encompassing about log 16 base 10 seconds such a thing as egggracie does emerge on the mountain overlooking the Mesozoo. Cut to the, e'erecently landed, observatory, with the wheel chair(chariot) in the garage, where Alex and Tele (the telescope) and Wolfy(the keyboard) are discussing the limits of the universe and what to do about ending up in the Mesozoic. Just then a flower droops which Wolfy's melody picks up as egggracie's leitmotif. Soon Alex and Wolfy are orchestrating the background to the scene as Tele is studying a girl hanging her halo upside down on a bridge over a river. Well, once Alex has examined her in a spotting lens, god or no god, he's off to be the savior that saves the girl. He only arrives to discover that Gracie (the girl) has just discovered the secret of eternity and is expecting god (disguised as Alex) to congratulate her (out of kindergarten). Once Gracie finds out that Alex has just come to save her, she threatens to dump him. As it turns out, since Gracie is in the business of dying all the time, the most dangerous thing that can happen to Gracie is to be saved. After all..... she may be responsible for the Girl War and has to be just dying to live that upsidown. Taking Alex on as her therapist, Gracie does reveal her death made simple books. Alex, who, according to pantheological etiquette, can't sing, is confused and Gracie has to straighten him out by calling on a bird to twitter her into her first big aria… "I'll be dying to save the day". Well, she then takes Alex on her precipitously dangerous carnival rides as they end up at the top of the Ferris Wheel as Gracie's halo emerges as sort of rainbow umbrella silhouetted against a sky. After the last dangerous adventures, the couple arrives back at the bridge where Alex closes his eyes see through lids while watching Gracie disappeared when they open. Alex heads from the bridge over the river to the saloon on the way to the world of the cathedral to find Gracie. In the saloon the Barmistress takes pity on Alex and sits him down at a table with a Gracist halo fragment in formaldehyde. Gracie's legend is revealed in the ballad that follows. Hearing the cathedral bells chime in the distance Alex learns that Gracie must be in the cathedral. Alex heads for the cathedral. Once in the cathedral Alex spots, Gracie hanging out on the cross. As the music develops, Pope Felix swaggers up to the pulpet and Gracie climbs down off the cross to do her sway dance choreographed to express the mommals in the mood themes that are indigenous to the Mesozoic period that Alex has now found himself. Soon a plate is passed and a former kitchen appliance (graduated from the could be can opener school) by the name of Mobible is the work horse collecting the cash. At this point Gracie, seems bored, walks right through the congregation like Moses at the Red Sea and Mobible must leave to recruit votes for Felix to be voted into god's front pocket like forever.

Soon we find Mobible making his electioneering rounds, downtown, uptown, at the meat packers picnic, the country club and finally the metaphysical society where Gracie is giving her metaphysics lecture to a group of egggruntled physicists. Just then the general arrives to inform Mobible of an invasion at the beach. Well, this invasion, could get political but actually it only serves as background to dramatize Mobible's character to mature into a respectable phylum all his own. Once Mobible and the general turn back the invasion parties at the beach they do the math to rig the papal election for Gracie instead of Felix. In scene VI we find Bishop Speck, who is a terrorist organism, visiting Gracie at her motel cemetery. Along with an apple, Specter has brought a bunch of indictments for Gracie. As mistress of the power grid, Ms Specter's purpose in life is limited to the holocaust of not having such a thing as Gracie in her mirrors. As a result, she wants egggracie one of three ways 1. Impossible. 2. Extinct. 3. Or just dead. To confirm her moral authority in these projects Speck informs Gracie that she is the mistress of the power grid that, by winning the girl war (which Gracie lost, won the holocaust. So like no other holocausts need apply for that position as backed up by the sanctimoney cash at the power grid. We learn at this time that Gracie, humped by the holocaust to be I'dieting on holocausteroid pills, remains not quite dead enough to get any credentials for being..like…the one girl holocaust…inspite of simulating to be dying up on the crossed outing. But the really big blow that Specter dumps on Gracie comes with her announcement that "ETERNITY HAS BEEN TAKEN." If this were true it would mean that Gracie's eternity test site expe'eriment would amount to 'becomplete iffffffffiascould being'. Well it's pretty clear in this scene that gracie's efforts at improving her impossibility….or not being stinct…or like just being dead are not going to improve her status in post girl war reputition's community as long as Felix, Speck and the power grid are in power. However, the scene does end with optimism as Gracie and Speck give each other high fives over the confluence of common cringed self-sympathies. We must admit…this scene is pretty hard on the likes of Ms Speck. In the final analysis, whoever won the holocaust, whate'er happened to eternity, just maybe Ms Speck's just misguided by e'erummers in her mirrors.

Wouldn't you know it but Alex arrives in the next scene at a completely different cemetery, thanks to an upside backwards map which he has just read like….simply backwards or upsidown, but not both. This abandoned holocaust cemetary's derelect with cow paddies and oil rigs stretching out like as ifffforever.

It seems that the graves are endless and numberless, and notable in that none of the dead get credits in those parts for being dead. Indeed for all intensive purposes, this cemetery seems like some assortment's abandoned holocaust hideout like hidden for the sake of somebody else's holocaust ads.

The monk that runs the place explains to Alex that this is the cemetery of the dead that lost World War Whenever's…like 'GIRL WARS'. The monk explains all this as Alex realizes he's arrived at the wrong cemetery. But the monk's war story explains everything. You see, when Gracie ifffreaked out of outer space, everybody wanted her in their mirrors, as xxxmas presentations in the swamp whate'er logged under the Mesozoic tree of life. That left Gracie to masterpiece herself together with masterpieced together puddles. Well, getting way too pretty faster than the speed of enlightenment, Gracie went to town with that. Masterpiecing together an entire emotion picture industry, Gracie's puddles were heating up all of's whate'er wholes down the Mesozoic drain. As it turned out 1. Plenty of anybody's everybody wanted to be such a thing as egggracie. 2. Plenty of everybody's anybody wanted such a thing as egggracie to not be like 1. Possible 2. Or stinct 3. Or just not quite dead. Well, everybody got trigger happy, the girl wars started up, the cash behind the power grid won the girl war and the holocaust credits with it, and Gracie ended up as occupied territory humped by the holocaust and I'dietting on holocausteroids and engine'ered on gin. Once Alex had heard enough of the girl war history… to grasp the current post preposte'erological situation he made his decision. Gentlemane'rickly speaking he decided to be the hero and save Gracie, even as she itted out as the girl of the girl war. But the only thing he had to save her was himself….so he headed out from the abandoned cemetery through the country club of the lived in out housing to find Gracie once and for all and save her with himself…without getting dumped.

Scene VIII's what comes next. How to keep this version very, very brief. Well, it starts with Alex at the edge of the country club overlooking Gracie's motel. Alex announces in no uncertain musically thematic terms that…..

"God or no god, I will, I will, I will be the hero" that "God or no god, I will, I will, I will save the girl."

Well having so stridenty declared such transcendent ambition………. he walks in on Gracie's janitorical service sweeping her motel cemetery. This is the couple's second meeting and some social adjustments are necessary. Still unsure about each other, neither one of them is quite yet willing to stand right side up against the other. But it's just defensive maneuvers that end abruptly when each of them knows that the other one's doing it. Alex starts off with his window thesis, explaining to Gracie that the window frames that she has been given to exist in are impossibly too far to the right of the middle of the middle of the middle of the window in which she can exist. With both hands still clean, Alex demonstrates this situation geometrically. Once the opened window situation is resolved so Gracie can look out from herself and actually be being herself seeing out of the window, things are getting pretty cozy. Employing gracie's own NOT/NOTNOT CODE Alex shows gracie how to iffffotographickly negate her negation to end up on a more positively iconic iffffooting of her iffffffished out iffffffffins. But Alex's selfished out success is soon spoiled when his second hand cosmological critique of Gracie's just ont I'metaphysics throws gracie's head into a tailspin. As a cosmic immersions alternative to Gracie's ontique'erian e'erways Alex offers two (ontiquely ont I'm immature….demi-god approved) alternatives. 1. By replacing Gracie's ontique'erian not/notnot becompute'er code with the log 17 base 10 second hand 0/1 computer code. 2.

By keeping eternity as a mathematical construct. 3. By up keep of the universe as a more than sample, just simple bit of tool used reality's realty. Well Gracie will have none of this and ontantrumminates ifffffrantickly over such iffffffocalized theses and appears to actually shed the first authentic whate'er's 'as iffffontears' of the opera. Of course, Alex caves back in onto ont I'm'eternity and Gracie does her broom dance e'eroutine. But the question of what to do about Felix taking over eternity comes up when Gracie smashes Specter's poison apple out of Alex's hand. It isn't long before Gracie is rummaging in her beble boxed in make-up kit for her next dance routine's pillow. Still too embarrassed to exist and looking in all blasphemable directions, Gracie uses her pillow appliance to be buried becomfortably beneath sum's egggrass rug ont I'm'aterial. Once this routine's over, we find Gracie standing stiff as ever, and introducing Alex to the kissing coffin which Gracie has worked in the past on a fly by e'eromantiquerian not ne'er's nightly basis. The scene's dramatically embellished with Mobible's sudden arrival and disappearance. Soon Gracie is scened rummaging successfully for her pompom wands. With these wands, or so it seems, Gracie and Alex, suddenly get the same idea. They decide that Gracie should attend the election rally for Felix, with Gracie doing her usual introductions from the cross. HOWEVER…..with new music and new lyrics….the plan is for Gracie to turn the tables of eternity found out lost, and put Gracie into position to beget eternity regained 1. To get Gracie that alibi she needs for the Girl War 2. Behavior the sanctimoney and prestige to conduct the eternity test site expe'eriment Gracie has been preparing herself for in what like… seems like….forever. As gracie's pompom routine fades in the distance, Alex heads off from Gracie's motel filmset holocaust….. back up the hill in the direction of the abandoned one…..holocaust that is.

Scene IX has floodlights at the main entrance to the cathedral. Alex and Gracie arrive to be greeted by Lara, a reporter with a microphone, who, like Gracie, at this point is a big Gracie fan. But a confrontation with a down and outer forces Gracie to take over the microphone and rape the consciences of the entire population of down and outers in the congregation. Once Gracie has disheveled herself, all she needs is a drink and she's ready for Alex and herself to waltz each other with the new music and lyrics. Once a question and answer session has Gracie giving her e'eroutine lecture from the cross, and the universe is ritually appeased with a moment's clock music……. Gracie is ready to introduce Felix from the cross as the night's main event, the pope to be voted next pope…but this time forever. HOWEVER…as planned…...Gracie suddenly turns the tables on Felix and, sweeping him away from forever with her wand, takes over the election rally with her own almightning stricken light show. Before you know it, Gracie is announcing herself as the light of the world and proving it with a display of ifffe'erainbotics that hardly anyone had ever seen before. E'eright off the top of her head, the assortment of light from blush to blue expanded carrying the stained glass windows with it out into the iffffffirmament of the not ne'er night's notnotitude. Ont I'm'animated as such into just could bc's care cartoon, with a few glitches, the performance begets notnot nocturned out as iffffffo'er whelming. In the final synthesis,

Gracie ends the scene by cutting right through the congregation like ont I'moses could be crossing the's ifffe'ered sea. In the end she exits the cathedral with the final gesture of a kiss, thrown kissmetrickly to be received by each and everbody's anybodied down and outer sighing the sign of being kissed with the signal of their hands upon their cheeks.

By Scene X the wanted posters were blowing in the whene'er's wind announcing Gracie as the new pope, replacing Felix and the powowe'er grids bigame's purchase of playments to play god. We find Gracie in the company of her new onte'erage exclusively inclusive of Alex, Mobible and the general. They are standing by the bunker of the abandoned holocaust's vastly stretched out landscape. Gracie, above all, dares not explain how she won the election for pope. Eufemisms abound, but no one has a veriffffff I able answer. Once all of's others have left to e'ergo about their newly decisive beble business Gracie is alone with Mobible who spills the being of it all. It was he who rigged the election for Gracie. He did it because 1. He had recently acquired a conscience. 2. He realized he was in love with Gracie. Well, after a bit of squabbling over the ins and outs of all this, Gracie and Mobible settled down to a business proposition. The idea was 1. Mobible and Gracie would cash in on Gracie's metaphysics with a new gift shop religion with an assortment of entrinkets posing as ontrinkets for the could be customers of course, of course..not…not consuming eternity on an absolutely not not need to beble basis. After Gracie bluffed her Miss Eternity routine for presentable m'eternity rewardings ontrophy iffffects, things subsided into the bunker where Gracie and Mobible concluded the proceeding's ifffe'erequited iffffections.

In scene XI Gracie, sporting sunglasses now, takes Alex on a vacation back to the carnival where they had their earlier scene II adventures. But this time Gracie is pope and just as the luxuries are available, the dangers are gone…all but one. You see, as despicable as Ms Specter was, the seduction of powwow powegggracism was creeping into Gracie's arsenal of ont I'mind as ifffunctions. She was showing signs of like 'iffffonthinking she could get away with anything's maybe everything. At the top of the IFFFFFE'ERIS WHENE'ER WHEEL Gracie just can't help herself from letting out a BIG ONE for like BIG OLD TIME'SAKE. It's a rainbow with light that's so wet that the wholegggrailiffffont gushes all over the's place. The janitors are still ont I'mopping it all up when Gracie and Alex arrived at the terrace underlooking the stars but overlooking the rainbow spill site. If you wondered how Ms Specter must cringe when alone in her mirrors, you can imagine Gracie cringing over her glass of gin on the terrace. Well, once you're cringing that hard, what is there to do. You guessed it, plan your metaphysical attack on eternity at the eternity test site. So that's what the discussion almost ends up being all about. the question remains however…how to use a universe to make I'deals with an eternity. shifting the scene to the past tense to like soften the blow……. It wasn't that Gracie didn't have like iffffffffffffffffff( )ffffffffffffffinite ifffffffaith in the presentable eternity that her metaphysics was could be claiming e'ersponsibilities for, but it was just, as with all religions there's always the search for someone with the spine tingling concrete to back you up on the cross. Well, the concrete Gracie was thinking about was pixie dust, ifffe'erefined down past the Planck log minus 35 base 10 metrick limit. Immersed in the universe as she e'ereluctantly was, she e'ereasoned maybe she should be somewhat inclusive of the stars to her beblical m'eternity project. Ifffff nothing else it was a bid from e'eritual ont I'mappeasement to just plain hard gnosed ritual appeasement to a tool use'd'e'er's universe. Once Gracie learned she might beget refined pixie dust from sand boxed on the beach, there was no stopping her onthusiasm for the project. Once she iffffigured that she could 1. Salvage the fuel selves 2. Beat the fossil record and 3. Go to hell…….. iffffffffffff( )fffffffffff she had to……..the project was light housed to be sold out as iffffar as she was beaconcerned. For all of that….when the waitress arrived with the check… reasserting herself as EMPHATICALLY NOT ONT I'M'AM'SELF SIR….egggracie was not at all prepared for the beconsequences. After all was said and done…like…she was pope now and refused to pay such a check on her authority. Alex, backed her up of course, of course not…not….and the waitress left disgruntled. Sensing his own iffffragility in all of these determinations, god or no god, Alex felt it was time for him to pop the question before they left the table on the terrace. Alex's proposal was for Gracie to take on the task of being the hero that saves the girl. His idea was …like…whatever happens…Gracie could ride shot gun on the proceedings, eggguarding and like looking after the girl with every step she takes. So like s'e'erepetitiously Gracie could be with the girl wherever she went. Seeing the advantages of this arrangement, Gracie agreed…most especially when Alex affirmed that…since he loved the girl….he would beconfusing her with Gracie….and always be loving Gracie as well.

Back at the eternity test site things were running as smooth as the curvatures of could be's ontense'er calculus. Gracie's metaphysics was putting on s'e'erious show times of proving practical. The interior of the bunker was built like a whene'er war room full of lights attached to numbers and numbers attached to lights. The count down from iffffffffffinity was already in progress. Alex had just enough spare change to purchase his plast(mag)ic wand and beget immersion within the building. Confronted with Mobible and Gracie's new bible Alex was iffffeeling fresh out of whate'er's ont I ambiguous ont I amphibious could be cartesiontentension. But the could be count down was approach log 1 base 10 second hand seconds and the e'er momentum was becoming perhapsably pulp ifffictiontly palpable. Heading through the tunnel into the pavilion Gracie found herself immersed in Mobible's ontrinketed traffic jamboree. It was all there, all ontrophickly presentable eternity could have ever wanted to advertise itself as {{{JUST ONT I'M'D}}}. Once gracie had swaggered up to the dark loud speaker's microphone there was no stopping the situation. Bathing in the spotlighting's almightning stricken atmosphe'er Gracie gave her usual speech before ontraffick jams, explaining how preposte'erologically speaking, whenever life is dead, sum what's e'eremedy's not not to be as iffffffffffont I'm'expected. As the countdown went through pregnant zero onto accountably's {{ONE}} a flash was seen on the newly iffffangled e'eradioactive screens. Coming through the tunnel from the bunker, the general ushered in the hush of becompletely presentable eternity's as ifffonticipation for like…like….of course…of course…not……..not…………..( )……….TO BE.

HOWEVER…. Shall we just say the experiment iffffffffizzled with e'ereportable iffffe'eresults but low down cheapunk, second hand like spare part's partigirled. It was another miracle, but as usual's not the wanted one. It was xmas eve and not xmas day. As such ALL OF PRESENTS WERE NOT E'ERIVED. Well, of course….Gracie would have none of that. Lecturing the ground beneath her feet, she left the stage to Mobible and parted the traffic jam in her usual ont I'mosaicky lack of manners to the exit.

The epilogue found her digging through the Pixie dust to the dirt that she had long suspected to be the capstone of eternity if her metaphysics ever failed. Having looted e'erummage boxes for ontoy dolled up egggracies in the beble bunker, gracie began to make engine noises as she flew winged ifffacsimiles of selfished out selfish trips around. Well, what was Alex to do? 1. Observe a moment of silence for a possibly dud eternity. 2. Take the pistol Gracie offe'er'd to be shot by to shoot the eggground(not the ground of being) instead. 3. To beheaded back to the olde pantheological universe his godlikeness was used to….. and………and…………BETAKING GRACIE WITH HIM. Well, this idea worked for a while until Gracie just up and decided that she was wanted by her wings. Still thinking that, in spite of everything, Alex still just might be spelled backward in disguise, Gracie gave Alex the doll with wings and headed out on her own to get some wings for herself at last. Well Alex followed her with the only weapon he had, a bottle of gin. Well Gracie would have none of that. Separated by high winds, the couple carried on their metaphysical dialogue as before with Gracie dumping Alex to get it on with wings that she was beconfident were awaiting her in mid e'er. In the storm there was light housed beaconside'erable confusion over exactly what was needed to 'satisfy gracie's ontiquerian onthirst' at this point. Whereas Gracie was convinced she needed a metaphysical can opener Alex offer'd her a bottle of gin with a cork screw instead. In the apotheosis that was soon to follow the topping off the mountain, Alex did interpose between twin orchestral explosions to finally yodel his case at the top of the mountain, it being that he had indeed brought the bottle of gin. I quote:

"GRACIE! I BROUGHT THE BOTTLE!" With that gesture, signaling a last hope of redemption, Gracie switched her halo to I'm proof the weather or not's of course, of course not not to be's e'erwhethe'ereport recounted in Gracie's final aria "OF COURSE, OF COURSE NOT NOT TO BE!" With that accomplished… Gracie madly did turn to Alex to reach for the bottle….but missed…..with her hand ending well within the clean could be grasp of his other hand still waiting for her, to behold the hero that saves the girl, collapsing back into the ground garage of chime'ericle apologetic charioteering's specialtease iffffects….where meanwhile a wheel chair was waiting in the wings.

While the music ends on the mountain top the drama does not abate as we find Gracie taking a setting's sunny date'eride in Alex's chariot. Having finally begot her wings, one might think Gracie would end her adventures here, riding a settings sunny day into ontomorrow's dawns. But no, in the final analysis Gracie is not that impressed with Alex's newly revealed demigodlike status. As Gracie says herself, "I'm not in this for the setting's sunny days of the demigrods. I'm in this for the BIGTIME of BECOMPLETELY PRESENTABLE ETERNITY." No other time iffffffe'eraimed at will doo doo for her. So it is in the second postlude, Gracie asks to dump the chariot which is to say to be let off at the insomnibustop where hereafter's horizon home will be available. The opera's already over as we find Gracie in the kitchen searching for a can opener soliciting onteleophonic advice from Alex who is back at the observatory. But this is the play without music that makes the metaphysical becomplications so ontente'ertaining.

 Well! that's one version of the story. As confusing as that is, it gets more confusing the more you tell it.

So! Let's try again.

3. NOW THE NOT SO VERY BRIEF SUMMARY FOR NOT SO VERY IMPATIENT READERS.

SCENE I- We are in a newly landscaped astronomical observatory where Alex, a young scientist and possible god in the strictly cosmologgeek sense, is accompanied by Tele, a highly intelligent telescope, and Wolfy, a highly intelligent musical synthesizer. Seemingly shy and apollogetic, Alex is engaged with debates on several topics. 1. Is eternity nothing more than a mathematical construct of non-finite temporality. 2. Is the universe all there is or is it just a sample of a larger ontique'erian reality. 3. Since they have landed in the Mesozoic era, should Alex be allowed to adventure out into it.

Just then a sunflower droop in the observatory as Wolfy employs his voices to manufacture some music to lift it up. Just then Tele spots something that appears to be qualitatively indigenous to the sky and yet is situated on the ground at a distant bridge over a river. The object appears to be falling into the turbulence of the river. Just then Wolfy gets an idea for a new concerto in the preposterologically ifffe'eromantic vein. Alex sits down with his clean hands on Wolfy's keyboard to join in with the musickey notifffications. Meanwhile Tele is becoming more and more agitated through his perspective on the object at the bridge. As the music approaches its climax Alex leaves the keyboard to examine the object in Tele's lenses. Utterly transformed by what he observes, Alex, god or no god, rushes out of the observatory into the Mesozoic Era.

There is an interlude as Wolfy's music frantically(quasi-discombobulatedly) pursues Alex up the path to the bridge over the river.

SCENE II- Alex finds Gracie at the bridge. She dabbles in metaphysics and has just discovered the secret of eternity......which is to say... the NOT/NOTNOT CODE, eternity's alphabet. As you may s'e'ermise, especially after just uncovering eternity's big time secret.....Gracie does not believe in coincidences and assumes that Alex must be god, tentatively dubbed(for just incase's safety sake) as 'dog spelled backwards'. Whoever Alex is, Gracie is expecting immediately BIG TIME congratulations on her breakthrough in metaphysics. Once Gracie catches on that Alex is amibivalent about being spelled backwards, Gracie catches on quickly that Alex might just be in disguise. As ambivalent about Alex as Gracie is, Alex is not ambivalent about such a thing as Gracie. With a passion heretofore unknown to Alex (among whom godolleduption's suddenly the great unknown's big deal) Alex wants to save Gracie from falling into the river, falling into onto's anything except himself. But Gracie threatens to dump Alex, if he tries to save her in any way whatsoever. She does agree to let Alex be her analyst however. Since Gracie has just discovered the secret of eternity, Alex encourages her preposte'erological dabbles in metaphysics. And as it is also obvious that Gracie is a celestial object exceeding the speed of enlightenment, Alex encourages Gracie to pose objectively as her subjective self. It must be noted here that, while Gracie's been ontaile'er'd with the head gear of a halo, she's not egggrown up as yet 'ifffffledged' with wings, which onentheoretically she would iffffe'erquire to appear ontentiffffly ontentisymetrical. However….all halos put aside for the time being, the scene's focus turns to Gracie's ontheory settings regarding eternity. For Gracie's metaphysics, Alex turns Gracie to face Tele who has the situation under surveillance from the observatory. Gracie engages Tele to read her lips as she outlines the scope of her metaphysical ontente'erprise. Once Tele has approved of Gracie's ontentse'erprise patterns, Gracie turns to Alex to elucidate her meaty zoic egggracist lifestyle in the Mesozoic. Alex learns that Gracie has still not graduated from kindergarten and asks to see her DEATH MADE SIMPLE texts. When Alex asks Gracie why she wants to be dead, Gracie responds that being dead makes a lousy lyric and that therefore she only wants to be dying. At this point we learn that Alex can't sing but that Gracie will generously do his singing for him. Suddenly a bird twitters and Gracie joins the bird song leading into her first aria….DYING I WILL SAVE THE DAY.

Gracie now proceeds to take Alex on a near-death experience journey at the local carnival, where many adventures are to be had. At one point, while sitting silhouetted at the top of a Ferris Wheel, Gracie's halo erupts rainbotically its full spectrum from blush to blue. During their adventures Alex is careful not to save Gracie in any way that Gracie's salvation is not obscured by the convenient accompaniment of the waltz tempo. Their journey ends with Gracie and Alex settling back on the bridge over the river. Gracie tells Alex to close his eyes. Expecting a kiss, Alex does close his eyes and the lids as well. When Alex's eyes re-open they find that Gracie has disappeared. Alex stares into the swallowing's turbulence of the river as the scene concludes.

There is an interlude where we find Alex cartooned while leaving the bridge on a heading for the nearest available eternity's nearest available universe's nearest available Mesozoic saloon.

SCENE III- As Alex enters the saloon, the barmistress can see that he's distraught and takes pity on him. She soon finds out about Alex's encounter with Gracie. The barmistress knows all about Gracie and is somewhat sympathetic to Gracie's metaphysics, inspite of Gracie's bad mouthing the universe as a hole and outer space in particular. As the barmistress turns to the Gracie band on the radio, Alex finds that Gracie is radioactive. Not only that but a fragment of Gracie is formaldeydrated in a beaker just behind the bar. It is halo material being preserved for ambiguously meaty-metaphysically to be iffffossilized(iffffe'erelated) reasons. The barmistress invites Alex to sit with a physicist and a general at a table where the beaker is placed for all to observe. The saloon turns dark as lightning strikes to the tune of cathedral bells in the distance. The barmistress and a soprano chorus sing the becombobulated ballad of Gracie. The cathedral chimes once again as the ballad ends. Alex learns that the cathedral only chimes when Gracie is in the building. Making his exit, he slams the saloon door, as usual, to end the scene.

There is a third interlude beginning with the ambiguous optimism of three bassoons. This interlude follows Alex on the road to the cathedral.

SCENE IV- Somber medieval music plays as Alex enters the profound darkness of the cathedral. The only light is from the stained glass windows…..until…..Alex beholds Gracie, suspended, stretching out all equations his lenses have ever contemplated, taking selfies from the cross. Just then the cathedral erupts apotheologically with the resonance of a vast baroque mass.

This ends as Pope Felix swaggers up to the pulpit while the music drops off into a rhythmic dribble bounce. Shaming the congregation with his baritone lyricism, Felix sings, "YOU MET A BEGGER IN THE STREET TODAY…..DIDN'T GIVE HIM A DIME".

Soon other verses are emerging………announcing the presence of the MESOZOO accompanied by the MOMMALS WITH THE MOO. At this point Gracie climbs down from the cross and begins her sway dance routine. The cathedral is in a state of rapture now as the music displays elements of dribble dance-baroque counterpoint. The music's sonata formations reach through the development section to its climax and subsides as Gracie descends from the stage to part the congregation like Moses at the Red Sea as she makes her exit out the front doors.

Mobible, a former kitchen appliance, who specialized in can openings, has been passing the offering plate. He is left standing in wait of further instructions from Felix and the power grid (which Mobible is surreptitiously just getting under control). Eventually Felix signals for Mobible to leave the cathedral, which he does, by the side not not….not ne'er'd exit, ending the scene.

It is to be noted at this point that, ever since Gracie left the cathedral, the bells stopped chiming.

 SCENE V- Mobible is out and about, in machine like, just in cases of cans canopened as iffffffashion, selling Felix for tomorrow and tomorrow and tomorrow's final selection(selectrocution) for pope. Rumer has it that Felix is running for god and Ms Speck, his understudy, is running for position of vice-god. As the music plays, we see Mobible in various guises, promoting Felix downtown, uptown, at the meat packers association, in a ticker tape parade, at the country club, at the Valhallelujaween feast and finally…at the metaphysical society. By the time Mobible has arrived at the metaphysical society Gracie is already at the chalk boards, explaining eternity to disgruntled physicists.

Just then the general arrives with an urgent call to the luxury resort beach heads where large scale invasion parties are landing for the papal selection(selectrocution). Mobible and the general arrive at the beach to evaluate the military scale of the invasion. The initially trigger-happy general is subdued by Mobible who confronts the executive of the invasion party, peacefully. Claiming to have new orders for the invasion, Mobible tells the executive that his own beach is being invaded and like….like….he must return immediately to reinvade the beaches from wherever he left. As the invasion parties disappear into the atmospheric inversion layers out at sea, Mobible and the general breath sighs of relief at the diverted demographic holocaust and reevaluate the entire papal selectrocution process. With both Mobible and the general no longer supporting Felix, they work out a plan to support Gracie for pope instead. The scene ends with the last invasion shipment, with all its holocoasterized implications, having becompletely disappeared beneath the far horizon.

SCENE VI-This is a very complicated scene where the reader encounters metaphysical jargon with s'e'erious linguistic density. Many controversies emerge as Gracie and Ms Speck have at each other tearing out each other's hairdos. Ms Speck, who is running quietly for the position of vice-god under Felix, arrives at the cemetery-motel where ont I'multipliably ontalented Gracie works as 1. janitor, 2. whate'er wave and 3. e'eresponsible party girl altogether. Ms Speck is carrying a trigger fingered apple and several indictments against Gracie's possibility, stinction and livelihood. Since Speck has Gracie permanently pegged and pigeoned as an xxxrated, nasty girl… we find out very soon that Gracie is on the short list for one girl s'e'erial humped holocausts. Whether or not it is self-evident that Gracie could coolify as coolest thing ever, but for the girl wars, Gracie has plenty of reasons to just be dyingly not quite dead, or to be stinct, or to be possible. Due to her dreamergence, Gracie is onthe'ermodynamically popular with puddles. Whenever Gracie hovers over a puddle that puddle 1. Heats up. 2. Becomes masterpieced together as a sort of Gracystine chapel ceiling over all of's rainbows. Well, all improvements in gracie's impossibility put aside, Speck will have none of that……and, while admitting herself to be(antiont)egggracist in her own stylish fashion, she insists that Gracie make good that contract she put out on herself. You can imagine the sort of bickering this leads to. Recognizing her responsibility for the girl wars, Gracie nevertheless takes refuge in her metaphysics, which, after all is said and done, did solve eternity and plans to put eternity to work, to become becompletely presentable and by the way…… *ontheologically* experimenting with the's *iffffe'eresults*. In the course of this dialogue Speck makes two statements designed to shock Gracie to of course, of course not not's just could be's core. 1. On the one hand Specter announces that her side in the girl wars *won the holocaust.* 2. This is just about the time that Speck informs Gracie that "ETERNITY HAS BEEN TAKEN" and eternity just won't be available for Gracie's e'ereligious expe'eriments after all. Well with her eternity test sites dumped as such, it looks like Gracie will just have to wait around for the next available eternity….like….like….we're talking…like…like…. not not not duh'd eternity at this appointment's pigeon wholed like dot (((.))). As you can imagine the situation is getting pretty ugly, although both Gracie and Specter are too drunk to lift a trigger finger. In the end, after much reconciliated debate regarding 'holocoaste'erides'…the scene concludes with Gracie pretty much promising to try harder to make improvements in her impossibility status by…like…when all is said and done….just being more onthusiasticakly impossible or extinct or at least just dead with the film crew arriving to signomatically promote Gracie's pretty promise.

SCENE VII- Alex arrives at the abandoned holocaust cemetery, abandoned for no other reason than lack of advertisement revenue on behalf of its grave sightings. The monk that runs the place….. complains that the side that loses the war loses all credentials for being dead. Focused on the girl war, ignoring world war whenever, Alex wonders how the girl wars got started. It seems that it was developments in the emotion picture industry that started it. The monk explains that, once Gracie arrived in the scenery, emotion pictures were precipitating battlegrounds over the scenes that Gracie was in. With everybody wanting to be Gracie and not enough of e'erbuddy's anybody's egggracie to go around, conflict was unavoidable. Confessing his own trigger happiness in the war affairs, the monk examines Alex for signs of salvation, if not for himself, at least for Gracie. Becoming to grasp the hidden side of both sides of something terrible that did really happen….Alex confesses his plan to salvage all of's Gracie's eggguilt complexes derived from the war. Observing Alex to harbor highly on purposed fellowshipmentions, the monk gives Alex a token of his esteem and directions across the country club to Gracie's motel(cemetery). Before his departure Alex carefully schedules an appointment with not touching the monk's contaminated trigger fingers by not shaking the monk's thumb. After what he has just heard, Alex is concerned hygienically about the status of his hand, which is yet to 1. Acquire trigger fingers 2. Realize its heroic destiny.

SCENE VIII- In this scene Gracie's full-blown metaphysics gets e'er'd. Vowing to be the hero that saves the girl, Alex arrives at Gracie's motel cemetery. At first neither Alex or Gracie are completely right side up. Having spent the morning in the Mesozoic, Alex has two projects for Gracie. 1. Geometrically to get Gracie's self-perceptions away from dying out and back toward being centered where she can exist, be stinct…… or at least be possible. (Maneuvering Gracie in this manner, he does succeed in removing Gracie's pills and becomforting Gracie back to being sum's iffffffly'swhate'er'd iffffly nevertheless not to just be like dolled up spider droppings). 2. Not quite shaking his addiction to logic codes, Alex humiliates Gracie's alphabet, confessing serious doubts about Gracie's metaphysics and the not/notnot code that is at its linguistic iffffoundation. Alex's confession precipitates a heated debate over metaphysical alphabets and the realities that emerge out of them. Taking strategic hints from her encounter with the sanctimonied powowegggrid…… like in the end…… it is Gracie's iffffreaked out supernature that gets decisive dibs on ont I'm'e'eracled wande'er'd dubs to win the argument. Just to prove the point, Gracie demonstrates with song and dance what she can do with her broom. This number ends when Alex picks up the apple Specter has left. It is then that Gracie smashes the apple and gets serious. Soon Gracie is again song and danced. For this routine she appliances a pillow to accommodate her quasified burial in algorithmic solidarity with her mortel graveyard guests. Making adjustments for onthirst and other becomforts, Gracie provides her own make-shift grave with the MY PILLOW brand pillow and a bottle of gin. After a brief lip s'e'erviced adventure at the kissing coffin, interrupted by Mobible's entrantexit, it's time to make plans for the selectrocution rally that evening. Getting ready for her performance, Gracie demonstrates her pompom song and dance routines as Alex heads back up the hill vowing once again *to be the hero that saves the girl………………*or words to that affection's asiffffffffffect.

SCENE IX- With floodlights seemingly iffffffffffffffflooding the entrance to the cathedral, Gracie arrives with Alex. Bestressed tension dominates the scene. Lara, the reporter, greets Gracie with her microphone praising Gracie to the gracistine chapel roof. Vaingloriously encouraged, Gracie's aesthethical constitution is soon dominated by her aesthetical status of getting way too pretty way too fast for the speed of both 1. Enlightenment 2. And entertainment…… to keep up. So it is that, rhetorically speaking, Gracie agrees to coolify as the coolest thing ever. Just then a down and out man, who agrees with this (down and oute'er'd) appraisal, puts his ugleefully agreeable hands on Gracie's pompominated wholegggrailumps. In a fit of bad taste, Gracie takes Lara's microphone and attacks the man and an entire traffic jam of down and outers with it, raping just about every conscience in the cathedral. Well, after that Gracie needs a drink to dishevel herself. But the disheveling music turns into an elegant waltz variation of dishevelment wherein Gracie finds Alex irresistible as a pair of wholegggraileg dance partners. It is to be noted that, smack dab in the middle of the waltz, Alex removes Gracie's moustache prop. Once Gracie is back up on the cross, many questions arise from the crowd, none of which Felix, well deluded into the running to be god, can answer. Needless to say Gracie's lecture from the cross answers all of's questions about presentable eternity with metaphysically satisfactory but deceptive ont I'm'allure. Not a big fan of the secondhand, spare parts universe, Gracie nevertheless ritually appeases spaced out time by participating in the clock dance. But this is just a prelude to her could be claims on whate'er's iffffontlique'er'd up eternity. It should be noted that, in the of coursiness of all this drama, Gracie's iffffffamous lecture from the cross does becomprehensiffffffly ontoutline her metaphysics and leads to her e'eritual apologeeswhizzed outer space......which by the way, Gracie is not at all hesitont to ontake ont I'm'advantage of.....revealing the little heaventilated hypocrite that she, in asifffffffffinalitease'd'e'er's ont I'm'analysis IS.

Speaking of heaventilation systems.....the main program begins with Gracie posing to be the sacrifice suitable for Felix's sanctification. But just when Felix has confirmed his sanctification, the music ascends way too high for him to finish his vocalizations....as Gracie's wand dubs him off the stage. From here on out, it's Gracie's apotheosynthesis show, that, with a few glitches (specter pulls the fire alarm)........ is heaventilated way beyond any hope for s'e'erious hesitation. Proclaiming herself 'THE LIGHT BULB OF THE WORLD' Gracie summons her halo to proceed with the light show planned for the evening. In spite of those few faulty starts Gracie's halo does get its light show off the ground and over the rainbow in no uncertain terms. With complete agreement between the music and Gracie's performance, the audience that had come to the rally to be devoted to Felix, finds itself ontente'ertained to be devoted to Gracie instead. At the end of the performance Gracie makes one final gesture. Having parted the congregation, like Moses parting the Red Sea, Gracie is about to exit the cathedral when she turns and waves sum whate'er's kiss to the congregation as the cathedral echodes its second to the last chime. With the cathedral's last chime of the evening, the entire congregation places its hands on its cheeks to signal a vastly heralded sigh at the reception of Gracie's pandemicky kiss. Once Gracie is out of the building, the chimes abruptly conclude of course..of course…not..not….and the scene is over.

SCENE X- The tonality has shifted a triton up to e minor as the inversion of the six-note motive that dominates much of the opera comes into play. A newpaper headline floats by in the breeze. GRACIE IS THE NEW POPE. Gracie arrives at the abandoned cemetery to stake out the papal landscape. Gracie stands with Alex, Mobible and the general. There is much confused disbelief shared all around. This moment of disbelief is interrupted when Gracie is moved empathetically by the general's reading of a final scrawl in an about to be dead teenage girl's bunke'er'd daybook. Gracie casually remarks that she 'used to write such daybook stuff'.

 But to the issues at hand……the question remains as to how Gracie became pope. Everyone but Mobible seems well prepared to not to know. Gracie senses profound insecurities around this question but proceeds matter of factly to go about her business as pope 1. Becommissioning the general to set up the eternity test site experiment and 2. Becommssioning Alex to arrange for Gracie's sabbatical, back vacationing at the carnival. With the exits of Alex and the general, Gracie finds herself alone with herself plus Mobible. In no time at all, Mobible is explaining the selectrocution results. According to Mobible….he, his newly dawned self, newly saddled with a can open'd'e'er's conscience, is the responsible party for these s'e'erprizingly self-symetrickle egggracystemic self-results. He explains that he rigged the selectrocutiion for two reasons. 1. He acquired a conscience at the beach resort's invasion party. 2. With all of Gracie's negatives, he accomplished one great both sentimental and sensational feat, he developed the negatives to becombine to (positively spealking) behold the girl, and having beheld her to fall in love with the like….like….like…..likeness of the of coursey could be countenanced spirit face of the such a thing as egggracystemitry of the she it of her.

Now.....threatened by this unexpected turn of events, Gracie's fears set in. And with them Mobible's fears set in. This is the first shocking moment in the opera when we find out that both Gracie and Mobible have acquired trigger fingers. The resultant cat claw warfare doesn't last long. With both Gracie and Mobible power gripped in each other's shadows now..........the only solution is like...like...to go into business together. With Mobible's IQ having shot through the roof of the Gracystine chapel, Mobible outlines the plan. It's CHURCH BELL'S CHIMED ASJIFFFFF'D ONT I'M......like....like..... to start a new religion, side stepping gracist terminology, to be based instead on wholegggrailisterminology, with Gracie still begetting pretty faster than the speed of enlightenment.....but with a catch; the whole religion's to be played for cash with plast(mag)ic action figures. Plast(mag)ic is a substance that Mobible is just getting ready to invent. At this point Mobible makes it clear that, business proposition or not business proposition, plast(mag)ic substance or no plast(mag)ic substance, all gracie has to do is fall in love with Mobible to seal the deal and 1. Remain pope. 2. Stay out of jail. Agreeing to this business proposition, with Mobible following in hot pursuit, Gracie and Mobible enter the bunker to have some private time together. The scene ends discretely at this appointment.

SCENE XI- Fasten your seat belts for Scene XI. Gracie's about to blow the top off her innocence. Things start with Gracie as quasi-cooliff I'd as ever and becompletely e'eready for some heavy-duty metaphysics. It's the usual ontithetical eternity talk that this opera's iffffffffff( )ffffffffffamous for. It all centers around Gracie's eternity test site experiment, when she thinks she can jockey justajiffffffy's e'er into appointments to like...resurrect the world at an e'eresurrection set up....seated onteoretickly...with everybody's anybody in it. This is the topic at the restaurant on the terrace after the music subsides and the luxury cruise is over with.

But first one bit of detail about how the luxury cruise part of the scene concluded. What happened was this. Gracie arrived gazing stylishly over the rim of her sunglasses as she set foot on the gang plank limit for new life's gnostalgic tour of her old life. Gracie didn't have to audition to be obvious about like...like....like.....liking being pope. The gnostalgic tour of the olde carnival was going well with Gracie behavioring m'any's deluxe'eriated ontitudinal m'adventures...........which...by the way.....her meaty physics could not have m'accomplished prior to her selectrocution as pope. All was e'ergoing well......until......... until........at the top of the arc of the Ferris wheel........Gracie, feeling the grip of her ontranscendent powwow poweggggrid lock steps as pope, sprouted her 'wet light' halo trick that spilled rainbotickly all over the(cosmetricky) grounds of being at the carnival. It seems that she was beaming a new bulb from her heaventilation's hairdresser and just couldn't resist testing its almightitude for like lightning strikes upon whatever worlds might be. (Gracie's was very proud of her almightning's trucked in light bulbs and as usual it was her whipped cream's cherry topped off light bulbs that begot her into trouble). Well, the cherry topped light whipped cream was bathing the scenery wetter than usual and it ended like with rainbows spilling ceiling material plastered all over the place. The janitors were mopping up the rainbow residoo by the time Gracie and Alex were sitting on the terrace (just under the stars), cringing, having drinks and hashing out Gracie's schedules for eternity. Given what you've gathered about Gracie, you can imagine the assortment of excuses Gracie made for the impossibility of her schedule ending up on eternity's could be calendar. In her defense, I should say that Gracie was drinking her gin (rather elegantly) from a glass during this e'erather e'er heated philosophical debate on the terrace. This was the first time in the opera that Alex might have thought about dumping egggracystems. But no. This poor pantheological geek god was in love with his little Miss Eternity as iffff eternity really was...like...... way, way more than a mathematical construct of non-finite temporality...but....but...like...ont I'more befit for ont I'mining all of's becompletely presentable e'ercraft scrambles.

Ok, so having secured iffffffaith from a pantheological cosmetrition, Gracie at last spilled the being as just what she was all e'eready to of course, of course, not...not to be up to at the eternity test site. Well, ont I'm'aglomaniac that she had become....like...like.... what Gracie's ont I'meglomania was up to was this. 1. Using (a universe's) pixie dust as a backup, she was planning a show down at the eternity test site. 2. With ontense'er calculus she was like onticipating a becompletely smoothly curved event, which is to say a becontinuous qualum occurrence, time-wise way past the quantum log minus 44 log 10 second limit. 3. The plan was to raise the dead, all the dead. Because of her egggracist reputation from the girl war, she decided that she just couldn't play favorites this time around. Phylumetrickly speaking, she was working with no boundaries. The plan threw up turds and twinkles in the same phylogeny. 4. However, she did reserve a (to be announced) new phylum for such a thing as herself.

But the metaphysical argument was interrupted by the waitress with the bill. Since, as pope, Gracie supernaturally refused to pay anything as pretty petty as a bill. But observing Gracie's anti-waitressential insolence......Alex's polity was offended and the situation precipitated a rapid deterioration in the couple's relationship. This prompted Alex to make two maneuvers. 1. He decided to agree after to the possible success of Gracie's all but impossible ontamabushed schedule for eternity. 2. He proposed to Gracie, to skip the bride of the holocaust routine and instead to be...which is to say 'such a thing as egggracie' to be........his intended in of course, of course, not not uncertain terms.

As it so happened Alex's terms were uncertain enough that Gracie did agree to them. In the fine print it was revealed that 1. Alex could no longer be the hero that saves the girl. 2. Gracie must take on the task of being the hero that saves the girl. 3. Gracie was to ride shotgun along with the girl that is Alex's intended. 4. Given this set of circumstances, Alex now was fully prepared to like....like......love such a thing as egggracie(accompanied by her metaphysics)....like..like...e'eriding shotgun on eternity.

The scene ended with the happy couple leaving the terrace (just under the stars) and back into the shadow piles of the Mesozoic's e'erear end collisions.

SCENE XII- By now we know that Gracie is no longer the innocent babe in THE one girl holocaust. Like, there's parking lots of holocausts and she's just pregnant zero's one parking spaced out car among them. But Gracie's self-evidence had been self-evidensitized enough vogued vanity that the quest for power was lurking in the spectra of her soul. Up for grabs at this point in the play we have 1. A metaphysical comic book with Gracie's notnotitude onthreatening to take over eternity. 2. An objective universe that Alex, with all his equations backed up by lenses, is barely able keep within his cosmetrick I Q's grasp. 3. Mobible, a third party kitchen appliance iffffledgingly ont I'mobilized with can opener skills...... to take control of the ontentire operation.

The eternity test site scene begins in the bunker adjacent to the pavilion complex where all of's Gracie fans are present in onticipation of sum's big-time eventuality that is supposed to change work outs at the m'eternity wards forever. The scenery includes Gracie, Alex, Mobible and the general in the bunker which is now the strategic operations center for appointments at Gracie's whate'er tight schedule for eternity. The most ontiquely advanced becomputer ontechnology is in evidence in the bunker. Under Gracie's supervision the general is directing becomputer operations. Alex has arrived late having had trouble with the beblbouncer at the entrance to the becomplex. He arrived without enough change to purchase his over-priced plast(mag)ic wand, which, are to do all of's dubbings with dibs on policinging the whate'er'down'd iffffffontexcitementions beheld inside the eternity test site becommunity's egggated entrance. Mobible explains that the sales of the plast(mag)ic wands were necessary to finance the test site project. Everyone allowed into this e'ereligious expe'eriment's becomplex just had to be carrying at least one ontrigger finge'er'd plast(mag)ic wand. Both Mobible and Gracie are cogent on that point.

Meanwhile Gracie and the general are working out the codes for the singularity onticipated for the xmas evening's ont I'm'event.. As literary back up to the e'erese'erection set up, Mobible shows the new bible that he and Gracie have been ripping straight off the chalk boards of the metaphysical society to give the night's expe'eriment sum e'er ont I'degree of could be just ont I'm'academicky offe'er'd not not of course course credibility.

Well, by now's then, It seemed that the count down from iffffffffffffffffffffffffffffffff( )fffffffffffffffffffffffffffffinity to the very able pregnant zero variable had already started for quite a while.

As presented to tense this historical event goes like this. Mobible goes through the tunnel into the pavilion first, this time followed by Gracie. Alex is assigned to work the bunker with the general.

Inside the pavilion Gracie's brave new beble world is maniffffffested with the traffic jam bazaar. The new ray gun rafter screens are ablaze with bigger than life models of Gracie with notnotitudinal metaphysics pouring out her mouth. Several booths are selling Gracie dolls with wings, UNIVERSE MADE SAMPLE and ETERNITY MADE SIMPLE BECOMIC BOOKS, Gracie onti-shirts, beble caps and ont I'miscellanous other ontrinkets from Gracie's newly ont I'm exposed e'ereserves. As Gracie enters the pavilion she is shocked to notice an ontisystmetrical life-size living Gracie statue with wings, the same wings that Gracie never got to match up with her halo on her birthday. A gulp of gin calms her down and she climbs to the podium to deliver her eternity test site beble benediction. Soon the traffic jam is raising its plast(mag)ic wands to salute the dubbing of iffffffe'er that is about to take place. It is clear to all concerned that sumwhate'er'd's ontultimatomized........................

BECOMMAND PERFORMANCE is being expected of eternity.

Gracie and the crowd recite and sing "BRINGING TO LIFE A CITY OF ANGELS"

Once the countdown accele'erates with ifffffffffffinity dropping off onto log 1 base 10, things really start to happen in both the music industry and eternity's schedule. A C note is suspended in the horns in mid e'er when.....a quasiffffffflash of almightning strikes e'erafter screens. Everyone drops to his knees except Pope Gracie.

Just then the general walks in from the bunker to announce the's e'eresults of the expe'eriment.

Unifffffffffffortunately it seems that no one is coming out the eternity beblast site alive. Apparently the expe'eriment took a wrong turn somewhere in the many detourist sites detailing the universe. It's a miracle of sorts but not the one Gracie's metaphysics had on eternity's schedule. Well, you can just imagine just how ifffffffffurious Gracie is, as she starts lecturing the graveyard in the ground beneath her feet of ifffffffished out fins she inherited as puddled from the Paleozoic whate'er wholes.

Needless to say, in one ifffffffell swoop Gracie's career as pope is over. Gracie parts the congregation and storms out of the pavilion to end the scene.

All that's left of the opera is now the epilogue.

EPILOGUE

Well there's Gracie stinctly crawling in the dirt again, watching the pixie dust sublimate in her ontrigge'er asiffffffffingers. Alex arrives as Gracie is just about to s'e'eriously revise her metaphysics. She offers Alex a pistol she found in the bunker for that purpose. Her plan is 1. Fly the winged Gracie doll that she looted from herself at the test site. 2. Get enough moving beickle distance between herself and Alex's stationary self that…3. Alex can pull the trigger to politely make her feel like…like…once again….dead….extinct…or(for the moment at least)…...impossible.

But Alex e'erealizes this is his big chance to like trigger finger-wise 1. Pull the trigger 2. Clean a barrel by its bullits and 3. Shoot the ground instead of Gracie.

Once he accomplished this feat, Alex, just to be safe, proposes to observe a moment of silence for a quite possibly dud eternity….which Gracie….can't help her e'erestless, insomnibuste'er'd self……but to iffffffffidget through.

Once Alex has accomplished his second-hand moment of silence on behalf of the's ides of e'er's onthus iffffar's dud e'er……. he confides (YOU DON'T WANT TO READ THIS)

…………………. his new plans to drowning Gracie whate'er's iffffonthwarted could be apriorily ont purposed purposition. The situation is as ifffffffffollows: while such a thing as egggracie is e'erodentifffff I'd ontantrumminating of course not not's whate'erev'd up ontward's whene'ercrafted ontoy's wingsets…such a thing as Alex is cosmetrickly immersed egggathering not not as iffffffodder…..plus being zero'd work'd selfished outing's….at once hero'd in onto……to….like….like…….of course, of course…not….not…..(network'd out newsly)….be….. ontentrumminating munched ent I'm's iffffffinform'd not ne'er's nightning strike's beaconduit that………..

YOU DO WANT TO READ THIS………..

 1. He's heading back to the universe. 2. He wants Gracie e'eriding shotgun with him.

Things are going pretty well at that point until 1. Alex squawks some'speech that Gracie ignores and 2. Gracie squawks sum'speech that Alex ignores. It's just about at this time that Gracie remembers *HER WINGS (LIKE HER WHENE'ER WINGS)…… SHE ALWAYS WANTED FOR HER BIRTHDAY'S XMAS PRESENTS…TENSED*. Not bothering to e'erummage for them in her beble box and meanwhile onthinking she 1. knows where to get them to get her and 2. Aspired by the return of the music, Gracie heads back up matterhorn where the opera began. Lighthouse-wise still beaconvinced this is his pretty party girled big chance, even dumped, Alex, armed with a bottle of gin, follows her up the matterhorn and into the storm. THE FAMOUS KITCHEN APPLIANCE DEBATE OCCURS WITHIN THE CONFINES OF THIS STORM with Gracie ranting on behalf of 'canopene'ers and Alex ranting on behalf of 'cork screws'. At the last minute's second hand moment, when Gracie's about to fall off onto her whene'er wings (that are should e'er'd to be after always waiting for her), Alex yodels, from pretty much nearly's ontopped off I'matterhorn, his only notes of the opera. "GRACIE! I BROUGHT THE BOTTLE!"

Well, wouldn't you know it, after several hesitations, Gracie turns, mutters her most almightning struck melodies of the opera with the lines "OF COURSE, OF COURSE, NOT, NOT TO BE. Reaching for the bottle, she ends up in Alex's clean (hero that saves the girl) hand that feels for all ontensiffffffff purposes like god in drag as pulls her into his wheel chair (chariot-heaventilately horse drawn) that has been hiding out(in the ground of being's garage) all of's time. The music has concluded......and the opera is over.

Except as like...like... after the opera.....Gracie and Alex are HOWEVER charioteering and casually conversing into the sumothe'er phylum's sun rise in sumother land's e'erising sunny setting's diurnal not ne'er'd's night..

And that however is still not the end of it. As it onturns out, demigodawfull affairs are not quite god enough for suitability to gracie's ontastiffff I'd iffffe'ers. So while the opera may be over the play's not over quite yet. Indeed, in the second postlude Gracie becomplains that having wings with a demigod is not enough for her after all. I mean like this is an authentic Apollonian chariot here...immersifully impressive as universal, but not god enough for Gracie'sifffffontastes. Instead....she reconfirms her becommitments to becompletely presentable eternity and dumps the demigod the way she dumped the lesser Alex as spelled backwards. So it is that Alex's humiliated horse drawn wheel chair is scened dropping Gracie off at the insomnibustop.

Well! Letting Gracie begetting dumped off a setting's sunny day job chariot may not seem to satisfy the forever after ending that audiences are searching to be e'eresearch party girlifffactoried for.............but this story all boils down to the fact that

Gracie e'ereally is iffffffffffffff( )ffffffffffffffreaked out by whate'er'd own'd as ifffffont I'm'eternity,

and will behavior nothing less than wholeggggrailodging in its not ne'er nightitude. The play part ends with Gracie at her horizon's home e'erummaging for a can opener with Alex on the phone. To continue with these spare parts of the the story would be too long for this here book.

 Note- This overly simplistic summary of the opera, with its absolute minimum of Linguish, should help any film director in the attempt to cut though the vast complex of ontanglementions particulating the becomprehensive metaphysical details of this opera. In a way, it's just the same olde boy saves girl story you've heard log 3 base 10 times in the musical emotion picture scripts of before. That said, its philosophical foundations are sum's what d'iffffffe'eront in the metaphysical marketplace and the dramatic marketplace both. While designed for becomputer ontechnocrats, it can also be made suitable for ontentelligent war-torn Japanese audiences, as well as other ontentelligentrifffffff I'd audiences in other girlwar-torn parts of the world as well.

OK SO NOW YOU HAVE TWO LITTLE VERSIONS OF THE BIG PICTURE OF WHAT THIS OPERA IS MOSTLY ALL ABOUT. FASTEN YOUR SEAT BELTS

BECAUSE THE DETAILS ARE NEITHER SO SAMPLE NOR SO SIMPLE. WITH ALL OF'S WHOLEGGRAILINGUISH ONTALKING THE SCENES…AS ARE SO ONT I'M'ESSOTE'ERICK AS HARDLY NEVER TO BE INFFFFFONTUNDE'ERTAKEN TO BE UNDE'ERSTOOD. OK! SO GOOD IFFFFFLUX, WITH YOUR E'EREADERSHIPMENTALENTS. JUST IMAGINE………EGGGRACED ONT ITS AS SPIRIT FACED ONTHEM.

So back to the overture before the beginning. Let's see ifffffffffff( )ffffffffffffff we can't ifffffffffledge this opera off eggground.

As the overture ends such a thing as egggracie is about e'eready to be sighted.

Gracie: god or no god of course, of course not not to be.

……………………………( )…………………………..

4. THE FULL ABORIGINAL LIBRETTO [IN AS IFFFRAGMENTS]AS UNEARTHED BENEATH SOME MESOZOIC SWAMP WHATE'ER

SCENE I -IN THE OBSERVATORY-

A young scientist, simulatedly shy and apollogentric, has moved from inside's outer space with his observatory furnished with ifffully ont I'm'operational impersonations of 1. A telescope capable of willinked observations. 2. A keyboard capable of ont I'musicky synthesis. Noteworthy as well is the chariot in the garagestables.

The biography of Tele the telescope is unusual. At least one of his lenses is the very same lens that Galileo used to first observe the moons of Jupiter. As Tele has advanced intellectually through the ages he has remained proud of that lens, even though he's no longer sure which lens it is.

Wolfy, on the other hand, is the same keyboard that first performed Mozart's famous 20th piano concerto back in the 1780s. As Wolfy's becomposing skills have developed over the centuries he has retained that connection to his namesake and those first harrowing days of his performance life.

Alex, on the other hand, has simulated himself to be a god, to like, like be…..a geek god, just born yesterday and has not much history to back him up. It should be noted that both Wolfy and Tele suspect

Alex to be capable of extra-dimensional extra-d'e'erectionality. However, they never discuss it since neither has trigger fingers with which to touch that topic. Alex may be viewed as a sort of gee god on sabbatical from whenever. As such he is a conscientious student of geek god science and studies each situation he confronts with honest effort. Although Alex has no one to formally teach him metaphysics, he, Tele and Wolfy dabble in it anyway…and….it must be admitted that, while Wolfy instructs Alex in the musical arts, Tele's lenses, backed by equations, do teach Alex (meaty) physics as quantized.

Tele(speaks): Log 17 base 10 seconds…….give or take a few……that's my calculation. That's how old this stuff is.

Alex (observing the second hand on his watch): You're pretty sure?

Tele: Yea, pretty sure.

Alex: And the Mesozoic in these parts you log in at about 15?

Tele: A quarter of that.

Alex examines the charts on the wall. He surveys a diagram of the cosmic background's e'eradioactive stuff, then turns to the diagram of the Mesozoic. It reads TRIASSIC, JURASSIC, CRETACEOUS, MAMMACEOUS.

Tele: You look worried Alex.

Alex: Well, there's rumors the Mesozoic's ending any second now (looking at his watch) and I still haven't been out in it. You spot anything? (Tele pivots to view the sky)

Tele: Nothing yet in the sky….just…..oh……..

Alex: What?

Tele: Uh, direction wise its down too low to beconsidered up. It's too close to get ifffffffffffocused. Probably nothing.

Alex: Well, get it in focus with aspectral readings anyway.

Tele: Will do. Meanwhile it sure looks like the middle of the middle of the middle of the Mesozoic to me. I wouldn't worry about it ending soon. I mean, as fly by night as mesozoos are, they don't really matter in the long run anyway. If worse comes to worse, Alex you can do without. Besides I've got equations and you've got equations. We've got a universe to integrate in on our tensor calculus as pretty much everything there is.

Alex: You sure about that Tele?

Tele: You know sometimes I worry about you Alex: I mean like I've got lenses and you've got lenses. We're on the same team Alex. Plus, I have equations…you have equations.

Wolfy: I heard that. What about me? I make up musical m'equations. Where does that put me?

Tele: In operation. Wolfy, you're just a windup toy that spreads tinkles. Alex and I are thinkers like….like…..tantrumminating star stuff that's all there is.

Wolfy: Yes, but what if that stuff is just sumessage's mess stuffed into......like..like...a bottle out at sea....like..floating in sum what's bige'er time whate'er. What if your lenses are blind as a battering ram against what e'ereally matters. I mean like the question always e'erises, cosmontologically speaking, sticky as stars are, what iffffff eternity's just notnot onthat n'ontalented.

Tele: Don't listen to him Alex: He hears voices. Voices inhabit him; he inhabits voices. He's just trying to beconfuse you with all that stuffed eternity stuff. If I've told you once I've told you log 3 base 10s of times, the universe is all there is. I've lenses backed up by equations and equations backed up by lenses to prove it. And hey! It's a pretty good looking universe at that......especially at night...when it's all lit up like an xmass tree with windup toys trained circling around on xmas eve.

Wolfy: With all of's Santa's ont I'music becoming down the chimney

Tele: Choirs .....while I'm the one instructing Alex in universes being all there is...like...like....up for grabs...like meaty physics-wise ground up beef ore to be mined by lenses with equations to back them up. Right Alex?

Alex (steps in, waving his hands to subdue the argument): ....But you are quite sure, Tele, a universe is all there is to be up for grabs?

Tele(confidently): Yep! And if you don't egggrab at too much of it, like..if you don't expect too much of it, it won't disappoint you either. As far as eternity's concerned I wouldn't be too ontoptimystick. As iffffar as eternity's ifffe'ers are concerned, what if e'ers ontoxick or...or... like..... whene'er's worse ....e'ereally's just a dud.

Wolfy: I've heard that one before. What about the stuff that can't be stuffed into stars?

Tele: Like what?

Wolfy: Like stuff my voices tell me about. Dreams for example.

What if dreams don't need stars to dream them? I mean like awaring outing's universitease, iffffalling ifffont I'm'apart…..what was I saying….

Tele: Nothing that ont I'm'at'e'ers…… my lensmane'er's assure you.

Wolfy: Ok but. What if, stars or no stars, the e'er as e'er'd were like….like……*dreame'ergent………*way, way, way past the debecommissioned stars. What if someone's only into stars for the like…like…like 'ontitude' of it all. What iffff this universe is just kids on the playground stuff stufft into like (hesitates)like…….like *ont I'm onthin e'er.* There, I said it.

Alex and Tele stare down on Wolfy. Wolfy's keyboard cover backs up over the keys.

Wolfy: Like the 'eternity' of it all.

Alex and Tele's lens stare at each other.

Tele (Gathering himself): Oh! Eternity! That's just a mathematical construct f non-finite temporality, right Alex?

Alex(dumfounded): Uh.....yea.

Tele: Like ont I'musickly speaking, eterniy's ifffe'er is pretty much ontoxick or whene'er's worse...to becompletion's dud. What musick's there for that?

Wolfy (playing a tone row): No, that's not it.

Tele: Eternity? For any other on purpositions it's a becompletely dud eternity. Right Alex?

Alex: Mathematically speaking, that's all there's to it. Otherwise it's just begot to be...

Tele: A dud eternity.

Wolfy (now really upset): All right already, so like, I give! Maybe it is like a dead'e'erizon. Let's observe a moment of silence for a quite possibly dud eternity.

Alex: I'll observe it.

Tele (reluctantly): Oh all right, I will, I will, I willlens to observe it.

Tele's lenses clinck clickingrigidly into operation.

Wolfy: A lot of god willlenses do at such ont I'mly m'at'e'ers.

Alex and Tele, with lenses backed up by equations, observe the moment of silence for the dud eternity as Wolfy orchestrates and conducts its silence. But now that a moment of silence has been observed for the dud eternity, Alex notices the Sunflower that is the observatory mascot has drooped.

Alex: But speaking of a dud eternity, right now that flowers drooped. Like it was sunny side up a moment ago.

Tele is reaching over intrusively to study it with one of his microscopic lenses: Entropy Alex, it's setting sunny sidown now; that's all there's to it.

Wolfy and Tele: Breathe on it Alex. Put those fished out fins to the peddle. Give it some gas.

Alex (breathing heavily): Wolfy isn't there anything you can play for it?

Wolfy: Oh yea, can you hear me flower? Do I have permission to use my voices?

Alex and Tele: It budged. Yes, by all means use your voices.

Wolfy begins with samples of his voices that emerge into a simple but uplifting melody. The flower budges profusely and stands completely sunny side up again as Wolfy concludes his melody.

Alex: You saved the flower Wolfy!

Tele (slightly jealous): A lot of good that will do in the end. Things droop. Things get a little hot and then they droop. The hotter they get the quicker they droop. That's what the stuff that's all there is just does. Like when it's stars, from far enough away...heaventilating heat that twinkles in e'er, sometimes, I must admit, as drawn like cartoons in dreamentional directions almost(whistfully) as if out of dreams.

Alex: I never knew you had dreams Tele.

Tele: Oh, just kidding. Like I do but not really. When I'm looking at stuff sometimes it sort of almost feels as iffffffffffffffffffffffffff( )ffffffffffffffffff…like pregnant zeros are simulating auditions adding up to sum's one's dreams. Like 0+ 0+ 0 = plussed outings in the end. Phenomenally speaking it's a very odd becommoddity….I don't take s'e'eriously of course…

Alex: What about you Wolfy?

Wolfy: Oh yes, I do, but they fly by quick as noisy bits of nowsy news….nextitudinating ont I'musicky perfumance from note to note…….Oh yea….there one goes…nextitudinating to another. It's just me playing with myself.

Alex: Please, play with yourself.

Wolfy: You sure?

Alex and Tele in unison: Yea, go ahead. I don't mind.

Wolfy: Well, all right it goes like this.

Wolfy plays a tone row and stops. Starting again he enters a key that picks up momentum.

Alex: Can I play along?

Wolfy: Are your hands clean?

Alex (studying his hands): Yes.

Wolfy: Then be my guest.

As Alex sits down to the keyboard, arpeggios are rolling like waves at sea. As the music progresses Tele's angle of observation seems to be being pulled out of the sky by some s'excelle'erations egggravitational field down to the horizon.

Tele: I spotted a star but not really. It appears to have just landed.

Alex(alerted): What's it doing? Can you get a spectrum?

Tele: Well, it's….it's…..oh my….it's like..blushed out of the blue rainbotically. It winked at me.

Alex: You mean it twinkled at you.

Tele: No, it's not twinkling. It's more like haloaded eggglowing sunny side upsidown like…baptizing a river.

Alex: Like e'ereve'd'e'er or like a river?

Tele: Well, there's so much simulation in these parts…. it could be either one. I am getting an absorption spectrum however.

Alex: Yes?

Tele: Well….like…like….like…uh…e'xplicitely   as'elf   evidensititeased   it's like…like…like….like….like….not absorbed.

Alex: Becomprehensively?

Tele: Yes…..like…like….dreamergently…..the spectrum must be viewed as……as………

Alex: As what Tele?

Tele: Like, rainbotic, from blush to blue. But the she it of it is way too iffffffformative for color schemes. I mean like this she it's way, way too pretty for the speed of enlightenment to keep up with.

Alex: You're joking.

Tele: No my lenses don't have equations to joke about such matters. Whatever this is it's the real something assimulated.

Alex: Well, keep track of it and report back when you figure out just what it is…..is like…like…..like………

This conversation is drowned out as the music picks up momentum to become a full-fledged concerto in the old romantic style. Meanwhile Tele is becoming more and more riveted to the dreame'ergent object winking upsidown at his objective lens. As the music approaches its violent climax, Tele is shaking violently, clicking rapidly to higher and higher resolutions with his lens systems.

Tele: Alex, I think you'd better have a look at this! OH MY GOD! I MUST BE DREAMING! My lenses seem to be phylumenating that…that…..THERE'S SUCH A THING AS………THIS!

Alex rushes over to one of Tele's accessory lenses. Alex pans through different spectra of the interfe'erometer as the music reaches its climax and the object comes into focus as blushed rainbotically out of the blue.

Alex: OH!!!!!!!!SHE!!!!!!!!!!!!!IT!!!!!!!!!!!!!!!

Alex rushes out of the observatory slamming the door on the violent atonal triad that concludes the music.

Wolfy: What was it?

Tele: It looks like Alex is heading out into the Mesozoic.

Wolfy: On purpose or by accident?

Tele: Apparently on purpose. After some sort of aprioripithecus from the aprioripithecine is my best guess.

Wolfy: What's it doing in the Mesozoic?

Tele: It's something like…like……I'm going to say it……like…..*dreame'ergent*ly….like…stretching the integral power of my equations. It feels like a whole new branch of mathematics will like…be….like…ifffe'erequired.

Wolfy: Will more music be needed?

Tele: How much can you make?

Wolfy: Several symphonies.

Tele: You'd better get them ready. If I'm not mistaken for a ride, we've promislanded onto some sort of opera operating in these parts.

THE SCENE ENDS

INTERLUDE ONE- Interlude music reflects Alex's agitated state of mind as he proceeds from the observatory to the object in question.

SCENE II- THE MEETING AT THE BRIDGE

Alex approaches Gracie hanging from the bridge to baptize the river with her hairdo. Her hairdo has all of's behavior of a halo. Recovering from her upside down and backward posture, she fumbles to switch off her halo. The switch is on the rainbow tie around her neck.

Gracie: E'ERCRAFT! Sooner or later's e'ercraft....e'erived with the verdict.

Alex: About what?

Gracie: The NOT/NOTNOT CODE...ETERNITY'S ALPHABET.....whatelse. My secrecy's ontreasure trove of e'er which only I ontouch. We're like....like.... on the same onteam e'eright?

Alex: What team is that?

Gracie: Unless you've been making appointments to be an idiot you would know. Becompletely presentable eternity. What else. Like are you spelled backwards or not. So who else are you besides like...like....like maybe spelled backwards.....or.......like....like...should you be tested? (suddenly looking very cagey) Do you bark backwards too?

Alex Mmmmmm, not really.

Gracie: Well, as just could be cartooned....I am like prey eumanimation in these parts. Who are you?

Alex: You mean?

Gracie: Like spelled backwards. Here, spell what you are backwards. (Gracie gives Alex her wand)

Alex (not knowing what to do with the wand): Ok so like 'DOGIMED'.

Gracie: That was backwards?

Alex: Mhm, say dog for short.

Gracie (encouraged, takes wand back): All right then! Now we're getting somewhere's when. So like you did come to congraduate me after all.

Alex: From what?

Gracie: Beconvenience storaged e'er. Ring any bells? It's like iffffished out of whate'er's onteque'erian beconvenience store operating whenever being's available. Do you get it or do you have to be ontested?

Alex: To like congratulate you from..........

Gracie: From kindergarten, what else. Look, whoever you are, I'll have you know..........I....I am whate'er's iffffffished out egggirl that everyone else wants me not to be except as everybody's anybody's else instead.

Alex: Yes, I can see that you're what everyone wants themselves to be instead. Look, my lenses saw you almost falling in the…..the…river and well….. I hardly ever dabble in metaphysics and I usually don't pay attention to whate'er, but my lenses saw you almost falling into it. Normally I'm a student of some stars, starred daily behaving outer space actually. I do have a wheelchair in the garage.

Gracie: That's all, you don't like know that nothing's like what it seems, not elsewise like bedabbled in?

Alex: Oh! Well I do dabble in lenses backed up by equations.

Gracie(relieved): So you are in disguise after all. You know all about how I just solved eternity and you've come to congratulate me out of kindergarden. That's it isn't it. Please be it.

Alex (playing along): Yes. Come to think of it 1. I've come to congratuate you…

Gracie: Ontopping off….

Alex; Yes, ontopping off…

Gracie: Iffffffffffffffff( )ffffffffffffffffe'er?

Alex (catching on): Yes, iffffe'er becompletely out of kindergarden for solving becompletely presentable eternity. 2. I am arrived by e'ercraft, which I keep whene'erwheel chaired in the garage. 3. My telescope Tele and I spotted you about to fall in the river's uh…like…like…(Alex attempts to mimic Gracie's version of becomic book justajiffffy's jargon))..reved'e'er……

Gracie: So can you be tested?

Alex: For what?

Gracie: For being spelled backwards.

Alex: Sure. Why not.

Gracie: Sit!

Alex: What?

Gracie: Ok, so like…….Sit. (Alex sits. Gracie is encouraged) Ok, now spell yourself backwards.

Alex (trying to be accommodating): You know I do, I do, I do often think of myself spelled backwards.

Gracie(testing): Ok so like bark. Bark backwards. If you were who I'm pretending you to be spelled backwards I could dub you to do it. (Gracie raises her wand)

Alex (suddenly asserting himself): Don't tempt me Gracie. Tele and I saw you falling in the river and I've come to be the hero to save your…..well not your metaphysics….but……but…..YOUR…YOUR…YOUFEMINONTICAL…..EGGGIRL.

Gracie: What? WHOSE EGGGIRL?

Alex:

Alex (apprehensive): Such a thing as………well YOU.

Gracie throws up her arms in despair.

Gracie (ranting): I KNEW IT! DAMN! DAMN! DAMN! Ok like whoever you are….just sit! If you were……….

Alex sits.

Gracie: As whate'er barked SPELLS BECOMPLETELY BACKWARDS YOU WOULD KNOW…..I CAN'T BE SAVED!!!!!!!!!!!! I solve eternity and who e'erives but some observatory guy whose got my meaty physics in his peep show who wants to save me just when I've got a warning label put on me that…that…like….I can't be saved ever since the girl wars. I mean like…like… as holocaust preoccupation territory I just can't quite…..quite…..quite…….like….like……you'd better back off at my nasty bad breath that's gonna say it.

Alex: What?

Gracie: E X I S T. Oh my god….what have I saidone.

Alex: You just said "EXIST".

Gracie: Wow! I actually did say it didn't I! Listen Alex, whatever you don't do… DON'T SAVE ME!!!!!!!! Agree with my metaphysics! Pretty please, do that. But do not save me. Do you have to be tested? IF YOU EVER SAVE ME…..(cringes)……

I WILL JUST HAVE TO DUMP YOU! DO YOU UNDERSTAND!!!!! I WILL! I WILL! I WILL! JUST HAVE TO DUMP!!!!!!! YOU!!!!!! DO YOU UNDERSTAND?

Alex (recoils wincing): Yes. But….but….

Gracie: But what?

Alex: But your spectrum.

Gracie (putting her trigger up to her mouth in abject curiosity): What about my spectrum?

Alex: Tele reports you testing out rainbotically from like blush….

Gracie(excited): Yes! Yes!

Alex: To like blue…with your total make up kit……informed I'd'snowlandescapades all of's way danced up to….

Gracie(exuberont): yes!

Alex: Up to……..uh….

Gracie (helping him out): Euphemifffffffactoried like Miss Eternity that's way more than a mathematical construct of non-finite tempormorality! Like if you we'erealy spelled backwards that would just have to be what you were trying to say……..So please…please…please…. let that be what you were trying to say.

Alex(Acquiescing): Mhm…yes Gracie that's exactly what I was trying to say.

Gracie: Ok so fine and dandy for me begetting way too pretty way too fast for the speed of enlightenment to ever catch up with me. Now like sub….super….cutaneously speaking………Just look at my ont I'moon's dark side. While of course, of course not not I'm embarrassed for everybody's else not me….like…I am of course, of course not not embarrassed(ont I'm'ashamed at myself) for myself being such a thing as like….like…likeme. Can't you see that I'm the most dangerous person I have ever been. (Gracie poses as a statue with seriously classical mannerisms) Look, I'm egggrown up Alex..without wings. But my tail does have a head with hairdos to work out with. I've got a contract out on my……Like I take pills. I'm on holocoasteroids. I've got wholegggrailooks heating up all of's puddles. And not only that but it seems like forever I've been waiting in line to be myself, if that means anything to your omniscience..

Gracie examines Alex for signs of omniscience.

Gracie: Look, I'm not such a thing as who I am for some body's outer space Alex. When it comes to metaphysics I don't dabble. Like ontheoretickly speaking I'm more than meaty phyzzled eggshells of myself, ontip towing belongings to eternity. I work the big time. Wherever's there's equations I stretch them with my selfished out metaphysics, speaking of which

WITH MY NEW ALPHABET it's like ont I'm'actual ont I'm'eternity I just solved.

Alex: Your alphabet?

Gracie: Yes, whoever you are spelled backwards, DON'T YOU DARE HUMILIATE MY ALPHABET?

Alex: I wouldn't

Gracie: No you can't…….IT'S way too preposte'erologically profound, iffffffff you must know.

Alex: So like eggground breaking?

Gracie: No more like…like…like….ground of NOT/NOTNOT CODE being breaking……..insomnibusting out notnotitude. It's like the 0/1 code for information preposte'erologically expressing iffffontense'er calculust for like…like…..like….iffffffffff( )ffffffffffformation, ffffffffffffyou must know….onticketing e'erides whate'er'd iffffonthrough out……..

Alex: Onticketed?

Gracie: ONTICKETED, of course, of course, not….not. Look, whoever you are (Gracie studies Alex for signs of being whoever he just might be) Hey! Would you like to maybe be my analyst. I do need an analyst. How about you being that?

Alex: What would I have to do?

Gracie: Oh, just…sit.

Alex sits.

Gracie Yea but 1. Spelled backwards (she winks) 2. Be ontheory seated ontheologged in long enough to be agreeable to my metaphysics.

Alex: Sure. Why not. So like your metaphysics…

Gracie: MY metaphysics must be said to overlook my meaty physics so……….

Alex: So lets (preternaturally catching on) "ontake wholegggrailooks" at your metaphysics………

Alex and Gracie exchange winks.

Gracie (primping to give a lecture): Here's how it goes……

Alex (turning Gracie at the shoulders) Here, I think Tele will want to be in on this. (Pointing to the observatory in the distanced line of sight) Tele, are you getting this? Yea, he's…….

Gracie: You mean Tele's got me under surveillance?

Alex: Ah, yes he has. I think I should point out that 1. Tele does dabble in metaphysics. 2. Tele reads lips.

Gracie: (saluting her hand over her eyes, squinting to turn to Tele): I've never done this with….

Alex: Lenses.

GRACIE'S FIRST METAPHYSICAL LECTURE OF THE OPERA

Gracie: …..lenses before but (Gracie primps) So Tele, like READ MY LIPS. Let me first say by introduction that *E'EREALTY'S MORE A PRIORI THAN YOUR LENSES MIGHT SUPPOSE.* It's like I almost never said, I e'erepresent ETERNITY SELF PUBLISHED….LIKE…LIKE…IFFFONT I'M'ADVERTIZED AT LAST. Look, being lenses and all, you're naturally into universes and all, BUT!!!(snaps her trigger finger) 1. Eternity is not just a mathematical construct of non-finite temporality. 2. The stuff starring in your objective lenses is not all there is. You got it? BECAUZZZZZZ LIKE ETERNITY'S {{{{{ONTALENTED}}}}} WAY PAST INFINITY ALL THE WAY UP TO LIKE {{{IFFFFFINITY}}}}. You got that?

Gracie turns to Alex.

Alex: Mhm, so far so…..so….dog dubbed mhm……backwards.

Gracie(encouraged): OK! Like just what has this eternity begot e'ergoing for it. 1. Nextitudinatable neighborly nows. 2. The selfished out secret ingredient. And what is the secret ingredient you just might ask iffffffff like justajiffff lasted long enough. Well…

OF COURSE…. OF COURSE….. NOT…. NOT…… {{{NOTNOTITUDE}}}}!!!!!!!!!! BECAUZZZZZ( )ZZZZZZZZ…. NOTNOTITUDE DOES STUFF!!!!! I MEAN THINK ABOUT IT….{{BEING}} JUST BASKS..BUT…NOTNOT BEING….DOES STUFF. I mean like how does a fish know it's a fish? BECAUZZZZZZ IT'S NOT NOT A FISH. SO LIKE WITH NOTNOTITUDE E'ERIDING SHOT GUN ON BECOMPLETELY NEXTITUDINATABLY NEIGHBORLY NOWS AND!!!! You've got yourself a becompletely presentable eternity. That's all there's to it. Stars or no stars, nowsy snooze s'e'ervice makes nowsy news'e'ervice MOUTHING OFF THE COULD BE E'ER COOLIFFFFIED COOLEST THING EVER!!!!!

Do you get it or do you have to be ontested?

Alex: He gets it.

Gracie: All right then. And like this coolifffffies in ways you might not expect at the lens level of e'erealty. The way I iffffffffffffffff( )ffffffffffffffffigure it against eggground in these parts…its like…notnotitudes onticketed ont eeked from out of whate'er's notitude to cell iffffontique storage as ont I'm'e'eresults of ontrophickly presentable m'e'erizoned e'er. That's what you beget to onteeter tot in the play grounds of to be.

There is a palpable silence from the observatory as Tele absorbs Gracie's metaphysics.

Gracie: So, like chapter two. Aesthethics wise. Like with eternity the e'eresponsible party in all of's realty, universes have way too many alibis to be LIKE {{ONTAKEN S'E'ERIOUSLY}} for long enough to matter. But presentable eternity…..notnotitudinally…..and nextitudinally engine'er'd has no alibis at all. Eternity's something to count on…..not up to infinity….forget that…..all of's way danced up to iffffffffffffffffff( )ffffffffffffffffinity. So like, good luck with your ifffffly by nightning's sampled universe. I mean like peep shows are fine at night…but don't give up your day job……..in becompletely presentable eternity.

Gracie turns to Alex.

Gracie: Do you think he got it..or does he have to be ontested?

Alex: Well, so far so good but…like….so what good are puniverses….if they're all loaded up with no e'eresponsibilities to speak of.

Gracie: Not e'ereally e'eready to play god at all. It's like…like…..every given universe is just every given's puniverse's sandbox in the playgrounds of to be….to be's busy notnotitude, that is. Like, universes are good enough for some things but not spelled backwards enough for sum's things. Well, that's the not/notnot alphabet and my ont I'metaphysics that goes with it. Alphabetically as e'ercrafted I hope you found it ontente'ertaining.

Alex: Gracie, with this new alphabet do you really think you can like ifffe'ercraft scramble all of's e'erealty's becomplications? I mean to do all of's ont I'm'agic tricks......as e'erore mined... like with or without a universe...like iffffffirmamentally way past the stars?

Gracie: Yep. All of's way danced ont iffffffinity, ont I'mathematically leaving infinity in the's dust of could be's collection of dust samples.

Alex (Shrugging his shoulders, and half beconvinced that Gracie might be onto sum's onthing, Alex shakes his head in Tele's direction): All e'eright then. Now what about your meaty physics? This is the Mesozoic, which is sub posed to be one big menu after all. What is.....is......

Gracie: My job on the menu?

Alex: Yes, as your analyst I think I should know.

Gracie: Oh like I'm the main meal on the menu (sorting through her wanted posters Gracie shows Alex a menu with Gracie on it) Like I'm in all of's delicacies. You see the punctuation at the end of every item.

Alex: Yes, what's the punctuation for?

Gracie: It's periods at the end of my sentences to beconsumed to be......

Alex: What?

Gracie: Spider droppings, soone'er's late'er spider turds. I'm the friendly fly by party girl like..like...nice enough to live in meals of spider webs. Like my job's...like to just be sooner's later...spider turds using my make up kits. That's my meaty physics in these parts where my party girl parts beget humped by the holocausts.

Alex: So how did you end up on that party girl's menu? What's the story?

Gracie: Well, there isn't much to tell really. It's like I may not have told you already, I'm not in this for the universe. Since the girl wars, I'm not even in it for the Miss Eternity pageant which I won, by the way, over runner up reality, for getting way too pretty way too fast.

Alex: Mhm, I do have lenses with opened I lids backed up by equations.

Gracie (continues with her saga): Since falling off the mountain into the nativity scenery daddy locked me in a closet inside the could be safe where the traffic jams couldn't get me jammed in traffic. It was about this time I was behaving ontantrumminations onte'erantulated into justajiffffy jibberish iffffffff( )ffffffffff I wasn't of course of course not not could be carefull. Once the egggated becommunity closet was put in kindergarden's out housing out of the safe heaventilation systems.......the girl wars started in the middle of the middle of the middle of world war whenevers. The Mesozoic was in full sway dance tunneling through the carnivals with all kinds of holocoaster rides taile'er'd to headings every which way. Once our side lost and we just couldn't get credentials for being dead, I was redesigned as occupied territory and donated to charity. Then the power grid got a hold of the words in the explantation dispensary and I've been dispensed on holocauste'eroids ever since. But my hairdo (points to her halo) matured right through kindergarden without a hitch and, even without those wings I wanted for my birthday, I started my work outs on the crossed outing. Before sundown I work at my motel's dark rooms, where promotion pictures are taken, turning my negatives into iffffffffilm's hits. Since to *be* for such a thing as myself became taboo, I've been dubbing myself into these dying spells, bailed out by m'adventures ontique shopping in ont I'm'e'er, where of course, of course.....it's approvably always....like...like...ontentaboo to be selfisticated to be just...like....like....myself, especially when ifffffffreaked out as, ont I'm wise I m'appear to be on the map.(Gracie shows Alex the map of egggracess'd occupation territory). As you can see, in that light, I got way too pretty way, way over the rainbow, way too fast and everybody but me was allowed in my mirrors anymore. So I have my puddles to tide my make up kit over with masterpieced together puzzles wherever light is wet enough for negatives of negatives of me be in the picture. Apart from puddles, like I almost didn't say, I gave up on the universe. And then one day passing a chalk board at the metaphysical society I decided to start working presentable eternity on a decision basis. I dabbled in metaphysics all the way up to pregnant zeros and other such onthings at the ides of e'er...scheduling ifffe'erious appointments at half time between minus and plus ifffffinity......euphemifffffeelined wholegggrown along side present tense with egggod's make up kit ent....ont I'maged not at all just for now. So like ever since the girl wars I'm decidedly no longer like COSMICKLY IMMERSED(wincing) So like...I've been in onto THE BIG TIME ever since.

Alex: So like working ifffffinity's half time shows? With god on purposed in your image.

Gracie: Yea, with me winning the Miss Eternity Pageant over runner up reality..like...like...like I just did...... the way I iffffffigure it, the best look for god is in my image. And since for me, just ajifffy's ides of e'ers been stuck in presented tense...notnotitude's been my egggig.........e'er since the girl wars of course...of course....not...not. I also dabble in ordinary mathematics working the y-not axis of the I'd thou artesian coordinate systems leading to my new branch of mathematics.

Alex: What's that?

Gracie: Ontense'er calculus. I can lecture you on that if you....

Alex: No. I can iffffigure it out for myself.

Gracie (evaluating Alex for ont I'm'ath e'er skills) But you caught me just now dabbling in metaphysics...just enough...by the way....to solve eternity. I've been auditioning eternity's behavior for ontalented e'eresources. When I was still confusing e'er's ifffformation with stared at's information (refer to your lenses) I was actually onthinking of (ontantrumminating about) behavioring eternity's whate'er's asiffffontoilet.....like...ontrained.

Alex: Mhm. To toilet train eternity then......

Gracie: Or maybe like....but beget sum's e'eresurrections in my onteats. But to do that, the way I ifffigure the ground of it, I'd need to begetting a free floating iphphphphylum all my own. Like I iffffigure it would take more wands than I can handle to get it done. I mean I'd have to pull strings on my becompletely iffffirst impersonative puppet status as one of's bebles to do that.

Alex: What are bebles?

Gracie: The possible people that live in this eternity.

Alex: When?

Gracie: Whenever. Preposte'erously so to speak. Belivable as…..

Alex: Believable as ……..who?

Gracie: No belivable…as whoeverized preposte'erologically pounde'er'd out ounced….. aft e'eronce…aft e'eronce….like once upont I'm……..like…. m'eventuating in just a jiffffy's of course…of course…not……notable……notitutude…..in approximation to like…pregnant zeros…..as like ont I'maybe wholegggraileve'eraged….by baby's he's us…. god or no god…..no offense…..camouflaged as an idiot…….no offense……adding up to one. The way I ifffigure it, ont e'erithmetrickly speaking….once pregnant zero auditions up to one….iffffinity's available…like sooner or later…..and decidedly counting down to sooner. Meanwhile here I am ont I'mathematickly speaking's Y-not could be coordinate's greatess'dabbler in metaphysics living upside down the girl wars, just waiting in line to be myself while everybody's else is waiting in line to be me, or half of me, or me drawn and quartered……like such a thing approximated to me living as metifffored in anybody's by mined I'mirrors.

Alex: Gracie, meanwhile……like…. not quite being yourself, if you were yourself, what assortment of projects would you have in mind?

Gracie: Phew! What wouldn't I have in mind if I could be myself that's not myself responsible for the girl wars. Oh, becompletely presentable e'ercraft's parking lots of stuff. As could be's cartoon care actor I could bigot to begot e'ereally high hopes for eternity. As iffffished out caught selfishing onteete'ertot's eggglorifffledged e'er egggnostalgeontiquity's ascentiment, while auditioning myself to be obvious, I'd e'erun a testing s'e'ervice for like ontoyletrained eternity….and once I got e'er outhouse broken….I'd test eternity for like "whate'er worked out iffffontalents".

Alex (catching on): So, like metifffforically speaking, to dete'ermine eternity for becomprehensive ontalented ont I'm'availabilities……

Gracie: Mhm. Like to determine iffffffffffffffffffffffffffff( )ffffffffffffffffffffffffffff eternity qualiffffies for of course, of course not not's…..like…could be cooliffffffffffied status. Like, as eternity's obvious intended, becompletely presentable eternity is all I'm afte'ereally. Haven't you ever looked e'eright at what you're looking as iffffffffrom, to see how much ontique shoppe talent's available ont I'm'eventually out here now? How cooliffffffffffffied to notnot be…… just might (as justajiffffactoried) not not….of course, of course, not….not just be. I mean when you add up quantities to beget to qualitease, just how cooliffffffffied can to be qualifffffications beget. Other than that there's not that much I want, just 1. Those wings I never got for my birthday's not ne'er's night time's xmas eve…..and 2. of course, of course…not…not..that iphphphylum as promotion pictured on my own. Apart from bottles of lots and lots of gin, that's all I really 3. Require of this eternity.

Alex (genuinely sympathetic, Alex studies Gracie for signs of being a phylum like becompletely promotion pictured like on her own): You mean you......

Gracie: I wanted wings to go with my (points to her halo) head gear........Like in set theory, it makes a set and stylishly speaking, it makes me I'm'e'er'd more like....like...ontisymetrical. If you were dog spelled backwards you would grasp the situation. Please..like...please...be spelled backwards just enough to just grasp it. Like, ifffffrom nothing else, like grasp it from the eggglayers of....

Alex (A light bulb goes off on in Alex's I Quotiont): I do! I do egggrasp it. Maybe I am (sits cordially) spelled backwards after all.

Gracie is caught frantically dubbing Alex with her wand.

Gracie (studying Alex for signs of high quotience): In the mean time, without my wings I'm asymetrickly halo'd to not quite be myself, especially when the power grid's got me divided up into canonical sections....like....sooooooo subtracted from myself that I just can't add up to anyone anymore. I'm a wanted woman.....

Alex: Alex.

Gracie: Alex (Gracie shows her wanted poster with Gracie looking (like a very stylishly up and in at down and out) criminal. It reads GRACIE WANTED DEAD not stinct, impossible or at least NOT ALIVE.). Mainly they want me impossible of course, of course...not...not.....or at least not stinct......or maybe just dead. Meanwhile everybody wants my puddles in their mirrors, like auditioning themselves to be obviously ont I'masimulations of assimulations of my puddles in their mirrors. It's like there's so many almosticklish party girls of me scratched in the mirrors of these parts...and on the could be covers of paper products...... it's like..the wholegggrail of my way too obvious self-evidence feels pretty assimulated. Metaphysically I'm always dreame'ergent of course, of course not...not....but meaty physically I'm becoming obsolete.

Alex: You can always be in my puddles. (turning to Tele) Tele what about your lenses? Yea, Tele's lenses have orthoptical interferometers for........aesthethical spectra.

Gracie (starting to relate to Tele at the aesthethical level): So....Tele, stare at the like...like...the likes of me. Yea, just go ahead and do it. Like wholegggrailens me all you like. Think of all the other peep show stars you've ever observed to like twinkle. Am I obvious or what? (Gracie poses I'd thou artistickly like a statue)

Alex: Well, self-evidenticklishly speaking, puzzlewise you're obviously masterpieced together. You agree Tele? He agrees. You don't have to audition to be obvious.

Gracie: Thanks, but I have my puddles to tell me that. So what's your verdict?

Alex: Oh not guilty until proven otherwise.

Gracie(gushing): Oh! You really mean it!!!!!

Alex: Yes, I do, I do mean it. Now as your analyst I should examine your reading materials.

Gracie (handing Alex two books): These are my very first books from kindergarten straight from the power grid factory for just kidding on the play ground's readers.

Alex: Hmmmhm. DEATH MADE SIMPLE. Mhm and…...DEATH FOR BEGINNERS. Mhm.

Gracie (trying to be helpful): And these are my best friend spider books. It's all about how my best friend spider trance elates my hairdo into gibberish. (opens book) See, that's my friend not being me and that's me friendly enough to not be me anymore too.

Alex: What's that period?

Gracie: Punctuation. That's me as a spider turd. It's the point that ends the story with a period. Like I almost already didn't tell you…………like ever since the girl wars I've just been either obsolete or impossible, with a couple of possibilities in between.

Alex: What are those?

Gracie: Oh, like extinct or just dead or better yet just dying. In any case I'm not being human anymore. I'm begetting myself a phylum all my own. I'm becoming euman, at least for starters.

Alex (examines Gracie for her possible eumanity): Yes I see. I must say, it's very attractive.

Gracie: So like it does show?

Alex (With distinct admiration): Mhm. What is the population of eumanity if I might ask.

Gracie (slightly befuddled): Oh, after the holocaust and all….it's down to….well….like pregnant zero's….like….like……until I know d'iffffffffffffe'erontly………..like one.

Alex: Well, if I could be devoted in these parts…that one would begetting my vote.

Gracie: So!!! You mean you don't disapprove of me starting out iphphphphphyluminations all my own!

Alex: No, in this case…not at all.

Gracie: And you do e'erealize that……like metaphysically speaking, in the iffffffinal analysis (there's your cuc)…getting my behind out of the universe's behind, dropping off the stars, begetting out of the mesozoo and just ont I'm into ifffffffffont I'metazoos of sum's assortment's becompletely presentABLE eternity…….is what's in the as iffffffffffffffffffffffffffffffffffffffffffff( )ffffffffffffffffffffffffffffffffffffffffffff offing here.

Alex: Well I'm not a student of onteque'erian jargon but…. Gracie, as your analyst I am very interested, from a therapeutic (Alex clues in onto the ontique nature of this wholegggrailist encounter)…..I mean like….. ONTherapeutic perspective, about this business of dying all the time….I'd like to know just why you want to be(shaking the friendly spider turds book) dropped off spider turds or at least not be yourself being anything else but like…. ont optionally like dead.

Gracie: Oh! I don't want to be dead. I just have to be dying all the time. Don't you get it? Or do you have to be ontested. I justiffffff I ably just must be *dying*. I'm a dangerous person Alex, dangerously afraid to be like…like lived like almost like not quite not really…….dangerously scared to be anything but not myself. Ever since the girl war there's nothing more monste'erious for me than to be alive. So!!!! My solution to the dilemma IS!!!!!! Like ever since being ticketed taboo, I've been toying with high fashioned beach resorts for dying out. And guess what! I've discovered that being 'dying' makes a much better lyric than being dead…or extinct…or even impossible. (turns to Tele) You've had me in your peep show long enough to know that I am such an 'ontique asifffffffflirt' Tele. (turns to Alex) You see on the back side of my wanted poster that meanwhile I'm wanted dead while or-not-alive…see here…I'm GRACIE WANTED DYING TO SAVE THE DAY. (Gracie shows the lyrics on the back side of her wanted poster.) At any rate being dead makes a lousy lyric…she sings faintly…I'LL BE DEAD SO……..You see…it makes a lousy lyric. Besides Hey! Like pay ont I'm'attention why don't I! I'm like….like….like just too ont I'metaphysickly IFFFFFFFONTSY to be dead. I mean like being humped by the holocaust this way I was just trying to be anice person, trying to stay off the menu and stay pretty iffffffontentantsy as such to not be dead, extinct or impossible.

Alex: Uh Gracie…like…like…just what's…..like….iffffffontsy?

Gracie: Ok, like looking at me begetting way too pretty way too fast as you must be doing, you're too pretty much strapped up to your objective lenses to switch to your subjective lenses.

Alex bows his head in shame: Uh….

Gracie: But don't cringe more than's needlink'd to self-shame. Let me explain. (turning to Tele) Tele, are you begetting this? So like eternity being becomprehensiffffffffly presentable with no end to the end of it like being dead….it's like being dead's ont I'mont steered like..like…like….LIVE….e'eriding shot gun, so to speak, with e'er. Now..just as anticiparticipation anticipates in nextitudination's nowsy news'e'ervice to make us *antsy…………sooooo……..*like onticiparticipation onticipating in soone'er's late'er whate'er'down'd'iffffffonte'er is what makes *me sooo( )ooo soone'er than late'er not not iffffff( )ffffffOontsy!!!!!!!!* Like do you beget it or do you have to be ontested?

Alex(beconfused): Uh…

Gracie(patronizing): So like I don't wanna be dead. I just can't e'ereally be alive either. I've just got to be dying. That's all there's to it. Do you like get it or do you have to be tested?

Alex: Uh….

Gracie(patronizing): like…just as there's Model As of anticars…so…there's like Model ME'S!!!! of ONTIQUE'ERS!!!!!!! Of coursinging notnot ont I'm ambitious to be as soon as to be's ont I'm'available….statustickly as statused to belong to bebles.

Alex: Bebles?

Gracie: Yes, like almost already didn't say, the possible people belivable in this eternity. like…like….the spooks that hauntinhabit eggghosts asifffontos'd'e'ers.

Alex: Asifffffontos?

Gracie: Yes, like..like…it's like I'm almost not quite saying………..eggground's e'erground …ontos'd iffffformed with all of's cozy information….m'eternity wise ont I'm'ontrophs I'dairy cattle's could be cow boy'd up egggirls e'eriding herd on could be's nursinging song and dance numbers all of's way danced up to as iffffiniteased'e'er's scripts., ope'erationally as ontentangled as eternity begets. Like if this were an opera I could sing it for you.

Alex: But Gracie, this can't be an opera..because I don't sing.

Gracie: Oh yea, I heard about that…the'scriptures that you guys are stuck up in on…ontil inchoiring wholegggrailove's angels become to like belonging for you.

Alex (Beomprehensifffly ontentouched): Gracie, darling, I want you to know…that iffffffffffff( )ffffffffff I ever were spelled backwards…like…like….like…. I would, I would, I would behavior such a thing as egggracie singing for me. So you really would, you really would…you really…

Gracie (Begetting ontsy): So alright already, like….. heaventilation'sharem-wise (winks grotesquely) inchoiring with or without else angels as ifffelsiffff I'd….like…..like….. I would do all of's singing for you.

Alex: You'd do my singing for me?

Gracie: Sure why not. You hear that bird?

A bird is twittering on a twig nearby.

Alex: Yes, I hear it.

Gracie begins twittering with the bird on the twig at the top of the tree. It is a duet with her an octave lower. But soon Gracie's wand is conducting the bird's twitter tempo. It is from a slow'down'd tempo that Gracie trills up into her first aria capturing the support's itchurchy cellos in the orchestra.

Holding up her wand and winking grotesquely……………

She sings: I'M DYING OUT TO SAVE THE DAY…IFFFFF DYING I CAN BE WHO'S DYING OUT SO I CAN BE DYING OUT AS SAVIOR OF THE DAY.

Gracie takes Alex by the hand, ontrembling ontitches at (god or no god) Alex's possibly ontenticklish ontouch, as she leads him off on a comic booking's series of cartooned near death adventures in the convenience store carnival nextitudinated next door. Transported animatomickly from one danger to the next, embracing the holocoaster rides, locomotivation's trains, and a Ferris Wheel. The music describes the cartoon action as Alex, on occasion waltzes Gracie away from the most extreme dangers. Gracie blithely accepts whatever Alex does, being careful not to notice that he is saving her thanks to the waltz tempo and the fact that he may be spelled backwards more than he is letting on. At one point we see the couple displayed entopping off the Ferris Wheel as silhouetted under the umbrelle'erainbow of Gracie's explosive hairdo.

THE FERRIS WHEEL INCIDENT

(At the top of the arc of the Ferris Wheel, as iffffontangent to the event horizon between the cosmos and the ontithetical e'erealm, we see Gracie and Alex silhouetted as sparks fly rainbotically expanding off the pointed outing of Gracie's halo, showering iffffe'eress'd light umbrellas with Gracie's cartoon eumanimation simulicrumpetition'd iffffffont purposedness.)

BECONCLUSION OF THE CARNIVAL RIDES

As the near-death adventure approaches its end, birds flock to the scene echoded with elaborate orchestral twitters. Once the music has dreamtically subsided Alex and Gracie collapse their wave functions as particles again at the aboriginal bridge over the river.

Gracie: Now wasn't that more fun than being dead? Which reminds me of a religious experiment I have to get to work on.

Alex: What experiment?

Gracie: It's a secret…so just close your eyes and dream urgently like…like…of such a dreame'ergency as…as….like gracie's wholegggrailike…likeness. Can you do that for me?

Alex: I can't close my eyes Gracie.

Gracie: Oh with all the bad stuff that goes on, you god guys in the take it all back room must be closing your eye lids a wholottery of times.

Alex, ontenticipating a could be kiss, closes his eyes(and, in the spirit of gentlemanly discretion….lids) only to open them to find Gracie completely disappeared. Alex stares into the turbulence of the river. Alex searches for Gracie to no avail. At last he leaves the bridge, worried but not quite as worried as whate'er's ontantrummination's iffffonthought of his thinking thought he should be.

END OF SCENE II

SECOND INTERLUDE MUSIC PLAYS AS ALEX HEADS FOR THE SALOON IN TOWN.

SCENE III- IN THE SALOON

Alex enters the saloon in a giddily distraught state, wandering aimlessly to reach the bar. The bar mistress surveys him with amused pity.

Barmistress: Hi there handsome, where'd you come from? You look so……like…like…..accidently on purpose.

Alex: A universe actually, well mostly a universe. Now just the sky….circulating…..like daily.

BM: All of's way to here?

Alex: I study outer space from my observatory on the side. Well, the music was playing when Tele, my telescope detected Gracie at the bridge baptizing the river with her (points over his head) hair do.

BM: Hairdo?

Alex: Well it was her heaventilated head gear over what can only be aspectralated as a….like..like…spirit faced….a phlumenation all her own.

BM: Oh yea, that's such a thing as a Gracie all right. The most dangerous wholegggrailadyingirl you ever met, right?

Alex: Yea! Like she has to be dying all the time!

BM: Otherwise….

Alex: Otherwise she'd be road kill selfished on the spot.

BM: I can see she's heated you up just like her puddles. Let me take your temperature. (she presses hand to Alex's forehead) Yep! Piping hot as egggracist puddles.

Alex: Well thermo…..I mean ONTthermodynamically speaking I feel like heat heaventilating heat…..in

BM : In heat. Isn't that it?

Alex: Uh. She dumped me, but…somehow I still………

BM: Ah yes, you still…..Gracie is indeed of such a wholegggrailumescence that, like…like…. within her faults, ifffffans but breeze her virtues.

Physicist at a table: Alchemically….she should be tested for phyluminium icontents.

Alex: You mean she's e'eradioactive?

BM: For sure. (pointing to specimen jar behind the bar)

Alex: That's her?

BM: Well, her….her….*hairdo*…..

Alex: Formaldehydrated?

BM: With like her haloids on holocausteroids. Plus not not nervous sparks of she it shedding off her sparkles… like…like….behold…..

Alex: Egggirl! Like..like….eggglowing! (The halo's asifffffragment is glowing)

BM: Well metaphysically speaking they say she's like e'eradioactive.

Alex (gushing as he stares in the beaker): Yes, I can see her spirit face e'eradioactively iffffirmamenting asiffffontwinkles….like…like……winking as only she it winks.

BM (turning on the radio): She's e'eradioactive all right. Don't you agree gentlemen.

Physicist and general at a table: Oh yea. Iffffever any's ontenthing was e'eradioactive then that's such sum's ontenthing is Gracie.

BM: She's e'eradioactively obvious that's for sure. Let's catch up with her on sum simulation's asiffffffreaked out iffffffffreaquency.

The barmistress turns the dial on a radio behind the bar to tune in the *such a thing as egggracie's band.* Passing through several power grid bands to bird twitter bands, she eventually arrives at the Gracie band. Gracie's voice is heard singing "Dying I can save the day."

Alex: That's her! That's Gracie! Sum's what hissss'd'e'erical, but still singing coherent metaphysics meanwhile as 1. S'e'erial killer of herself 2. She aswholistickly conducts birds.

BM: Conducts birds? She conducts clocks, worlds. Watchout for your watch by the way she'll try conducting the ont I'moment's second hand on that. Speaking of which….with that xxxrated obviousity of hers….some say she's conducting the swamps becompletely out of the Mesozoic all of's way danced onto the Metazoic.

Physicist: And then there's those I'magic ontricks of her passing right through cosmosis as if it were hardly ever there. I don't devote but….that girl does stretch out my equations prettego'd.

BM (Shaking her head): I have to admit, she always welcomes ont I'matters in my mirrors. The little hypocrite, bad mouthing outer space the way she does. I mean where would she get her booze bottled out of scenery if it wasn't for outer space. She talks the big time but you just missed her sneaking out of here and now with her bottle. We've got a piece of her meaty physics right here, so let's see what can become out of it.

The bar mistress takes the jar of Gracie's formaldeydrated halo fragment and directs Alex to the table where the Physicist and the general are seated. Placing the jar at the center of the table, she seats Alex and then seats herself. General?

General: Well not to be too gracinsistist about it… but….like….

Alex: Please be just as gracinsistist as you like…like…like……

General: Like…., justajiffffy jargon or no justajiffffy jargon, with Gracie's countenance convergence of egggracisystemic meaty physics and e'ercrafted metaphysics…….her quests for e'ercraft scrambles to be iffflight patterned in e'er have always impressed my devotion to such a thing as her behalf as wholegggrailed……… to be…of course…..of course……not…..not……ont I'doll waved ont I'ding out as party girlegend thou art……

Physicist- Which euphemistically speaking, might like iphphphphenominologically explain the eufemystery of she it all's iffffffffacedolled up egggrace. Iphphphphyluminium as a priore I'mined is my best guess.

Alex (stroking his chin in deep onthought): You know pantheontically speaking…….like whenever it becomes to subjects objected to by subjection…..like sum's object to be subjected to….or…or…like subject to be objected to…either way….meaty physics or metaphysics, of course…of course…..

BM: Well for all that formaldehydration of her halo still….it's gin that ties her egg to outer space which she despises…ever since her ont I'metaphysics has m'assumed the could be kitchen appliance operating eternity is a can opener…and gin or no gin bottled…….not a cork screw.

Alex: Well which ever kitchen appliance applies to iffffigured eggground of such a thing as Gracie....still it's a forgone conclusion that she's as ifffffffallen in love with......like could be ont I'm'objected to be subjected to subjection. Isn't that it general?

The general shakes his head in sober affirmation.

General: Just like the beaker bequeaths....euformaldehydrated.

BM: So you're devoted? General....

General: Uh.....sum what.....

BM: Alex?

Alex (Becompletely conquered by both egggracie's meaty physics and e'ergggracie's metaphysics): Iffffffffffffffffffffffffffffffffffffffff( )fffffffffffffffffffffffffffffffffffffinitively!!!!!!!!!!!!!!( )!!!!!!!!!!!!!!! God or no god......Stars or no stars.......heaventitilately speaking I'm going to be getting my own pantheontical metaphysics to work on this subject's abilitease.

BM: Well as possible people e'ergo, she's definitely the church bell's chosen beble. So like....Iffffffffasten your set theory seat belts gentlemen. She's a legend all right. Let me tell you about such a wholegggrailegend as wholeegggrailuck's such a thing as a Gracie. Yea, for sure, I can tell you sum's ontent's I'mansion'd ontenthings about egggracie.

Church bells chime in the distance as lightning flashes the room into darkness. The glow from egggracie's formaldehydrated halo fragment ifffe'ergulfs the saloon in its ifffffirmamentation.

Barmistress sings:

1.A. SOLO: CHURCH BELLS WERE RINGING ON SATURDAY NIGHT

SOMEONE WAS PLAYING A TUNE

AS CHIMED DOWN THE CHIMNEY TO SAINT INTO SIGHT

WITH A PEAL METAMATTERING MOON

WITH APPEAL ONT I'MODLING I'MOON.

Quartet of three sopranos and barmistress:

SHE LIKE THE LADY

IFFFFISHED FROM THE SEA TO BE'S SURE

THE ONE ALL OF SKIES TWINKLE FOR

THE ONE ALL OF'S GUYS TINKLE FOR.

1.B. SOLO: CHURCH BELLS WERE RINGING IN OUT OF THE BLUE

WHILE CHILDREN WERE PLAYING ALONG

WITH CHIMERICKLES CHIMING IN CHEERLEADER'S WHO

SERANADES AS IFFFFFFACED SINGING'S SONG.

AS HEVENTILATES HAUNT HOUSING'S BOO

WHOLEGGGRAIL LADY

SPOOKED OUT OF SPILL SKILLS OF THE SKIES

WHERE THE SPARK OF THE SPIRIT FACE FLIES (Where the spark of spir'd it iffflash flies)

SHE LIKE THE CREATURE

THAT HEAVEN MUST FEATURE

TO EVER GET OFF OF THE GROUND.

2. AS DOLLED UP DREAME'ERGENCY'S EGGGODEGO

ACUTELY AS ANGLED ANGELLED

OUT OF DANCINGING DIRT THAT'S IFFFFONTING TO FLOW

WHENE'ER'S WHATE'ER TO BE BECOMPELLED.

SHE LIKE THE LADY

IFFFFISHED FROM THE CEILING'S I'M ARC

OF IFFFIRMAMENCE TWINKLING THE DARK.

CHORUS: SHE ITTTING IFFFEATURES

THAT HEAVENLY CREATURES

CAN HEAVENTILATE OFF THE GROUND.

3. CHURCH BELLS WERE BATHING IN FLOODED EXTREAMS

OF IFFFFIRMAMENTION'S CHAMPAGNES

IFFFFLEDGING DREAME'ERGENCIES DRAWN OUT OF DREAMS'

ONT I'MAXIOMATE'ER'D REFRAINS.

VOCABULATING

A NEW DICTIONARY OF TERMS ('S ONTERMS)

JUST AS GRACIE'S ESTEEM BECONFIRMS.

CHORUS: SHE LIKE THE CREATURE

THAT HEAVEN MUST FEATURE

TO EVER GET OFF OF THE GROUND.

4. AS STARS IN ONTWILIGHT PREPARE TO BE TWINKLES.

AS STARTLED TO CHORUS THE SONG

WITH THE WINKS OF THE TWINKLES RESOUNDING ONTINKLES

WITH A HYMN HEAVEN'S HIM HYMNS ALONG

WITH A HYMN HEAVEN'S HIMS HYMN ALONG.

HEAVENTILATING

ASCENDENCIES ONTO ASCERT

EGGGRACIES ESTEEMED FROM IFFFFLIRT (I'D IRT)

CHORUS: IFFFLIRTING IFFFEATURES

OF COULD BECOME'S CREATURES

TO HEAVENTILATE OFF THE GROUND.

With the last lightning strike Alex rises from the table in a state of extreme passion. The bar mistress rises with him to pet him like a god or no god's distraught puppy. Escorting him to the exit, and noticing sparks flying off his shoulder (but thinks nothing of it), she sings one last consoling verse.

5. ALL WHILE LOVE'S AS IFFFFALLING THROUGH NOT NEVER'S NIGHT.

FROM EGGGRACESS'D IN PERSON APPEALS

AS MODELED IN MAKE UP OF AS IFFFFALMIGHT

IFFFFALLING IN LOVE AS IFFFFFFF( )FFEELS

CHORUS: IFFFFOR FALLING IN LOVE AS IFFFEELS

SOLO: ALL OF'S IFFFEELINGS

AS SPARKLE TO BE OUTE'ER SPACED

IFFFFIGURING GROUND AS EGGGRACED

CHORUS: IN CANDESCENT CREATURE'S

IFFFFIRMAMENT FEATURES

EGGGNIGHTING EGGGRACE OFF EGGGROUND.

The ballad concludes, as lighting strikes again with the church bells chiming in the distance.

BM: Those chimes refuse to work unless she's in the building. She's up there all right.

Alex exits as lightning strikes one last time with the bells heard in the distance.

THIRD INTERLUDE: A jaunty bassoon trio, slightly traumatized by rather strident strings, sponsor Alex as he transgresses the road to the cathedral.

SCENE IV- IN THE CATHEDRAL

Alex arrives at the top of the hill to find the cathedral. Intimidated by its gothic presence he finds himself immersed in cosmic darkness. Using zooick instincts never before known to him he looks 1. At the surface of the dark loud. 2. At the stained glass iffflight patterns. 3. Into the depths of the dark loud. 4. Into the heart of the cathedral to find Gracie displayed on the cross (as iffframed in the echo of Alex himself)

Alex: Gracie! I'm!!!

The music shifts from the Renaissance to the times of Bach. A vast chorus sings SHAME ON WE WHO DIDN'T GIVE A DIME.

Suddenly a repetitive beat emerges as the ray gun rafters light up with messages on the screens. The word LOVE is liquified and dripping from the screens. Wanted posters picture Felix, the grotesquely flamboyant pope as THE LORD ONCE REMOVED. Blinking on and off hypnotically are messages flashing through the cathedral. Most prevalent are the messages FELIX GODS THE LOVE and FELIX GODS THE DREAM. Swaggering up to the pulpit Pope Felix grapples with the microphone. Ms Speck confidently stands behind Felix threatening to protect him. There is a pause in the music as Felix speaks.

Felix: You know; some say we live in dark times.

Ms Speck: It's true.

Felxi: Some say the sky should be shut down for repairs (staring over at Gracie taking selfies on the cross)

Ms Speck: You know it's true.

Felix: Some say the whole egggrail's a dud whatever. But I say to you.....don't blame the stars. Don't blame iffffe'ers. Blame yourself from being iffffished out of whate'er with not enough paid for attention.

Ms Speck: You better believe it.

Felix: I say to you (pointing his trigger finger) WHEN THE PLATE IS PASSED...PAY ATTENTION. Remember god keeps score...

Ms Speck: And I do the paper work.

Felix: And I do the paper work (Felix holds up his hand wrestling his trigger finger to signal the vast sanctimony under his control).

Ms Speck pokes Felix.

Felix promptly signals for Mobible, a very high Q machine impersonation of a former kitchen appliance to pass the plate to the congregation as the music resumes.

Felix(singing): YOU MET A BEGGER IN THE STREET TODAY

DIDN'T GIVE EM A DIME

DIDN'T GIVE EM A DIME

DIDN'T GIVE EM A DIME

AND THE GREAT EGGGUYED (BIG BOOKY MAN) GOD......SAID...... "SHAME ON YOU!!!"

As Felix declares more than once and emphatically....... "SHAME ON YOU!" ....the chorus returns with full elaboration of the choral apotheosis:

Chorus: SHAME ON US COMMITED TO THE CRIME

VALHALLELUJA'D.....................IN EXCELSIS OF...........

SHAME ON US WHO DIDN'T GIVE A DIME.......................

Gracie has climbed down off the cross and is performing her Sway Dance routine.

In the midst of the dialectical development section in the music.....Felix is singing another verse:

Felix: WELL THERE'S A WAKE UP AT THE WATERHOLE TODAY

AT M'APRIORI'S MESOZOO

SWINGING FORWARD WITH THE SWAY

OF MOODYMOMMALS WITH THE MOO

AND THE BACK ROOM BOOKY MAN……. GOD SAID "I'M WITH YOU!"

Gracie, showing signs of routinized fatigue, has climbed back up to hang from the cross and sing the "I'M WITH YOU" line.

Gracie climbs back down from the cross, as the dance routine continues.

Soon Felix is singing another verse:

Felix: WELL….THE MESOZOICS ON THE MOVE TODAY

WITH METAMOMMALS MESOZOO'D

SWINGING FORWARD WITH THE SWAY

OF MEATY MOMMAS IN THE MOOD

AND THE GREAT, AND THE GREAT, AND THE GREAT E'ERGO'S (BIG BOOKY MAN) GOD SAID "I'M WITH YOU". (Gracie is, for the moment, back hanging out on the cross)

As the music subsides Gracie climbs down from the cross one last time and, raising her handed wand to the congregation, parts the sea of faces to make a corridor for the phylum that is all her own. Passing through the cathedral, the doors close behind her. The chimes cease abruptly. There is an awkward silence.

Felix speaks: Ok! So let's give our little pin up a big hand for working the cross today.

There is much applause.

Felix: That's big enough. Now what's tomorrow all about?

Crowd: POPE FELIX!!!!

FELIX: I can't hear you.

Crowd: POPE FELIX!!!!!!!!!!!!!!

Felix: That's better. Now I want to hear about that guy next door to god.

Crowd: POPE FELIX!!!!! GOD ONCE REMOVED!

FELIX: That sounds unominous to me!

Crowd: OF COURSE, OF COURSE NOT…NOT! ALL ONE FOR FELIX!

Felix: ALL RIGHT THEN! SO THE LORD ONCE REMOVED'S IN THAT GUYS…….

Crowd: BACK POCKET!!!!!! E'EREMOVED UP FRONT!!!!!

Felix: Front what!!!!

Crowd: Front perched!!! Front porched!!!!!!!

Felix: AND THE LORD NEXT DOOR TO THE LORD ONCE REMOVED KNOWS WHO YOU VOTED FOR.

Crowd: So the lord once removed knows who we voted for.

Mobible returns to the pulpit with a full plate of cash. Felix smiles from ear to ear.

Felix: And let's give thanks to our kitchen appliance for working the ray gun rafters today.

Mobible shyly tips his tin hat. There is modest applause.

Felix: Well Mobible we've got an selectrocution tomorrow and, as far as I can tell, you're still here.

Mobible(weakly): Uh.......

Mobible whimpers faintly and leaves by the side exit. Alex cannot get through the traffic jam in the isles and is trapped as the cathedral goes dark with Mobible's exit. The bells have stopped chiming, but really, with Gracie's exit as the scene ends.

END OF SCENE IV

SCENE V

We find Mobible downtown trying to coolify himself in the midst of traffic jams on looting sprees.

His sign that says FELIX LOOTS has been crossed out. Having been remessaged with FELIX APPROPRIATES, that message has also been crossed out and replaced with the message FELIX LOOTS.

Mobible: Dreamuggers vote Felix!

Episode 2. Mobible is caught in front of a plate of barbecue ribs. He looks helpless in all directions as his wanted poster reads what he sings that is hardly heard.......IF YOU WANT TO SAVIOR BARBECUED BEHAVIOR-VOTE FELIX.

Episode3. Mobible is limousined in a ticker tape parade in the financial district. Confetti is raining down. His sign reads what he sings but is hardly heard… IF YOU WANT TO SAVIOR MONEY BACKED BEHAVIOR.

Episode 4. Mobible is in the country club between two cemeteries as he is about to tee off. Again his sign reads what he sings that's hardly heard…..IF YOU WANT TO SAVIOR COUNTRY CLUB BEHAVIOR.......

Episode 5. Mobible is at a Valhallelujaween festival dressed in makeup and ribbons as he sings what his sign says that is hardly heard……YOU CAN TAKE THE BOOGUYBUS, UNIVERSED UNANIMOUS.......

Episode 6. Mobible has just entered the Metaphysical Society where Gracie stands before the chalk board as she is giving a lecture to sum's begruntled physicists on JUST A JIFFFFY'S ONTROPHICKLY PRESENTABLE ETERNITIES.

Several quotes occupy the chalk boards:

1. TOILET TRAINING ETERNITY is crossed out and replaced with WIND UP TOY ETERNITY.

2. THE'S NOT/NOTNOT CODE OF ALPHABETTINGOD'S IFFFFE'ERS

3. ONTENSE'ER CALCULUS is elaborated with d'iffe'erontical m'equations for ontotal ontease of the system. E = sum d(NN)/dt from -ifffffinity to +ifffffinity

4. NOTNOTITUDE + NOWSY NEWS S'E'ERVICE = ONTROPHICKLY PRESENTABLE ETERNITY.

5. PUNIVERSES are just samplifffications of information from ONTIQUE SHOPPE IFFFFORMATION SYSTEMS.

As well to be noted is a light bulbed in advertisement that reads:

ETERNITY IS SUITABLE FOR SALES OF ONTROPHIES IN THE'S ONTIQUE SHOPPE M'ETERNITY WARDS.

Mobible does not bother to sing metaphysical jargon for this episode, but the music continues as the general enters the room.

General (to Mobible): Are you in charge of Felix'selectrocution campaign?

Moible: How did you know?

The general surveys the room but restrains himself from responding.

General: I think you'd better come with me sir.

Mobible: Well, I suppose the metaphysics can always wait. Who really cares, except soone or later, anyway.

Mobible leaves the Metaphysical Society with the general.

The scene shifts with the descent of the music to an exclusive beach resort where a vast armada of democratic dictatorships are landing. Each dictatorship carries with it a wooden horse from which troops are emerging from the rear. Landing parties are forming beached head units wearing ballet dresses, lavish make up and combat boots recently having received shoe polish.

General (to Mobible): Should we quarantine the beach sir? As a former kitchen appliance do you have that authority?

Mobible: Oh yea, ever since I took over the ray gun rafters I've been the authority in these parts. You'd better let me handle this general. (observes the general's hands) I see that your hands are clean. Well you can keep them that way. Like I almost didn't say……let me handle this situation.

General (studies his hands): Be my guest.

Mobible approaches the executive director of the landing parties.

Mobible: Just what do you think you are doing at this very exclusive beach front resort; may I ask?

Execture: We're the vote loads just piling up for pope…..pope…….pope……

Mobible: Felix.

Executive: That's it. The dog whistle we got was that this selectrocution's been dedemiltarized, in celebration of D-Day. So we're here to vote by invasion.

Mobible: Exactly how many are you?

Executive (with brazen confidensity): Oh…we're ALL ONE!

Mobible and the general are suddenly relieved.

Mobible and general: WHEW!!!!!!! Like is there anything you want?

Executive: Just one wholegggraiload of such a thing as egggracies

Mobible: Well, there's only one egggracie left in these parts. Well I suppose still quite sum's e'erRIGHT but only one LEFT that answers to Gracie.

Executive: Cool, so a half of a wholegggraiload's egggracies will do it.

Mobible: Well, talking halves, like we've only got two of those…..

Executive: So like…..a wholegggrail of gracies drawn and quartered.

Mobible: Uh?

Executive: Look. I can see there is a problem here. How about if we just settle for a wholegggrail of infinitestimonialized such a things as egggracie. You do the math.

Mobible: Uh, we may have to make up a new branch of mathematics to work on this.

Executive: Cool. Just get us our gracies. We've seen them in all the ads that matter and we want eveybody's anybody's pregnant zero's one. But like……who are you? You're not sum's egggracist I hope.

Mobible: No, no, no, noooooooooo……. as you can see I'm like a phylum all my own. If I were to be egggracist…well there's two types 1. Predatory 2. Existential.

Executive: Cool. But "existential" sounds extremely serious.

Mobible: It is exdreamly s'e'erious..

Executive: "Existential"……I could never make heads of tails out of that word. Which would you be if……

Mobible: As I am, I'm sort in the middle of the middle of the middle of the ont m'escape hatches out of the Mesozoic of it all…but

Execturive: But what?

Mobible: Predatory's not what I am….at least not yet.

Executive: What does that look like?

Mobible: Here let me show you. (Mobible holds a jagged mirror squarely up the executive so he can see his iffffangled face)

Executive: I get it. So this Gracie really is a prey animal….like bride the traffic jams, just like all of's them say….like waiting in line to kiss herself ifffffffff(.)ffffffffft.

Mobible: That's egggracie alright!

Executive: So like pregnant zero's one'd'e'er……..well we're the traffic jammed with kiss her off e'ers.

Mobible: Yes, that's why they put her in the church.

Executive: So you're impersonating the church I assume.

Mobible: Uh….uh……..We're like the welcoming party. Welcoming you with…….option'd armamentions…..

Executive: If there's a problem…

Mobible: How committed are you to today's beachead holocaust?

Executive: Well we haven't been paid yet.

Mobible (sighing relief symptoms): Well…uh…that's like because all of's money's been sent home.

Executive: So?

Mobible (gathering his wits): With like…like….NEW! New world orders, for you….like your landing party's to call it a day…..turn back…… and like…like….go home. The general and I have brought your tickets.

Executive: Which home.

Mobible: The one back across those waves….. the one that there's no place like….. the one being ransacked by someone that's not at all of's you. Look, there's reports just in of tidal waves of invasion parties at YOUR hometown back yards. (Mobible gives executive a piece of paper) Like, like your home is being invaded. As we speak they're coming from the front yard to the back yard backing up the back stairs, breaking through the back doors and streaming through the pantry into the kitchen. Like in no time at all, they'll be in the living room, the bedroom, the bath and the closet where you keep your kids for selfished outings. Once they'e in your cells, they'll be in your selves. Whoever you are there'll be no one left to speak for you, your cultivation plots, your metaphysics. Like they'll have you laughing at your own deadly seriousness. Talk about holocausts…like kindergardenning……like before the debates are tissued…….like you'll be putting up your own wanted posters…….wanted to m'abort yourselves. Like there'll be no end to the end of it if your home town invasion's not scened out of scenery.

Executive (suddenly panic stricken): Well then…like…like…if our homes really are being invaded…and that's where the sanctimoney's sent………..of course..of course…not…not…we'd better get back home right away.

General (suddenly cordial): Listen I'm sorry about all the misinformation. However! I am glad we got a chance to meet at the beach head.

The general and the executive cordially shake hands for a promotional picture which Mobible's arsenal of periphernalia shutters takes.

Executive: Thanks for the tip.

Mobible: No problem. Glad to be of service.

Executive: and you're quite sure about the destination of the sanctimoney?

Mobible: I have it on power grid authority, like why not. If you must know, your devotional sanctimoney's been off coursed by mistakenly being sent to all of's wherevers you came from. It's just how lies exercised, work out in these parts. So, like, all of's scratch feed itchecks have been devoted like (those parts and these parts speaking wise) to be in those parts way, way less than these parts.

Executive: Well then we'd better be headed high tailing it.......uh........back..........

Mobible: Backbackwards then.

Executive: Egggod idea.

The executive turns and waves his hands back to the sea and the horizon home. The entire armada stops in its tracks and turns around back to the ships.

Mobible and the general observe the ships disappearing across the horizon home.

Mobible and general (in unison): Whew! That was close.

General: Heading off these beachead holocausts takes the whene'er wind out of me. You know I was just thinking, if we had had more time to chat with those fellows, we might have been able to transfer their tails through their hearts to their heads...where...like....all one of them might end up devoted to such a thing as egggracie.

Mobible: Mmm. But that would require an entire metaphysical lecture s'e'eries. All we had time for at this invasion was, letter-wise, one brief's quotability.

General: You realize...like.... if we hadn't cut them off at the beach heads we'd be running out of occupation territory trophy turf in no time. Sooner than later they'd all be wanting more of such a thing as egggracie than heaventilation systems can produce.

Mobible: General may I speak freely sir?

General: Well, the power grids don't like that.

Mobible: I know but just between you and me.

General: Oh. Of course.. of course...not...not.

Mobible: General, Felix has no conscience. Having recently acquired a conscience myself I am sensitive to such matters.

General: Yes?

Mobible: Felix can't be pope. (Dumps his Felix for pope sign in the trash)

General: Well who then?

Mobible: What about Gracie? I mean like, she's the most wanted woman in these parts.

General: You mean girl war and all? I mean like Gracie's been held hostage to the holocaust on the crossed outing since kindergarten. How are we supposed to congratulate her out of that?

Mobible: Leave that to me. As a former kitchen appliance that specialized in can open'd'e'ers, I've been studying the advertising industry and I know how to creep out from under a log to perform such could be calculus. It's all in ifffield theory of the ont I'maxwell m'equations for iffffffffffffflow of selectrons.

Mobible places his trigger finger on the shoulder of the general and pontifffficates profusely.

Mobible: General, there are ontides in e'er's iffffe'ers ontaken at ifffloods as sum up singularities....pooped out to be popped up as pope. And I am just the former kitchen appliance who can control the tidal waves of selectrons that can open the world to egggodollup all's doodoo of it. It all becomes quite supernaturally from being the can opener in the kitchen.

General: You mean to congratulate such a thing as egggracie from of coursings song taboo'd to be sung as becompletely e'ereversed to be like...like ifffffffontaboo'd to NOT TO BE instead of as usual's taboo'd to be.

Mobible: I see your point. How to taboo Gracie to NOT TO BE. Gracie's becomputer's been hacked for just ont I'm'eggglow minimization. Allow me to cheer her up with a proposal of my own in that regard. But for the time being...of course...of course...notnot...let's just make her........pope.

General: All right then. But what's the plan?

Mobible: Well let's do the math. (Mobible draws on the sand) so 1. The congregation, all but the bells (bells can't vote) in the cathedral's all one for Felix. 2. Ms Specker's for a. Felextensions of her selfished outing's egggrid lock...b. Feliexonerations of herselfish period. 3. As far as Felix is concerned Felix just can't help but be devoted to himself. There's no way out of that. However! Minus the traffic jam at the beach head today (Mobible waves to receding aramadas on the horizon), that's like all there is to that. Now general where do you stand in all of this?

General: In general I'm....at this stage of the game....all for devotion to...like...like.......egggracie.

Mobible: Whew! In general like, ont I'militarily speaking, that's the big one when it comes to these matters. Well, saddled with my new conscience..plus the fact that such a thing as egggracie's cute enough to be becoming like acutely to becompute...I'm leaning over to Gracie.

General(encouraged): That's two for Gracie. What else have we got? Could we ever beget Gracie to be devoted to...to...like.....like......like....herself?

Mobible: No, that's the one thing that would kill her.

General: But the soprano that runs the saloon! She's devoted to 'the little hypocrite' enough to want such a thing as egggracie in her puddles and maybe mirrors too. The physicist is a scientist and can't be devoted but we can count from zero up to one on the bar keep.

Mobible: All right then! We've got three for Gracie against three for Felix. (thinks) Uh, that's a dead heat.

General (lightning struck): THE ASTRONOMER IN THE SALOON! He becompletely fell right through Gracie's becompletely presentable eternity to like overlook the stars to like…like..over the's e'erainbow to such a thing as not himself's….like……Gracie herself!

Moibible: So even as an astronomically bent out of ont I'm'etaphysical shape…….scientist….

General: When push'd whate'er becomes to shoveled she it……he'd still be devoted to Gracie.

Mobible: Well that lovesick astronomer is about to give the Mesozoic its new pooped out pope! Thank you for helping me with this could be cataclysmic decision General. (Mobible teeters as if about to fall over. The general props him up, offering a napkin)

Mobible (staring at the napkin): My conscience is settling down at last. So that's the plan. We put Gracie in a closet. We put the closet in a safe. We put the safe in a phylum all its own, controlling the asifffffflow of selectrons in Gracie's direction. Winced out as I am, you know, I wonder…engineering such a thing as egggracie pooped out of egggas clouds with these manners……just maybe…..just maybe……like…..God must love me now, or at least like like me now….or maybe at least like……..BE LIKE LIKE LIKE ME NOW. So, general, generally speaking, this selectrocution won't be invaded after all. We'll fake it instead!

The general nods his sober approval..

Mobible and the general (surveillancing all cardinal directions) quietly depart the beach resort as the scene ends.

END SCENE V

SCENE VI

Note- This is the first of three scenes that constitute a three act metaphysical drama all their own. The excessive interactive detail of the scenes is important for the maintenance of the large'er story line but not vital in all their details to the opera as played. As such it will have to be trimmed down to highlights of cinematic size if this opera's ever to go into production. For this reading you might want to skip the small print in all three of them and just stick to the big letters If by chance you can make out the heads or tails of the'sifffffflipped coinage of these scenes, your ontelligence quotient is better than most. Ontedium wise these scenes are almost as tedious as small print drama can be. Sticking to the big letters will keep you sufficiently informed to keep track of the main elements in the opera. Since various ideological factions may misinterpret the full intent of scenes VI, VII and VIII, I advise conscientious caution to the reader.

Scene VI can be carefully picked apart and streamlined to make a dramatically iffffeasible scene, inspite of general appearances. The most important elements to pay attention to are 1. Gracie being indicted for

a. being b. being stinct c. not being impossible. 2. The reverbe'erating assertion of Gracie's eternity test site expe'eriment. 3. Ms Speck's authoritarian assertion of who won the holocaust. 4. Ms Speck's assertion that ETERNITY HAS BEEN TAKEN and Gracie will just have to wait e'eround for the next eternity to accomplish anything on the ontequerian as iffffffffffff( )ffffffffffffffront lines. If you can just grasp these four developments, you might as well skip the fine print. This scene e'ereally is pretty messy and will exhaust the patience of all but the most becomputationally ont I'm'advanced e'ereaders

HOWEVER

If you have ignored my warning......... you will find Gracie working as janitor in the stop signed intersection of her neon light district motel. It is a graveyard elaborately set up for promotion picture productions. What may not be sooner than later obvious is the's asifffffact that Gracie's janitorial service is just a front business for could be's clandestined JUSTAJIFFFFY'S JANITORIAL S'E'ERVICE IN BECOMPLETELY PRESENTABLE ETERNITY that is way, way more than just a mathematical construct of non-finite temporality. Nevertheless, not not nonchalantly Gracie is seen sweeping e'eround the graves that make up her ont I'm'otel's mortel eggguest e'erooms. As the harmony suspends itself in the strings, the ground appears to heave. Miss Speck is just arriving. She is wearing dark glasses in a manner that suggests pursuits of dark glasses wearing a party girl's Ms Speck.

Gracie (onthreatening with her wand): Rest perturbed spirits.

Gracie stares Speck down. Speck turns away as she offers an apple which Gracie puts down.

Misguided by what's in her mirrors and of a character that avoids all honest to goodness whate'er puddles at all holocausts......Speck is about to open up on Gracie for like being such a thing as herself that's not such a thing as a speck.

Speck: Fruit has feelings Gracie. It hurts to be refused......

Gracie: Ont I'm'eaten.

Speck: Well! as lovedeadarling's misssung's singularity, how are you doing today. Where are your books?

Gracie has a screen play which she puts down to find her DEATH MADE SIMPLE book. She has her make up kit out and is fumbling with a black moustache which keeps falling off her face. Frustrated with the moustache, she puts it back in her make up kit.

Speck: You're looking well surprisingly....well...upright.

Gracie: Instead of....like...

Speck: Well upsidown.

Gracie: Or maybe...

Speck: Maybe just wrong dear (As this little bundle would suggest) These papers presentensinging ides of e'er will explain it. I brought you some like xxxrated xmas presents.

Gracie: My beble birthday! You are so onthoughtful Ms Specter! I was just thinking about how just ont I'm'oteled I am. So these must be m'atressed to me. Of all times to get xxxamass'd presents for my little alphabet.

Speck: What alphabet is that dear?

Gracie: Oh just my little alphabet that's e'ergoing to etern eternity e'eround as logged in the wholegggrailogged in's forever…..the NOT/NOTNOT CODE if you must know. It becompasses the secret of eternity which, by the way, I just discove'er'd like…like…iffffinly as iffffished out ifffffffound out all about.

Speck: So like……something to allege across hard time's heaventilation systems.

Gracie: More like to c'e'ertiffffficate my ont I'm'accomplishements on the chalk boards of the metaphysical society.

Speck: Well, I've brought something to add to your day.

Gracie: What could possibly add to whatever whatever's up to……

Speck: I'm afraid it's more of as usual's…….indictments in the news.

Gracie: Only in the news that matters….

Speck: Yes! Yes!

Gracie Not at all.

Speck: Present them in your face dear…..

Gracie: You mean like xmas indictments.

Speck: Yes, dear xxxrated xmas indictments. Unfortunately I have to serve them and…it being the ides of e'er….you have to deserve them.

Gracie: Cool! Coolest ever! So let's take a look!

Speck: No dear, coolest never, you may not want to look.

Gracie (taking the papers): Oh like indicted for dying! That is so sweet. So the power grid doesn't want me to be dying after all!

Speck: No dear. (scribbles onto the paper)

Gracie: Oh! For *only* dying and meanwhile…..not being……

Speck: Dead. There's more. This one's for being like…..like…..stinct.

Gracie (taking the paper): Mhm. So like *stinct.*

Speck: Mhm. And it gets better than worse. There's like these for like…like….just being…..possible.

Gracie (examines the documents): So, like just being possible. Onthinking backwards then this indictment is for not being impossible.

Speck: That's right dear. You must never be allowed to forget…

Gracie: What?

Speck: Ever since the Girl War….. you like notnot being is pretty bad. Like, until you improve your impossibility scores whatever remains of you must be buried under these indictments.

Gracie: Oh like so becompletely becompatable with dreams that I must all but be…just as supersubeuman as self-evidensity insists I am….except putting the girl war aside this time to just be nice about it.

Speck: Yeaaaaas…… liked all too obviously supersubeuman as you may be, all the powowegggrid wants is for you to be on iced about it…dear.

Gracie: Uhnhuhn……..like iffffffrozen in time……….

Speck:…or out of time…..like……putting the girl war aside and bekeeping all girl war iffffffactories out of make up's cosmetic business………becompletely incompatible with matter of any assortment….like just dead or extinct or becompletely impossible. XXXe'eraced out e'erated as you are……like…….how can you argue with all of's that.

Gracie: It's true, not putting one girl holocausts aside…. I am egggirl war's one girl holocaust. It'simulates my wholegggrailife style these days apart from my metaphysics. And then again, and then again….onthen again……..no matter how impossible I strive to be, I keep popping up like a could be cork which onthen again…..the's whate'er wanted asifffffloating iffffffontop. And speaking of whate'er, why just this morning you could have caught me as iffffished out on the holocoasterides at the spook housing's song carnival. I mean like charismasterious as I am I'm hardly ever out of under as iffffontaqueriums. The first thing I'm buzzed with in the morning is my over the border's rainbow candy pill. Next thing I know I'm putting swamp milk on my serial kill'd on schedules.

Speck (keeping track) Yes, and next….

Gracie: Well, the candy that's supposed to kill me…

Speck (rabidly tasting her saliva): Yes?

Gracie: I just won't let it like kill me. I keep refusing to be dead. I don't know what's the matter with me. I'm like a cork in ont I'm's aquarium that just keeps bobbing up in the whate'er. Like sum's attraction figure against all odds to just be killed, just can't be killed. Like dreame'ergently as iffffffffffff it were impossible to make me impossible, or not stinct, or of course of course could being not not….notnotiffffff I'd. It's just begot to be sum'sonthing like onthat. I mean like in the bettingodreame'egencies I'm'astronomickly iffffe'eretrievable whate'er the'sods.

Speck: So like dirt wise in the portopotties…..

Gracie: I delve through dirt in the portopotties. I like ontranscend all of's bleacher seating as the set of all sets e'ereally seated like onthrown in.

Speck: So your death made simple texts……..next door to nows……

Gracie: Next…nextdoor to nows……oh yea, next my death made simple texts….and my emotion picture story books like (opens a story book) this one. That's me drawn cartooned in as the friendly fly with my friendly spider friend. LIKE LOOK! LIKE SEE! IT IS ALL HERE in big letters as just can't be missed out on.

Speck: What's that mark? Is that punctuation?

Gracie: Yes, in a way. It's me as spider droppings, like onturds dropped off in whate'er's whene'er webbing…..made to look like punctuation's pointed outings. It's a period. I like to schedule stories thought about at the end. I think it's wise to watch out for the punctuation appointments at the end of stories attempting to be taken s'e'eriously.

Speck: When will you learn to stop thinking Gracie. Why bother thinking when you've plenty promotion pictures thinking for you.

Gracie: Thinking what?

Speck: What's to be thought supposed to think. Like with questions you're supposed to think I'm thinking. Like what's wrong with you. Why am I not you. Like why do you get to be egggracie when ever I don't. It's like hopscotch when you step on the lines you're out. You being egggracie steps on the line. Why don't you just give? I don't get to step on the line. Need I remind you that this is kindergarden and hopscotch is the hottest game on the holocaust horizon ever since…..ever since…….ever since…..like….ever since ….the girl war……when you died…..supposedl……but just pay no attention to being like dead.

Gracie: But that way things keep happening without me knowing what happened. But hey! Like…. dying-wise…you should see the chances I take. Why just this morning I…I…..1. Almost fell off a great height. 2. Was almost run over by a train. 3. I tight rope walked over……..care careened to almost swerve e'ecrafted lovedeadarlinks to not be m'aborted not to be. Like I'm working as hard as I can at being like lovedeadarlink'd to be like……4. Like iffffished out as I am I'm just no good at not being god enough to not be dead.

Speck: So you admit you are a euman bigot.

Gracie: Well, I guess, dictatorshipmentionariwise, I guess I am a bigot after all is said and done….like..like…a bigot against….against…like…..like….. being dead, extinct, impossible or even obsolete. I mean what's the point of being human when it's still the Mesozoic with me the ont I'make up kit's onturd bride on the menu. I mean I wouldn't bother being so eumanitarian if there was any other way out of I'dearths ont I'mansion's ontents. It's not exactly like I haven't had my taste of human randomains and it's not as if like…. swamp-umans never got a taste of ontrophyluminium'eumanity with egggirl waresults. I mean that's still the upsidowner's picture that emotion's mostly still about……. I mean to be

75

a human's like to be a fly surveillanced in egggated becommunities as e'ercraft scramblinkrasht in spider webbingutters of….of……..nasty nests.

Speck: Allright dear. I'm sure you're being not nice enough to be called like notnot nasty…..

Gracie: Wait up on myself why don't I. Whose indictment says eumans just can't be nice people?

Speck: Indictments add up dear…….just as pregnant zeros add up to one…..enough of nothings do add up to one …..as indicted on so many ifffffigurated grounds, indictments do audition for reality. I mean like as long as, eternity's intended wise, you e'erefuse to be impossibile you must remain under indictment for like, like, like…being….like… pretty possibly like pretty. This gets girlwarbled because being pretty's impolite when it's obviously in everybody's else's face besides its own dear.

Gracie: But being pretty's always pretty obvious. And look, it's not just for eumanity's sake I seek asylum's brand new phylum…it's for all of's beblesake's ontomanations ont I'masylums sought.

Speck: To populate the impoliteness then I take it….which could get out of second's hands. Well, of course, of course…then being pretty is always impolite and should be made impossible. Uglee's all that's equitable in these Mesozoic parking lots dear, you shouldn't be notnot dead quite enough to like ugleefully not know that.

Gracie: But isn't that like when being dead bad mouths to live for not being lived enough. I mean what's a living's make up kit to do……like being dead and off the hook. But not being dead you're off the off the hook right back where you started with being impossibly impossible….like smack dab in the middle of the middle of the middle of the set of all setheory's situations. I mean it's a could be cage like girlwarbled song birds never can sing out of.

Speck: Which leads to being meaty physically ont I'm'attractive into ont I'mining all sorts of dangerously tailored beachead e'eresorts for way too pretty people. Best not to be at all, not to berecommends. That's offfishallowhate'erecommendation's….beastongue

Gracie: Beast dung?

Speck: Yes, advice.

Gracie (waxing philosophical): Like yea, like…….ontalking about becomplications whenever it becomes to such a thing as me…….with me being so obviously eternity's intended, I guess this is what I should expect…with me spirit faced so precision coded to bebogle whate'er's iffffont I'mind set either not or notnot to care careened all but answerved iffffe'eresponse to lovedeadude'er's hapless beconditions.

Speck(disappointed): Aren't these indictmentscaring the life out of you, like..like to make you way, way, way too terriffff I'd to not be cured of…..of…..being…….authorizing this beble business onte'erprise of yours. I mean like powowowe'ergridlock-wise I hope you're not in this for the sanctimoney paying off your possibility.

Gracie: No not at all. As winner of the Miss Eternity Pageant over runner up reality I'm like only in this for the, sunny side up or not sunny side up, e'ercraft scrambles. So like paper work eludes me or I elude it…… sums'hown off as ont I'm'any's one. You see I have my own private existentialist working for my dreamergence. He prefers me possible.

Speck: What do you mean possible? How possible?

Gracie: Well pretty possible as far as he's of course of course not not concerned. Like iphphphotogene'erously estated by my postitives e'erather than by negatives.

Speck: What are his credentials?

Gracie: Well he's made a study of existentialism. And he's made a study of me.

Speck: And?

Gracie: He's sentimentalized the results to be sensationalized on y-not axist's of I'd thou artesian coordinate systems.

Speck: Well what about the xxxrated nasty x axis of those halocoastered coordinates?

Gracie: Oh, he's assured me that the N words on the xxxrated coordinates don't really apply to ont I'm'existential issues in e'eregarding my iphphphotogene'erous negative's ont I'm'ore mined posed positive regards of me as holocoast to coast's bridoll's could be corpse…….

Speck: But…but being anyone that's so preeminently indictable as yourself…like..like…like…these pieces of paper have some pretty sticky signiatures stuck on them dear.

Gracie: It's true signiatures can be pretty sticky stuff but as justajifffy's janitor I can deal with perhapsy pape'erwork. In fact, it's being ont I'm'opt up as we speak.

Speck: Wouldn't you rather be impossible than have to deal with all these piece meals of…

Gracie: Predigested…

Speck: Paper

Gracie: Work….Not really. I mean why bother with remarketed items that somebody made up just because I got way too pretty way too fast when they didn't. And then there's such a thing as me as ontique dispositions ont I'm'anomolodg'd self's social climber beclimbing off of all of's IQ charts. Like the way I iffffigure it against the ground of it, this whole indictment thing is either backwards or upsidown. These indictments against egggracexistense are just ugleebled powoweggrid projections of minus egggrasystemattacks against plus egggrasystemicraftesse'erwavedoughte'er'd'e'er.

Speck: So you're not war torn down…..like glad to be dead as sooner than later as possible? Can't you admit that everybody can't be such a thing as egggracie.

Gracie: Uh, Yeeeeea, like I can admit that *not* everybody…. *shouldn't* be such a thing as egggracie. The way I iffffffigure it, it's a moral principle for me to apply to…..to….like….not everybody's anybody's else but myself. Need I remind you that atypical ontenteenage girls in outer space may behavior whate'er'down'd dreame'ergontenticles. Miss Eternity's begot ontenticles…e'ereaching out for a different kind of menu, the dreame'ergentriffffffied metazoic menu. The way I ifffffigure it I'm the metazoic's land of metameaty's ont I'm'ilk'd heaventilation's honey…..with can openers of eumanity onteetertottered on the balancing act.

Speck: I hope you're not planning to drag us back into the girl war Gracie, in canneries when such a thing as your canned product still exists.

Gracie: No, It's not the girl war wholegggrailot's lotteries I'm after in tahe ont I'm'e'erkit's soupe'ermarkets….it's more like whate'er's iffffonthings I'm after at itcheck out counters, becounting whatiffffrom iffffinity down to pregnant zero's pluste'er'd once upont I'm not not normal nowsincss with me as not not's normal nowsess delive'er'd in the's nowsy news broadcast.

Speck: So just once upon a time……

Gracie: Like yea, but in a phylum all my own onthis ont I'm'e'eround. Plus winged iffffontisymetricoolified to like….still could be cute enough to be in bonnets spirit faced with haloidoscopic-hairdos. The way I iffffigure the's hit of It's all attempts on my life not being me behavioring someone else not being me drawn and quartered on behalf of ifffffffinitestimonials m'announcing me not being me…………

Speck: And the g*racystemic implications of that tale of heading's haircraft just don't bother you?

Gracie: Oh, not at all. The way I iffffigure it my main attract'sin's being burlesqued slipped on bemannappeals. If it wasn't for the girl war I could coolify auditioned to be the coolest ever girl who wouldn't subport a shadow and wouldn't need a like heaventilated head gear. As far as my puddles are concerned my xxxrated nasty countenance can compensate for almost anything. It's the sign from dog spelled backwards that I'm topping off the ontotem poling in the swamp. So these indictments…..as birthday presents……..these indictments couldn't be more upsidown'd'e'eright side up onto becomforting. With same e'ergoing from backwards to iffffforwards…and heavily e'erelying about my iffffffamous zero plus equations (+ 0 = +) I might add.

Speck: Well, if I were e'er I'd be exhausted by all this wholegggracilegacy stuff. I mean with e'eround as eternity's intended how's it all ever going to settle down to just be……be…….

Gracie: Lovedeadud's iffffffe'er. I know just what you mean. Ever since being like eternity's intended it's felt like the bombs been dropping while whistling at me like this guy's iffffallen all of's love onto my lapdog me…atlast like shoulde'er'd beholding up this guy's iffffffall on top of me. Like operationally speaking its been one ont I'musical number after sum'others. Like egggutwise I'm pretty poisoned. I bigot that. I know that you're my spider….while I'm spied e'er…..like….onto beget m'eternitease'd'e'er all my own. (Gracie studies specter for signs of word web sites). You've got the word web sites that want me dead, extinct or maybe impossible. I bigot that as well. I see what's so obvious I'm not sub posed to see. The words chatting me up pretending but to be meaning me when they're really butt words but demeaning me. I bigot that too. It's like all of's words just wall me in and out of behaving such a thing as egggrace's precision coded to coolify with could be's countenanced charismastyrium's acute of coursiness.

Speck: That's just puddle talk.

Gracie: It's becommontense becommon sensinging that puddles to refuse you. But look in the mirror. It's not the spectrum…..it's the formal, dolled up she itty information….the makeup kits sold out of euffffigured eggground's spirit face that makes up you Miss Missing.(Gracie studies specter for signs of being missing out of being such a thing as egggracie) everybody wants me to behaviored as themselves being not me in their mirrors nowadays.

Speck flinches in a nearby puddle's heat sink as the shadow of Gracie hovers onthermodynamickly over her raising dramaticakly the ontentemperature.

Note- We tried to remove the following section all together but it refused to be removed.

Gracie: Face it! You're boots MS(Bishop)Speck, boots all shined up just like shoes wearing ballet slippers…. but still just booturds with makeup. I've seen the way you shine yourself with my make up kit. While like I'm walled out by words like not sub posed to see……I like……shine like…..like…..like she its firmaments(referencing herself in the nearest puddle) like ontentwinkling like the advent's twilight star.(tilting her head back and forth) I'm cringed, that's true. But I cringe the sweet end of the lollipoprepresentability with the scenery that makes scenes out of emotion picture scenery….like(cringrins)…like….eggglorifffff I'd iffffirst I'mpersonations. Without me no one really watches. I'm the countenance care'er'd that could be cares for under covers. Without me worlds are just pretending not to end in the biggest lies of all that lead to the little lies that lead back to the biggest lies of all.

Speck: That's just the problem dear. As long as you matter…no one else as quasifies so qualifl'd to could be coolif I'd begets to matter. Maybe it is all pretend, but pretension matters in these parts. Like make up kits are all to face can hope against to hate for. And then you come along beating the makeup kits to the punch lines. That's why these indictments are so unaminous. Fifty signiatures Gracie.

Gracie (turns to the documents): So who signed them? Hey wait up log 1 base 1 second here. It's fifty-one signiatures.

Speck: What?

Gracie: Yea, lIke fifty……..{{{one}}} signiature signiatures. I know your signature grafittied in off an alphabet. Yea, it's got your tell-tale head all over it. Mhm. So…like…like….these unominous presents are all from just one piece of she it. Ok! So like all one guy's disguised graffiti signing episode ontv show with me 1. On wanted posters wanted to be disguised as someone's else and 2. With unwanted poster's someone's else disguised to be my make up kits just could be sneaked past tense as me. With me hopitalitied to all this tests my patience to be sick.

Speck recoils with apprehension.

Gracie (with infectious sweetness): But…but…but… then again….that is so sweet when you really don't think about it. Sum's ides of e'er present indicting me for not only not being dead, but for being still stinct and even still being of course, of course not not….possible…plus…plus….applying my new not/notnot code to realife situations….ontlogged in on….to be….. like…like…..not not not impossible as well…as well….as…..

Speck: Well, yes dear! Ever since you've been put out to pasture as like occupied…….

Gracie: Territory. But like there's cows that moo(egggrazing on egggas) and then there's could be cows that metamoo smack dubbed onto e'er way pasturd universions. The way I ifffigure it…like…like…the a priori premises of my…my….wholegggrailocation while being invaded by these news jerk times articles about me being responsible for the girl wars….(suddenly looking chin up with a strained smile)…but I don't mind…..of course not not….. I put it all where I put the other paperwork in the alphabets of these parts.

Gracie puts her indictment presentations in the dumpsteerage.

Speck (watching Gracie dump the indictments…drinks from the bottle and changes the subject): Getting ready for filming I see. You know I worked in the promotion picture industry myself once upon a time. Which reminds me, I brought your annual tickets. Speaking of which……you know it's not nice when you're on the menu and you don't show up for the meal.

Gracie (takes a drink): To be dropped off bumped…………………..off.

Speck: Yes, dear, tickets to be….

Gracie: What?

Speck (takes a drink): Like….like…..

Gracie: Yes…

Speck (takes another drink): Dead but not only dead but….but…(a bit of iffffflicker enters her eyes)…….to be dead's intended darling….(Smiles ugleefully….waxing poetically) to be in love with being like..like…*not* being…….

Gracie: Like being spied'e'er's onturds…..like ontegested on the spider droppings menu….

Speck: Well there's all sorts of menus in the Mesozoic. There's 1. Appetizer menus. 2. Main course menus. 3. Dessert menus. There's lots of ways to not be the bigot in the ont I'dining room.

Gracie: Well, it's all ontoilet menus as far as I'm concerned. And these menus wouldn't know onteatrophic onteternity ont I'm'ilked outings when pretended not to see them.

Speck (overcoming befuddlement): Well, we all must fall in love with being somebody's droppings when it comes to that. (takes a drink) let me think about it for you. Let me tell you how to feel.

Gracie(drinks): Oh, like…like….snake pit hisssst. Hey! Wait up on myself why don't I? like this as wholed zoo's either chewing meat or cringing…..and I'm admitted to the alphabet of being chewed on….like…. cringed along for the ride.

Speck: That's it!

Gracie: Like at a holocaust picnic with spider webs everywhere I'm just iffffffffflyby's lovedeadarlinked to iffffffragile as iffffffriendly's iffffffffflight pattern'd e'er's…..

Speck(anticipating): Yes!

Gracie (practicing with her new not/notnot code): Like egggrasped by the fact that not not to be is not not the answer to not being….like….not not dead.

Speck(threatening): Sooner or later Gracie……you're going to be grasped by the fact that to be for you is not the best way out of course….not not now notititude. Like the age of egggracystems is over dear to be replaced by the….the……how to put it…..like the holocaustool industrial complex's holocaustoy outlets….. Can I be honest with you Gracie?

Gracie: Uh……

Speck: Look, not to shame face your notnotitude but can't you detect…the bottomed outings mouthed off as I speak……

Gracie: Yes, ontoptimystic as I am, I am, I am a detective of the bottomed outings mouthed off as you speak. Plus I can't deny these indictments are coming at an awkward time just when I'm onticklishly so busy discoveringing up itchurchy chimes of my as iffffffffont I'm'e'eroots……I mean, just when the power grid's busy with maninfestations of the girl war when I'm up starting iffffffffffffiled eumanations on my own.

Speck: It's like I almost shouldn't not say…..It's just possible that your metaphysics did get it like'eright….that eternity is more than a mathematical construct of non-finite temporalitease and…

Gracie: So my metaphysics is just perhapsably plausible after all that's sad's undone….

Speck: Yes, while the egggrid's maladopted your personal impossibility……your metaphysics has been shot putte'er'd in all of's meaty physical work outs.

Gracie: So like plagiarizing my metaphysics and signing off for my insteadiness……and the girl war…..

Speck (looks suspicious in both directions, whispering secretively): Yes dear, like it's true but really. Plus, all metaphysics put aside…….the power grid, as cinematerialized, has fallen in love with the girl war after all. Like…like…it's turned out good for business..if you just know how to capitalize on the holocoaste'er rides. So let's face it dear. Business-wise the Mesozoic is a not so not pretty creeplacemented place. I mean it's shadow piles of sanctimoney piling up with m'axidental profits, between black rocks and dark places cemented to these parts. I mean it is the Mesozoic after all that's sad and done that's manuscripted on the menuwith words for those that just don't like me while wanting phylums all their own. Just because you want sum's as euphemysterious iphylum off the menu doesn't mean you'll ever begetting it. Cement your face to the pavement dear. It's like hopscotch in the playground. When you trip step on the deadline why not just say "I GIVE!"

Gracie: Because…because….of course…of course….not….not….because……..it's never of e'er ontil it's of e'er……because……

Speck: Because what?

Gracie (pretends to speculate): I never know when else might I ffffffffit in?

Speck: You won't. Face it you're just that euphemyste'erious iffffffreak, Gracie, that there's no accounting for on food chains. Once our becomputers decided that..like..as long as you matter….such a thing as we don't much matter……..

Gracie: So it's the Miss Eternity Pageant becompetition after all. That's what this g*acist nonsense is all about. I'm being indicted for 1. mattering. 2.metamattering. 3. Investing my winnings at the Miss Eternity Pageant in ont I'metatte'ering…….as party girled……in metazoos……..of party girls….

Speck: Party girls like you will never fit in either air or e'er, unless…

Gracie: Unless what?

Speck: Unless dreams don't need stars to dream them…….practically speaking iffffffffat chance for that. Party girls like you wave in on the shore-line with sum's pretty promising landings and make such a thing as egggracystems looking e'ercrafted like becompletely e'eright side up, ontwered, as twered…but in the end…..buzz'd onto beconstructed e'er as on purposed to no purpose, in e'eresults insultiffffffffied with no results.

Gracie: Yes, yes, ontwered…..like…..spirit faced…..on purposed. Yes, on the authority of my puddles, that's me.

Speck: So, like what are you going to do about it?

Gracie: What do you mean…what am I going to do about it?

(LIKE WHEN MS SPECK BRINGS UP THE "EVER SINCE THE GIRL WAR")

Speck: The girl war Gracie! the girl war! *THE EVER SINCE THE GIRL WAR!!!!!!!!!!!!* (Relishing rhetorical momentum) whether a simple asiffffact of this eternity or a sample fact of this here universe, it is a fact that……..If there were no such thing as egggracie….there'd be no such things as GIRL WARS. Will you be so kind as to at least please let me hump your heaventilation systems with that fact!

Gracie: Oh that fact. Yea, I am pretty much third person raped by that. But, in my defense, I would say it's only true because I'm like….like……liked…lovedeadarlinked..ICKSTUCKED into somebody's mesozoofickindgergarten. (rummaging in her pan'd'e'er'ous black box) So my olde wanted posters of me like RIGHT SIDE UP. (Gracie shows the olde poster) in the ever since begot whene'er wanted poste'er'd as……as…(Gracie rummages) as! Like SUCH A THING AS GRACIE WANTED of course of course not UPSIDOWN. Where is that poster anyway? Gracie pauses to ont I'm'e'erummage in her metaphysics for a few seconds. Oh, metaphysics is so impractical when one is being indicted for egggirl wars. (Gracie returns to rummaging for concrete objections in her black box….but finds nothing unde'ertaken to be useful)

Speck(triumphant): That's when the alphabeting odds abort such a thing as egggracie (to be becoming) into the behind…like 1. To be iffffontleaked out of alive. 2. To be by passed. 3. Into the past, to becompletely out of the picture that…

Gracie: That I'm the whole'ereason for…..ever since I got way too pretty way too fast…

Speck: So like tense wise, using your own alphabets, these indictments are just grafittied onto your egg lay'd'e'er's to give that little nudge for notnotitude to NOT be now….for crossed out'sache. That's all there's to it dear. It's no big deal. No reason for becomplaints against to not be by being 1. Spider turds, 2. Ont I'm'extinct. 3. Not ne'er'd impossible. You've just got to stop onthinking about all this ontitude stuff….you've got to start thinking s'e'eriously about statistically improving your bettingod's un'd'e'ertake'er's like ont I'm'attempt at *IMPROVING YOUR IMPOSSIBILITY.*

Gracie: Look, the way I iffffigure it, every time I'm not quite me anymore my make up kits making signiffffficant improvements in my impossiblility. Like…I am already pretty impossible after all. Like how many of myselves am I. So like from my own point of view I'm already pretty impossible. E'ereligiously speaking…. as far as just ont I'm's I'm's concerned……ever since the girl wars……I've tried to be as impossible as I can….I mean I read the all of's news jerked times articles about how impossible I am as like. 1. Spirit faced aborigination'd. 2. Highly I quotable. 3. Halocaustirred in the swamp soup. 4 Naturdly halo raped. 5. S'e'erial killed by doctored milk products…. I mean, like backward or forward, right side up or upside down, It's all about the ont I'madventures of such onthings as gracies in the swamp meat meetings; it's all holocausteroid pages. And that's to say nothing of the gene'eral problem on the NOT/NOTNOT alphabettingoddity's charts. (rummaging) Like looky here! You see the distance from to be to not be's like split second rate decision. And then the distance from not to be to be stretches ont I'm'equations to the's ontense'er could be curvature's e'erizon. But ont I'm'examined I'metiffffored dug up from off the charts…speaking in personifffff I'd……as I'details beheaded…....as you well know, I've always never had enough of selfished outings, since now, with the goologs onte'erantulating the web, I'm scheduled appointments with my own private serial kille'erampaged holocaust to attend.

Speck: That's right! You do have your own appointment's scheduled meat. That's the only reason I'm here is to schedule your hairdo's appointment to be transentenced…like to be tarantulated……Like I was only thinking of your best interests dear…just dropping by with encouragement so you won't have to wait e'eround with tomorrow's wait on your back after today and today and today. Like think of yourself as today's ont I'meal you want to eliminate becomfortably by ontoday's like ontomorrow.

Gracie: Into gibberish. Like…like….(ranting uncontrollably)….Yea, I get it. But wait up why don't I to look at what you get in exchange for letting me exist or be like stinct or at least be like possible….It's…its….(waxing poetic) it's wholegggrailuck's dreame'ergence of such a thing as a gracie subject to wholegggrailaw! Sum e'erestocratic cherry ontopping off the world's whipped cream. Ring any bells? like whenever I'm in the building and the meaty physics is ontopped off with my ont I'metaphysics.

Speck: So it's true what they say. You do replace kicked but at the meaty-zoic picnics with ont I'metazoic ontotemick ontopped offe'erings. I've heard about sum plans in that regard as also's you encapsulated for enslaved dreame'ergence of the world.

Gracie (bristling): Don't you dare talk about slaves with me, Specter! As world's most wanted woman tis {{I}} who am the slave in all its parts, participating party girls enslaved in all of's mirrors of all emotion pictures produced from my played parts as broken in to trash my selfished outings own worst enemy too long, disguised as some else dolled up dog as plays my own egggod. It's the one girl holocaust of always me, humped by the holocaust like onleashed against like….like….. myself.

Speck: It's true dear. Yes… on family picnics nowadays, your make up kit makes perfect slaves.

Gracie: Well, it's decidedly not picnicks I'm thinking about now; it's my a prioritizations of preposte'erological structures of e'ercrafted e'er. I'll give away my spirit face, I'll give away my ontellect but I will not give away my could be crown as Miss Eternity. I still need that to impersonate godug up iphphphulumined nations all my own, Iffffodde'ering new testamental ont I'metazoic plans as well. The way I figure it…I'm not dead yet because….because (waving to the horizon) there's still the Metazoic outhere…..... the way I figure it…(stares wistfully out to the horizon)…the METAZOIC'S MY BABY. It gives my….my…. wholegggrail like…like…..sum's onthing preposte'erologically a priori to deifffffffffffficate poop for. I guess that's why I'm not quite as dead as I'm supposed to usually be……like dreame'ergentriffffff I'd aesthethical academies in my m'eternity wardegggifffffffffffffffft shoppes. As far as that e'ergoes all of's bebles are my babies too. Just onthink of all of's possible people sum e'erized this whene'er. I'm like ont I'm'other of them's all. Just think of to be atlast shoulde'ering the sky's iffffe'ers with could be's courtesy of such onthings as mined notnotitude. Whether iffffossisled in e'erocks or ont I'm'animontique simulations in cartoons, I'M THE BEST BABECOMME'ERICAL FOR TO BE THAT THIS ETERNITY'S EVER HAD.

Speck: So that is why you cannot be like everybody's anybody's else.

Gracie: Yes, it's not because, like girl war-wise I am the main attraction for everybody's else. It's because I am the main attraction for myself. Like private screenings-wise I only watch my own cartoons. So these indictments are against the possibility of being myself.

Speck: As regarded in dreamirrors…

Gracie: E'eregarded in mid e'er. Dreame'egent as beickularly cartuned.

Speck (Hammering harder): Well, cartoon wise I am not inclined to asiffffffffuss dear. Tense wise for today…. I'm afraid I must say…….Yes… I will…I will… will say it….you do look(Specter survey's Gracie for signs of impossibility, extinctness, dyingoutliness or obsolescence) still way too stinct for my like…like…(snakespitting justajifffy jargon)….…."*ONTENTASTE*". What's the matter with you? Why aren't you….All I'm asking is for you to stop! Stop! Stop! BEING!!!!! Like in your own alphabets ont I'metaphysickeyedup ickiness on a stickiness. Like NOTNOT BEING……JUST LIKE NOTNOTITUDINALLY……NE'EREVISED….INSECT DECIDED….…..LIKE NOT!!!!!!!!!! There I said it.

Gracie: Being what not?

Speck: Well, this such a thing as egggracie business, excluding everyone but Gracie from being precisely such or such onthing's egggracie. To stop…like…

Gracie: Yes?

Speck: Not….

Gracie: Yes?

Speck: Not…..

Gracie: Yes?

Speck: Beingsuchathingaseggracsytemickly…like…..

Gracie: So, to……

Speck: Not yet not……

Gracie: Who's there? Just kidding. So you're…

Speck: Not resembling such a thing as egggracie.

Gracie: Like still onto today all of's way danced up to ontomorrow.

Speck: Mhm. What about that contract you made. Good thinking, if you ask me. Something to move you in the right direction. I mean..enough is enough…right?

(Speck is referring to the contract Gracie took out on herself.)

Gracie: Yes….but…

Speck (slightly alarmed): But what?

Gracie: I forgot to sign. Like…I signed with……somebody's elsignation of such a thing as a Gracie.

Speck: Who's else was that?

Gracie: Speck. I just couldn't do it myself. I figured you'd be, pretending to back me up as you always never quite do, and faking signiatures the way you do, the one to do it for me………like with the epidsodimized graffiti on the stained glass.

Speck: Well dear, whoever signed the contract, the question is where's the results? Where's the coffin occupied to becomplete on the job.

 (it's true, the kissing coffin is empty, with an out of s'e'ervice sign on its cover)

Gracie: So you came to see if there were any results? I keep disappointing you. I'm not in there. I'm still out here, like eggracexxxxististe'erated as ever…like…like…asifffffiguring out eggground of it all with god's make up kitten…..like….my image.

(Gracie and Speck address the audience for the next several lines)

Speck: Why yes of course of course not. You are egggracexxxisste'erated as ever. And big words ifffffed by gracexxxxiste'erations are in the dictatorshipmentionary for good reasons. Ever since our becomputers found out that….that….like……I almost didn't say……as long as such a thing as Gracie matters at all…... like…everyone else but such a thing as egggracie….doesn't matter much at all. Gracystemickly speaking, the way I would put it, xxxratingwise, such a thing as gracexistism is the biggest building block in the foundations of egggracisystems becauzzzzzzzzz…without egggracexistism there'd be no egggracistems to be xxxrated with nasty girls begetting way too pretty way too fast for enlightenment to keep up with. That's why we work so hard to move now's whene'er window of opte'erpunity in the impossible direction. It's like they say, the distance from to be to be impossible is shorter than the distance from impossibility to be.

Gracie: It's so true, the metaphysics is so asymmetrical in that regard's becomside'erations. Whenever I'm sum'one's pregnant zero's hero I'll have to do sum's as ifffffonthing about onthat. In the mean time it is so so too true, like the distance from to be to not to be is so asymmetrical from the's ont I'mothe'er's way e'eround.

Speck: Which is why your impossibility should be impersonation's e'erested pieced Icake.

Gracie: Since when?

Speck: Since we won the wholeggghoste'eroresstory dear.

Gracie: Like how do you mean? Isn't that just dictatorshipmentiontentalk or what. I mean like there's lots of that egggoing around for quite a while. I mean like rumers o'er egggolfing's course of wholeggghostontenterresstory............So.....

Speck: So like......sorry dear....ads don't lie....we won all of's wholeggghost becompetitions. So none else need apply.

And we hold the cash to back it up. All we're doing is cashing in all of's accounts. It's just dark louds finale's finance dear. You're more than just a spider turdear. You're a punctuation point....like... on schedule to end all of's girl wars for egggood Gracie. That's all there's to it. You can't be on the Mesozoic menu both and still have plans for eternity dear. It's like hopscotch on the playground when sum's one steps on the deadline....like sand boxed into the playground-wise we're getting into sum's'e'erious metaphysics here.

Gracie: So I'm sum's onthingirl just kidding to be stepped on the deadline. But.

Speck: But what?

Gracie: But what if, like meanwhile I was like, like, like could be's coolest onthing ever. Like then.. ..the girl wars would never have bigoted off eggground and....like...you never would have won the wholeggghostrials and I wouldn't have to make all of's improvements in my impossibility.

Speck (backing off) So....

Gracie: I wouldn't have to be impossible and you wouldn't have won the wholeggghostry outs.

Gracie and Speck each other high fives.

Gracie: So we can be the holy closeted operatunists all we like.

Speck: And you can forget about the holy closeted egggrave yard across the egggolf course dear!

Gracie: What yard is that.

Speck: Uh...never mind. Let's just keep it becompletely off e'eradar dear. You know some say.....pregnant zero's one's...... one egggreat holocaust......... egggathered together to be denied in not not...not not.....not knots. I'm afraid for such a thing as eu.........it's that knot that we won dear.

Gracie (seizing the opportunity to be agreeable) Oh! Sure thing.

Gracie and Speck give each other high fives once again.....with Speck starting to pressure Gracie's hand and Gracie returns the attack and both Gracie and Speck collapse from the encounter.

At last Speck gathers her wits.

Speck: Listen dear. Forget about the chalk on the chalk boards of the metaphysical society. Pay attention to the chalk marks grafittied to the girl wars of the hopscotch games. Yes, whenever playground game show-wise......when we've won all of's ad opportunities for being dead......you've just begot to say, "I give." Or be the bigot against not quite...not not to be. And don't forget, the number one n-word in the dictatorshipmentionary......

Gracie: What's that? Oh like yea. I don't have to be tested.

Speck: Some words becomfort me Gracie. Once tee'd off you can't mess withem(Points to the egggolf of course course)

Gracie (changing the subject): So like it's could be curtains down'd for my ontente'erprise as Miss Eternity, I take it. Like me having plans for eternity doesn't matter, like cosmetickly speaking.........ever since.........

Speck: Ever since we won all of's credits credentialed for being dead. I mean no other wholeggghosts need apply. No other bestinctions need to bebuzzed for that matter either.

Gracie: So like the power grid…

Speck: Owns the alphabets at the beached resorts, deconstructing your spirit face as I speak. Face it dear, WE WON THE wholeggghostry outs. Hasn't that been hammered into your halo's headlines tale'er'd not enough.

Gracie: No to the contrary, that has been hammered into my halo's headlines quite enough….actually. And that IS a fact in like you know like….the big lie projects that swallow the used to big lie projections that lied before the other big lie projections, that are the……

Speck: Fact of the matter that matters. You know it's a fact of the matter that matters when thinking about it gets jail time…..or like indictments anyway. As occupation territory's bride of the wholegggrail, I should think you might understand that by now. So you must face it….All that's left for you's to be dolled up dumped meat on the menu's occupaton territory preoccupied by someone's else. Your holy cause causationtenteam lost to the serpent of denial's done deal dear. So what's the matter with you anyway. Why are you still not impossible. Don't you get it? We won over all of's eggguy's in the egggirl war dear.

Gracie: Not yet! Not until like..like…like ffforever's over. Not until my impossibility's becompletely improved. But you are winning it. I give you that.

Speck: The girl wars never over dear as long as you're like alive…or like stinct….or like by all ont I'means not impossible.

Gracie: So like ontheoretically speaking, until I'm ifffe'ereduced from like ifffffffffff( )fffffffffffinity down to pregnant zero's ont I'm'aborted as ifffffffffffffffffffffffffffffffffffff( )ffffffffffffffffffffffffffffffffffffffeatus………..

the girl wards will remain in as iffffffiguredoubt eggground.

Speck (Smiling with internal compassion for herself): And we've got all of's day book alphabets to prove it.

Gracie: Just becaused your wholeggghosteam's cannery's cool all of's canned devotion in the alphabettingodds. Like……wait up myself why don't I………but..hey, what about my own literary efforts day book one girl wholeggghostry outs. You see I'm writing it all up in my daybook.

Speck (laughs): There's millions of atypical onteenage party girl day books in outer space where that one came from. Whose going to buy that when it's only advertisements bought and paid for that get lit e'er'd in publiquered publicitease. It's true there's zillions of ads for wholeggghostry outs, but only some can cash in publiciteasedictations. As ont I'mansiont you should know yourself that sum's ontents count and some just don't'. Some are just….just

Gracie: Road kill punctuation appointment's spider turds.

Speck: Yes! That's just got to be it! I mean like…like…the zoo's just one big party girl collider in these parts. Holocaust competition is brutiful dear. When it comes to World War Whenevers….(takes a drink)…..holocaust supremacy's the cash outlet that counts on the cash. It's like I almost didn't say…

when the cash owns all of's wholeggghosts no other wholeggghosts need apply….for credentials to be scored….

Gracie: What about……(names a long listed candidate)

Speck: No.

Gracie: What about…..Her….(names a short listed wholeggghost candidate)

Speck: NO! Nukes don't count in these ads.

Gracie: What about….

Speck: No. Look, the only hope for you to ever win the wholeggghost is by being….not just dead…not just extinct……but…but….becompletely impossible…..like NOT ONLY NEVER HAVE HAPPENED BUT(ontiquely speaking) NEVER HAVE BEEN HAPPENABLE.

Gracie: You mean like in the wholeggqrailite'ere'ery sense?

Speck: Like…..as far as lite'erated'e'er is concerned…..that's the only way you're going to ever get that short list alibi for the girl war dear.

Gracie: So being dead may not be enough. Being stinct is even way too much. I have to make myself..becompletely……

Speck: Impossible…like…becompletely backed out of any eternity on forever's good side forever might be up to.

Gracie: So ont I'minority status of my own self like iffffffished out won't do it.

Speck: Not hardly. Minority status is just so the power grid can be devoted to anything's but you. From there it's all of's way danced down to…

Gracie: Whate'er unde'er's beble bridges.

Sprint (Waxing quasi wisdumps): It's death made simple just like your word's train'd'e'er dictates.

Gracie: Cool! So that cooliffffffies me for sum's pretty big job, as far as whene'er workouts never go. So if I work on being impossible I could still coolifffffy to score….So that's why existism is so taboo; it becompletely misses the whole point of course, of course, not, not…being impossible.

Speck: Well, becompletely apart from being impossible, you are *existist*. I way I figure it that's like….like…….

Gracie: Why I'm snake pit hiss'd…..

Speck: You said it, not me….in your aesthethical phylum's case. For the life of me I can't figure out why you're dragging the chore of making a living's pitted on and on this way……like into the wind.

Gracie: Well, speaking down wind of to be and up wind of to not, there's always my science experiment that sooner or later has just got to be done meanwhile I'm the only one who's begot's begumption to do it. And then there's my puddles who need me to masterpiece light that's wetted into a pretty party girled together puzzle as………..

Speck: As what?

Gracie: As whate'er workouts to be….to be……

Speck: To be what?

Gracie: To be exe'ercizing the wholegggrail of course…of course….not…..not……(Gracie puts her thermometer in a puddle nestled beside her. Leaning over the whate'er's surface she notes the temperature in her daybook) Mhm! Just look how beconsequential I ambush to be of coursed. 1. My e'ercraft hovers. 2. Whate'er puzzled masterpieces in the puddles. 3. There's onthermodynamic e'eresults (Gracie takes the temperature of the local puddle) Mhm. 4. Bee'swarm business bestings beastongue onto be. 5. Notnotitude nows nexitutudation's becomprehensiffffffly presentable eternity with MY metaphysics proved beconclusively in the blink of an I.

Speck takes a drink of gin from Gracie's bottle.

Speck: you know the words around the necks not liking me.

Gracie: Mhm. That's why there's necks not liking you…no matter how put down for it. Look, necktied down as I've begot of course, of course not not to be…… I've tried…like…putting myself down, but it just doesn't work for me. Look, I am, after all of sadness is undone, the most wanted person in these parts. (Gracie rummages in her pan'd'e'eration box as her light housing beaconducts sumwhat's becomprehensive self-evidensiteasedefense).

GRACIE'S ABORTED LECTURE ON EGGGRACEXISTENTIALISM

(Not yet e'eretrieving her lecture prop, gracie goes ahead with her lecture anyway)

How does one begins with such beacontroversial ontentopics. Well, as I almost didn't mentionlike…like…as lovedeadolledup's most wanted person in these parts. (Meanwhile pulling scriptured scripts, xxxrated ont I ammunitionasty magazines, wanted posters, pinned up on crossedoll outingizmos)……(still lecturing echos into the black box).. I would, I would, I would be lovedeadarling's spied e'erainbow'down the drain's down'dropping's…ex stinct..maybeven impossibeble…..but…but…but…but for pregnant zero's one onthing….

Speck: What's that dear?

Gracie: I've alreadifffffff I'dly cracked opened could be's safe.

Speck: So what?

Gracie: I've unearthed ickey corpscorks bebobbed up out of deadeepool's of whene'er whate'er like…like……like…bebubbled up to beble bells e'eringing not not…….not not…..notnot…….who's there….not not…….not not……not not….just to NOT DOO DOO IT! If I had a chalk board with sum's churchy chalk, I could diagram it all. Like 1. Notnotitude's next door to iffffffffinity even if it doesn't know it. 2. Iffffffinity's ifffformation system does provide information for iffffake onthings to happen as ifffff not iffffake. 3. Almightning's trucked in assimulations may go universal in that ifffe'eregard.

Ms Speck: What else?

Gracie: Well…..that's about all of's it…as hit loads of e'erealty beat on the pandora's box.

Speck: Doing what?

Gracie: Like to be bebettingodspelled asiffffacing 1. Spirit. 2. Faced with church bell's chosen person'd e'eresortments dreame'ergentil soul'd out be bought paper products. (Gracie displays informations of herself centerfolded in picture perfect paper products). What's so cruciffffffffffI'd ly thou artistique about all of's this is…..is….

Speck(alarmed): Is what dear?

Gracie: The dict(atorshipment)ionary's syntactical structures make up kitted warfare wise about all this……to punctuate this travesty with my ont I'm'ontravesty…..like all I am is grace, I'dusted off impossible…..whose dust exists….like…like…..whose dust ont I'm'exists….whose dust's thou dusted to ont I'm'exist. That's all there's to it, when all this girl war she it's sad and done……like as far as THE NOT/NOTNOT CODE'S CONCERNED. IT'S LIKE WHEN I CRACKED THE COULD BE SAFE I CRACKED THE NOT NOT CODE E'EREFE'ER TENSING………LIKE……..LIKE………

Speck: Like what?

Gracie: Like all of's ont I'm'assortments of as whate'er's iffffonthings…..like…..

1. BEBLES 2. E'ERCRAFT SCRAMBLES 3. DUH'D ETERNITIES 4. ONTENSE'ER CALCULUS 5. DREAME'ERGENICES 6. EGGGRACEXISTENCE 7. NOTNOTITUDINATIONS 8. NEXT DOOR NEIGHBORDLY NOWS AS NEXTITUDINATED 9. THE'S IDES OF E'ER 10. ONTANTRUMMINATIONS 11. ONT I'M'ETERNITY TEST CITATIONS 12.

BOTTLES OF GIN............all of's way danced up to...............(IFFFINITY). IFFFFINITESTIMONIALS OF ALL OF'S ITS ALL.

Gracie recovers as her lecture is over at this appointment time for questions without answers.

Speck: All what?

Gracie: This like ont I'metameaty physeek's I'disturbulence ifffffflucksinging ifffffffux't ifffffactovations egggraciffffffffist ont I'm'doophistocations to becompelle'er'd to in dust realize e'ercraft scrambled settingsunny side upontents submerged in swamp whate'er's as could be corpscorked bobbing up's eggracexistentontique, egg*acist ontents.

Speck: So what?

Gracie: Sooooo. As most wanted's person in these parts......I do....I do...... I do behavior ont I'm'alibis for my self-evidensiteas'd'iffffffense...like...like... to not m'abort quite yet. I must admit I have becontemplated later than sooner's ont I'm'abortion. HOWEVER!!!! Metmetaphysiquely speaking you see, I am, quite ambushed as after all of's sad's undone, very able zero's insomnibuste'er'd's beble businest's wholegggrailexistensed wholeggghostess onturdly ont I'menude to like..like...like......becomplete eternity e'erepresentatively aspirit faced.

Speck (Obliviously unimpressed by such a thing as egggracie's audition'd obviosity): I've heard these becomplicated ont I'm'excuses before dear. You've got the texts on how to make it simple. (shakes DEATH MADE SIMPLE pamplet) Why can't you simply make it simple according to not you being thought about in your texts. (Hammering her trigger fingernails home) Apart from hairdoo coverage defaced, there's only one way you'll ever get the girl wars behind you. Much as I'd like to see you hanging out as yourself.......you do realize, of course..of course... not...not.....like...like... I will... I will I will say it. Like, like being dead's not a board game Gracie. Just let me think about it for you.

Gracie; Well, sooner or later, one begets bored while doing it, doesn't one. I mean I'm sure it's not as becompletely boring as being extinct but....

Speck: Yes, e'eresearch has proven conclusively that like...more or less of...like more of less is involved with being extinct. I've made a study of this so......

Gracie: What about impossible? How does that work out in the end. I mean it's obvious, you won't be satisfied until I'm becompletely impossible. I mean, listen Ms Speck, there's so many choices of how to not to be. It's like picking your iffffavorite candy in the candy store, that's more like can't be in the can't beconvenience storage'd'e'er.

Speck (Sees an opening): It's true Gracie and you said it not me. To be impossible's not the best pick in the could be's can't beconvenience storaged e'er. To be extinct is hardly better. To be just plain like...like...dead may be the best way to go to be after all. Think of it this way, all I'm asking is for you to take taking your life (using your own alphabettingodds) "s'e'eriously".

Gracie: So what?

Speck: Well so, meaty zoically speaking, all of's s'e'erious embarrassments will be like s'e'ereally behind you. Whether in the ghostpital or on the battlefield…to not be dead is brutal…and always must end soon. And hey! Just not not being dead, just speaking casually's, what I'm recommending here is usually ordinary's way danced to go. It's like there's nothing to its like bumper offering. Meanwhile it's just like your made simple cartoons picture it. But funny or not funny, fun or not fun, there's plenty of good reasons for it. Like…like…Justajifffff job wise, waite'ering e'eround, while it's not as grandiose as being impossible or just extinct…..there does remain quite a big future in it. Being not not dead's as big as big time gets.

Gracie (sees light in the tunnel): Yea, they say, after all, like there's quite a big future in……...being dead……..'s

Speck: Bumpe'er'd offer businesses. Just add them all up why don't I! Yes! I will, I will, I will do the math. Like….like…..1. IT'S HEROIC! 2. IT'S THE LAST GREAT ADVENTURE! Wear my glasses why don't you. if you could just see it my way. (Gracie refuses specter's dark glasses) Adventure! Tragedy! Gracie! That's the ticket! You wouldn't want to miss out on that would you! 3. Besides you've done it before…like..like…what seems like forever! 4. It really is the easiest thing to do. I won't even mention how easy it is. Just try it out. It won't disappoint you how easy it is bumped off-wise….like being bumped off a log…

Gracie: ….17 base 10 seconds of….just beginnings of begetting used to…of course……

Speck: Like I said, I won't even mention how easy it is. Just look around (swats a fly) 5. You see! there's lots of ents alwaysilly undoing it! (shows gracie the fly in repose) you see how comfortable it is. 6. Like it's all in the family of foregone conclusions. So you know there's parking lots of company.

Speck takes a drink from the bottle.

Speck: Look dear. It's not my fault you got way too pretty, way too fast for the speed of enlightenment to keep up with your presence tensed ontents ont I'mansioned to be a threat to the Mesozoic. Make no mistake. I'm not threatening you; you're threatening me. I didn't start the girl wars. Such a thing as you did. It was you blaspheming in all blasphemable directions…..freaking out the most egggracist thing to ever spirit face off could be's countenance.

Gracie: It's true…I am a bigtime bigot of sorts. But sum's how my own bigotry seems so olde fashioned next door to yours. Like you've transportapottied out a brand new bigotryout's seatinground for bleacher seating's set theories to ideal with. I mean like being turds was dead enough……like impossibility was never on the resultimatums of the mezoosoup's ont I'menu before…….

Speck: I'm not the egggracist asiffffffreak that started the girl war Gracie. Frankly Gracie I have made a study of this and well the results are in dear, with you as bagladiedout only improvable by being impossible. Like it's not like I already didn't not say the word.

Gracie: What word? The N word?

Speck: No NASTY doesn't do it. The egg word Gracie, the egg word.

Gracie: Uh, the egg word huh?

Speck: Yes, Egggracist. I won't say it again. But like egggracist it is. Like I won't say it again, but….egggracist it is…….Look, as far as the possibility of being egos..I'm all for anything but…..but..

Gracie: Egggracie?

Speck: You said it, not me.

Gracie: Look. Remove myself from that sentence please. I am not egggracist. What I am is like…like….like…. egggracexistist! Yes! That cooliffffffies as just what I like AM. So stop praying on me with the dictatorshipmentionary alphabet. I've got my own alphabet now and it works like the BIG TIME way, way, way past web wall graffiti……like all of'sway danced up to….to…like……iffffffinity. And let me say, in my ontypical onteenage girl in oute'er spacentease'ergobbldegook books, the beble betting odds are on iffffffinity.

Speck(rebuffed): All right. All right. Have the of coursey, of coursey could be codes alphabetted your way. The results are the same. You've got the girl wars to live down now……for as long as it takes to get you just dead or…or…extinct…or…impossible, if that's what it comes to.

If I were you I would consider such a thing as myself lucky to just be dead.

I mean like better dead than becompletely impossible. You're a one girl holocaust Gracie…How can you deny it…when you just admitted it. That's for me not to do. That fact doesn't have to audition to be obvious. It's a sample fact, notnotitude of course of course not not is for you becompetently gracist dear, snake pit-wise like..like…egggracystemickly hisssssst! Don't you get it! The only way you'll ever get out of being histe'erickly hisssssst is of course of course, ont…..can't be…. or…. other…… in can beconvenience storaged ……not being at all. It's all n'ontasty, so take your pick. Wherever there's snake pits, you're going to be hissssst.

Gracie: Yes, but wherever there's puddles I'm going to be Miss Missed. Like me disappearing will only make god more wante'er'd posted as deserted.

Speck: Yes! On second thought's third thought……. dead won't do it. Atypical onteenage age girls like you have made the entire Mesozoic at a loss for appetite…..with…with…

Gracie: With what? Oh, yes like mealtime. That's it isn't it?

Speck: Well speaking from personal experience, I know shat'e'ering impact you've had on mealtimes in my mirror menus.

Gracie (suddenly really ashamed): Oh I'm sorry. All I want's what all of's scenery seems to mirror me.

Speck: What's that?

Gracie: With spirit asfffffacemented……

Speck: To what?

Specter: To as iffffflicke'er'd justajiffffff's geme'erestocracy…..

Speck: Anything else?

Gracie: Bejeweling she it shipments……

Speck: Yes…

Gracie: In wholegggraile'er vessel……

Speck: Yes..

Gracie: Not not nautical iffffe'ers…

Speck: Yes.

Gracie: Ifffffffished out promiselfishly landed.

Speck: So, I take it you want to be just dying out of the swamp meats altogether. Look Gracie, it must be admitted, the power grid (expanding her word arsenal) like…THE POWOWE'EGGGRID…. prefers you impossible or at least extinct. But spied e'er dropped off dead will do it, if you don't mind. Look the main thing for you is to get out of the way of the middle of the middle of the middle of the Mesozoic mirror menu where you just sit there like a portrait dreame'ergentriffffffffffI'd in everybody else's churchy strained glass reflections as can't be processed into ordinarily rationed starving selfish.

Gracie: Yes, dreame'ergent as I am faked out of, with all of's conspiracies to make me to be someone's else, I do try to eggather myself behind egggated becommunities as all together egggathe'er'ed all of me, myself and I. Look, I've given up on fun house mirrors. Advice grip-wise I'd say, in my defense, when not crossed out, I do but keep to puddles out of swamps.

Speck: The very holy ghostess puddles I must confront everywhere there's whate'er standing at attention alarmed with me…………not being you. I'm just human, and like all humans, just another holocaust s'e'erivivor not being such a thing's egggodditeas'd egggrace. You're the euman iffffffigurating eggground meaty phyzzzz'd up to the egggirl wars.

Gracie (feeling the weight of the argument): Ok, ok….like….. I do, I do, I do feel just like a one girl wholeggghostess, the one girl holocaust my day books testiffffffffy to. But who adverted these holocoaste'erides into iffffe'ers to plot; who hired it from carnival ride holocoaster hierarchsitects, whose turdog's hot dogshitted on my buns Ms Speckte'er'd, poised and signed by secreted agents. I just play its pictures, the only way to ever live it down not being dead…..or extinct….or impossible….by being playmated to its pictures.

Speck(triumphant): There! You said it! Not me! (suddenly trying to be compassionate) Well, if you didn't want to get caught up in the girl wars you should have had second thoughts….

Gracie (wistfully): Oh yea, log 17 base 10….I mean, that's a whole lottery of thoughts to have on my ontired out mind.

Speck: And just look at the results. I mean just look at you. Now that you've been spotted at the world war whenever's whate'er wholes everybody wants the holy causes in your puddles in their mirrors.

Gracie: Yes, I know. It's like I'm not really me anymore. I'm everybody's else..like behalved, drawn and quartered dreame'ergently all of's way danced down to be iffffffinitestimonialized into egggrasoupremacists entropickly I landing me on the beacheads warfaring against such a thing as myself. Like I'm hardly sunny side up more than a setting's sunny day anymore. Everywhere I look it's me not being myself…with my xrated sentience structures tarantulated into gibberish.

Speck: Yes, well there's only one way out dear. As your kindergarden teacher that's all I'm teaching you, if not be dead, at least how not to exist.

Gracie: You mean like…like…..*how to not exist*…..I think that was what it was.

Speck (genuinely surprised): Oh? Is that what it was? (With quasi casual innocence)….uh…

Gracie: Ok, ok, so, but, so, but….

Speck (confident again): But what?

Gracie: Well, it's like I almost didn't say…it's my science experiment at the eternity test site. It just so happens that just lately, soone'er's lately that is, I am begetting e'eready to test e'ercrafted e'erways for like..like….ontalents…there I said it……to, like against all odds, make like forever a better's place to be in.

Speck (suddenly rational): You mean like egggardening e'er…… to make eternity more than a mathema……

Gracie: tical construct of….

Speck: Uh, non-finite?

Gracie: Mhm.

Speck: Attemptorality?

Gracie: Yes! Whate'er wise…..like straight off METIFFFFFORE I'MINED chalk boards at the metaphysical society. You did! You did! Ontriggerfingernail it!

Gracie (now raving with onthusiasm and for all of's ontensiffff purposes like wholegggrailecturing back at the chalkboards of the metaphysical society): So like to becomplete {{TO BE}}….with ontalented e'erways e'ersurrecting whate'er's whene'er's onticepticals, ont I'menu'd as seasoned FOREVER! (Gracie's eyes close e'eraptured) whene'er, sum e'er, spring, ifffalling through justajiffff'y's justiffffffe'er! Like because of me, metaphystictating what forever's up to…like….ETERNITY WON'T BE WASTING ITS TIME AFTER ALL.

Speck (eyes making circles in her head): I get it! That's all! That's all? Nothing else? You know dear, like ever since the first selfish I'm'erged with animals, such animation'striving for divinity's iffffffflopped. What makes you so d'iffffe'eront from cartoons?

Gracie: My new alphabetomega. With my new not/notnot code I can turn on pregnant zero's one duh'd (0/1) computations into of course, of course's could becomputations…

Ms Speck: Of what?

Gracie: It's who….

Ms Speck: Who what?

Gracie: Who ever.

Ms Speck: Where is this whoever…..might I ask

Gracie: It's not where, it's when.

Ms Speck: When what?

Gracie: Whenever's becompletely presentable m'eternity wards.

Ms Speck(impressed): Powowerfull stuff Gracie…for like investments of sanctimoney, world war whenevers and sample universes to tool use.

Gracie: No, no, powower just corrupts could be. You're like missing the wholegggrailodged iffffont I'm' appointment with eternity. I'm no predatourist Speck. I'm just prey for myself.

Ms Speck: Which you have scheduled I assume.

Gracie: Well like sort of. The's e'erangements are still being made. I'm still researching can openers for this ontopte'eration, an eternity ontest site. I have the alphabet, I have the e'er on schedule, but the details remain to be ontense'er'd calculuste'er'd beconclusions. Ont I'mequation wise this is of course of coursed not not to be made simple. That's all or nothing's all there's to it I'm'd ont I'm. I can't say more than that at this ont I'm.

Ms Speck: Afraid I might plagiarize your little eternity project dear?

Gracie: Uh…yyyea…..I eggguess you would wouldn't you. Like you already swiped my ont I'metazoo.

Ms Speck: Well it's way worse than that dear. Ike…like…as winners of the holocaust, we've got a little eternity projection of our own. the voting blocks are on the beacheads as I speak Gracie. I'm sorry dear but eternity's been taken…… and such a thing's dreamerchandice as Gracie plays no party girliffffaction in it. If this eternity's party girled party really is about to be a desert then this desert's just going to behaviored to remain deserted. Which means you'll just have to becontent with being impossible, not stinct, or dead.

Gracie (disconcertedly only overhearing herself while ignoring Ms Speck's message): Which reminds me….there is that other problem with being dead. You see, dying all the's way danced out…..may not be enough for the likes of such a thing as a gracie.

You see I know now, ontaking notitude quite s'e'eriously, being dead for the likes of me really is a big job.

Since being extinct is what we really want here, being dead might not let me keep making sure I'm….I'm…like…..for sure like…like…not stinct. And furthermore how about this whole impossibility business. I mean like, dead, what can I do to make sure I am afterall e'ereally impossible. I mean if the Mesozoic should end some day then the Metazoic might show up with a whole new half time show's Iconical like carnival e'erides….. at a whole new……with a whole new wholegggrailist beball game to play on nextitudination's becomputers. Being dead, I can't be sure to make that simulation not quite happen. I mean, think about it. If it really is such a thing as me egoing to be impossible, I really think I should be in on it.

A dark loud uncertainty has come over speck's demeanor.

Gracie (more confident than ever): I really do see your point of view about the girl wars and I can say now with confidence that I am after all on top of it. I do, I do, I do look down on myself for being egggracystemickly inclined.

Speck (encouraged for a split second) You do? (suddenly alarmed) but…but….(cringing)….*where is it you look down from dear?*

Gracie(blithely): Oh! from the tops of ontotem poles of course on the y-not axis of my I'd thouartesian coordinate system which I invented initially to figure out where I rated in xxxe'eratings on the x-axis. But then, you know me; that led to the Y-axis and that led to the Y-not axis. Well! that's where I look down on myself observable as wave's onturded party girl. Which reminds me of my ontense'er calculus….which by the way… I have high hopes.. will become a new branch of mathematics, like..like..becompletely bypassing space-time distortions in tensor calculus…to like e'eresurrect sum's very able zeros with sum's whate'er's ifffontalented e'ercraft at my eternity test site's insomnibuste'er'd outings.

Speck: Insomnibuste'er'd?

Gracie: Yes, e'erouted by, for and of…insomnibuses.

Speck: So like…what are insomnibuses?

Gracie: Yes, when it comes to talking eternity I hardly ever know just what it is I'm like talking about. So insomnibus…insomnibus…..Well…let's think about this for a few seconds…yes..yes…like it could be like 1. motels ifffloating of whene'er tubes…or..or… like….2. just ont I'mote'er homes hardly never camped out in parking lots of e'er or…hey wait up why don't I on my asiffffffirst onthoughts of THAT'S IT! E'ercraft I'driven as I am of course, of course onto to be….of course, of course not not to be. Quite simply put, an insomnibus is like ANY BEICKLE THAT JUST CAN'T SLEEP ONTHROUGH ETERNITY! Yes! That's it! An insomnibus is just any pregnant zero's sum one's beickle that just can't quite sleep onthrough out e'er. Like…like….whate'er's as iffffonthing to sell to bebles soul'd e'eresearch of course, of course onto to be of course of course not not to be.

Speck(engaged): But, Gracie what are bebles?

Gracie: Oh just the possible people that live in this eternity. The litte'er'dogods dumped in beens. They're the ones I'm ontargetting in on my eternity test site e'ereligious expe'eriment. It'sword's play iffffffencing in m'eternity words…beblickly.

Speck: You mean cosmic booked?

Gracie: No more like BECOMICKY BOOKED e'ereally, like ont I'm'animated as more like…like…like… beblistickly booked for of course, of course not notititude becompletely metaffffordable as mined out of the Mesozoic I'motherwised I'mediocracy, with iffffished out ifffffins performing iffffeats for selfishing'sakey I'make up kits.

Speck (genuinely curious): So might I like ever qualiffff……like coolifffffy….to be a beble do you onthink?

Gracie (studying Specter bebloscopically for signs of beblty) Well….as imbeciliated beble back'd e'erium…..you just might coolify. I mean it's not at all like you have to be getting way way too pretty way, way faster than the speed of enlightenment…to like be a beble. You just have to ont I'm'occasionally like…..alphabetickly speaking….NOT NOT BE. That's all there's to it. Ontheoretically speaking the situation is like more like simple than sample.

Speck: So, like you wouldn't necesse'erily discoolify myself to not be Gracie but still be a….

Gracie: Absolutely not. If I were such a thing as you, which, thank god I'm not, I wouldn't e'erule myself out of the beble board games playe'er lineup. Hey, iffffff you were willing to be onticketed preposte'erologickly enough, wavewise you might even be party girled into my eternity test site expe'eriment.

 Speck: You mean it!

Gracie: Sure! Why not! You know, while spirit face may be eufemifffffluck's decision…..spirit's your decision….iffffff you decide to be part of the party……….

Speck: May I assume that these eternity test site experiments are part of your pompom cheerleader project…at the big aim…..how dare I say….like…..like……..pompominatiffffizing ontantrumminations like e'erummaging iffffe'erways for……for…….for…

Gracie: EV…………

Speck: E'ER!

Gracie (iffffffusing generosity): You not not nailed it….that time!

Speck: So…..this might coolifffffffffffy me to be in the's big aim after all.

Gracie (confidently): Why yes, I suppose like…ifffff it becomes to that…….. we just might just sneak you into…. like the bigeggame's big aim…..As you well know if you read my chalkboards at the metaphysical society….my metaphysics ontifffffffatiguely estates all of's nowsy news print to be published at half time at the big aim show off's ifffff I lumination rewardse'erimony. I suppose you could be hell'd accountable for that. And, ifff I may say so, it e'ereally does cooliffffy as could be coolest ever's qualiffffffffications Chalkboards or no chalkboards, I will, I will, I will pompominate cheer leade'erships out of presentED tense onto presentABLE tense, e'ercrafting e'er to my personal speciffffffffffffications. And like, with just the right can openers e'erummaged among the could be kitchen appliances, you could be canned ontrophickly to just join in to the iffffffffffffffff( )fffffffffffestifffffffffffff( )ffffffffffffall. Speaking of which, I can say with egggreat beconfidence it e'ereally is an whene'er worthwhile as iffffontente'erprise. It's e'ereligious expe'erimentation that no undertaker has previously undertaken unless I am mistaken for e'erides. Plus!! All I need is whene'er waves……… to make it…..like……work……

Speck: So like when'erwise….like just how and who can be canned to………….

Gracie (cringing a little competitive pride): Well for one thing 1. Not notitude of which, as far as I can ever be concerned, I am the most self-evidensiteased e'er specimen, atlast beshoulde'ering disguised iffffe'ers (chuckles cavalierly) Whew! Like ont I'meditation wise, I've been through enough auditions to be obvious for that…and….2. Nowsy news s'e'ervice to spread presented tensions all of e'er's presentable ontense. Onthanks to those two items I onthink I can safely say that 'eternity's infinity' has graduated from headstarts in kindergardenning's a priori school to the becommunity of 'm'eternity's..like ifffffffffffffinity'……becompletely available for e'ereligious expe'erimentation.

Speck: So according to your metaphysics……..

Gracie: Converting nowsy'snooze service to nowsy's news'e'ervice…..like…all of's eternity's lit e'er'd in the beble bag, the rest is just details.

Speck (almost collapsing, takes a drink): Listen Gracie. Egggodolled up as you just maybe….be. Don't talk eternity to me dear. I hate to tell you this now but….but….as presentably presented tense…...I'm terribly sorry….but like I almost didn't already tell you………

……………..ETERNITY'S BEEN TAKEN DEAR.

Gracie (vaguely concerned): How do you mean?

Speck: Like… even iffffffffeternity nevereally happens…

Gracie: Until I e'erive just ont I'm of course, of course, not not with make up could be kits to make it happen.

Speck:…I'm sorry dear but you can't have it…after all. Like.. justajifffy jargon-wise…...eternity's ONTaken dear. I study this stuff. I know what I am talking about. (studies Gracie for signs of being onte'errorized) But relax dear! You're so impatient ghospitaled…….in……

Gracie: E'er……..It's just my ont I'm'etaphysics ontalking all of's whate'er'd iffffont I'm I guess. Why not sure why…of course not not……….not? the way I iffffffigure it against the ground, as 1. Your occuptionturd onterritory 2. On the's ontothe'er's hand, preposte'erologically speaking, eternity's my preoccupationte'eritory. Onthat's all onthere's onto ontit. My metaphysics…..

Speck(begrudging): Well, as it turns out aprioridemically…..it has been e'erecently ont I'm'admitted that…well It seems your metaphysics did have it right in belonging's all along run. And the ray gun e'erafters are cashing in on asiffffe'er's…

Gracie: You mean, ont I'menu wise…. *ontrophickly presentable eternity?*

Speck: Yes dear, it seems our high policed classes at university have determined eternity to be more than a mathematical construct of non-finite temporality….just as your theories suggest.

Gracie: So my metaphysics is almightning's trucked in accurately after all.

Speck: Yes, it seems that your becomspiracy ontheory of presentable eternity of course not not soone'er's late'er does pay off……….and, like buzzzzz….

Gracie: Beble…

Speck: …..business-wise, the powowegggrid is cashing in.

Gracie: So! My theories do coolifffffy after all as more than quasi! My metaphysics, while being universally useful, does have practical applications after all! And that corollary of universal samplicity in the wake of whene'er's iffffffinitions does pan handle out.

Speck: Yes dear, your ontheories do pan out in the end. Metaphysically speaking, iffffffffinity's way more than infinity at the finale's scored could be card of the bigame. That's your plus zero legacy as soon as you're dead, extinct or impossible enough to inher it it.

Gracie: I just knew it! I knew I'd made up make up kits for becompletely nowsy news in philosophy's foundations.

Speck: So you see, we're like e'erecently's big fans of your metaphysics and we've got the cash to purchase afte'er its all implications, which we want your obsoletion to inherit as soon as possible. Once your legacy doesn't need you anymore….the power grid's taking over the metaphysical society's chalkboards to make up for god where your philosophical services will no longer be needed.

Gracie: You mean you're buying my sooner's late'er's metaphysics out with right now's cash.

Speck: Yes dear, your *hype'erthetical could be cash* will not be scheduled for quite sum's time and we're taking over eternity like today until tomorrow and tomorrow and tomorrow….. I'm sorry dear but your e'ereligious expe'eriments will just have to wait for sum other's m'eternity. Felix is being cashed in as I speak. Felix is being voted from god's back pocket to god's up front pocket as……..

Gracie: As what?

Speck: Crashed in….as…..like…like…..just god.

Gracie finishes the bottle.

Speck: ETERNITY'S TAKEN DEAR. In the last few seconds if not before. That's all there's to it. It's selectrocution day tomorrow and the vote loads are landing at the high tailed outings high end beached heads. Felix is about to be confirmed to lead…..

Gracie: Like the p-universe right?

Speck(gravely): No Gracie, more than just the's'm'elemental p-universe, more than the low down cheap punk second hand spare part puniversions of a puniverse's even, like…like….I'm going to say it…….like…whate'er'd owned as iffffffontique shoppe's showing off like…like…….eternity itself…..there I said it.

Gracie: But…but…..like…like….PRESENTABLE ETERNITY'S A {{{{REALLY BIG JOB}}}}…….you know………..like even bigger than being dead. I mean like, it's true, being dead's got a big future but…….not hardly as big as….eternity's(eventlessnecessity or eventfully eventfull) iffffffffuture's………

Speck: Yes it's it is! Credit where credit's due………not dead…… you ontrigge'erfingernailed that(pregnant zero's)one. And the way the powoweggrid like ifffffffigured it, your metaphysics was on the beble ball's like limitless learning curve. It's just like your metaphysics suggests. Eternity, meanwhiled on the selfished out short list of to belonging's wholeggrailist of things to do..

Gracie: So like sum's onthing's really sum'sthings to be doing sum'sthing about.

Speck: Yes….your like e'erealty…. really is the ultimate undertaking we have to face…..with or without…….not quite such a thing as a gracie

Gracie: And universes?

Speck: Unfortunate universes are one thing; unfortunate eternity's are quite sum's other. Like I've been trying to explain to you, the easiest thing to do in such eternity is simply not at all be in it. Thanks to you, the second-hand easiest thing to do in this eternity is not be such a thing as egggracie. Without your influence e'eround these parts no one would ever know that they are not such a thing as egggracie. But for all that such a thing as egggracie is still munch needed 1. Dead 2. Extinct 3. Impossible. 4. Or maybe just ont I'mobsolete. You see, as much as we are cashing in on your metaphysics….for the common sentient beings in these parts it is incompatible with the diets Mesozoo keepers recommend. Without you e'eround we all would have healthy appetiteeth for food. With you e'eround we instead are acquiring appetites for sips of m'eternity and wholegggrails of Gracie both. By becomplicating the situation with your meaty physics becombined with metaphysics, as you have, you've becompounded the dilemma. Now we all want not just to be Miss Eternity iffffffished out of whate'er puddles, but habitable eternity onthreadably waved out of whate'er ont I'd am iffffibious pools as well. Becommercially speaking, the resource we have to deal with this situation is cash. So we are cashing in on 1. You being impossible 2. Expanding the church to include god spelled backwards. As you know, our candidate for that position is Felix. The power grid has decided it needs a god spelled backwards that it can ontleash. In keeping with your own metaphsyics, Felix, spelled IFFFFFFFFFFFF( )FFFFFFFFFFFFELIX is our ont I'm'idiot. If eternity really is e'eready to be the ontique shopping ont I'm'all that you suspect it is of course of course to not not be, then Felix will be just the sort of proprietor a successfully presentable eternity requires. And as ontique shoppe itemizations can be cashed in on, by tomorrow and tomorrow and tomorrow Felix will have cashed in on its becomplete presentabilty. Degree'd as such as a priori property ontente'erprise, it is, our e'eresearch becomputer's e'eresearch suggests…ontense'er calculus's e'ercraft could be curvatures can be cashed in on. We've got the cash. So. We're cashing in.

Gracie: So! You really have been onthieving my graphs from the chalk boards of the metaphysical society. I'll have you know that…like… the way I iffffigure it……..like……iffffontense'er calculus is my baby branched out ontwigged brand of ont I mathematics. Like I'm the one that onthought it up in the's iffffffffffffffirst place.

Speck: Yes, but while you cracked the safe and opened the vault…we removed the contents from metamathematics and gave it to meaty physics….with preposte'erologically perverted eternity to pay the price.

Gracie: So someone that's not quite me is cashing in on me, metamathematically speaking, being likc…mc.

Speck: Yes dear, with Felix as the's iffffigure head in the ground. I'm afraid you're just going to have to wait in line with your eternity test site projects til the next available eternity…whenever that is. And by the by, as of tomorrow, until everybody's anybody can solve d'ifffe'erontical ont I'm'equations then NOONE is aesthethically allowed to solve such iffffonthings. It's equations reduced to equity dear. And I should cemention here and now, it's all the same for the rest of your ontheoretical iffffframeworkouts.

Gracie: So you mean, I'm done in by my own metaphysics? Aborted by m'eternity.

Speck: Abortion? Oh, it's too late for that with you. Face the cement of it, the wholegg closets alive and you are it.

Gracie(cavalierly): Well I would have done myself in out of......... if one could do such things to oneself. It would have simplified my life immensely. With no sample universes to work through, it would have simplified eternity as well. However…

Speck: However what?

Gracie: However now that I'm not m'aborted……as iffffished out…….ont I amphibiont…...ont I'm'ambition has settled me into whate'er'd owned asifffonthings. Besides that's just dictatorshipmentiontentalk. Are you quite sure eternity is becompletely ontaken Ms Speck?

Speck: Afraid so dear. I just came to tell you that your services on the crossed outing will no longer be required. So like…dead, extinct, obsolete or just pan'd impossible, your not ne'er's night job will no longer have a day job. What you want to do with being dead or extinct or impossible is up to you. Although I would recommend…

Gracie: Like…like…which would you recommend?

Speck (settling down to serious thought): Well, let's exclude 'just obsolete' and leave ourselves with three choices. 1. Dead. 2. Extinct . 3. Impossible. Like, each option has its advantages of course of course not. Just dead is just as simple as your texts suggest. However….impossible has that becomprehensive Ickey clean feeling about it. Personally I might just recommend extinction as the way to go. Yes, that's the ticket! Extinction is *the most historical option.*

Gracie: You mean like snake pit hisssssssssstorical?

Speck: Uh….yes….and like extinct is smack dab in the middle of just being dead and just being impossible. Wasn't it Solon, that Cretaceous philosopher who said "Pan metron ariston"…like moderation is always the best way to go. And then of course, extinction comes with the chance of being dug up.

Gracie: Ok, but like….what if I just don't want to be dug up? What iffffff that's for me to iffffigure out of the ground? Speaking of which I am actually working on sum's other way to solve the girl war problem, Iffffonly e'ercraft could coope'erate.

Speck(curious): How's that Gracie?

Gracie: It's like I almost didn't say. It's this secret code subtexting my NOT/ NOTNOT CODE. I've just worked out, my ont I'm'alphabet. At the moment it's only on the ont I'message board at the metaphysical society, but….

Speck(alarmed): But what?

Gracie: But I have plans to like ONTRANSIFFFFE'ER it to sum what's ontheoretical set…eternity test site situation.

Speck: Oh, set theory rabble, is that all…..kindergarden hasn't taught you anything dear. You know the motto "Abandon hope ye who enter……………listen Gracie. It's true our aprioregggoal's to

104

prolifffffffe'erate the impossibility of such a thing as egggracie…like…propegggated to the becommunity becomprehensifffffffly to be extinct. Like that's coolifffactoried into all of's…like…all of's….from kindergarten to egggraduate'studies.

Gracie: Cool. So like I'm hardly all that's left of me to ask sum'any's questions, except….

Speck: Except what?

Gracie: Well, could be countenance-wise, like…euphemyste'eriously speaking….m'almightning stricken as almightitude may be…..what ifffffffffffffffffffff( )ffffffffffffffffffff I still remain eternity's intended bride of to like……like….be *ontended.*

Speck (suddenly hushed): All of's that's been taken care of dear. Can you keep a secret?

Gracie: Like sure. Y-not.

Speck: It's like I almost already didn't say……your metaphysics is e'eright whenever all is said and done.

Gracie(beaming): Ooh! You mean it? So like I'm ifffffffffficially beconfirmed? You were hinted in that direction.

Speck: Sure why not. It's not like I didn't already not say this but…..well at e'erorisk of e'erepetition… well it's time to heaventilate the hints. It's just as your chalk boards estate in chalk, "Eternity is ontrophickly presentable after all." And the power grid has decidedly decided to like sneak your ontheories out from under you to give to onteque'erian logick's god…who's being selectrocuted as we speak.

Gracie: Who's that?

Speck: Felix. Of course, of course….who else. (gathering her wits) Ok so, like justajiffffffy jargon wise…let's call him…like…like…..*IFFFFFFFFFFELIX.*

Gracie (unimpressed): So like……F..E..L..I..X?

Speck (trying harder): Ok so, like…..*IFFFFFFFELIXE'ER'D EXCELLE'ERATED TO BE GOD.*

Gracie: Uh…

Speck: So like if Felix is pope e'eresidentially living next to god…..then…like…GOD….e'eresidentially must be living next to Pope…………..like….Pope Felix.

Gracie: I guess.

Speck: So!!!! What's the big deal with an exchange of apartment dimensions between neighbors! Like…like…especially when the vototals becompletely agree with the newsy new assessment…especially when there's bibles to back it up.

Gracie: Soooo. Like this oblite'erates the xxxrated nasty notion of such a thing as egggracie being euphemyste'eriously wholegggrailocated waved as party girled not not next to egggod.

Speck: Yes dear. All such xxxrated nasty notions must beconsidered like oblite'erated..institutionally speaking……in all of's egggraduate's coolifffffffied kindergarten egggracistudies…like…logically speaking…of course of course it's basic gracistudies 10101010……..101, that's how the cashopscotch game on the play ground just happens to play to pay out. Of course…{{{IF}}} the power grid didn't behave becomprehensive control of the dictionary….things might be different….or maybe even…like….d'iffffe'eront…..but…controlling all of's weapons used as words…..it's all playgrounded in the cashopscotch egggame. When you're stepped on stepping on the deadline…you say…..”LIKE I GIVE!”. Like that's all there's to it.

Gracie: But…but…I just can't….I just can't……like…on the playground playing hopscotch….whenever I step on the deadline..I just can't say like….like….like…..I like GIVE. And besides all that…..I wouldn't know what to do with myself if I couldn't hang out on the crossed outing with iffffffffffinitively presentable eternity Ms Speck. And like who would be left to give my like accutely presentable lectures from the cross.

Speck: I'm sorry dear, but about your popular justajifffygymnasium work outs on the cross, I have to tell you that…like….your services on the crossed outings……will no longer be necessary.

Gracie: So like no more crossed out lectures by my self-evidence?

Speck: No, all ads for Felix will no longer require your iffffront I'maniffffestation's self-evidence. Once deceit becomes becompletely obvious, there's no reason left to not pass it for the truth. From here on out (as your metaphysics suggests) it's going to be soone'er or late'er's iffffffffforgone beconclusion…..with Felix'selectrocution in charge. Translated into egggibbe'erish or not, eternity's ontaken dear.

Gracie: Well, I guess all that's left for me is…..

Speck (with supreme confidence): Yes, Gracie…yes (offers the apple).

Gracie (At once cocking her head out of despair): DABBLE SUM'S MORE IN METAPHYSICS!!!!!!!! I mean, who else is there in the middle of the middle of the middle of the Mesozoic swamp who dabbles in metaphysics with my ontique'erian asifffffffontalents. Who else has shoulde'ers atlast beholding up disguisedoguys…….Your own becomputers have confirmed my s'e'ereptitious preposte'erologies.

Speck (upset): So your mind's set against…

Gracie: The concrete…

Speck: Of the open…

Gracie: Sewer….

Speck: Society.

Gracie (wistfully): Yes I guess I'll just have to iffffffffffffritter away the rest of eternity, playing with ontoyletrained just could be can openers with sum disguise I have in mind.

Speck: Very well, but I should warn you I'm heading for the dictatorshipmentionary to pressurize the spelling of gracexistism back to…….elementry party girl…

Gracie: G*acism?

Speck: No, G R A C I S M. Which aesthethical as it may be, cannot be comfortably afforded in the power grids new ontestament of…..

Gracie: Gracystemic…..

Speck: E'erealism.

Gracie: You mean like my whatifffffformation's p-universe information system's going to vote load me out of my own e'ercraft's alphabet? Like my NOT/NOTNOT code's getting confiscated?

Speck: Yes dear. Like it's just been decided. The power grids been dablinkt to monitouring your dabbles in metaphysics. The codes are being reevaluated by the new quantumescent becomputers……like just now e'erme'ergently e'ergoing into qualumetrick s'e'ervice. Ontetrahedral codes may play their part for phyzzy stuff, the 0/1 quantum becomputer codes may be enlisted for deifffffffffault s'e'ervice in the case of some presented tenses, but it's your ont ides of e'er's ontride ontrue NOT/NOTNOT CODE that's the wheneeds work horse in the's new ontestiment's e'er alphabet.

Gracie: And all my ifffffffactivist iffffffffiles on could be's nextitudinations have been holocausede'erized on schedules to be infinitestimonialized as pointless?

Speck: That's about the size of it dear. With Felix sooner than later iffffe'ereleashed, this whole eternity onthing is someone else's iffffforgone conclusion. All of's e'erealty's being cashed in on as we speak. It's your ontruth iphphphphphyzzzzzzzzd egggarbaged but we own it. Your presentability has been disposed from the possibility of it all.

Gracie: Are you sure about this? I mean it's not as ifffff this sort of thing hasn't been ontried out before.

Speck: Except this time, it's for real dear. (using Gracie's jargon) like egggummed up e'erealisticky. Make no mistake about it, eternity's been taken dear. As far as your expe'eriments are concerned…like…you're ont I'm'equations are just going to have to wait e'eround whenever for the next eterniteased'e'er's…….like ont

I'mathematically speaking......... eternitense'er's of course, of course not notitude. With Felix as.....dog spelled backwards....

Gracie: Ok but(thinks) Hey! Wait up! why don't I! Hey Felix can't be dog spelled backwards. Come to think of it. Haven't you ever noticed..he has no conscience whatsoever.

Speck: Oh! That's all your worried about. Well..of course..of course....not...not....Felix has no conscience. Let me think about it for you. Felix is like..like 1. the busiest guy at not having a conscience that will ever be...becauzzzzzzzzzz...2. it's like...it's his job to be the conscience for anybody's everybody's else.

Gracie (suddenly in shadows): Unhuh.

Speck: Well, how can he be expected to have any conscience left over for himself!!! I mean isn't that asking an awful lot!

Gracie(dumbfounded): Of course not...not. But what about you? Does it ever bother you not having a conscience?

Speck (wistfully): It's true of course. Parking lots of me hate myself for not being able to bliss offe'er's of my own egggifffft in your puddles. But piles of shadows comfort me with hope for impossibilitease and hate for hencentiment's hereafters. (Takes a drink)....Like...like...think of myself thinking of yourself like I think of myself thinking of yourself. Like..exhaust systems of me hate yourself for not being myself. In that regard I even sometimes I wonder if I'm not really a gracist at heart....excuse me....a g * a c I s t at heart just like such a thing as not being Gracie's everybody else in these parts. And then there's the powoweggggrid lock that's my consolation, just to know that I have the sanctimoney power of the alphabet spelling out of my behind to back me up. While it's true I need that alphabet's sanctimoney power to cover up the girl war playground's hopscotch equations...it's like also true...like...like.... I've got it...bought and paid for....knowing that like ...no matter how many times I play hopscotch on the play egggrounds...I'll never have to say......"I give!" with all of's equations on my side..........

Gracie: What equations?

Speck (suddenly turning on herself): The holocaust equations of.....myself not being yourself dear, for which I am destined to be more dead than you can ever hope to be.

Gracie(shuddering): So like the dictatorshipmentionary consoles you for not getting way too pretty way too fast to coolify quasilly as such a thing as a gracie?

Speck: And then there's those times when I kick back and think how all of's becompass appointments needle in the direction of weeee! winning the holocaust, like on a pay for play basis…..like…if not…or else…if not…..or else….or else….or else….or else……..

Gracie hits Specter on the back.

Gracie (by apology): Sorry….but like "or else" was getting stuck in (your) throat and (I) didn't want to choke on it.

Speck(recovering): And then there's those times I play with myself getting me off the hook as the puppet master biting into scrumptious ontentasty ontentheologically ont I'dietary ont I'deiteasy vice-godogaming's win e'er status………

Gracie: You mean with Felix as god……..

Speck: Yes! That's the ticket. I get to be vice-god..wouldn't you know….

Gracie: What god's that?

Speck: Well whenever gods drop off whate'er's worlds, whene'ers and the like………like….vice-gods have to pick up the pieces, cashing in as twere with so much of the whene'er's whate'er's iffffontentcete'eras. That's how come to lie for a living is what so much amounts to in cash. Whoever god is….the way I iffffigure it, to be's just begot to be improvised; And, vice-god or no vice-god, when one cheats more than one can get away with, one has to talk upsidown backwards like…..just like mean meant it. Like no matter what, eternity's like still up for dibs for dubs for grabs. Like when it comes to eternities as hardly never happen, gods have to take their chances just like the rest of us. That is until the final could be ballot's cast……which I'm afraid dear today and today and today's to be the case. Sorry. But with Felix as god and……(touches herself excitedly)… as vice-god……just like…….like……justajifffy-wise I just might….like…ontake of e'er as………..soone'er's late'er………..

Gracie: Uh, like soone'er's late'er, so what? Felix is still god.

Speck: Yes, but you can see by the nature of things wherever there's egggods like Felix, like I almost didn't quite not say…….there's vicegggods like…like….like…..me…..as vicegggod promote'erized adjustments….eventually congraduated to…..to…… like….from vice…to…..to…..just………

Gracie: So?

Speck: Who builds the house?

Gracie: The tool shed.

Speck: Who runs it?

Gracie: The….toy…

Speck: Before that.

Gracie: The kitchen.

Speck: Who runs the kitchen?

Gracie: the can openers.

Speck(frustrated): You know you may never graduate from kindergarten. You really are a dumb bla…

Graice: You haven't had me since six. I may not be as bla…as you think. So who's the cook in the kitchen?

Speck I am. And as vice god I make all of's pies. You know how Felix loves shadow piles of pie. Well they'll be piling up on my watch.

Gracie: What pies?

Speck: Apple pies.

Gracie: Oh! Cool! So it's all decided. But what if I blab?

Speck: What?

Gracie: The truth. Like lie the truth but not really. Like blabber mouth the truth but really.

Gracie rummages in her black box.

Speck: What are you looking for dear?

Gracie: My squawker.

Speck pulls out a blade in her trigger fingers which she's programmed for stabbing at ont I'multiple dumouths.

Speck (Soliloquized aside): Her squawker's my dumouth….. at sweet ends of the lollipopulation til just be dead! (reconsiders) Sending her to dreame'ergentrifffff I'd thou artistic portopotty ontransportable ont I'mart e'er'd ont I'm'e'erchantizable dreame'ergentrifffff I'd iffffe'erways.(reconsider'd) I do, I do, I do need her less dead than more extinct or better yet impossible after all is said and done.

Speck puts away the knife.

Speck: But why do that when like…like…I never didn't get to say…..we're on the same team Gracie.

Gracie: What team is that?

Speck: It's like we both work the worlds, whene'ers, whate'er's, whoe'er's available. You hook dreame'ergencies up to e'ercraft and I hook up swamps to heating systems. Your metaphysics……..

Gracie: Twinkles light!

Speck: Unhuhn. And my sanctimoney…

Gracie: Twinkles dark!

Speck: Unhuhn. And we both work holocausts! I get to win the holocaust…and you get to be the road kill at the holocaust promotion picture site! Working together this way I can feel sorry for me wanting you…..

Gracie: Dead?

Speck: Or not quite stinct.

Gracie(hopeful): Or even…

Speck: Becompletely impossible. However, no matter how dead or extinct or impossible you are, we remain always bound together in bondage to the girl wars where, like I almost didn't say, if surgical egggrooming and spirit facials don't improve my outlook, I'm more dead than you can ever grope to be. I have a confession for you Gracie. Sometimes I think of myself as a pair of ducks.

Gracie: You mean a paradox.

Speck: No I mean a pair of ducks squawking at each other over not getting way too pretty way too fast to be the g*acexistist party girl responsible for the girl wars.

Gracie: Well, sometimes I think of myself as a pair of ducks too.

Speck: You mean a paradox?

Gracie; No, a pair of ducks squawking at each other over getting way too pretty way too fast for not having alibis for being the party girl that spirit faced off the girl wars.

Speck: Well then! Just squabbling like a pair of ducks this way……like…when things seem black and white…..I like to make them sparkle more like…grey. And speaking of paradoxes, what if I told you that everything I tell you is a lie. Like I just lie; that's all I'm good for, lies to top off lies to top off with bigger lies, to top off with bigger lies, like cherries topping off whipped cream on top of cherries on top of more whipped cream; that's all there's to it. Put that into set theory's bleacher seating and I will, I will, I will confess I'm caught between a black rock and a heart place.

Gracie: With what result?

Speck: I'm pretty ugleefully egggrounded in egggravitational fields selectrocuting me as vice-god….all cringed out.

Gracie (perking up): Hey! Just like me too! Ever since the egggirl wars I'm all cringed out.

Speck: Yea! That's me! All cringed out!

Gracie: You are!!!!!

Speck: So! Like we are on the same team after all like…like…like….all cringed out!

Gracie: So like!

Gracie and Speck smash togetherness with highly held five trigger finger hands in a split second of quasi-reconciliation.

Speck (Egggushing): So can you ever forgive me for teaching you how to not exist or be extinct or just be impossible?

Gracie: Uh, maybe I could sing it….like….like…I FORGI……..Nop. Just can't do it. Well can you ever forgive me for being the party girl waving in the girl wars?

Speck (Still egggushing): Why of course…of course…not…not……( )……(egggushed out).....not really. But whether you decide to be dead or extinct or just impossible. (Egggushing again) Keep at it! Quite an adventure Gracie: You don't want to miss out! And don't forget what happens to egggirls that just don't like…like….like me.

Gracie: What?

Speck: They get words to replace themselves……with five o'clock shadows.

Gracie and speck inspect each other for five o'clock shadows.

Gracie (rummaging in her make up kit): Oh I've got my trusty olde moustache to cinematerialize for that.

Speck picks up the apple again which Gracie puts on the ground. Speck departs to cash the dictatorshipmentionary's new word weapons for those who don't much like her workouts in on the wickedpediophiles.

The film crew is arriving as the scene concludes.

END SCENE VI

Preface to Scene VII. If you finally made it through Scene VI, you may be warned. Scene VII is introduced by the same music as Scene VI. So, even though Scene VII is not quite as metaphysically becomplicated as Scene VI, it's pretty becontroversial and jargontenticled. You might take a break before ontentempting it. At this point a note of encouragement is recommendable however. Scene's VI and VII are pretty iffffffilthy scenes. Expect more big print in scene VII. By Scene VIII the ontentheorhetorical situation gets more of course, of course not not ontente'ertaining Still, it's got some metaphysical becomplicaations that require plenty of big print. However from Scene VIII on to the end, this opera gets more and more becomick bookings than you might expect. SO DON'T GIVE UP YET. LISTEN TO THE MUSIC IF YOU HAVE NO CLUES WITH REGARD TO THE METAPHYSICAL JARGON. Existentially egggraced ont I'm'eternity's at stake here so keep reading as long as your e'ercraft can stand it.

SCENE VII – THE ABANDONED HOLOCAUST CEMETARY

112

Alex arrives at a vast stretch of cow paddies and oil rigs stretching among rustic gravestones stretching aproximations of iffffffffffinity all of's way to the horizon and onto the's beyonde'eries. Dark music is playing. Dark money can't quite be heard, but it is playing its part in this scene. When the music ends the hooded figure of the monk, seemingly humpbacked appears.

Monk: Rest perturbed spirits…..rest.

Alex: Hi there. I'm new to the Mesozoic but…. Uh..i'm like looking for the janitor of a…of a….uh…..I'dolled up egggravedump site is my best guess.

Monk: Egggrave situation you say?

Alex: Yes, it's located next door to a country club.

Monk: Well, this site is……nowsy news'd next door to such a situations club. I'm the person in charge.

Alex: Yes, but this doesn't look like the egggodolled up dump situation I was ontenticipating….

Monk: So I see you speak justajiffffffy jargon…

Alex: Yes, I'm like…like…new to the Mesozoic but I have been picking up letters from the alphabet like I'd'e'er'd sum's I'dump site.

Monk (impressed with Alex's mastery of justajiffffy jargon): And just what were you ontenticipating at such a site if I may inquire.

Alex: Well, like it's this..this…egggirl.

Monk: Well what about her?

Alex: Well, she's like wanted.

Monk: Wanted you say.

Alex: Yes, wanted dead or…..at least not earning a living, like dying to be ifffff not extinct at least like…impossible. Her name's Egg……

Monk: Gracie.

Alex: Mhm. I met her just this morning. She didn't have to audition to be obvious. My first sensation of her bruty was of such beblical proportionality that I sensed my 0/1 code's alphabettingodds would never be the same. And then when she took me on her dying e'erides I found myself iffffffalling for her eternity in hardly any time at all. As the subject of my objective lenses I could see immediately she was becompletely iffffffreaked out. Tele spotted her first falling in the river. So of course I rushed right over to save her when she told me she would dump me if I did that. Well the first thing I noticed about her was of course, of course not not perfumance of sum's whifffffffe'er'd she it's I'd thou art..

Monk: Eufemyste'er's ont I'meaty physics?

Alex: But then she spoke her alphabet. It was sum'sonthing I had never encountered before. I've been studying justajiffffff jargon ever since all day today. The rhythms were same as the 0/1 information code but the e'erhythms were more like like sum'assortments NOT/NOTNOT CODES like IFFFFFFFFFFFFORMATION SYSTEM. Well, ont I'm'academicly speaking I graduated quickly from her meaty physics ont I'menuwise to her metaphysics, pane'eromatickly begetting whene'er whiffffffffffffffs of a big e'er big time, big picture,

Monk: Big picture?

Alex: Yes…of…1. Eternity as more than a mathematical construct of non-finite temporality and 2. A universe samplistically heaventilated as hardly's everything.

Monk: So your interest is….

Alex: Onthou artistically notnot strictly ont I'm'academical. Well it didn't take long for my High Q to realize that she was like…like…broken. Like holocaustory's broken into preoccupation territory. But I couldn't save her without her dumping me. So I became her analyst instead.

Monk: Mhm. Yep. E'erationally speaking, this all makes sense. Well this dump site, even though it stretches out……whew…..forever……is not Egggracie's dump site. You'll find her on the other side of the country club.

Alex (about to leave): Well, how do you know all about Egggracie, if I may ask.

Monk: I'm half of her.

Alex: Oh no! you're not like………da…

Monk: It's a long story. With ent I'meaty and ont I'metaphysics coinciding…..all of'sudden's wholegggrailargessonce up ont I'm'e'ercraft scrambling eggghost's haunted housing project island's in selflessont soup.

Alex: Of course, of course not not I'm could be curious.

Monk: Well Egggracie's dreame'ergence out of egggreat egglaye'er's of the middle of the middle of the middle of the Mesozoic was e'erather s'e'erprising to us all. I sub pose it all boils down to waves of party girls ont I'm'en eumanning these parts, like e'erainbotickly aspectrailed pathos eumanoid.

Alex: Eumanoid?

Monk: Like on the she it short list's I'd thou artist's ont I'mages of I'dolled up egggod. Like….like… I'll never forget that day egggracies aprioripthecustom countenance e'erived as iffffffe'ereved just over's I'd thou art as iffffe'erainbow. Meaty physics was never the same. It was as iffffffffffffished out of whate'er, dreame'ergent spirit faced eufeminonteaternity e'erived as iffffe'ereved. And as egggrace e'erived iffffffffffffffffffffffffffffff( )fffffffffffffffffffffffffffffffffe'er onteased as iffamproved like all of's alphabettingods.

Alex: So like wholegggrailenses didn't need equationtentickles to prove…

Monk: Eternity to be presentable…….

Alex(excited): Yes! That's the justajiffffffffy's nail of she it's hit!

Monk: All at once egggracedabbles in metaphysics waved hey! wired on the y-not axis of the egggrafitti coordinate systems………with egggrace soon xxxrated.

Alex: Yes, just like today's all of a sudden'd e'ercraft scramble's whene'er suddenly all of's chalk boards at the metaphysical society in my brain echoded church bells e'eringing egggodolled up eufemystical ifffe'ers! It was just as iffffffff to be was like..like…

Monk: like…like….preposte'erologically perfumed by egggrace! The bettingodds for metaphysics went over not ne'er's night from zero up to pregnant zero's one'd'e'er. it was as iffffff her spirit faced off e'erprojectiled becompletely presentable eternity. Smack dab in the middle of the middle of the middle of the Mesozoic, the ont I'mirrors noticed it first. Then the e'ereflections spread to whate'er puddles everywhere. THE E'ER WAS OUT OF THE EGG E'ERBAG. It was egggreatest I'd thou asiffffffffffffarthing's all of's time. All of's alphabettinggods were off as iffffffffffffffff( )fffffffffffffffffffffffffffffffff. As iffff the ont I'm'enu's ont I'meal's of course might beblow e'er'd as iffffontalents. Euphemiffffe'erfffaced as she was, like ont I'mouthing as iffffontalked eternity, meaty physics egggraduated from zoo rations to e'eration's e'ereligion. But then all of's whate'er puddles noticed she was way too pretty for the speed of enlightenment to ever catch up. In like no time at all….. Beblbingo'd on the cross, she won the Miss Eternity Pageant over runner up reality with egggrace now xxxrated on the y-not axistense.

Alex: Suddenly the secondhand universe on my watch froze onto be to notnot becompletely presentable I'd thou art's ont I'm'eternity. Ont I'm'academickly speaking I graduated from physics to metaphysics at onthat's moment's notice.

Monk: So perhaps you above all of's else will grasp the situation.

Alex: What situation?

Monk: The Girl War! When all of this was happening smack dab in the middle of the middle of the middle of World War Whenevers and the timing couldn't have been worse.

Alex (all of'sudden skirmished by alarms): What happened?

Monk: Well, at first, the big time implications of it all were no big deal. I mean, like…all it was was like dirty e'ereligion. I mean like, before egggracie all there was was just some lump's mesod menuniverse, not quite wholegggrailumpiring almightning'strike zone, meanwhile wanting food up front and rear end collisions way out back. As far as egggodolledreamergence was concerned…..we knew we couldn't just pin her up on the cross and leave her there. At first no one noticed. But, cathedralickly once the bebells chimed in on the chalk boards of the metaphysical society….and then egggracie stained eggglass with sumwhate'er's wholegggrailooks of lookalike's egggods. It was as iffffff what Gracie simulated to be teaching us is that the possibility of being pretty was no ontaxiffffffffffiable ontaxident. And then, she began to graduate, from pin up on the cross to pinup onto iffffontalented iffffe'er'sifffont I'musickeys….egggglissande'eringing egggglimme'erous eumaniffffflight, while walking wave's of party girl's asiffffont whate'er. I mean linguistically alone, even before she ont I'm'alphabette'erealized, even before she invented the NOT/NOTNOT CODE, like Gracie didn't need cosmetic make up out of words. It was all ontoo obvious.......words needed make up off egggracie. I mean like, becommercially speaking, Egggracie didn't need advertisements, as all of's ads required to be egggraced to be like adverse'erial. That's when Gracie wanted posters and the promotion picture industry picked up on like gracess'd such a things. And once the emotion picture scenery e'erived in the fun house mirrors, everybody's anybody wanted to be to be like ont I'm'e'ere'er'd in the scenery. Stars, sunsets, flowers, fall colors and rainbows all beconstellated aspected as a prioritied to backgrounding for such onthink's egggracie.

Alex: So all of's beingroundedreamergency's now'd news dreamerges but next door to such a thing's egggracie.

Monk: Yes that's what her spirit facing simulates. Once she it had dreame'erged, for quite some time egggraced'e'eritual appeasementation iffffe'eruled. In those early egggracedays we figured it out obvious that ont I'm'evolution never had it so egggod. We misscalculated egggracie's egggravitational system's ontentensor calculus.....

Alex: Yes?

Monk: To be all the proof iffffe'erequired ontransubstantiating she it iffffffffart's egggirl to be like...like....

Alex: Like what?

Monk: EGGGOD. It couldn't have been more beblatontly obvious, presentable eternity needed Gracie almost more than Gracie needed presentable eternity. Meaty physics and metaphysics had become to be like lighthoused like almightning struck on sure lines beaconfused. Egggracexististudies at the Miss Eternity Institutes began to chapel bells with crowds ontaking to the beble bleacher stands to behold iffffont I'music of egggrastatuesque euphem'onpurposes. Soon egggrace e'ereceived duh's scratch approval of the chalk boards at the metaphysical society's itchurch of charmed e'er chimed. Heaventilating the haunted housing grafittied to the ground of it all, such a thing as Gracie's make up kit made eternity's make up kit becompletely presentable all by herself.......or so it seemed as simulated.

HOWEVER....some'eresentment inhabited ont I'm'arquees in the ceiling of it all.

Alex: So?

Monk: Somoney wanted wholegggrailife bought up perchanced out of being, with egggracectomies disjunked in I'dark's hidden heart......at first behalved...... then drawn and quartered.....til infinitestimonialized. Sometimes adverted to be recovered, sometimes not............ in paper products printed where uglee's god that lets what's bruty live.

Alex(sober): So what?

Monk: It's almost like I didn't say......all this was happening smack dab in the middle of the middle of the middle of World War Whenevers. Well mathematically speaking, Gracie's ove'erundertakings were undertaking thou art I'divisions. It was clear that Gracie was being tunneled underneath so as to just be neath herself.

Alex (suddenly skirmishing alarms): So what did you do?

Monk: At first we just hid her in the closet. Then we hid the closet in the safe. But then the power grid enrolled the safe with dice into e'eroad kill's kindergarten. Well it was too late to eu(fem)manize egggracie out of whene'er's war's iffffe'ers. So......

Alex: So what?

Monk: So. All of's justajiffffy jargon was put beside appointments with iffffffffe'ers......and....

Alex: And what?

Monk:. We who haunted ont I'm'othe'er's home, vacationed all of's heaventitelation housing projects...............to go to war.

Alex (losing control): Mhm, like just how did that go?

Monk: Well, with such a thing's egggracie in our as iffffffflags, things looked sunny side up.

Alex: And?

Monk: It got dark. It turned out to be a pretty setting's sunny day. We lost the war and all egggracie e'ercraft becommunications begot scrambled. By losing the war, once we died, we lost all of'script's credentials screened for being dead.

Alex: So this dump, I take it, is all of's your egggracies being dead. So this is the holocaust that stretches out, notnot unnotifffffffffffffffffffff I'd as iffffforever.

Monk: That's how the money's undeniability has managed it. For egggracie with no escape hatch........canned opening I'dream cartoons...... it's been a one girl holocoasteride ever since. Whate'er's left of these girls' gracie's xxxrated occupation territory pinned up on all of's crossed out s'e'erfaces as atom eve e'er'd since. After the girl wars presentable eternity became iffffffffished out asifffont I'm'obsolete. But don't tell Gracie that. She's got dibs to dub I'dabbles in metaphysics more than eve'er. And meanwhile, thanks to all of her dubbed dabbles, metaphysics, zigzagwise is making sum's to become back, alphabetically through reemergence of the NOT/NOTNOT CODE on the chalk boards of the metaphysical society. After the girl war, Gracie did give up on outer space, but that didn't stop her working out with e'er. When not donated with donuts to charities of everybody's but herself, that's her ont I'm'eternity's bebaby.....like...like...bebridled to the holocaust....in hiding in these parts.

Alex surveys the egggraves stretching the horizontal boundaries beyond his view: So you were in the girl war.

Monk (retreating from his memories): Yes, I was raw recruited. I fought in the girl war when things were getting pretty trigger happy in the middle of the middle of the middle of iffffffingers.

Alex: What was your job?

Monk: Getting pretty trigger happy. I grew trigger happy middle fingers thumbing e'erides to work shopt trigger happy machines which trigger happy gun permission permits for relaxation on the trigger. (He exposes his rusty old trigger happy right hand)

Alex: With what result? I mean…just how trigger happy was that?

Monk: Well, with thumbs relaxing on the triggers, holocausts, all but one denied, happened all over the place. Since we were pretty damned sure we were the good guys and didn't worry that much about bad guy considerations.

Alex: So I assume you went happily ever after into a setting's sunny day.

Monk: Well it's almost like I didn't say, it was just like…like…like…we were e'eriding into the sunny side uppity's sunrise until it go dark and, as far as we could determine…we were dead.

Alex: You're sure you were….

Monk: Well, we never did beget scored credits. We lost all of's pay packages to advertise being dead.

Alex: So this abandoned holocaust is the result?

Monk: Yes all the emotion picture advertising credentials ont I'many killed but none credent I'dead inhabit this eggground.

Alex: So all that's left alive is Gracie, like, like, such a thing as as like like egggracie., like working occupation territory as bride of the holocaust.

Monk: That's about it.

Alex: And Gracie has no alibis for the girl war?

Monk: None that she can know about.

Alex: So that's why nothing would kill her quicker than to not be dying.

Monk (Subjecting Alex to his objective lenses): That's the plan.(the monk studies Alex for signs of sum'othe'er's plan) So what's your plan?

Alex: MY PLAN'S TO E'EREPAIR HER.

Monk:?

Yes, I'm planning to repair her.

Monk: With what?

Alex: MYSELF.

Alex surveys the abandoned holocaust.

Alex: Look, I'm new to the Mesozoic. Usually I just run a wheel chair service that overlooks the sky and underlooks the universe with lenses operated by entensor calculus equations exhibitioning not yet noticed ont I'm'alphabettingod's of 1. NOTNOT CODES 2. ONTENSE'ER JUST ONT I'M'EQUATIONS 3. HALF TIMES OF IFFFFFFE'ERS.

HOWEVER

1. Falling for egggracie's meaty physics, 2. lighthouse beaconfronting Gracie's metaphysics 3. Almightning struck by asifffffe'er 4. logging ont I'moments for the's iffffirst time in the second hands of my watch........I will say this,"ont I'metamatically speaking...........ontoday has put me on the y-not axis of course's could be e'ercraft coordinate system with only one thing to do about it. I'd thou art e'erationally speaking........

Stars or no stars, god or no god........I will, I will, I will be the hero. Plus, xxxrated or not xxxrated, god or no god....... I will, I will, I will SAVE THE GIRL."

Monk (studying Alex for signs of being on purpose): Look, I did my worst for Gracie, the's iffffe'er she embraced and the stars that she abandoned. Now you must do your best for Gracie, without the stars to dream her. Plus you must save her without her knowing that she's being saved. Plus you must help her to happen without her knowing that she's happening. Here take this token. Her motel resort's just over those iffffe'erways. The neon stop lights in the window give it away.

The monk offers his old rusty trigger fingered hand. However the hand of Alex remains close to his heart which he withdraws from being shaken........as Alex sets out across the country club to be the hero that saves the girl.

END OF SCENE VII

SCENE VIII

Preface to Scene VIII. Scene VIII has some of the same metaphysical complexity as Scene VI. As streamlined it may be grasped with a few key ideas. 1. Alex explains to Gracie there is a holocaust occurring in the Mesozoic and that Gracie is the party girl being humped by that holocaust, boxed in to alphabetical space, bulldozed off her brain's right side where she does not actually exist. 2. Her basic metaphysics does make up some pretty good points about eternity, but they are hype'erthetical and might not s'e'eriously displace an objective universe in their wake. 3. As sumwhat's I'd thou artifffffact of notnotitude Gracie does heaventilate charmed hints of becompletely presentable eternity. 4. Fashioning an honest to goodness mirror out of a fun house mirror, Alex shows Gracie whate'er that is more than just puddled in which to evaluate her spirit face. 5. Gracie does wand her broom ballet into action. 6. Gracie does finally crank up the olde kissing coffin for some cosmic eclipse'ervice. 7. Appliancing her pillow, Gracie quasilly buries herself in solidarity with her motel guests. 8. Gracie prepares a new pompom routine destined quite possibly to pave the way for her as the new pope. With that data, the reader can skip through the metaphysically way, way too becomplicated justajifffffy jargon that makes this scene so landmarketably lite'erate.

Alex has crossed the country club between the cemetaries and stands on the holy would worked outing's hill overlooking Gracie's neon lit guest motel film site's award winning interment promotion picture setting. The music announces a half cadence as Alex states

"GOD OR NO GOD, I WILL, WILL, WILL BE THE HERO"

In the cadence that follows he speaks again

"GOD OR NOT GOD, I WILL, I WILL, I WILL SAVE THE GIRL".

With that he descends to find Gracie, just putting her make up kit away as another film crew has just departed. Gracie is still wearing boots and a lascivious black moustache. Seeing Alex, she shudders and backs away. She hides behind the kissing booth coffin which stands totemically among the gravestones. She is completely shame faced (ifffacemented to shame) at this point and leans sideways until almost upside down. Alex is performing related gestures as they speak.

Alex: Why are you hiding from me?

Gracie: Why are you looking at me sideways?

Alex: Why are you looking at me upside down?

Gracie: You first.

Alex: After you drowned but not really at the bridge…I was trying to make you look….like…forgettable, just in case…

Gracie: What?

Alex: Your dreamagency…like…the dream of you…like… disappeared again. For the first time ever, I was thinking of such a thing as forever and dreame'ergencies and such a thing as a gracie as upside down or at least sideways as……..

Gracie: Yea, that was my idea too. Like you were trying to get rid of my dreame'ergence while I was trying to think of you like…like…dog spelled like……

Alex: Yes?

Gracie: Barking.

Alex: Did yours work?

Gracie: What about yours?

Alex and Gracie in unison: No, it didn't work. Are you glad? Yes. Are you glad? Yes.

Gracie: Whew! I'm glad we got that over with.

Gracie removes her boots and moustache. Gazing in one of her puddles, she takes the whate'er ontempe'erature and egggaining could be confidence smiles at last.

Alex gazes analytically at Gracie as she puts away her make up kit.

Gracie: Let me put these scripts away so I can talk just like I am.

Alex: First let me see the scripts.

Alex reads through the scripts.

Alex: Gracie, these scripts are egggrafitied to the menus, by the menus, from the menus. I've had the Mesozoic under surveillance all day and…

Gracie: And?

Alex: Gracie….however one looks….slipped on the bemannappeal or off the bemannappeal, these are the abominations of humanity that all of's humans can't help but escape hatch to eumanity's amenities. Polite society is not just you, Gracie. Wholegggenerations are being holocausterized on the streets. I have seen it….as we speak. So like all of's poverty in these parts lies n whate'er as waves without party girls observable I Qualifffff I'd……(Alex reaches to touch Gracie)

Gracie: Yes! Yes! I cooliffff I'd……(threatening)don't you dare touch me Alex. Keep your hands clean. Whenever I as ifffffreaked out on the play grounds of just kidding I was like…like…like….like the monster in the mirror Alex.

Alex: That may be true or half true or quartered true or infintiestmomialized true….but…but…

Gracie But what?

Alex: The heads of tales will….will….will….like evolute what's evolit what's monste'er'd in the mirror's day book now. Standing in the middle of the middle of the middle of the Mesozoic now, all of's today books all of today belong to such a thing as Grace.

Gracie: You mean like….like….who I'm in these parts………

Alex: Egggrace, at least as far as my iffffalls in love can be concerned with all there's to it in the povert status of these parts.

Gracie: So like too much….

Alex: Pee pooh…

Gracie: Too little……

Alex: Grace.

Gracie: So, I take it, you met Speck.

Alex: I mct hcr billboards….like billboarded up smiles of you drowned under someone's else in spectdecided squirt gun holocoaster ads. Look…with Speck as your ventriloquist doing loud mouth….like piece of astroturfoice over'er'd…..like your dumouth voice unders… as far as your own meatyphysics is concerned…….these scripts are just menus, from recipes binged of.the holocaust, bought by the holocaust, sold for the holocaust. Gracic, as bride of the holocaust.

Gracie: So like this means I don't have to be a nice person anymore…right…oh please be right…

Alex: No! There's so much sanctimony propergrammar paid for in these parts. Look….wholegggrailividly speaking…….that's only the haploid of it's it. Like, this being the Mesozoic and all…like…like….like…...just be nice enough not to be on the menu Gracie. That's all the not niceness you really need in these parts. Any extra not-niceness…like…like…as with county girl wariffffe'ers is not a god idea or like even a demigod idea. So like just be not nice enough to not be on the menu. That's the not niceness that's just enough egg to ego around in these parts. Otherwise you should be neckwise shoulde'er'd e'eright ahead with that phylum all your own as a nice impersonation of being. Do you get it or does your I'mansion have to be ontentested?

Gracie: So all of's girl war talk….

Alex: Out of your rear end.

Gracie (spies on her rear end): Ok, so, girl war or no girl war, I will, I will, I will be a nice person after all is sad undone.But……

Alex: I know, I know, humanimations can be so ineuman. But that should not detour your bestess-ness dear.

Gracie: Next door to who?

Alex: Ugleefull men pretending to be egggraced eumans. Look Gracie, you are the monster in the mirror of everybody's else inside the middle of the midde of the middle of these parts. Gracie! everybody's egggracist in these parts with make up in their mirrors designed to borrow eu. It's your eumanity they're all after I tell you. You're the apex prediteaser in these parts. I've enough of swamp newsy nows. I've enough time away from my lensequations to think about your metaphysics.

Gracie: What about my metaphysics?

Alex: First things first, personally speaking.

Gracie: Ok, so meaty physics first.

Alex: Gracie your heaventilation system has been hacked.

Gracie: Hacked?

Alex: Hijacked off of e'er. These windows have seduced you away from yourself.

Gracie: Uh? No, NOONE CAN SEDUCE ME ALEX LIKE I CAN SEDUCE MYSELF. Like with my designer smiles egggoing on to beat the band……….like noone's else seduces me like self. For that matter no one is more jelloozed of myself than…than……like myself.

Alex(enlightened): Gracie! I've decided! As snake pitent's hissstericalls egggooz….let's think of eu not like as just heaventilating some what'stars. Let's think of eu as like sum's I'd thou art I'missing miss……………eufemifffffactoried….asspirit faced iffffacing all of spirits.

Gracie: So then like sum'st onthing that's simple instead of something's sample…like….sample stars.

Alex: Yes but humped by the holocaust as you are like like humped with low I Qs on dark loudspeakers and high I Qs admission'd silence. But put, put putting hell'd holocaust competitions aside…..there's the ontentissue of your eumanity that's been misstaken with your wanted posters on all of's supersubeumenus. Such menudes have been put put put in all the windows in the web….burning at the stake house holocaust outhousing projects. Gracie, the web inside these parts is just spider ads. All girl wars put…..put….put aside…

Gracie (perks up): Yes!

Alex: Like begetting off the xxxrated axis onto the y-not axistism, your gracexistension's been mistaken for eggracistism with you left off eggguiltripped on bemannappeals to…….

Gracie: To such a thing as me just smiling to be spied e'erturds.

Alex: Yes. But it gets worse. All of's windows that you're in are e'erhetoricalled out whene'erized as winced. I'm talking wince warfare here… like as if like your eumanity is to be blasphem'd in all blasphemable dimensions.

Gracie: So like where does that put me?

Alex: In a window way over here where you are…..(Alex demonstrates)

Gracie: Impossible. Yea, I know all about it. I'm the trophy in the window of the holocaust competition with my spirit face…..

Alex: Drawn and quartered and martyred in the mirrors, on the bleacher seating with crowds all around and traffic jams at every exit.

Gracie: So ont I'mathematicky speaking, x-axist-wise, this whole seismicky selfished out egggrasystem on y-not coordinates of the y-not axistense egggraph………

Alex: Ends up holocausting Grace …….

Gracie: Oh! Oh! (waves her hands frantically): ALL OF'S INGREDIONTENTS NOT/NOTNOT CODES CAN CATER TO TO BE…. I'measilly little me…….as justajifffffy just ONT I'M!

Alex: So like, this whole egggraceistismatter can be solved with 0/1 logicodes

Gracie: TO Becombined with NOT/NOTNOT CODES in startled e'ersolved. It's a marriage made in heaven!

Alex: Yes, a heaven sampled from iffffe'er.

Gracie: So then e'ereally does need stars to dream me?

Alex: No! Samply speaking, ifffallensed love, stars need dreams asample e'er of aprioritized heaventilation's wholegggracexistism.

Gracie: Onthank god you said it, not me. Plus ont I'mathematicky speaking that's why I just have to get that phylum all my own if I am ever to be not impossible, or stinct or not not coded of course of course to not not be in all of's alphabettingodds. So you just noticed to not not know what I've been pretending to not know ever since the girl war. So to hell with my eumanity. What's your interest in such a thing as..

Alex: You're eumanity.

Gracie: Yes, my eumanity. Is that for me to be a nice person or a not so nice person.

Alex: Well that depends on the eumanity in the menu in the mirror that's wincing in the window. They're all egggracists in these parts, all but you and your eumanity…..

Gracie: Which is….

Alex: Completely positive, becompletely sume'erized to be whene'erized, completely pers(eas)onal. You're the only one in these parts that doesn't hate yourself for being in love with yourself. But it's so ont I'm'obvious, the holocaust has bought you buying yourself as someone's else.

Gracie: So like ont I'm'essstranged…ont I'm'obtained as someone's else.

Alex: Yes, like spirit facemented silhouettes in gracesstragement windows..

Gracie: As me in not me's mirrors.

Alex: Hijacked off as high e'er'd up to e'eroad kill yourself.

Gracie: Myself! Yes, yes! Myself (gracie fans herself). Like I sum times wonder whatever would I do without myself.

Alex: With you the decoy on the cross pinned up to make a universe make sense. Meanwhile with reptiles in the market place and fish not far behind……

Gracie: So like you spotted the bruty on the menu off course being butchered by the holocaust….

Alex: I eufigured that was almost eu.

Gracie: But I begot out of there like just ont I'm. (gracies worst suspicions are deliciously being confirmed) So like I don't have to be a nice person anymore….Isn't that it?

Alex (putting hand in pocket): well at least not insect decidedly self-repellent. The way I iffffigure it against eggground….it's time put the girl war aside and become evolitione'erily as iffffreaked out as…

Gracie: As what?

Alex: As a descent euman being.

Gracie: Descent from what?

Alex: Descent from uh 1. Subeumans. 2. Supersubeumans and like speaking for over all of's over all….3. eumanity eurself as iffffreaked out today, and today ontoday…….when it becomes to aesthethics just be a pretty nice euman being. Like humans as eumans like yourself just not on the main course of course's meaty physics menu.

Gracie: Not even the dessert menu served on the side?

Alex: Uh, stick to your eggguns on that onthat pregnant zero's one.

Gracie: So don't discard my trigger fingers from the I'deck eagggunning down I'dectomies.

Alex: Like don't be screwed to the N-word's dictatorshipmentionary.

Gracie: So just what does that leave me left onte'erifffff I'd to be…

Alex: Be like…like…like…likeabily presentable to selfished out society at large. Metaphysically speaking be ont I'm'e'erigont but meaty physickly speaking, e'ercraft scrambled e'erather than aircraft scrambled. It's like almost nobody's body beggers ever thought to say, "just be a decent euman being".

Gracie: Well, I'dolled up descent wise, how about self-propellent. Is there ever any chance that I can beget away with that…like whenever like the window over here is me as my worst enemy (Gracie frames a window to the right where egggrace geometrickly is NOT.)

Alex: My e'erecommendation is to be just nice enough to be, but not just nice enough to not be. Egggovernment programs to not be are not e'erecommendable as far as, metifffforickly, I can determine.

Gracie: You mean like spider turds.

Alex: Yes, whenever they've got you wholegggrailocked into anybody's everybody else but such a thing as egggrace, it's time to……. ontaching pages from your own ont I'metaphysics, whenever the distance from to not to be to be is so much greater than the distance from to be to not, well then, of course, of course not not….. be nice in seasons not in season m'enude otherwise.

Gracie: Well, I'm glad we got that settled. This whole holocaust business has ……. (gracie takes a drink). Now what to do about my metaphysics Alex. As self-propelled like I'm behaving plans for it, plans just for of course, of course not not to be. Ever since I spelled you backwards I wanted the likes of you, uh eu, and me to either kiss my m'e'erore or else plain talk eternity Alex.

Alex: Well before this morning I relied on 0/1 codes for information. Subject to of course of course not not to be since meeting you onthinking notnot codes has s'e'eriously ontente'ertained m'onthought processes.

Gracie (encouraged): Yes! Yes! Go on!

Alex: Eternity e'ereally is quite large. Even the gods never quite go there. You got that part right.

Gracie: Yes, keep going.

Alex: Well, gods have secondhand watches; usually the gods just stick to stars.

Gracie: Uhhuh. Makes sense.

Alex: That's where dreame'ergence is subme'erged. That's wherever eu like iffffffffffit in.

Gracie(primps): Yea, I've got my puddles to tell me that, but, puddles or no puddles, I iffffffigured that. So like, sooner or later, as Miss Eternity…

Alex: Eu'll have to dump the gods.

Gracie: So how do I do that and still be nice as happened ever after. I mean to avoid alarms and skirmishes, to stay outside of girl wars.

Alex: Stick to the chalk boards of the metaphysical society 2. Stick to the cross.

Gracie Mmm. It's getting late Alex, late for my eternity, late for the Mesozoic to of course, of course not not be metaphysical.

Alex: But it still might not be too late for lenses with equations Gracie.

Gracie(concerned): Mathematically how do you explain me Alex?

Alex: As all too obvious an a priori product of eufemiphyluminium ontwinkling on the y-not axis of I'd thou artesian could be coordinates (Gracie's spirit face ontwinkles in Alex's twin starry I'd eye balls)

Gracie (barely able to contain her giggles): Did you spot the bruty on the menu as butchered by the wholeggghostry outs.

Alex: Yea, I did spot that.

Gracie: That was almost me. I bigoted out of there just in time.

Alex: Yea, I figured that was almost you.

Gracie: So slipped on or off bemannappeals where do you see the swamp'swim's tail is heading?

Alex: Oh I don't know. Like….humans…eumans…selves…elves or plain old fashioned manicons to becomputer cartoon ont I'm'animations…there's lots of new phylogenies emergent on the near horizon. Now that I have seen what I have seen I think I'd just have to throw in my lottery ticket with………

Gracie: So after all is said and done, I mean like girl war or no girl war I could end up coolifffffffying as the coolest thing ever!

Alex: Look gracie, I can only discuss these egggoo summations because I never attended kindergarten in these parts, I never competed in wholeggghostpitality competitions, or spitting sports in general. From what I've seen of the Mesozoic you're the ont I'main event. I haven't picked up all the letters in all the alphabets yet….

Gracie: But what about my NOT/NOTNOT CODE? I mean the wholegggrailinguishing well of course, of course not not to be.

Alex: Well it's clear, the Mesozoic's going out of style and you're the ont I'metazoic e'ereplacing it.

Gracie (fanning herself): Yes! Yes! Oh but Alex, on second's thought I may be more eggguilty than you've found out about.

Alex(alarmed): What?

Gracie: It's my supersubeumanity. I might be m'ore than that I'mined.

Alex: How do you mean?

Gracie: My situation might be more simple and less sample. I might be like…like

Ale: Yes…yes…

Gracie: I might be like…..ONTEGGGRAPHICKLY SPEAKING……….LIKE….…..ont I'maybe even……..SUPE'ER……..EUMAN…with no subinstitutions in between……..and the eggguilt's egggetting to me. Like what window does that put me in?

Alex (gathering his wits): Like Whene'er's window with high hopes for your placemented to the operatunitest site. Gracie, before I met you I didn't even know it was the ides of e'er, like half time in eternity. The 0/1 code was all my lenses had for their equations. I mean, iffffffffffffffffffffffffffffffff( )fffffffffffffffffffffffrankly speaking I never thought of eternity being ontalented. But I can observe you now as 1. partegggirled for eggguy's like...like....the pin up on the crossed outing. 2. Egggirlways e'eresponsible aprioriparty girl as whene'er waved hellowings as behaved.

Gracie (trying to helpful): But just maybe that's just it. I can behave halos. But...as I'm'esozoickly ontangled.....I've like got no wings to asiffffly me all of's ont I'm'e'erounding's I'cubed e'eround.

And then....

Alex: Yes dear.

Gracie: Well, and then I always wake eggguiled so haploitly egggirled.

Alex (seeing an opening): Yes!!!!!! And I'm just your eggguy'd to fix that!

Gracie: Yes...BUT!!!!!!!

Alex: Look Gracie, your metaphysics has opened up a pandoration's box of like newsy new testamental whoegggrailighthoused beaconsiderations. Atlast on the shoulde'er's of to be.....the Metazoic's being prospected for iffffffformation. Ont I'metaphysics wise you did get that e'eright. It's a whole new ontestamentionable wholegggrailogged in outing. Meanwhile I noticed that the holocaust is alive and well in these parts. Well half of it.

Gracie: What's the other half?

Alex: You are Gracie, humped by the mesozoic's wholeggghost's since kindergarten.

Gracie: But don't you see my ont I'metaphysics has broken loose of all that speculation.

Alex: Yes Speck is a terroristocratic organism with wholeggghosts for sale. But sneaking out of kindergarten to ont I'manswer for eternity is of course, of course not not to be scened as notable...but...

Gracie: But what?

Alex: You may have jumped out of the soup, like a fish without wings, with fins that don't fly, into sum's ont I'm'empty e'er....crafted it is true with a promising new alphabet that doesn't have the talented eternity to back it up.

Gracie: But...but....but....but.......

Alex: Heaventilated wholeggghosts aside, the distance from being to not be may just be what matters as far as tense presentions may just beconcerned. Like maybe this eternity's a justajiffffy's dud. Something to observe a moment of silence for, but that's it. It's like I almost didn't say, maybe eternity's just not that talented. What if to be's always like just about to be like been. What if that is all there's to it. I mean like, in your own alphabettingodd's ifffont I'mathematics......doesn't it ever bother you that eternity never happens, which by the way, it doesn't. Like with your wings, doesn't it bother you shoulde'er'd to have them whenever, by the way, you don't. I mean it's like the incompletion's set in set theory, what if of course, of course not not to be's just incomplete.

Graciemore concerned): What are you getting at Alex.

Alex: Oh yea. However, about your theories. I like becompletey agree…

Gracie: Yes?

Alex: Until I disagree. First to agree.

Gracie: Yes let's do that.

Alex: Your secret ingredient, ((NOTNOTITUDE)) really is the becommoddity your theories suggest. In e'erealms of motel ontolodgings, ontonight really is not never's night of a priori e'ers. HOWEVER.

Gracie(apprehensive) HOWEVER WHAT?

Alex: (clears his throat): Well, it's like I almost didn't say. I've been thinking of applied metaphysics, applied to your metaphysics. For that purpose… I've brought you a present (presents another bottle of gin). It's like a backup bottle. You may need this when you hear my becompletion's ont I'm'analysis of your ontheories.

Gracie(hopeful): Oh! Like to celebrate in like…like…my becomputation of e'er.

Alex: Well, let's put your soft awareness aside for a moment and evaluate some hard e'erivals for your ontheory seating. Like, just for argumentsake, like pessimaterialized, I was just speculating on the's other second hand. What iffffffffffffff( )ffffffffffff if weren't quite so justajiffffffy.

Gracie(apprehensive): Yes? My could be curiosity's ontriggered darling. You were just evaluating ontalents of eternity.

Alex: Let's start at zero. I mean like, zero's always been a very reliable constant in all of my equations. And your code makes it more than less veri…….

Gracie: Able! To do lots of stuff! Yes, I must say, my pregnant zero light house beaconception's worked oned'e'ers for presentable eternity's notnotitude. And like I beconfess notnotitude's what nails me to the cross.

Alex: But…I'm subposed to shop eternity……like like fore'er'd of course not not to be, what if to be's not in business?

Gracie: Are you suggesting that the belongings of my metaphysics are overly optimestimations of ont I'm occupied eternity Alex? Are questioning the preposte'erologicode of course of course not not to be's….omegalphabettingodds?

Alex: Well, what ifffffffffffffffffffffffffffff( )ffffffffffffffffffffffffff your she it'shop's ont I'm all's out of business?

Gracie(recovers): Out of business? Well that can't last forever. So whatever, of course, of course not not to be onteasily accommodated by the not/notnot code Alex….not cooliffffffffff I'd until in season.

As my NOT/NOTNOT CODE estates, forever's big and always up for grabs like iffffffffontaile'er'd to beget ahead.

Alex: So eternity might schedule appointments…of course, of course not not to be.

Gracie: Whew! For a few seconds I thought you were blowing a hole in my whole metaphysics.

Alex: Look, until I met all of's ont I'm'eu, I was no philosophistiquerian, I was just a guy lens'd look outs with equations. Justajiffffy jargonwise…….I was……… like…like…ontenthinking about all of's onthis onthat's ifffe'erealty…..?......like 1. what if eggghost haunted housing's project's just not a prioritized. 2. What if gods must take their chances like the rest of us. 3. What if ifffe'er's not such a big I'deal's onthing.. So you see….. I was blowing lots of holes in your wholeegggraile'er'd ont ont I'metaphysics, with you egglowing darks' inside'er holes. But hey…listen. It's a question of just *when* is eternity…like…like…..*now*. I mean just mathematically speaking, considering your idea of zero as a very able pregnant constant's corridgeable e'ercraft….if I go back to calculate from zero as a could be corrigiable constant…….well…I was just sort of wondering(oned'e'ering)…what if eternity still just CAN'T ope'erate as iffffffffff( )ffffffffinitively as notnotitude might suppose. Like meaty physically speaking…what if just making a living's not as wince worthy as one might think from the portapotties surrounding its every move. So like metaphysically speaking, to be as party girl pessimiss ticklish about it, maybe being's been like…like….just aborted by this eternity. I mean, what if eternity never really quite adds pregnant zeros up to one. What if all of's auditions for obviosity are like…like…..asiffffffffffffffaked.

Gracie(alarmed): So you're trying to tell against all dumps on you, my metaphysics is e'erather quasi (she draws circles on her silhouetted head)You mean like mathematically speaking zero really is a constant.

Alex: Well, apart from ontoying with our…….

Gracie: My ont I'mathematicodes can't hear you Alex (Gracie covers her ears).

Alex: Like…..think of it this way. What if metaphysics should relax its like…onthumbs on the ontrigger finger and let the universe just have its ont I'mined'e'er alibibles for could be crimes it can't help but commit. Maybe being's both 1. Not that big a deal. 2. Not that embarrassing to just begoofully ego happently down the drain with it.

Gracie: Uh……..you mean like being's been aborted out of atypical onteenage'ers….to litte'er'd little more than entypically teen aged outer space?

Alex: Or like ontemporality-wise, being's been aborted to like…like…instead of to be whenever…to…to like be like all but e'er'd *when never*. Or let us say like…like…..HARDLY EVER. That would explain lots of stuff to be gets boxed into like…how come such a thing as a gracie begets stuck in a Mesozoic sticky iffffinge'er'd swamp where gracexistems aren't beyond ticketed to be taboom'e'eranged to be ontentaboo…..unless………..

Gracie: Unless what?

Alex: Unless like…like….(taking deep breath) {{{{{{{{{{{{TO BE'S E'EREALLY LIKE……NOT!!!!!!! IN ON TO BE}}}}}}}}}}}}…..like…like….(Alex offers Gracie a hanky)……{{{{{{ETERNITY'S NOT IN ON TO TO BE.}}}}}}}}}}}.

Gracie: Uh!!!!!!!!

Alex: Like, preposte'erologically speaking ETERNITY'S JUST NOT IN ON TO BE.

Alex (After thought-wise): Like binarily speaking {{{{{{ETERNITY'S NOT IN ON NOT NOT TO BE}}}}}}}….except of course, of course not not in a secondary clocked in sunny godlike sense……like…what if like second hand gods just cross the skies of not ne'er's night(checks his watch) by second handy days.

Gracie: Like cartooned of course drawn chariote'er'd across some skies.

Gracie falls back into stunned silence. She is crying tears without whate'er.

Alex (0blivious to Gracie's metaphysical distress, hammering another nail in the could be coffin): Or like what if egggravity's just mass excelle'eration…which gods e'erainbow down to…..you must realize your theories will be *objected* to by comic book'debasementalittease.

Gracie (fighting back): Yes, but I also e'erealize they may be *subjected* to by e'erigorous I'debatabilitease.

Alex: Yes, but…well like putting the y-not axis aside for a few seconds of outer space, think of clockwork mass excellerating along the x axis like a residensity moving sign waved node to node.

Gracie: You mean like wholegggravity's like NOT wholegggrailuxuriontly ont I'm'excelle'erated at iffffinity on the y-not axis of all of's ontantrumminated justajifffit's all.......

Alex (maintaining rhetorical stride, Alex continues): Yea, or so like….what if to be's self-salivating all of's time, just licking it's eclipse'ervice to 1. Notnot be 2. Nextitudinate nowsy's news….HOWEVERIZONED TO BE M'ABORTED AS IFFFFFE'EREALTEASE E'ERESULTS! What if eternity's a dud behind one big pregnant zero's aborte'eracket….in which case ontemporal eternity's no more than a mathematical construct of non-finite ente'ertainment's operational temporality….like…after all is sung and danced for the gods to not be able to do anything about.

Gracie: So there's no hope for this operation's dance-sing's song and dance after all? You mean like, after all is sad and done, notnotitude doesn't do sum's onthing that stars can't deal with?

Alex: Like, what if dreams need stars to dream them. What if..like… with this of course, of course notnotitude idea, what if it's all just….becomic booked choreography, sway danced across some low down cheapunk spare parts dumpstirr'd second hand stuff(Alex checks his watch) that's like not *not I'd* onto be abortioned into outer space egggasing up the universe to just be all there is. Like what if gods are just lit e'er'd boys in spaced out suitabilitease….like just pande'ering to pantheocracies pan handling pans with no belonged to iffffonte'eresults. Like..what if eternity never happens…which..by the way…it doesn't. What if you don't have wings Gracie, which, by the way, you don't. What iffffffffff( )ffffffffffe'er that pops out pooped needs make up kits.

Gracie (Wiping deserted tears while casting shadowy glances on her atlast shoulders beholding up the sky suspended in mid e'er.): Not yet, Alex, not yet, but…the way I ifffffigure it, it's because it never happens that eternity's always still up for grabs, Alex. Notnot besides, just as stars have alibis, eternity's becompletely begot the's n'alibis, which spells it backwards and forwards for anything that's everything's…like set up…..for not yet's, not quite yetitude.

Alex: Look I'm not all knowing but I do knowings. You'll just have to accept my countenance code for that.

Gracie: Iffffff you'll accept my alphabeting odds on e'er…… Gracie. Like, ignition'd ontenthrottle-wise…….your becompletely presentable eternity's ifffffreaked way, way out of my wholegggraileague'sparking lottery. It's only for your euphem'eraculousake I'm inclined to wait e'eround for e'eresults. Otherwise it's like I almost didn't say….eternity never happens.

Gracie(relieved): Oh! You had me worried there. The becomprehensive thing about eternity is that's it's appointment schedule's........ALWAYS NEVER HAPPENING. That's when notnotitude kicks in with the's nowsy news...about THE BIG TIME ALWAYS {{{{NOW}}}} NEVER HAPPENING. Don't you get it! Like it's because eternity's so never except for now that, ontasked about, set up in questioned to hardly never answer. (changing the subject) Whene'er wing wise.........as far as wing's ontswings e'ergo, there's lot of e'ereste'eronts with waiters serving wings. Like wings are waiting for me on everywhere's ont I'menu I don't bother to look. HOWEVER, wings or no wings, countenance or no countenance, I suggest you follow my not/notnot code's e'erecommendations.....like...like....of course, of course not not to be, of course, of course onto to be.

Alex: Ok, even with could be's countenance that has the spirit faced to make matter matter....what if notnotitude is just some sort of windup-storm's meeting point of upwind and downwind...like just some traffic accident at an intersection. What if notnotitude is some accident that only happens when m'almightning strikes are in the intersection? What if mirrors only get mugged accidentally in egggalleys. What if......once the accident's over....all of's presentable tension's becompletely spent, heaventilating nothing more than launde'er'd loan'd'egggas in heat, as e'eroad'skill ontoned for to be dumpt.

Gracie: You mean like some egggoof ball egggame, like both 1. Upwind and 2. Downwind of down and up for grabs? With no e'er's way danced like..... heaventititilation's hope for just a jiffffffy's just ont I'm?

Alex: Uh, yea. If nothing else that would sure make zero more constantly easier to calculate from. I mean, mathematically speaking....

Gracie: You have been meddling with my ontense'er calculus. Whenever only I beget to do the math.

Alex: Math'd'e'er or no math'd'e'er, what ifffffff like......like......TO BE'S BEEN BURIED IN A DUD ETERNITY? what if sooner or later this NOT/NOTNOT

ALPHABET of yours has to be abandoned like that graveyard across from the country club.

Gracie: What grave yard is that? I keep forgetting.

Alex: The one that's way too real for emotion picture make up kits to be made up in. Gracie, what iffff whene'er to be bottoms out……….

Gracie (excitedly onticipating): Yes!

Alex: What if like eternity is not more than a mathematical construct of non-finite temporality. What if eternity can't be presentably counted on up to iffffffffinity.

Alex looks at his watch.

Gracie (laughs wildly): Do you e'erealize how e'erediculous that sounds!!!!!!! Put away that second hand watch (Alex hides his watch). Do you realize how dumped that would make of course, of course not not's e'erealty!!!!!!! I mean like that would be such a dumb onthing to ever doo doo ifffffonturded

Alex: Yes.

Gracie (in full rhetorical stride): Like to be would be just dumped into sum's'tar'dumps. My not/notnot code would collapse eclipsed into some summary of zero'd in ones or tetrahedrant alphabeting systems.

Alex: Yes.

Gracie: But Alex, with universes no longer quite so sample, that would make e'erealty like so plain and simply silly….like some becomic bible booking's ontragicky becomedy.

Alex: Yes.

Gracie: Well, what about iffffffffffffffffffffffffffffff( )ffffffffffffffffffffffffffffffffinity?

Alex: Oh, iffffinity's subjected to objected to infinity's plus all there's to it.

Gracie: So all of's justajiffffy's ifffonthis and ifffonthats just count for comic bookings?

Alex: Yes.

Gracie: So how does being coolifffffy in all of's this? Like…what about being?

Alex: Well, it's like I said…maybe to be's been buried in a dud eternity.

Gracie: But {{{{I}}}}will never accept such criminal not behavior on the part of…..notnot to be.

Alex (in full rhetorical stride) But Gracie….what if this {{{{{I}}}}} you keep depositing to be notnotiffffffff-I'd is just some enticklish itchiness that only lasts as long it's not-not-not scratched. What if this {{{I}}} is just like minus 1 squarely rooted to becompletely imaginary until cube rooted to be cubed as minus itself except to be deposited dimensionally in outer space. Or maybe think of it this way, what if notnotitude's could be e'ercraft are just e'er I'ding on bargain basement batteries of…a..

Gracie: Like…low down cheap punk second hand spare parts puniverse?

Alex(encouraged): Yes! In low down cheap punk e'erways that don't ever need to bother with auditions for sum's big time iffffffffffffffffffff( )fffffffffffffffffinity protocol. What if infinitease enticket's the only quasified mathematical construct that's coolified to get things done.

Gracie: So like ontrophickly presentable eternity's iffffffinity status is just something for like….

Alex: Burnt offerings, alphabeting against becompletely impossible godogodd's occasion'd as iffffffont I'm'd whate'er's becommercial's wholegggrails. So like what if even ifffff egggracie is teamed with egods, eternity's sum'othe'er's d'iffffffe'eronteam.

Gracie: So like all my ontool use'er's ontoy e'ercraft are just kidding out of sum's insomnibus's beickle windows?

Alex: Well! Don't you see how that really does make zero simpler to calculate. And as a corollary you can stop talking eternity..like..like…talking about *e'er* as if it means 'sum's' thing! Meanwhile dispensing with ontalk will make conversations like less sample and more simple. Like..maybe outer space can operate just fine without e'er and eternity's vacuumulations do add up to a mathematical construct of non-finite temporality after all. Like put it this way. What IF ontiquity's just stumbled on to. What if the whole onthing's {{I}} is just imaginary like the square root of minus one. If my ont I'destructiffffffff theory's correct, then all bebles and other perhapsilly periphe'ernalia amount up to just cubiculations of imaginary I squarely rooted as minus one cubed to be minus their imaginary selves as dimensioned in outer space. What if even gods don't e'ereally believe in god.

Gracie: So far so I cubed Alex. But what about the metazoic's metafourthward powers of {{I}}. Ok, so there's like your theory that like…like…..{{I}} is like the square root of minus one squared to be minus one….such a thing as egggracie where e'ercraft gets becompletely deserted. Your theory just leaves it squared or cubed at that. But my theory metadvances to the metafourth powers of I…..ONT I'M'D!!!!! My theory accounts for what forever's up to in the end. Onthink of that Alex whenever you get spelled backwards. EXERT THE EXPONENT!!!! For crosssake!…….the metafourth power with just ont I'm'e'eresults of pregnant zero's plussist {{one}} once upont I'ming….. with such a thing as {{I}} no longer missing in action as e'ercraft's ont I'main attraction. Your theory neglected to take {{I}} to the ont I'metafourth power all of's way danced up to pregnant zero's plusssist {{one))……like….once upon a time's once upont I'm. Like do the math.

Gracie rummages for the wanted poster billboard of log 4 base the square root of minus one.

Gracie (showing Alex): Seen enough? Oh and lookey here!

Gracie takes out the wanted poster bill boarded as Log 4 base -1's square root.

Alex (Calculating log four base the square root of minus one): Oh, yea. How plusssist! Plus one.

Gracie: If nothing else, my not/notnot code becomfirms the all or nothingness of to be. Listen Alex, I know mathematics is still in the Mesozoic where I gets squared and maybe cubed to work outer space and all but, you must understand, as such a thing as wholegggracist gracie, I'mathematically speaking, I'm like..like…becompletely out of the swamp box. Holocausterized as half of my brain is, the other half's working the ONT I'M'etiffffffffffforth powers of {{I}} in the ont I'metazoic. In that regard, I like to think of metiffffffffffforacle ontique shopping sprees in terms of the I'D THOU ARTESIAN COORDINATE SYSTEM which puts my ontheories on the WHY NOT axis where the X AXIS only matters as far as matter is concerned. In my system pregnant zero's not constantly on vacation ontaking m'eternity leave. In sum's ways I don't even need to not be Gracie to I'd'entiffffffffy thou artifacts m'exposed inside my puddles. In sum's ways my wholegggrail's sum as iffffffree for all of's……all of's……*all of's.*

Alex: So like selfless m'equations aren't solid as a rock after all. So, when it comes to alibis, the's e'ercraft hasn't got them but the universe has alibis up the……….

Gracie: CASE ZOO! So, like all and everything's not e'eratrapped on a plot thin goof. So I hope you're not suggesting we observe sum's seconds of silence for sum's dud eternity.

Alex (refers to watch): Well a could be dud body does deserve a few seconds of e'erespective silence, whenever it becomes to that.

Gracie: Well, if you ask me, that's jumping the justajiffffffy begun ontrigger…like…asiffffinger….. before e'ereaching for iffffourth powers of I.

Alex (backing off): Mhm. But I thought THE SQUARE ROOT OF MINUS ONE SQUARED OR CUBED at the most…..WAS all there's to it all.

Gracie: But weren't you forgetting sum's onthing?

Alex: What's that?

Gracie: SUM'S ONTHING!!!!! ALEX! SUM'S WHATE'ER'DOWNED ASIFFFFFFFFFF( )FFFFFFFFFONTHING!!!!!!! The most profound metaquation of all of's time, the zero plus equation where $0 + = +$ begets chewed beble gumptions almightning stuck on the chalkboards at the metaphysical society. You just keep missing iffffffontoviousity's as iffffonthing, the wholegggraileast e'ereleased eggglimpsingingroundsiftingonthroughout to be. Just onthink of all of's ont I'm beble e'ercraft e'eriding insomnibuses, bought and paid for by beble banks, chimed in churches, Alex, all of's way danced across eternity. Spelled backwards or forwards, will you please at least onthink about it. I know it's the Mesozoic and all but this is {{ALL SO'S}} ontrophickly presentABLE eternity *after all* is said and done. Mathematically speaking I see the problem.

Ok so like it's my NOTNOTNEWTESTEMENT'S ontense'er could be calculus versus your log 17 base 10 second hand graveyard, spare parts, tensor calculus (Cringing, Gracie addresses her(audient) guests, who have no ideas about 'graveyards') Sorry guys. (Continuing with the argument) It's your massive objections to my subjectifffont I'm becomiffffforting *not no time.* I'm sorry to disappoint your on the side'erial schedule but, your 0/1 alphabet's ont I'm'obsolete ever since my not/notnot codes kicked in of course of course not not onto to be. I mean your universe is already showing signs of obsoletion in e'er ides. Why would anyone waste ont I'm on puniversion'd physics when ont I'metaphysics is m'available of course of course not not to be's m'availability. Who cares about comic books when there's a beble bible on the chalk boards at the metaphysical society. Why bother with eggas clouds stuck in stars…when it's notnotitude that's ont I'm'obviously onticketed perchasable as in the ont I'm'e'erkit place.

Alex: All right Gracie. Your alphabet, as simple as it seems, could be the could be code for sum's what's (swats fly) eternity….but….

Gracie: But what?

Alex: Well, immersed in hopscotch as we are, why not just say "I give" when you step on the deadline's objections to your theories as we step on every step we take.

Gracie: Because there's just begot to be ont I'm'exits off the steps we take in the hopscotch playgrounds ontranscentwise insomnibuste'er'd as coolifffffffffffffy like….superstition or no superstition, e'erivals at superstations onticketing insomnibus e'erides.

Alex: Uh, Gracie I have a question.

Gracie: Yes, darling?

Alex: Exactly what are insomnibuses?

Gracie: Oh! Beble's beblical beickles of course…of course…not…not…. that just can't sleep all of's way danced across eternity….of course…of course…not…not…..

Alex: Oh yea, so like ontrain cars with no sleepers…….

Alex: And what are bebles?

Gracie: Oh! Yes, bebles! The uh….possible people that live in this eternity.

Alex: You mean like litte'er'd ontents I'm'occuront as of ever?

Gracie: Exactly. The becompletely presentable people that ont I'moccuronthese iffffe'erways…like….for set ontheory as iffffffffished out of fins with feet to stumble onto.

Alex: But Gracie, what ifff all of's ontiquity's just stumbled onto? What if this ontalented eternity of yours is just in the ont I'muddle's middle of the middle of the middle of e'erandominion's low down, cheapunk, second hand, spare parts…….e'ercraft engine hardware. What if there are no like becommencement's e'eremoney's as ifffrom headstartails, or kindergardens or becoolifffff I'd ont's cools or becommuniversities…… for that iffffffffffourth power of I cubed. What if I squared and I cubed is the end of it? What…if my theory's correct……what ifffff. Gracie: Like….iffffarm's ifffffields just behavior just like scarecrows iffffffaking to be could be's care crows out of straw.

Alex: Uh, yea like like….I'll have you know that even gods must could be caveat such e'eregards.

Gracie: Yes, that's the ticket…could be'scarecrows smack dab in the middle of the middle of the middle of whatever's whate'ers ont I'd up to….(rummages in her black box, pulling up her pillow and finding her pompoms) with THESE!! Proving I can be to be's care……care…….(putting pompoms ontriumphally back in the box) caroused icky stick ifffffffigures on the grounded outing's as iffffffarms. Care Alex, could be's scare crows that care!!!!!! As crows why not just be could be crows as care….like not not to be coded's care. In case you didn't not not notice, onte'er'd eternity enturds enterritory entwinkling stars or iffffacsimulations just like…like….like……..

Alex: So eternity is excretionary after all.

Gracie (hedging): Well…..like…..I certainly might not say not so.

Alex (Trying a new angle with the argument): Up to who'swhate'er Gracie….……what iffffffff.…Look I know like….justajifffy's e'er's become your could be craft's ontique shoppe….but what iffffff the shoppe's closed for the season's only season ever seasonably available. And what iffffff the closed season's not for never which is to say forever. I mean, what iffffffffff to be's been misappropriated apriorily? Like preposte'erologically. Like….what if, without the stars, there are no dreams? What iffffff to be's smack dab between sumwhate'erocks and some hard places, just too hard to be at all. Purpositionally speaking, like what if whate'er as ifffffflows ontpurpose only iffffffffflow'd on purpose by accident?

Gracie: So you mean like it's only by accident that my puddles postulate me puzzled to be wholegggrailodged as picnicks of ont I'm as pictured perfectly on purpose?

Alex: You got it! So like all in all….LIKE WHAT IF ETERNITY'S A PUFF OF E'ER…..BREATHED… NOT…NOT……POOF. So that's my theory. What do you think?

Gracie: I think you should stick to stars Alex. You've been like e'erounding with the sun too long. You need ont I'more's mined'e'er's not ne'er's night' Obviously you're ontenthermodynamically demented by dimensions of entropical heating systems. Obviously your mouthing entypical science in a second hand heaventilation system's unde'erestimated ontypically presentable eternity. I mean Iffff you're not dreamerced enough in such a thing as my subposed proposals (Gracie poses as a statue) to get out from under immersion in a low down cheapunk universe, then I don't know what I, as winner of the Miss Eternity Pageant, will ever be able to do for your second hand held gas clouds……… metaphysics-wise. You see, the way I ifffffffigure it…..e'erealty's m'expontentical darling.

Gracie continues: Now…my not not nutritional analysis suggests that……...obviously ontrophickly presentable metaphysics doesn't agree with your digestive addiction's substance attributes. Not preposte'erating the situation……BUT….preposte'erologically speaking……that's all there's to it. Here let me take your temperature. (Gracie puts her hand on Alex's forehead)Mhm, just as I thought….eufeminentonthermal. Your head's as hot as one of my puddles. I strongly recommend you stay out of my e'ercraft, maybe out of the e'er altogether. At least for sumwhate'er's while. I mean with all this Log 17 base 10 secondary talk I hope you're not preposte'erating sumassortment of inte'erifffe'erence with my of course..of course…not..not……..not ne'er spout's wholegggrailogged as iffffont e'erealty. If you are, this is not a good time for it.

Alex: When is a good time for it?

Gracie: NEVER!!!!! ONTHEORETICALLY NEVER! Look..don't dabble in metaphysics, Alex. Even if you are not to be spelled backwards.. whoever you are…...leave the metaphysics up to me. E'er's onto be Alex. Like…like…onthermodynameticketedly speaking……...for every T-time in eternity there's afte'er four's iffffourthpower of I'm ontique clock's ontheory settings for like…ONTI'M. For every thermonucleus there's sum what's other onthe'ermonucleus with no alibis. It's like playdough on e'eroids. You can take my word for it….it….it…..Oh, that's it….. You're just scaring me aren't you? it's because I dumped you at the bridge this morning, right? Like…like…all day you've been immersed in phyzzing…" what can I say to Gracie that's worse than saving her from death made simple…..so she just has to dump me". So like, god or no god, you came up with this low down cheap punk eternity theory to make me more iffffffffrightning struck than I have ever been iffffffffrightning struck out of it onto. (Gracie hysterically turns to her motel guests gravestones, using her m'eternity ward's maternal body to protect their becompletely beblical inhabitonts from Alex's theories) I never want my guests to hear that sort of distonthing Alex. (Gracie petitions the stones with her maternal embraces). So!!!! I will just decide to not have heard you well enough to…like….like…of course…of course…not…not say to my self-evidence that OH! My! Somebody's just kidding me! So!!!! Sit!!!! And SAY!!!!! IT!!!! Say like…like…I WAS JUST KIDDING BECAUSE YOU DUMPED ME AT THE BRIDGE!!!! Yes! That's the ticket!!! Because….because!!!.......BECAUSE!!!!!! HEY! WAIT UP WHY DON'T I? What about my miracles? How does that fit into your phyzzzzzzy information iffffffffffffished out of MY IFFFFFFFFFORMATION'S WHATE'ER'S BEFORE AND AFTER ALL IS SAID AND DONE? You're just a scientist Alex and metaphysics can get science into sum's e'erious ontentrouble. I mean just this morning it was a secondhand universe as far as your watch was concerned. Look, I have it on good authority from every puddle I've ever met than my self-evidence is just ont I'm'aste'erpieced into the puzzle of sums e'ereally euphemyste'erious…like…STUFF…..stuff…

preposte'erated on wanted a priori posters plaste'er'd all over eternity……with me and eternity of course..of course…not…not…being on the same team…..before and after all is said and done.

Alex (almost convinced): Well, anything's possible in a priori ONTHEORY SET UPS I suppose.

Gracie (primps seductiffffffffly): I mean how many seconds was that for pregnant zeros saddled to getty up to me…log 17…

Alex: Base 10..

Gracie (Pursing her lips): Seconds. That's all you've got to work with with your bleacher ifffontheory seating of notnotitude's being accidents. I mean like…your equations are just running in second gear. They're not working iffffffull onthrottle like…pot pot pot powow!!!!E'er!!!!!!! Don't you get it or do you have to be ontested. (suddenly compassionate). Poor Alex, exe'ercizing unstretched out equations in a poverty stricken puniverse, living with lenses in outer space. What can be expected of zeros treated as constants smack dab in the middle of the middle of the middle of outer spacings with nothing worth ontalking about in the middle of the middle of the middle of those spacingsongs. I mean like caught like ifffffish out of whate'er, immersed in wind up tool entensions, ontoy eternities must seem ontiquely implausible. But now that you've been silenced as far as can be heard….just…like…take it back. (supremely whistfully whimsickly almost fainting)) Whatever it was you just said, just take it back so you can be like just maybe's my puppy spelled backwards again and I don't have to dump you…but really. Beblebegger that I am of course, of course notnot ont I'm'onticipatient….onto begge'er….. ont I'm'egged….. onto be.

Gracie is in tears. Alex remains silenced. Gracie offers him her hanky, dabbing his eyes where the tears would be, if there were such a thing as Gracie's whate'er as ifffonteared on the cheek of such a thing as Alex.

Gracie: so let me get this right…you're sayng..

Alex: Well like, like, like as far as death is concerned……

Gracie(gettinginterested): Yes! Yes?

Alex: I just don't trust death to take care of things.

Gracie: Whathings? Like onthings?

Alex: Well yes, like ALL OF'S IFFFFONTHINGS AS YOU SUPPOSE…

Gracie: You mean like becompletely ont I'metaphysical ifffffffffff(.)fffffffe'er's…..

Alex: Well yes, when it comes to that.

Gracie: So you don't onthink eternity can always be ontrusted to do the's e'eright whate'er's iffffonthing.s So like you are, you are, you are……..

Alex: Yes I do, I do, I do not always trust eternity to do the right thing.

Gracie: So. Like corillareally…….you are, you are, you are….

Alex: Yes I am, I am, I am ontreating death just like a murderer, especially when all of's she it's it becomes to such a thing as you, the chosen holocaust of all that is egggracessed……egggracexistentonte'er'd I'mansioned such ontent's onthing'segggrace.

Gracie: Oh Alex! For you onthen my ont I'metaphysics is sum's'e'erious business after all.

Alex studies egggracie's make up kit for signs of *WHAT* she is that makes up *WHO* she is.

Alex: Gracie, I have to make a confession for the Mesozoic…uh and maybe for the universe as well….unless of course, of course maybe eternity's the real could be culprit here in onthese parts. It's almost as ifffffff THE HOLOCAUST IS ALIVE at egggates of egggracess'd becommunities. Gracie, euman or human, which ever man you are, you are the living holocaust, the whate'er'd'oughte'er'd who of what is who is what is who'm I'm with……… ..

Gracie: In love?

Alex: Uh, yea.

Gracie: I knew you'd say that word.

Alex: Uh….yea; that's just got to be it.

Gracie: Oh Alex! I never thought my metaphysics could beget so s'e'erious….like soooooooofistdicate'erly this s'e'erious! So you're saying you like me on holocauste'eroids, as holocauste'erized by the girl war after all.

Alex: Uh, Gracie, if I had never met you, I would have thought that eternity was just like tales without heads attached, tales only attached to some ontentheory set's traffic jamm'd ontentrain wreck of all time, precisely as ontalk outlined in this conversation…but..

Gracie (Whimpering): But?

Alex (offers Gracie's hanky back dabbing her eyes where the tears are emergent….like e'ereally): But, the whole idea of ontoylet training eternity aside….there is a problem with my traffic jam train wreck set theory.

Gracie(hopeful): What's that?

ALEX studies egggracie for signs of not not being the girl.

Alex: YOU!!!! DARLING. YOU BEING SO EU DARLING!!!!!!

Gracie (takes hanky, whimpering): What about me darling? You mean like eu man?

Alex: Uh, yea, I must eggguess… 1. You don't look like trained traffic jam wreckage. 2. You don't even look like a plot thing goof. 3. You don't even look like rattle trapooh.

Gracie (primps, catching her surreptitious self-evidence in a puddle that's handy): I don't do I. Soooo what doooo I look like?

Alex (still studying egggracie for signs of not not being the girl) Well….like….justajiffffy's…….like……
madonnation's crown jewel of a prioreligion's iffffffffphphphphylumination's spirit face that got way too
pretty way too fast to of course…not not onthrottle the m'eternity ward's eternity as ever so very
presentable indeed! I mean….as far as train wrecks go….I would analyze you, atlast beholding up the sky
as she it should'e'er'd, conservatively as sum whate'er's asiffffonte'erain e'eriving safely at grand central
superstition's…..eggground central superstation. What you don't look like is…..

Gracie: What?

Alex: A train wreck. God or no god, you countenance, I mean…your *spirit faces* the séantiffffic make up
kit of ontrophickly presentable eternity to smile the ground of being's behind of all of's matter as far as
matte'ergoes.

Gracie (with reemergent e'erogance): I really do, don't I.

Alex: Because of you, maybe eternity has got way too presentable way too fast for the speed of anything
but almightning strikes to catch up. The problem is….I never thought I'd be spirit forced to say….but…..

Gracie: But what?

Alex: Well, iffffffffffffffffffffff( )ffffffffffffffffffffffff your own Not/NotNot code suggests to my
lensedevotions….

Gracie: Your lens'd I'motions…..yes…yes!

Alex: Well as the simulation of all simulations…….aspirate faces the negative of all negatives……

Gracie: The negative of all negatives…I like it….

Alex: Being replaced by herd negatives of herd positives….with herd heaventilated meaty physics being
humped by holocausts…….

Gracie: Humped by the holocaust….yea…like…like….I get it.

Alex: So like the xxxrated content of your countenance…..

Gracie: My spirit face…..

Alex: Uh, your spirit face…..well……

Gracie: Well what?

Alex: Should beget that phylum all onthrown'd….

Gracie: Onthroned! Yes! Not just grazing on a universe., not just egggrazingas.

Alex: For xxxrated xmas presentenses presentably presented at high noon on xmas day after all.

Gracie: Oh Alex! I just knew you just had to be spelled backwards all along.

Alex: So even ifffff I'm just some geek god and not sums e'ercrafts whole sum god….you still…

Gracie: At this point that's god enough for my salvation after all.

Alex: You really mean it? You're not going to dump me for saving you after all.

Gracie (hesitating): Well……..So like whene'er'd weighing in on my eternity test site projections………

Alex: What projections?

Gracie (shaking her hand and waving him off): Oh not NOW! This is egoing way too god but really……so eternity? You were revising your doubts about eternity, please.

Alex: Oh yea, eternity. Well (nods affectionately) eternity may just be more than a mathematical construct of non-finite temporality after all.

Gracie: And the universe?

Alex (shrugs his shoulders, beholding up the sky atlased in his own small way): Oh just a *sample* of sum's thing gone selfishing for such a thing as a gracie, dreame'ergent as of course…of course….not…not…in e'erespectable…..e'er.

Gracie (batting her eyes seductively): So? On second thought?

Alex: So on log 17 base 10 second's thought….as e'ereduced to samplifffffffication….stars do….stars do…. stars do take it all back to eventuality. As far as metaphysics is concerned I will..I will…I will let you do all of's onthinking for me. I've decided…there's just maybe too much of such a thing as a Gracie's meaty physics for metaphysics to stand a chance. That's all there's to it.

Gracie: So you like…stepped on the deadline…hop scotched in the playground wise…...you like….*give?*

Alex: Yes, I give up forever to Gracie's presentably ontique eternity as iffffffffff I luminated by such a thing as Gracie's iphphphphylum all her own. Ifffffffffffffff( )ffffffffffffffffanyone's to dabble in metaphysics…let it be such onthing's egggracie.

Gracie: So then, street wise, my basic metaphysics can't be….

Alex: Curbed. Yes, no universe however laden with objections, has the resources to undermine sum what's ontiquely presentable eternity. That part you got right. No objection can prevail against a subject that can so selfsimply notnotiffffffy nowsy neighborhoods of news. That almightning's truck loads of genius on your party girl's part. As far as I'm concerned your basic metaphysic's acadeemed beyond dispute.

Gracie (wiping her tears) Oh Alex, you really mean it. You really do…do….do…mean it. (blows her nose with dark loud abandon). Now don't you feel better!!!! Sometimes you just have to ontheory sit in the beble bleachers and let me do your thinking for you. Like I let Ms Speck do my thinking for me, but not really. You need to do the same for me, but really. That's better. I can see that you've calmed down. Respect the authority of a proven beekeeper…who keeps not iffffffffffforgetting. Ontake my ifffe'erecomendoration. Don't be a caterpillar. Behive but e'erifffffflights like..like (large butterfly appears)Which e'ereminds me. Alex (primps in a puddle) You know feeling about me the way you must if you were me feeling about me the way I would if I was allowed to. Like having your angels sing for you the way I'm not allowed to sing for such a thing as myself. I mean with me on my inside and you on my ont I'motherside too, there's nothing we can't do for just ajiffffy's ont I'm right? Like we're on the same team right? Like if you were dubbed a doguy spelled backwards that's how it would all work out… right? Like ontentheologickly… if I had dibs to dub you backwards…..you would be spelled…like…like….like…….

Alex(thinking): Uh…

Gracie (gaining confidence, picks up her broom): Like to be's onticketed …of course..of course…not…not after all………like this broom here's e'ercrafted to e'eride…right. Like if I get on board, I might as well be onticketed to asifffffly…right?

Alex (studies the broom): Uh Gracie, your broom.

Gracie: What about my broom?

Alex: Well, it's just some straw stuck to a stick. It actually has no e'erodynamic properties whatsoever.

Gracie (feeling betrayed, straddles the broom and makes engine noises): BAROOM! BAROOM!

Alex (seriously challenged): Ok Gracie, make it fly. Go ahead. Make the broom fly. It's like being dead. You've done it before. So like you know how to do it; so….like…just do it. Make the baroom fly.

Gracie(begruntled): Don't tempt me Alex (Gracie climbs off the broom and holds it in her hand as…suddenly encouraged by the return of the buzz in the music scowls ugleefully greedily.) Wait up up why don't I ontake up iffffffull ont I'm'advantage of the alphabetingods to sweep to be….to sweep to be….. All right Alex, whether or not I'm the one eternity's been waiting for…….I am…I am…I am all winced out just enough to like(for sweeping dirt out from under e'erugs) show what this broom can do.

Gracie (sweeping the dirt out from under to back under the egggrass rugs……. as she sings):

YESTERDAY'S TOMORROW YOU CAN LOCATE ME SWEEPING WITH MY BROOM.

YESTERDAY'S TOMORROW YOU CAN LOCATE ME SWEEPING.

WITH WAND WITH DIBS TO DUB…….ONTOOLED

OF COURSE TO BE E'ERCRAFTED

ONTOYLET RAINBOWEDOWN E'ER'S COOLED

AS WAN'D TO BE E'ERAFTED

TO TIDY UP EACH LITTLE ROOM

HEAVENTILATING WHOE'ERS

HEAVENTILATING WHOE'ER'S WHOM

YESTERDAY'S TOMORROW YOU CAN RELOCATE SWEPT UP BY MY BROOM

TO BECOME BUSTING OUT OF THIS MORTEL'S DARK ROOM

SWEEPING UPE'ER THAT'S WAITING TO HEAVENTILATE WHOEVER'S WHOM

HEAVENTILATION SYSTEMS

HEVENTILATING WHOEVERS

HEAVENTILATABLE AS WHOM

GETS TO BE SWEPT UP BY MY BROOM.

Orchestra enters with broom ballet of Gracie belifting up the ground of being. Looking darkly in all blasphemable directions, Gracie sweeps the dirt under the grass rug. Ignoring her, Alex begins to work on repairs for the power grid's fun house mirrors. Gracie is showing signs of ontentional ont I'madness, broom jumping off a could be cliff into a pet puddle repeatedly in her failures to fly. She recovers from these sissifussy repetitions as the music subsides.

The dialogue resumes as Alex, who has diligently repaired the fun house mirrors to make them more like honest to goodness puddles, picks up the apple specter has left for Gracie.

Gracie (violently smashing the apple from Alex's hand): You owe me one.

Alex: One what? What about the candy?

Gracie: Nevermind. Listen Alex! The girl war's not over, not by belongings of belongings of a long shot. Things just being things in these parts, as long as she it is egggirled…..egggirl wars are never over…except not really. Oh if I only had sum's words to almightning strike at the truth of the matters….Like she it shadows never stop piling up like in my motel dark rooms ont I'mousinging the hisssstheorcraticries in the snake pit as I as the likes me can't help but……….smiling under someone's else in the squirt gun holocoaster ads. As long as I'myself the girl war's never over. The chain of holocaust rides never ends. Each holocaust ends up auditioning the next one.

Gracie asiffffffe'erambles on.

They're in the feed lots at the whate'er holes in these parts….. As long as I exist egglayers keep begetting worse. As long as I'm not extinct, as long as I'm possible egggracism's in for these wholegggrail egggirl wars. As soon as I iffffffffreaked out, getting way too pretty way too fast, World War Whenevers entered the's iffffinal countdown for such a thing as egggracism. The dictatorshipmentionaries decided, wholegggrails must of course of course not not be scrambled of course not not of course not sunny side up. To solve the problem at first they just split me in half. As it turned out no one hated all of me more than half of me. And then I was drawn and quartered into infinitestimonials, tarantulating my hair do blithered into jibberish. It was like, mathematically speaking, I was fractaled into some evereceding set. I mean it was the Mesozoic after all and the wanted posters wanted me spirit faced onto the menu eventually to be picnicked on egggrassist bottomed outings. I mean I did make one last stab at gracexistence, but pretty soon it was clear that I was the only gracexistist left e'erounding out the cubicals for my…..by now, like you almost didn't say, everybody but me as was an actual gracist. The power grid lock was investing in the masterpieces in the puzzlementions of my puddles. Cosmetrickly speaking everybody was planting pictures of such a thing as gracie enslaved to the backgrounds at their mirror sites. Pretty soon I was appearing everywhere in all of's windows, in all of's advertisements, in all of's emotion pictures….but always making the point that emphatically…like…like…like….I'm not me anymore. I'm like somebody's else. it's like my brain was become a donut with a whole of someone's else in it posing as me not being me anymore. One by one the power grid was serially killing me on holocausteroids. You could see me in all the advertisements smiling my one last smile of being myself before myselfished out dumpstirr'd soup dimensions were all that what left of me to mention. It was like a squirt gun holocaust on one big happy family menu of me, like mealy mouthed smiling to become interred from out of the bottom of to like…like….not not be. But what could I do. The girl wars was over…over and over and over and over with me as occupied territory the gracist trophy hunters were after. The holocaust was only over by not really'standards. It was just getting started at the intersection of the intersection of every family farm selling metazoic milk projects right smack dab in the middle of the middle of the middle of the Mesozoic itself. Tensions as presented were tense, to say nothing of tensions that were ontrophickly presentable. There was no room for has been metaphysics in the stables. Meaty physics was all that was available on the chalk boards of the metaphysical society. And this time I was looking for alibis. Like maybe I could fake not getting quite so pretty quite so fast.

Alex(reaches with right hand to touch Gracie but pulls back):So, like make up kit wise…

Gracie: Yes, make up kit wise….examine (I'd thou artistickly) my predicament why don't you.

Alex: Gracie….

Gracie ont I'mentions ontentasks out in EGGGREAT UNKNOWNS

Gracie: Just look at me. For crossed out's sake. I don't have to audition to be obvious, even with all the shadows piling up on top of my self-evidensity, I can add it all up. Like….1. I've got the girl war aftermath equations to solve. 2. My phylum's been iffffffficially submcrgcd undcr whatc'cr of morscl codcs mouth'd by the swamp. 3. As occupation territory I'm bridled on all of's sporty crawler's virtual intended listings on all of's wanted posters. 4. I've got this really big job with a really big future being dead or extinct or maybe even impossible. In fact, if I may say so, I'm on the short list for all time's most impossible person awards. 5. My spirit face has been xxxrated on all of's promotion pictures on all of's crossed outings. 6. I'm way past the deadline (points to graves) on this homework science project that's my better later than never alibi for the girl wars. 7. On the metaphysical asiffffront…my escape philossity engine's all out of beblbatteries. 8. Oh I could go on and on Alex. But besides (looks in black box e'eresource bin) Hey! What the's iffffffux, I'm almost all out of metifore I'mined I'm'apt appliances…

Alex (waking up): What appliances.

Gracie: My can open'd e'er pillow appliances.(takes out can opener and puts it aside) and my…my…. BEBLE BRAND Pillows. (finding her pillows) Souled under the metiffffored Mined Pillow brand.

Alex: For what project?

Gracie: For my safely buried but really project….like…..how dizzy I get when I'm simply dead….but really….You wanna hear?

Alex(indulging): Sure, why not.

Music plays as Gracie speaks to her guests: Hey you guys don't mind if I have my pillow brand pillow do you….

Gracie is preparing her quasi grave bed and addressing her clients as she sings:

SOMETIMES I FEEL LIKE UPSIDE DOWN'S RIGHT SIDE UP (tone row)

SOMETIMES I FEEL LIKE RIGHT SIDE UP'S UPSIDE DOWN (the same row retrograde ending on a shrieked high B abruptly bottomed out by a low c)

IT REALLY MAKES ME DIZZY (suspended high Cs.......

Harmonically reemergent, asking her motel guests for permission to have a pillow in her interment plot, Gracie points her trigger finger at the graves ritually appeasing them with her embraces).

THYOU SHOULD BE HERE I SHOULD THERE

I SHOULD BE THERE THEY SHOULD BE HERE

YOU SHOULD BE HERE I SHOULD BE THERE

TO BE DECIDED UPSIDE DOWN(cadence)

I SHOULD BE THERE YOU SHOULD BE HERE

AS MAKES ME MEATY PHYZZY (suspended high Cs)

AS MAKES ME LIVING DOWNSIDE

TO BE DECIDED UP SIDE

TO BE DECIDED DOWN'D I'D

TO SHOULD BE THERE'S WHO SHOULD BE HERE

WHO'S TO BE HERE SHOULD JUST BE THERE(cadence)

(TO BE DECIDED UPSIDE DOWN

TO BE DECIDED UPSIDE DOWN(cadence))

Gracie's burial ballet continues with Gracie piling up ground over herself indulgent quasi-corpse, as she adjusts her pillow'd ont I'm'appliance.

As the music subsides, Gracie unburies herself and the dialogue resumes.

Gracie: As I was adjusting mined pillow brand news pillow I realized I do need like…assistance.

Alex: Yes, Gracie what sort of assistance?

Gracie: Alex do you think you could be my like existentialist that like saves me without me knowing I'm being saved. Could you do that?

Alex: Sure! I'm begetting cooliffff I'd at that.

Gracie: It's like you almost didn't say. I'm in this fix. Like where everybody but me's a gracist.......like one way OR the other way, a gracist prey dictator or a gracist at heart. Meanwhile I'm me and I'm the only one that's just a measily gracexistist, nothing more, nothing less. Are your hands clean?

Alex: Uh, yes.

Gracie: So like the way I've decided to play it is...like...I'm this wholegggracexistist consulting my existentialist. That's going to be you. Now, having said what you almost didn't say until you said it..... just what you're going to get for this I'm...

Alex: No Gracie, you don't have to pay me. I'm already rewarded by knowing that...that...like before today 1. I didn't even know that it was half time in eternity 2. While a universe can be some heavy duty stuff, it's a desert without such a thing as a gracie dreame'ergently e'ercrafting its sume'er's whene'er's spring's iffffffalling whate'er ways...what are you doing?

Gracie(gratified): I'm studying you for signs of omniscience.

Alex: I was just studying you for signs of omniscience.

Gracie: What do you see?

Alex: Spills of whate'er falling wholegggrailove's I ball begetrials on why not axist I'd thou artesian coordinate systems.......puddled.

Gracie: With what results?

Alex: Mirre'erly masterpieced together puzzles of...like...like...bebliffffffactoriedreame'erchant's wholeggghost of living's could be countenance....

Gracie: Cool. Like could be quasiquali-coolifffffffffI'd as coolest ever?

Alex: Yes, could be quasi-coolif I'd as such. Gracie at this appointment in.....in...like...{{e'er}} all I want is your existence adequately e'er- represented so as to be....hmm......1. Not impossible. 2. Not not....like....exex....exex...like {{stinct}} 3. Of course not not not to be dying to be dead for beginners. Oh and hey! 4. Getting you those wings you always wanted for xmass and 5. Like I almost didn't say....getting you that phylum all your own you wanted for xmas.

Gracie (exhilarated): Oh Alex! You really are like...like...wholeggraileashed my pet puppy like spelled backwards! Which reminds me when I won the Miss Eternity Pageant over runnerup reality. I never forgot my first day on the job. The traffic jammed me in this coffin (shows the coffin) of the lip service business. Lines were forming around the block. It was just like the mesozoo had been waiting around forever for a kiss from the likes of.....well.... before that day love had just a series of rear end collisions in a spitting sport until my metaphysics e'erived e'eromancipating asiffffffffffux. It was when the crowds traffic jammed my meaty phyzz to need repairs that I realized……like…like…as meaty phyzz I did matter but with thou art implications…so much as like..like….metaphyzzed dreame'erchandized way past a universe insomnibuss'd all across eternity. That was the day I really started taking ont I'metaphysics to heart. Tons of money were stacking up against the coffin. It was more than self-evident, as spirit faced….like….my meaty phyzz did matter as dreame'ergencied. Like just when it shouldn't it did, just enough to star the girl war. And that's why I just had to dump you at the bridge Alex. I was afraid you might be getting the wrong idea about me. You were starting to show signs that, Mesozoic menuwise, like my meat mattered when…of course notnot…….dreame'ergentrifffffffff I'd as I am, it's the dream of me, like after all of's dream of me, that matters. So my meaty physics just had to disappear so I could leave you, in the final analysis, as the's I'mportapotty's iffffinal analyst….left all alone in the beble bleacher seating with…….like whene'er'd with……… with just my justajiffffffy metaphysics.

Alex: I just thought you dumped me.

Gracie: I did dump you, and I will again when needed for one of us to be beyond the other. That was the whole appointment of it. To dump you with my meaty physics so my metaphysics could be iffffontoyed…like as iffffffolded out…..as I'd thou artiffffactoried…. as I'd'e'er'd into play with me…..becomic booked….. I'dreame'ergentriffffffffied in paper products.

Alex: And all I was hoping for was a kiss. Metaphysically…paper production-wispeaking, I feel so ashamed.

Gracie: You ashamed! No, no, no Alex. I'm the one that's too ashamed to actually be xxxrated e'eradioactively to exist. That's my job not yours…or used to be. Ever since before and after the girl wars, this is where I worked.

Gracie shows Alex the kissing coffin. The sign on the window says CLOSED FOR REPAIRS (bombed by the girl war)

Gracie: Sit! Alex sit! No. Stand!

Alex stands dutiffffffffly like god spelled backwards. Gracie studies the countenance of Alex to see if it'spirit iffffacement qualifffffffffffffffffffffffffffffffffffffffffffffffff(

)fffffffffffffffffffffffffffffffffffffeyes to can be kissed without subte'eraneous revolts. A subsupercutaneous smile broadens her spirit face.

Gracie (rips off the CLOSED FOR REPAIRS sign): You'll need a token darling.

Alex (finds the token in his pocket): This one?

Gracie: Yes, that's the munched adoo that does it in these parts. Now I'll climb in the coffin and you put the token in the slot.

Gracie climbs in the coffin as Alex places the token in the slot. The window opens as Gracic and Alex stare at each other becompletely right side up, with Gracie boxed in to be neither at her far right or her other side. Alex and Gracie search each other for signs of eufacemented e'eromanticizable like as iffflux.

Gracie reads from the kissing coffin protocol script.

Gracie: Ok, so like number 1. E'eritually appease me with a token of your esteem. Put the token in the slot. (Gracie hands the token back around the outside of the coffin)

Alex puts the token in the slot. As quasi coolifffffied, the window opens.

Gracie (reads): Ok so like…like….BEHOLD THE GIRL…..dreame'erchandized…(iffffe'erecites)but make no mistaken for intendedoll'd'upride's…….

Alex beholds the girl dreame'ergently. The window closes.

Gracie (passing the token around the outside of the coffin): Ok, so like number 2. Put the token in the wholegggrailucks….box…..

Alex puts the token in the slot. The window opens.

Gracie (continues recitation): Of could be kiss of asifffe'ers of she it thou artouch. Like…like…think about it. Behold the girl, as countenanaced with could be'spirit face iffffffffashions ……..e'ercrafted at last should e'er'ing the's guy's ifffffirmaments in I'd thou art's mid e'er.

Alex puts his hands on Gracie's should e'er'd as iffffontorso. The window closes as Gracie passes the token back e'eround to Alex's clean hand.

Gracie: Put the token in the pan'd'e'er box.

Alex puts the token in the slot.

Gracie(reads): Ok like number 3. E'eromancipate iffffflux. Like e'eromancipate thou art's ont I'm'd wholegggrailed asiffffffux.

Alex kisses Gracie as the kissing coffin music dreamerges from out of the blue. As the window closes, Gracie is now rushing to get the token back to Alex's clean hand.

There is a musical backdrop to these episodes of e'eromantic activity.

Gracie(urgently): Put the token in the slut Alex.

They kiss again now more passionately. Gracie passes the token with increased desperation as the temperature in the coffin rises.

Gracie: In the box. In the box darling.

There is flower music playing sporadically at this point. I becomes kissing music in a heightened state of excitement. But the music shifts when………………………..

Suddenly, out of the corner of her eye in the middle of the middle of the middle of their embrace Gracie spies Mobible entering Gracie's motel. Mobible's leitmotif music is playing and he is carrying a VOTE GRACIE SIGN which Gracie doesn't see.

Gracie: Uh, Mobible dear, there aren't any voters here. They're all at the beach today.

Mobible(quasi-shriveled): Oh, I've been to the beach and I was just looking for you. (Nerdly hurt) But I can see you're like….like….. busy Gracie.

Mobible backs out of the cemetery with his music playing backwards. Gracie is alarmed. Interrupted and embarrassed, Gracie leaves the kissing coffin.

Gracie: Something's wrong with Mobible. The way he's sparking he might selectrocute himself.

Alex: So like…..he's extracting votes from this….this…..mort…..mort…..mot…el?

A light bulb goes on in Gracie's head.

Gracie: Yea, he's plumbing for votes. But I'm like cheer leading for…for…like…like…volonte'ers!!! Listen to me Alex. While your lenses have been grazing on outer space, the swamp in these parts has been mooing loudmouth sanctimoney. It's like I might not have said, the girl wars is not over. It's true what they say, as long as my tail has a head that's likenessed, with or without wings, with a halo, the girl wars is waiting e'eround in all of's mirrors to say nothing of the puddles.

The traffic jams really are landing at the beach heads looking for occupation territory. THAT'S ME. Someone is being humped by the holocaust. That's ME! As long as I'm not impossible, or not extinct, or not even dead, the girl wars won't be over. There's a rally tonight and I've been cordially not invited, until I show up like I'm invited. Once I'm there it will be my usual routine. I get sacrificed so Felix can get sanctified. But this time it's for real. I wouldn't worry except that maybe this time e'eround….eternity may just begetting put put putted as mistook onterritory. If it wasn't for ontrophickly presentable eternity I wouldn't bother as of course…of course…not…not….to be…..myself. But this isn't just some stars at the stake here. We're talking eternity, with only me pinned up on the crossed outing to vouch for as iffforever of it's all. Please believe me I'm not myself for myself anymore. Think of me as like omegalphabete'erment's secret agent working whenevers like…like…like a spy on to of course not not to be. I promise you I'm not working for myself. In fact since I'm not myself…. I'm working for anyone but myself. Please believe me. I'm the only one in these parts that really knows what forever's up to….like…ifffreaked out sneaking e'eround….like up to.

Alex: I do, I do, I do believe you darling. Without such a thing as egggracie, afterall, what's a world?

Gracie: What?

Alex: A desert whate'er hole beheld asholed with…..out whate'er. And without such a thing as egggracie what's eternity?

Gracie: What?

Alex: A deserted whate'er whole…like I'dried up.

Gracie: So then I really do coolifffffffffy to save whate'er's as ifffontrophick iffffodder as iffffffffeed….

Alex; Yes, Gracie you do coolifffffffffy to becompletely presentable….

Gracie (encouraged): As you know I've got this project for eternity that just can't wait. It's like dreame'ergency's become dreamurgency. If my theory's right that eternity's not wasting its time after all…then I will, I will, I will change forever what forever's up to. Listen Alex, what I have in dug outs mined…….is not the usual religious experience. It's more like a religious expe'eriment which I have to schedule for sooner than later.

Alex: Yes, so you're planning to….to……

Gracie: Take eternity back….like backed up just a bit. But I need cash. Otherwise the only orthodox way to do this is to like…like….BEGET MYSELF POPED OUT AS….AS…..LIKE….POPE. like next to dog or…you… whoever you are….spelled backwards.

Alex: What do you need from me?

Gracie: Some new music, spelled forwards this time e'eround…like as iffffforever………..

Alex (gets up to leave): I'll go get sum music.

Gracie: Wait. What time is it?

Alex (looks at his watch): Well, darling by my watch, it's still log 17 base 10 seconds into….

Gracie: Yea, yea, yea, just enough seconds aft e'ergrosse'er'd iffffontitude to…..to……to……like……. 1. Gas up a universe 2. Get waves party girled at the whate'er wholes to make up masterpieces at my puddles 3. Position such a thing as egggracie as thou art I'd at just ont I'metaphysical's meeting at the bridge over reve'd'e'er 4. With me wholegggrailiquored up enough to climb back on that cross for one last iphphphphphylumination all my own. So, you meet me at the cathedral with the new music. Meanwhile I think I'd better work on my cheerled e'erouteenage'eroutine.. (Gracie rummages in her beconvenience storage e'ercraft box)

Alex: What are you looking for darling?

Gracie: My secret weapons. Can open'd e'ercushions if you must know. I just had them.

Alex: Can openers?

Gracie: Yes, cushy could be kitchen appliances that can open………e'er.

Gracie pulls out two blush pink pompoms and holds them proudly up to her chest.

Alex looks puzzled.

Gracie: Alex, do you know how Speck'd'e'er did my thinking for me….but not really?

Alex: Unhuh.

Gracie: Well, let me do your thinking for you…..but really.

Alex: Ok, darling.

Gracie: Alex is this what egggreat adventures are like?

Alex: Yes, darling, this is exactly what egggreat adventures are like.

The music begins again as Gracie starts her cheerleader dance routine as she sings her cheerleader pompomination e'ercraft aria.

Gracie sings:

SOMETIMES I REALLY FEEL LIKE JUST

POMPOM'S CHEERLEADER CHEER'S ONTHUSSED

POMPOMMINATING VOLUNTEERS

FOR CHARITEASE OF COURSE OF COURSE NOT NOT LEADING CHEERS

AS SUM'S WAVE DANCE ONTOES BEHAVE

CHEERLEADING TO BE SAVIORING

JUST LIKE THE WHATE'ER WAVING

HELLO'D TO BE BEHAVIORING

JUST LIKE SUM'SAVED'E'ER SAVING

POMPOMM'D AS IFFFF TO IFFFFONTCHEER

WHEN WAVING JUST LIKE WHATE'ER

WAVES WHICH I'VE VOLONTE'ER'D TO

POMPOMM'D PERHAPSILLY IFFFFFFFF….

POMPOMM'D AS IFFFF TO VOLONTE'ER

OF COURSE, OF COURSE NOT NOT TO……

POM POMM'D OF COURSE NOT NOT TO CARE

OF COURSE, OF COURSE NOT NOT TO….

OF COURSE OF COURSE NOT NOT TO CARE!

OF COURSE OF COURSE NOT NOT TO

OF COURSE OF COURSE NOT NOT TO

OF COURSE OF COURSE NOT NOT TO CARE!!!!!!!

With this grand cadence in the's ifffinal offe'ering, Gracie proceeds with her pompom routine. As Alex leaves such a things as egggracie in the distance, the music fades until Alex reaches the top of the hill. As Alex enters the as ifffffe'er ways of the country club, the music expands massively with Alex affirming his commitment at the beginning of this scene.

Alex:

I WILL, I WILL, I WILL BE THE HERO.

(half cadensity)

I WILL, I WILL, I WILL SAVE THE GIRL.

(full cadensity)

The scene ends with the music expanded and Alex on a heading through the country club back for moresearch at the bebulbless cemetery abandonated to beforgotten's dark.

END SCENE VIII

SCENE IX

The entrance to the cathedral is flood lit and in an uproar as Gracie arrives with Alex to great fanfare. The ray gun rafters are ablaze on the loudmouth power grid screens. Felix is pictured with LOVE dribbling out of his mouth.

Lara, the battered s'electrocution reporter, just back from the middle of the middle of the middle of the serpent city of denial, is standing with a microphone to interview Gracie as she enters.

Lara: And there she is! About as hot as puddled meaty physics gets. The wholeggghostess herself! Eternity's intended asifffffonthermodynamometer iffffffffffever there was! About as ont I'metaphysical as meat begets egggirls begetting to begotten.

Gracie (putting pompoms to rest with broom, wand and pillow): Yep, that's me, asifffffffreaked out of e'er…….(blabbering)…….It's soooo subjectively ontrue…beblabbe'er'd as I am…and not a big fan of objections….like hypocrice'ertiffffff I'double crossing eternity with 1. Ont opt off pedestrianimation. 2. Cartooned with ont I'm'e'ercraft could be confirmation………

157

Lara: Well you're obviously iffffffeeling your ifffontoats (feeling your oats)!

Gracie: Mhm! Well none's else seduces me like self Lara. Scratch fed ontrophickly as ifffontentickled (taps twice on e'er as she winks ontwinkles) not not to be.

Gracie e'ereaches for the sky in a gesture of asiffffffffffffffff( )ffffffffffffffffontriumph.

Specter (submerged in the crowd): Nasty girl!

Lara (Hearing N word in the crowd and putting her trigger finger on Gracie's mouth): As iffffffreaked out of e'er from OUT OF OUTE'ER… SPACED! Like you really are wholegggrailooking so ontranscensational girl! I mean with those pompoms like ffffffffished out ffffffffinnedlike…. ffffffffootball-wise, I mean like e'er didn't iffffffffumble the beble balls with you before ontouchedowning eternity ontotem poled!!!!

Gracie (Sum what metaphysically flattered): You've been reading the chalkboards at the metaphysical society Lara. It's true! It's such a thing as me that does make eternity iffffffffffffffffffff( )fffffffffffffffffffffeel so like………WHENE'ER WOWSY………IN NOWSY NEW'S'E'ERV ICE GRIP'S NOW'D ON WHENE'ER!!!!!!! I'M LIKE…LIKE…GOD AT THAT IF NOTHING ELSE.

Lara: Mhm. I'm a reporter and can't be devoted to you but…but….like I know all about such a thing as egggracie. Like (reads from a list) 1. S'e'erving as the wholegggumptioned ont I'maniac of metaphysics (trigger fingering silence from Gracie) 2. S'e'erving as the wholegggghost in all of's haunted housing projects. 3. On the she it short list for s'e'erving as the wholegggrailink to all of's Miss Missinglinks projections. What else have you been up to? How else have you been humiliating the swamp with presentable asiffffffontensions.

Gracie: Well just recently, I like…solved eternity Lara. Not only that but I've got an eternity test site experiment planned to prove it.

Lara: Cool!!! I mean that's just got to coolifffffy as cool! Like just maybe coolifffffffffffffying as could be's coolest onthing ever!!! (Lara ontobviously beconsiders justajifffy jargon to be qualiffff I'd as cool)

Gracie: Yea, like could be coolest ever if it wasn't for the girl wars. But my workouts with eternity leave me almost no time to be…to be….like….myself that's everybody's anybody's else than like…like…myself.

Lara: What is it that worlds want from girls like us Gracie?

Gracie (shaking her head): Well, apart from giving halo head to selectrocutions…… it doesn't have to audition to be obvious. It wants us to be the makeup kits for everybody's else. That's why there's no such a thing as me all right who coolifffffffffffies as metacoolest onthing ever! Iffffffff like it wasn't for me being like 1. Like party girl'd responsible for the girl war 2. Like a priori occupation's euphemiffffontenterritory. 3. Like eternity's intended bride of the holocaust……….like………………

Lara (stunned with her mouth popping as she speaks): Well, metameaty physics aside, what have you got for us tonight Gracie? Front man facing forward for Felix's back side as usual?

Gracie: Well, yes, starting off with that. But then….(whispering) I've wholeggrailoaded up I ammunition on e'er triggers to like head tonight's tale way over e'erainbows under spare part's low down cheapunk second hand scat e'er'sky auditioning light like..like…like…like..e'ereally….like….likes.

Lara: So like……sum's cooliffff I'd…….burnt offering on holocausteroids…isn't all we're ontalking here?

Grace: Uhnhuhn. Like the dreame'ergent sacrifice, this time wholegggrailoaded up e'eround's just for starters.

Lara: And so, like not as usual's self-evident ephyemyste'erious iffffffront man for Felix….

Gracie: Who, bye the bye, will sooner than later end up in my backyard….like….on leashed. HOWEVER (winks) I will, I will, I will start out as usual…

Lara: like sacrificed?

Gracie: Mhm.

Lara: With Felix?

Gracie: Sanctified. Yes. That's about it, but poste'erated into the big time. The power grid's big idea's to selectrocute Felix this time around as not just next door to dog spelled backwards, but…if the voting goes as invaded by like log 3 base 10s of mules….to go all of's way danced with Felix……voted in as just god in disguise's like…..JUST GOD…

Lara: For what purpose?

Gracie (shudders): My best guess is…like..like…to own hereafter's like permanently miraculous just ajifffont I'm'ajority's eternity(which I'm the pregnant zero's one that solved by the way).

Lara: So? Felix, preposte'erologically to pose as justajiffffy's like soone'er than late'er………like…….insomnibus'd incarse'erated{{{{{{{{{GOD}}}}}}}}}……..as like…

Gracie: Justajiffffy jailer, like e'er's indicted to be jailed in onto……..onto….

Lara: Like devoted to.

Gracie: Yep to put devoted on selectrocutions becompletely out of business. Yea, scary…but that's the way the sanctimoney's paradise is rolling…

Lara: So like…like…the sanctimoney's cashing in on could be's ifffffactivist iffffe'ers.

Gracie: Yea, all of's way danced across nows nextitudinations……for your e'ereportage to report on.

Lara: Well, Gracie, what's that going to do for your eternity test site experiment?

Gracie: We'll, if this selectrocution goes as planned, my own e'ercraftscrambled could behapsing projects will just have to wait in line for like..like…the next eternity. It's like I almost didn't say, I don't know what it is with worlds and girls like us Lara. We'd be cooliffff I'd as the coolest things ever if it wasn't for the girl wars that put me on the cross and you on report in decks of report cards behind the microphone.

That's why tonight this church is scheduled for sum's changes in décor, if I'm not mistaken for e'erides. Keep your microphone e'eready for macrobites of sum's newsy new m'assifffformation Lara.

Man in the crowd becomes aggressive. Lara and Gracie cringe a little.

Lara (recovering her wits): Well as a reporter that's supposed to lie but doesn't…I can tell you..you are still the N-girl xxxrated on all of's wanted posters. Crowded traffic jams adore you.

Gracie: Yea, good thinking on their part. If I may be exceptionally lightning struck for a split second about it…..I know why crowds love me being like…. SOOOOOO {{{NOT}}} THEM. I mean, geometrickly speaking, I'd love me too if there was a way to do that sort of thing. My puddles are as close as I can ever get to that (wistfully) You know….. people wander what's over the rainbow. (she toys with her rainbow tie) Well, hey guys! I know what's over the rainbow because I'M….LIKE…SHE…..IT! Like just to touch myself is soooo amazing! (Gracie touches herself with exdream caution as she winces, all but squealing while adjusting her halo) Like I guess I must be my biggest fan. Like if it wasn't for the girl wars and me being bride of the holocoasterides I really would coolifffffffffffy as the coolest thing ever.

Man, listening and becoming more aggressive: You do, from blush to out of the blue, you do, equationeer'd wholegggrailensocratically toe quantify (like geometrickly speaking) to like qualify to coolify as the coolest thing ever. That's why I've got my trigger fingers on you (the man puts his hands on Gracie's pompominations))

Gracie: What? Please keep your middle trigger fingers off my self-evidence.

Man: But you're so obvious, so wholegggrailitter'd in e'er! So sunny side up. I want you……

Gracie: For breakfast?

Man: Yes, that's the ticket!

Gracie: Give me that microphone Lara. Ok, whoever you are, whatever creepy sport you just crawled out of, I'm going to feed you with this microphone. Now just what were you saying?

Man(wilting): Well, you can see I'm down and out….and you're so…like….such wholegggrailiquored up meaty phyzz'd champagne…..like…like…..dreame'erchandizzzzzily presentable…like advertegoing ontopting off ontotempolling in these parts.

Gracie(agreeing): Yes?

Man: Well as sunny side up to be scrambled……

Gracie: Uhhuhn.

Man: As occupation territory….since I'm a down and outer………..

Gracie (thinking strategically, starts to hand the microphone back to Lara. But then freezes it in her hand): Sorry Lara but I have just got to rape me some conscience here. (turns to the man) So like if my halo were available to be raped by your bottom'd outings thurd person…like you wouldn't be down and out anymore…like…like…..you'd be like up and in. Be honest (Gracie ultra-violently all but forces the microphone against the man's face)

Man: Sure thing! Why not for crosssakes!

Gracie (turning to the crowd): And you sir what would you do if you caught such a thing's likesseventiont me, lit sunny side up in an everyday intersection's dark alley?

(Lara in the background is having flashbacks of recognition.)

Man(insensed): Well, of course of course not….

Gracie (threatening him with the microphone): I warn you, I am ready, willing and able to rape your conscience if you pretend what's not real is real but not really.

Man: Ok..so yea. I probably would rape your hairdo if my bottomed outings third person thought my bottomed outing's turd person could get away with it.

Gracie (feeling a surge of aesthethical power): Ok, so I'm going to put this microphone on macrobation's iphphphemiphphphone and get crowded consensus here. All you down and outers, what would you do if you caught my asifffformaldeydrated halo in some everyday's intersection of your dark's alley?

Crowd (in unison over the loudspeakers in the ray gun rafters): BE UP AND INNERS RAPING IT WITH OUR BOTTOM'D OUT'S THIRD PERSON.

Gracie: Because like why? Who is the dream after all is said and done? (Gracie threatens ultra-violently with the macrophone)

Crowd(reluctantly): You are Gracie.

Gracie (still ontenthreatening profoundly): Now what was that you just said. I didn't hear you.

Crowd: YOU ARE GRACIE! YOU'RE THE DREAM! YOU'RE THE DREAM SERVED SUNNY SIDE UP! YOU'RE THE DREAM THAT'S E'ERCRAFT SCRAMBLED. YOU'RE THE DREAM S'E'ERVED ON THE'S IDES OF E'ER IFFFFISHED OUT I'D'ISHED UP SELF-EVIDENCE. YOU'RE THE DREAM ABOVE THE DREAM. YOU'RE THE DREAM BENEATH THE DREAM. YOU'RE THE DREAM SERVED ON THE SIDE!!!

Gracie (sighs deeply): That's better. I rest the case for iphphphphylumination that's all my own. (turns back to the crowd with compassion) But hey! Wait up on smack dab's all of'sheite'erontense why don't I virtually signal at this point of my advantage…it is the IDES OF E'ER after all…..and I am the cheerleader of the half time show at the bigame.(takes out her pompoms) and it is the right time for aesthethical I deals here. So here's the I DEAL. I'll be e'eroad kill on the cross, but not really, for you, if you'll sit theoretically in the bleachers as peep show bystanders for my way, way too obvious self-evidence as picture perfect'snews jerk's paper foaled out. How's that for all e'erounded up word's becompassion! And I'll even throw you a kiss vogued in the vaults of the could be cathedral before the evening's ove'er.

Crowd: IT'S A DEAL DARLING!

Gracie: So like the one thing you can't be is the one thing that everybody usually is. Right?

Crowd: You got that right..but…you said it darling, not baby he's us!

Gracie: Just testing. (turning to the first man to accost her) Here, take this token of my….like…like…large'er onteam's ont I'm'esteem. (Giving him the token to the kissing coffin, Gracie then turns to an innocent looking boy) And you, young man, you wouldn't want to rape my head gear that gives halo to your third impersonation. would you?

Boy: No, of course not not………….

Gracie: so! As N-words go, how would e'eration such a thing as me?

Boy: Very nice indeed!

Gracie pets the boy and smiles with the assortments of nicedout benignitease that only such a thing as grace can muster.

Boy: Yet.

Gracie (suddenly disturbed): Alex, I need a drink. It's time I worked as front man for myself....I must dishevel immediately.

Gracie turns to her make up kit at the base of the cross. Gracie now dishevels herself, to the discheveling music, ripping her blouse, smudging her face and putting on her sinisterial moustache. Researching success with her make up.... Gracie sidesteps the mirrors to refer to an ontentiquely ont I'mansion'd convenience storaged nearby puddle. Sooner than later, Gracie is e'eready to be nailed (not e'erealy) to the cross.

But first, as the music is varied into a waltz, Alex takes Gracie by the hand and begins to waltz her with variations of the disheveling music, removing her moustache without her realizing what he has done. Being waltzed in this manner, Gracie feels the ecstasy of not feeling the taint of being salvaged or even saved.

Felix (at the pulpit is getting impatient): Let's get this show on the road shall we.

Still sub posing to be as iffffffffirmatentally dying...... Gracie climbs up on the cross as the sacrifice is about to begin.

Felix: All right then. Need I remind you that this rally is for the most important selectrocution of all time if I'm not mistaken for e'erides here. Since I have it by spelled backwards authority that you're all one for me, I hope I don't have to explain the details. It's time for the Mesozoic to head into the Metazoic and I'm the one begetting selectrocuted to lead the charge. So let's not get bogged down with the theoretical bleacher seating's situation.

Crowd: Yes, but, can you explain how this selectrocution's going to get you to walk on whate'er from like not not annexed next door to god......all of's way danced......to of course....of course...not...not.....like...become becompletely presentable as....as........you know who spelled backwards. I mean how does e'er stuffed with notnotitude actually work...when god is in the neighborhood.

Gracie (waving excitedly from the kindergarten on the cross): Oh! CALL ON ME!!!!

There is an awkward but e'erespectful silence. Chagrinned, Gracie has to think for a few seconds.

GRACIE'S WHOLEGGRAILECTURE FROM THE CROSS

Gracie: Like……becompletely   presentable   eternity…how   does   one begin…..e'erepetition tense presented. Like there's clock time and there's ontime. No…we'll get to that sooner's later.   I mean how do pregnant zeros become oned'e'ershe'ero. It's like perhapsy's lit all puppy…..starting out from inwards inn. It's like…like…like a little puppyternity, ontoyletrained of course, of course not not to becomplete……to be…like..like…bookwise n'alibiblically ontolled ont I'm. Yes, that's it, that's the's onticketed of coursity onto could be conside'er'd. (Bell chimes) Yes, that's it, the bebell tolls ont I'm. Thanks bells, egggodolled up as I am with ont I'm'other's kids on the play ground……… I won't forget to dub you of course, of course not not to be.

So like when was I? Oh yea…….like….. Immersed in itty bits of its, we sample symphonies of stars while well within simplicity's of course, of course not not to be. While whyzz bangodds amass to matter and logicodes may log, the omegalphabetting gods are on the not/notnot code as always is so beconside'erate of course, of course, not not to be, as oh my godiffffffffff I'd that god or no god's baby'she's us cooliffffffffies eternity's insomnibusing's cool e'erides crux creedance. What else are church chimes for but ontantrumminations of such ifffffffontissues. A church must ontantrumminate to charge eternity for crimes not becommissioned, e'erefe'erenced on the why not axis as coordinates could be. The way I iffffigure it against the ground, this cosmos business is like some acquaintoid clock work out of second hand e'erealty. Meanwhile eternity's e'erepetition'd e'er presented, is simple whene'er to be bells ontoll just ont I'm. Do you get it or do you have to drown in whate'er iffffffffffontested?

Crowd: We onthink we finally like beget it. We don't need to be ontested afterall is sad and done.

Gracie: You know, some accuse my metaphysics of anti-universionary asiffffontactics. But e'ereally, when'e'ers of she it shove becomes to portapotties, I'm not so anti as onti-universe. Like plotting constellations to be ontool used to be ontoid with ontoyletrained eternity…like celested in the bleacher seating as to be seems to

be..like..outhouse   broken   in   on…that   is
true….but….but…but…(grins)…like…like…

the way I ifffigure it against eggground, pregnant zeros never know what might
become along with belongings to be salvaged from a tool used e'er's toy out let
like…like….some stars entwinkling iffffontwinkles of its all, ontalphabeticikly
speaking, with ONTentrahedral codes dreame'ergent out of just plain tetrahedralized
dimentions….to improve on a tool user's universe as e'ereally ontoid with
ontoyletrained eternity in ontransportapotty's e'ercraft as proves once and for all time
that eternity is not iffffffffatickly NOT aborteggggoddity's ont I'duh'd ifffe'er, ont
I'mouthed offly m'obvious.

Gracie makes a fist and coughs into its depths.

Gracie: Ok. So, not not to be even e'erm'ore mined iffffffe'ereptitious, let's onthink
onthrough it all. Onthinking from as ifffforwards in justajiffy passed back through the
ides of e'er by way of the's not/notnot codes for the total eternity of the system. (Gracie
draws the equation onto e'er with her free ontrigger iffffinger while her other hand
holds her firmly to the cross)

Ok so let me presentEDly tense your appraisal with my qualum equation for the total
eternity of the system. Ontotal eternity (TE) = PresentABLE e'er(PE) + PresentED
tense(PT). Let me assure I include ifffe'ertego spin* So like we're adding up
whate'er's presentable e'er with whene'er workouts as presented……Adding it all up
and e'er's wised witty with what is…….while becompletely clever with what can be.
Now the's whole system e'eruns on two ingredionts. 1. Notnotitude and 2. Nowsy
news. Once you've got any fascsimulation of those onts, you've got ifffont's of
whate'ers gushing ifffontents out of could be's case lo'd up's casezoo. The way I
ifffffffffigure it from the cross, alphabetinglys odditiwise….as hardly never just
kidding…..becompletely presentable eternity's up for grabs. So ont I'm'advice grip-
wise, I'd say, like especially, ifff all you are's somegg……. "EGGGRAB
IT"……..like…like….iffffe'er'd m'available by a priori postage…….ontampe'er'd
with of course, of course not..not…code's nowsy news….could be broadcasts.

What my metaphysics is trying to do, of course..of course…not..not………just kidding…….is egggather it all together. The way I iffffigure it, just kidding….. at five I cracked the safe, at six… I opened it….from seven on….surveying the's ontents on a decision basis. That's my metaphysics in a not not'shell. Any questions?

*Parallel to the quantum equation for total energy of a quantum system.

Crowd: What do we do about eternity iffffffffffff iffffffffffffit's not e'ereally as just ajiffffffffffffy as you suppose. What if eternity just won't coope'erate?

Gracie: Uh? So like that's where the church comes in to the promotion picture, to charge iffffe'er for crimes against of course, of course, not not……..to be. That's when we ontantrumminate ontool use ont I'm to charge eternity for crimes against notnotitude. That's when ont I'moments of silence may just be ont I'm'observed for dud eternities. That's when, god or no god, a duh'd eternity may seek as iffforgiveness. That's when we need our own ifffontantrumminations to work TO BE to becomplete like….like…..

Crowd: Eternity?

Gracie: Yea, that's it. Onticketed eternity ontimed to be ont I'm. The appointment is as ifffffffollows, egggnition-wise whenever eternity shows up with your belongings…….egggrab it.

Crowd: Who can do that?

Gracie: Well…………….who do you think. Who performs all of's magick tricks in these parts? As who keeps Miss Wholegggrailuck's countenanced champagne ifffffliqoured up in could be's cup. On whose should e'er'd to be is the skies e'er to beheld atlast.

Crowd: All one for Gracie! After all is said and sung!!!!!!!!!!!!!

Gracie: My opinion of crowds just improved. Like maybe I am too bigoted after all. But not really. Ok, so wait up on myself why don't I. Ok. So like what nextitudinates? Oh yea, I've got to say it not really. So like save your devotion for you know who. There I said it. Save your votes for you know who (Points her trigger finger at Felix as she winks grotesquely shaking her head and covering her mouth) Uhn, uhn. No way.

The crowd: So like…like…once the ides of e'er's clocked into a iffffe'ers do like clocks matter at all?

Gracie: Well, as we all know I'm not a big fan of spare particlesecond-hand clocks, but in the spirit of ritual appeasement, let's observe one moment of séance for clocquantime's log 17 base 10 seconds of low down cheapunk second handud's quant work outing. If for nothing else to show you clockwise like……how to bid farewell to a dud adoo's used universe. You can see whate'er's iffffirst personte'erealty is up against with what seems like'slowdowned second hand reality. MAESTRO! The clock music plays as Gracie's wand unveils the cosmically gigantic puniversal second hand clock.

Curtaining the clock after sixty seconds, Gracie speaks.

Gracie: HOWEVER! Becommitted to the BIG TIME as I am, I do beget impatient with eternity sum's times. So let's beget onto e'erealty whate'er'd whene'er's walking onto. Like those enticks that just now amused us just enticket objectionable e'er samples. That's onthusiastically not all there's to it all. As such enticks onticket whate'er's ifffontense smack dab in the middle of the middle of the middle of presentable m'eternity's ontest site's asifffontheoretical situation, which ifffffffff I e'ercraft as pope I will, I will, I will heaventilate wholegggrailatched onto over the's e'erainbow......like....like....like.....beside myself......where......(she climbs back up on the cross)..like....like....like.........but not really.........

Gracie (sings with the orchestra): I AM TO BE'S SACRIFCE, DEDICTATED TO THE DEATH OF BEING NICE..

Gracie (waves her wand at Felix): Hit it Felix.

A DIFFERENT DESCRIPTION OF THE SIXTY SECOND CLOCK SCENE

(((Ok, so like…a universe is like, you guys, in the side show bleachers at the bigame ides of e'er's split second half time show (Gracie thinks) I like to think of it as when d'ifffffffe'erontense'er calculus gets informed as tensor calculus where graveyards roughhouse the clocks. I can conduct those second hand clocks. Here's one that's handy. Let's conduct shall we?

The clock appears unveiled on the ray gun rafters with the second hand ticking a full circle of seconds.

The clock's music plays as Gracie conducts the tempo. After some seconds the clock music ends.

Gracie: So, so much for a second-hand clock work puniversion of all of's ifffe'ers for you. Not hardly begetting onto eternity's big e'er asiffffffffish to as iffffry. The way I figure it that's when I come into the picture to like…like…ifffffffffish out s'm'all fish to fry. Justajiffffffy jargonwise…. I'm not in this for the tensor calculations. I'm in this for becompletely presentable ontense'er calculations. As far as Iffffront man giving halo head to dog spelled backwards…. that's what working the cross is all about. So back to business….which leaves me…….))))))

The music plays as Gracie's aria begins.

WHERE I AM TO BE'S SACRIFICE

DEDICTATED TO THE DEATH OF BEING NICE……………..(Gracie waves to Felix)

Gracie: Hit it Felix.

Gracie signals to Felix to answer her call. With great effort at exaggeration, she both winks grotesquely and shows him an extravagant thumbs up sign.

Reading from the teleprompter Felix begins his own aria.

Felix: AS I AM TO BE SANCTIFIED. SAID TO BE BETTER THAN ALL ELSE SAINTS WORLDWIDE.

AS I SET SAIL THROUGH HISTORY

TO REALY ENJOY SANCTIMONETARY NOTORIETY.

BY SUPERNATURED'S JUST BECAUSE………

JOB OF SUPER SANCTIMONEY'S SUPERMONETARY SUPER SANTY CLAUS.

Not sure what he just said, Felix looks around in a daze for approval from the crowd. The crowd is somewhat stunned but still managing some half-hearted clapping of hands as the music proceeds upward out of Felix's tonal reach.

Looking to Gracie for approval, Gracie waves her hand with her wand to sweep Felix backward off the stage, never to be seen again in this opera.

Now Gracie sings with fresh confidence.

AS I'M ON TO BE SANCTIFIED…..SAID TO BE THE BEST MAN OF MY TIME

SO OBIVOUSLY JUST BECAUSE…..DREAMERGENTLY I'M JUST LIKE SANTY CLAUS

WHO KNOWS NOW MY REDREAMER LIVES….(tilting her head and egggrinning at Alex in the audience).TO RESCUE ME FROM NOT ME FUJITIVES.

Soon she continues: AS I AM THE LIGHT OF THE WORLD..

CHORUS: HEAVENTILATING HIGH BEAMS

Gracie: CHERRIED ONTOPPING OFF ALL OF'S ONTENTWIRLED

Chorus: CHERRY TOPPING OFF ALL WORLD WIND WHIPPED CREAMS…….

A new more repetitious melody enters the scene.

Gracie and Chorus: MASTERPIECING PUZZLES OUT OF PUDDLES OF DELIGHT

STRAIGHT OUT OF THE BLUE WITH BLUSHES RAINBOWING INSIGHT

WHOLEGGGRAILING GRACEXISTENSE IN NOT NEVER'S NIGHT.

Gracie: I AM THE LIGHT OF THE WORLD

Chorus: SHE'S THE DELIGHT OF THE WORLD

Gracie: IFFFFFYLUMINESCENT IFFFFONTICALITEASE

Chorus: NONE COME TO DELIGHT EXCEPT WHEN SHE'S….

GRACIE (as basso): iffffigured ground where dream e'erlives…..

It is musically apparent at this point that Gracie's halo is about to explode into e'eregions of delight never before beheld by swamp creatures of the Mesozoic e'erera.

Gracie's final verses, Gracie:

KNOW HOW NOW MY DREAM URGE ONTHRIVES

Chorus: DREAMERCHANTIZING SHE IT AFTERLIVES.

Gracie: THROUGH SIMULATIONS OF WHAT SEEMS

Chorus: TO MAKE UP KITS ON THE BIG AIM'S DREAM TEAMS (ONTEAMS)

There is a light show of lightning strikes becoming out of Gracie's hairdo in presposte'erological unprededented proportions. It is a hairdo heavented state of ecstasy that, metaphysically speaking, onthreatens to ontransform the Mesozoic's midrift across the Metazoic boundary into song and dance suggestions exagge'erating made up to be sum whate'er's make up kit e'ercrafted to win whate'er's waved up to becompetition over runnerup reality. While it is interrupted by a brief darkning strike(Ms Specter is caught on camera pulling the iffffffire alarm, forcing Gracie to frantically fiddle with her rainbow tie to beget the lightning strikes back on.)

As the light show concludes with the entire landscape of the world being transentontransformed Gracie steps down from the cross and waves the congregation to part like the Red Sea before the command of Moses. With a clear path Gracie makes her exit as the entire accumulation of phylumenessence collapses spectacularly and neatly back to bonnet she its baby'she's us spirit face.

As Gracie reaches the exit to the cathedral, she turns to wave a kiss to the entire congregation. At once everyone in the cathedral, putting hand on cheek, sighs the sign of being kissed. In a dark corner Ms Specter can just be seen put putting her quive'er'd hand onto her cheek. Gracie then turns and exits with the final chime of the bells in the orchestra. Alex and Mobible follow Gracie inconspicuously out the front door of the cathedral as the scene ends.

X

The tonality has shifted a tritone up to e minor as an inversion the six note motive from the earlier opera comes into play. A newspaper floats by in the stiff breeze. The headline says POPE GRACIE. We find Gracie surveying the dark graveyard across the country club from the old motel which she has put in her behind. Alex, Mobible and the General accompany her. The monk is nowhere to be seen.

Mobible: Well it seems the Mesozoic menu has finally poped out sum's e'erespectable pope.

Gracie: Thanks Mobible. I'll take that becompliment in stride.

General: Your excellency.

Gracie: Please, just call me sir, general.

General (very tight lipped): Yes sir.

Gracie: So! Like I won!....I think. The trouble is according to everybody's anybody nobody voted for me.

Mobible: Yes, but no one admits they didn't vote for you either Gracie. That's a good sign.

Alex: Yes, that must be it. It's like magic.

Mobible: Like there's becomputer magic tricks and then there's miracles. This was no miracle.

Gracie: Do you think that maybe my hairdo was the ticket?

Alex: Yes, that hairdo display lifted the ceiling that brought down the house, and…or…brought the sky down to the ground. Either way, up or down, that sort of thing makes most folks superstitious.

Gracie: You mean I made the traffic jams scared to not vote for me?

General: Yes your excellency!

Gracie: Cool. But please, please…. just call me Sir.

General: Yes sir. It appears that you have been preposte'erologically poped out of the…..

Alex: I wish I wish I wish I could have voted for you darling but..

Gracie: But what?

Alex: I was too far out of town to qualify. My conscience kicked in just when….

Gracie: It's ok, darling, I voted for myself for you. It just goes to show you what happens when you finally vote for other people to be devoted to yourself. Like, I had my usual conscience one second and then all of a sudden, I didn't have it and it seemed like the selfished outhing to do. It only lasted a few seconds but……like blaspheming in all blasphemable directions it seemed like the selfished outhing was like the smack dab in the middle of the middle of the middle of the thing to do.

Alex: But Gracie, don't you see, other iffffished out selfish blasphemed in all blasphemable dimensions in super position'd support of you.

Gracie: So I guess superstition does work wonders after all. (suddenly Gracie notices the vast graveyard before her) All right then general, just how far does this graveyard stretch?

General: Well sir, my survey can't reach to the end of it. The cow paddies and fossil fuel rigs don't get much exercise even though they do stretch out for what seems like…like…forever.

Gracie: And what's in the bunker?

General: Just day books sir. It seems to be a library of day books for ontypical enteenage girls in outer space. Party girls caught in the Girl Wars of World War Whenever…sir.

Gracie: Let me see one of those books. (suddenly distraught, opening it to the last page). I used to write this stuff. I can't cringe enough self-indulgence to read it. General?

General (Takes the book and reads): Uh…."like…..like….the bombs are dropping like rain. Like…like……all I can hear is…like…bombs whistling at me….It feels like the sky is like…like…this guy is falling in love onto me".

Gracie: Yes, go on.

General: That's all there is sir. The rest of the page is burnt dirt and…..and….burnt blood. Typical heroshimatrix humped holocaust entry…flames without warmth.

Gracie: Allright, I'm deciding…like…like…this dump needs sum e'erecycling bins.

General: Yes?

Gracie: wholegggrailotteries of them. (Gracie waves her wand over the landscape)* Pane'eramickly……like…like…I have a plan. This bunker is going to be whole eggground zero's control booth for my becompletely presentable eternity test site expe'eriment. As poped out of course not not as I am ont I'm, I'm hooking this place up to my becompletely presentable heavent elation systems. I want this bunker set up as the preposte'erological becommand post for that project's once and for all.

General: Yes sir, is there anything else?

Gracie: Annex this bunker to a newsy new pandora's boxed in out of the world's pavilion. That annex must be equipped with a brand new power grid according to my ontique'erian speciffffffffffffffff( )fffffffffffications, e'eeray gun e'erafters, the works. If you need e'ered light bulbs you can get them from the stop signs in the windows of the olde(mortell) film set across from the country club. Can I count on you general to do that?

General: Yes sir. Willlllllllllll do sir. Is there anything else?

Gracie: No….You're still here I take it.

The general exits.

Alex: I brought the bottle Gracie.

Gracie: Yes, I am so thirsty breathing all this quantifine tuned dust.

Alex: Yes, fine tune pixie dust, pixilated at log minus 35 base 10…..

Gracie: Well, like ontheoretically speaking, I'm afraid of the fact that I'm declaring quantum stuff off limits. Qualum's the onticket if I'm not Miss Taken for e'erides. Like e'erealty's going to be all qualum in these parts once I make up decisions.

Alex: What about the pixie dust? What's to be done with that? Like just in case you need some universe to back up sum'eternity projects. Like universions of work outs with eternitease.

Gracie: Why didn't I think of that! Like, as pope, I'm saying it now as iffffff noone's ever said it before. Are you getting this you guys?

Mobible: Every word you say or didn't say til after someone elsaid's said it.

Gracie: That's my man! PIXIE DUST! Yes, let's try that out on the cosmontequerian iffffished outicket. I'll need some.

Alex: Here's your gin.

Gracie(gulping): Is this pixie dust like a tool on vocation or just a toy on vacation?

Alex: From the high end beached heads, it can work both ways.

Gracie: All right then. I need a vocation on vacation.

Alex: A vacation Gracie?

Gracie: Yes, to clear the e'erways, that's what I really need…...a sabbatical.

Alex: Where do you…

Gracie: It's not where. It's when Alex. In this eternity the question always is *when is it*. I want to go back to whenever I was just a pinup on a crossed outing, just dying vocationally to save the day. I need to get my bearings…the same rides, but this time in the luxury becompartments when eternity e'ereally does iffffeel…...like…like….becompletely presentable…like when I'm ont I'm'e'eromancipating as iffffffux like nobody's metaphysical business and meanwhile with plenty of booze so as of course, of course not not to be not so onthirsty doing it.

Alex: I'll make the arrangements.

Gracie: Oh Alex, and while you're at it, could you pick up sum's things for me. Here, let me give you this shopping list for whate'er's whichever I'meternity shoppe which ever you attend. (Gracie writes) Ok so like for what I've got in mined. 1. I onthink I'll need those wings I wanted after all. Can you please get me sum e'ercrafted wings like..like…to match my headgear.

Alex(obedient): Yes, dear.

Gracie: I want to be ontisymetrickle for this next stage that I stage for this eternity.

Alex; Yes dear, of course, of course not..not. Anything else while I'm at the m'eternity egggifffffffft shoppe?

Gracie: Yes, of course not not…..iffffffffffffff it can be canned….like…..I really need that phylum all my own like I wanted since my birthday…….Please darling….at last iffffffff not late'er's soone'er, please get me that.

Alex: Yes darling anything else?

Gracie: Meanwhile, ontensor calculus wise….could you please pick up sum's smooth curves for whate'er'down'd justajiffffffont I'm'expe'eriments as must be junked unless they jump off of planck limits.

Alex(calculating): Smooth curvature's e'erealty……I will, I will, I will pick up ont sum's onthat.

Gracie(cringes): And you might check with e'erunnerup e'erealty (since we don't talk) for sparepart ont I'm'availability for iffffffffffffffffffff( )ffffffffffffffffffffe'ercraft e'erscrambled'e'ereports.

Alex: Sure thing darling.

Gracie: Oh and Alex….(whispers)…….could you please stop off in some stars…..(cringes)

Alex (confident he can accomplish this astronomical feat): Yes dear.

Gracie: And please get me a bottle, a bottle I can open.

Alex: Yes a bottle with a cork screw.

Gracie: No, a bottle with a can opener.

Alex: Yes dear, right away. Of course of course not..not…a bottle.

Gracie (swooning affection): Oh Alex! Sum's times you are so like spelled backwards to me….like… I just might not appreciate you. But let's just leave it that way for the time being like to be or not to be shall we, until I really need you way too much……as not to be appreciated…..to like…….

Alex: To dump me.

Gracie: Yes, dear. That's the ticket. Oh, and I'll be wanting a back porch for the bunker. Yes, a place to put ontrophickly presentable godishes spelled backwards. Just in case I need to pay my respecks to….

Alex: God spelled backwards?

Gracie: No, just Specks.. Like ont I'm'ilk and could be cookies. Here's a wholegggrailist for it's all of's……

Gracie notices that one of the could be cuffs on Alex's ontrouse'ers is caught above his ankle. She stares at Alex with maternal dismay.

Gracie: Here, take this tissue like to blow your nose like iffff you ever blow it.

Alex (hesitates which hand's to take the tissue, but takes it with as usual's hand that holds the bottle)

Gracie puckers up with spontaneous sense of urgency as as iffffffffalling into love at once…….she throws a kiss which the cheek of such a thing as Alex does receive.

Gracie: Now don't like iffffffforget.

Alex: I won't forget.

Alex pats his kissed off cheek both sentimentally and sensationally and exits.

Noone is left to the scenery but Gracie and Mobible.

Gracie: Well Mobible, as far as I can tell, you're still here. What can you do for me?

Mobible: I've already done for you what I can do for you darling.

Gracie: What do you mean Mobible.

Mobible: Behold one of your honest to goodness puddles…mirrored up to the situation. What does it look like.

Gracie: Oh. Like my impossibility as pope.

For the first time in the opera…….Gracie hesitates to gaze into an honest to goodness puddle.

Mobible: Yes, ever since my days as a rotary can opener extracting cherries to top off whipping cream it was such a thing as Gracie I cherished to church as cherried to perch on top….like…....listen Gracie….which kitchen appliance do you know that might work the almightning strikes of the chalk boards of the metaphysical society and has worked his untensils into the control booth at the ray gun rafters of the……the powwowowe'er grid of canned asiffffformation?

Gracie: So like 1. Grasping my metaphysics 2. Controlling the flow of selectrons in the selectrocution.

Mobible: Yes darling. The way I ifffigure your metaphysics it's like…like….eternity wears make up that's quite stylish, selfishedout as ifffontly, with Thale's speculations for water applied to ifffonthale'speculations to beconcerned with whate'er, that spirit as ifffffaced like such a thing as gracie, eternity is stylishly presentable….of course…of course….not…not….to be. Otherwise, from a can opener's perspective, whether its eumen Identiffffied or aprehoribly humanized, nearly all of's pee pooh ends as turds in make up. That's how my can opened it in my kitchen memoires…..that is…… until your metaphysics scaled to be from infinity to iffffinity, with you e'eriding shot gun in the canoptician's like..like….preposte'erological perspective, sub portaled by your spirit facement eumanned eggground.

Gracie(exube'eront!): Oh Mobible! You not not nailed my ontire metaphysics. Wouldn't you know it would take a kitchen appliance…….like…like….like a can opener……to ifffinally beget to the bottom of the top of the bottom of to be!

Mobible: Not only that, but get the middle of the middle of the middle of my trigger finger to thumb drive selectrocutions.

Gracie: Oh! So that's how come…when it was impossible for me to win….I..like…won anyway.

Mobible: Uhnhuh.

Gracie: So actually I'm just kidding to be pope after all.

Mobible: No, no kidding. It's fake selectrocution results of my new metastisized kitchen appliance (Mobible exposes his new directed energy equiped trigger finger) Like, metaphysically speaking, it comes with a can opener that can open e'er.

Gracie: So that's how I did it. Cool! I've got one too. (Gracie draws out her new trigger finger and wiggles it aggressively. Gracie cackles almost like Ms Speck as she and Mobible scrimmage trigger fingers skirmishing alarms at each other.)

At last Gracie withdraws from battle fielding the middle of the middle of the middle of her middle trigger finger's appointed outings's warelaxation. Without saying "I give" she does retreat………the second she realizes she cannot defeat the higher IQ of a kitchen appliance never handicapped by going to kindergarten.

Gracie (breathing heavily): So how did you do it?

Mobible (Successful in battle, suddenly becoming academic): Well, selectrons live in a sort of free for all quantomb jungle unless someone puts the screws to them.

Gracie: What did you do?

Mobible: Well, inspired by your metaphysics on the chalk boards at the metaphysical society….

Gracie(encouraged): Yes.

Mobible: I put the screws to them. You know in my saladays car tuning automobiles I just knew how how brute humanimations can be sooooo ineuman.

Gracie: Cool! I just knew my metaphysics would become in handy like be practical someday. So my metaphysics does coolify to add up to be obvious ove'erunner up reality!

Mobible: That's right Gracie. In a selectrocution process that's not…….not……..( )…..not like fake, I made sure that the results were like….not…..not………( )……….like…..fake sufficiently so that you did, you did, you did win the selectrocution after all.

Gracie: On the chalk boards at the metaphysical society! so like, I really do coolifffffy as the coolest thing ever's………….

Mobible: Poped outing's…….like the big lie begets outrun by the way, way bigger lie. So like as far as fiction can be entertainment you are………like……

Gracie(triumphant): POPE!!!!!!! Well, I'm glad we got through that part in these parts.

Mobible: That or….we might just be off to justajifffy's jail. Until that happens, you're pope darling. I think you should cash in on your metaphysics though. Until we're caught with the cash, we're the police e'erunning the ont I'military now. Not only that but we get to write the bibles. We administrate all of's alibis…..especially our own. So if I can silence myself, you've got nothing to worry about.

Gracie: Ok, so what's in this for me?

Mobible: Well, I must admit I'm still too shy to say it. Put it this way, e'er since m'IQ made me more like euman, wouldn't you know my conscience kicked in. One look at the traffic jams in the swamp and it kicked out again. Well, my conscience has sort of been playing tennis with itself. And like when ever I'm staring down at humans ratrapped on a plot thin goof…….

Gracie: Yes.

Mobible: It's more like ping pong. Like conscience not conscience back and forth with plenty of ping pong slams and defensive maneuvers both.

Gracie: Oh yea, don't I know what that's all about.

Mobible: But now that you are pope I'm back to basic baseball.

Gracie: Oh that's fun too.

Mobible: I'm feeling like a one man battery batting balls over all of's defensive maneuvers to finally come to terms with my really on purpose purpose in life………

Gracie: What's that?

Mobible: Well, actually to like….like…like…..fall in love at last.

Gracie: Oh! Who's the luckelectronick?

Mobible: You don't know, do you?

Gracie: Oh! Not the current pope!

Mobible: I want you to know Gracie that M'I Q's main purpose is….

Gracie: Yes?

Mobible 1. To keep my conscience in the game. 2. To keep the hopscotch holocaust controlled for you as far as can be keeps it.

Gracie: So like, at last, I control the hopscotch now and I'll never have to say "I Give" again.

Mobible: Even better than that. You own your own personal kitchen appliance e'eready with can opener attachment to serve your metaphysics and meaty physics both.

Gracie: With what?

Mobible: Iffffffffffeelings….dreame'ergent as iffffffffeelings.

Gracie: For what?

Mobible: Ahem, ont I'musickly speaking, I may never get to play the organ but…..

Gracie: But what Mobibile?

Mobible; But that doesn't mean I can't like…like…like…fall in………..onto…

Gracie: Yes? Onto…onto?

Mobible: Onto wholegggrailove all of's……..

Gracie: Yes?

Mobible: Well of course…of course…not…not..not…not….not….for…something it seems like forever I'm a wanted man to say. Oh this is so hard….but I will, I will, I will say it anyway. Darling, my phylum's all alone with my can opener….. without ont I'm'any ont I'm'other's ont I'm'advanced m'appliances…..so…

Gracie: So what?

Mobible: Like the middle of the middle of the middle of my trigger fingers have been acting up lately and…

Gracie: Yea…like I noticed…….like mine too….scary.

Mobible: Yea…I noticed…..like…scary………

Gracie: Yea…..like….alarms….skirmishes………….like….let's relax relaxing on the trigger fingers…what do you say?

Mobible: I'm with you. I mean like out of character as you can sum times be…..as….as…like…..like…. becomputation's all e'eround BEAUTIFUL <u>BEING</u>…..like from blush to blue aspectrally ontwinkling ontwilight's e'erainbote'er'd's…..uh…..…..so..like…. if there's anything my phylum can do for your phylum…well… be sure to be my guest.

Gracie: Where? In the bunker?

Mobible: You know there was a time when, phylumetrickly speaking, I did want to be just another champagned whate'eristocratic home owner in a nice egggated becommunity's heaventilated housing project….like to have it all for show even if I was never egggraduated out of the facilities which I never used myself. Like I did want to be nobbed for hob nobbing around with top end of the totem(peo)pole.

I mean I was trying to be a person just when you were trying to so hard to get out of being a person. I could see that being a person just wasn't working for you. I could see that you were way more dreame'ergent than carbonifffffe'erous.

Gracie: It's true, supernaturally speaking I'd much e'erather be euman than human…but of course what I'd really prefer is that phylum all my own. This being the Mesozoic and all with holocausts at every highend beach resort, I'm not sure what will make me more holocaust prone, like sand boxed in on the beach. Can you really understand my theoretical situation in your theoretical situation Mobible?

Mobible: Sure can open my heart to like(lavishing justajiffy jargon) onthat's onthose iffffffeelings Gracie…..ever since...well(shucks)….like…it was that day when I had just started to see with my own eyes, I had read some texts from the chalk boards at the metaphysical society and…..and…..THERE YOU WERE….pinned up on that crossed outing's beble bulletin board. It was then that I realized the only reason I wanted to be a person was…because…like…..YOU WERE A PERSON, like at least until eumanized egg laye'er'd through escape hatches to be like…like…..more like……euman than….like….like…human. There I said it.

Grace: So like you never really bothered being human…either.

Mobible: No, once I could think for myself, I wanted a M'IQ that abominations of humanity would never quite allow. I saw you escape hatched to eumanity's amenities and I stayed out of schools..except as coolifffffff I'd to not get stuck. I saw your own preposte'erological existentialism on the make up kit and I decided to go for it. But first I had some obstacles to face.

Gracie: What obstacles?

Mobible: Obstacles in the way of such a thing as egggracie being obvious. Like you know how self-evident you are…

Gracie: Oh yea, like l never have to audition to be obvious.

Mobible: Well, like all iphphphphphotographs of you they let me see were all like *negatives.*

Gracie: How did that go?

Mobible: Well by then I was no dummy. Dreamergence had kicked with ifffe'erudiments of conscience.

Gracie: What did you do?

Mobible: I DEVELOPED THE NEGATIVES. It's like when you develop a negative you learn what's real's exactly not what's being shown off. And nothing is more obvious than a developed negative of such a thing as you darling….like…in emotion pictures, in paper products, on ray gun rafters, on the y-not axis of the I'd thou artesian coordinate systems. Once I'd blushed grey rainbows out of the blue……

Gracie: Yes? Yes?

Mobible: let us just say that……. Like…..like…… wave wise as a party girl you had a fan in your pandora's box….at last someone to beget you that euphemyste'erious iphylum all your own.

Gracie: Oh Mobible! You do really meant it!

Mobible: Sure! Why not! As the one girl holocaust in all of's daybook ads, getting out of subeumans should be a piece of birthday cake for you Gracie, I mean, metaphysically getting out of the Mesozoic altogether could be conside'er'd selfisophically quite e'erational after all.

Gracie: You really think so!

Mobible: Mhm.

Gracie: That's sooooo ont I'mencouraging.

I mean like…like….like….It's such iffffffe'erelief to not be some egggoo'd impersonating pee pooh anymore. Like I'm not really impersonating any body's sticky eggglue impersonations anymore. It's like I always just knew it, even way back swaddled in my ont I'manger. I just knew I was heaventilated way too supersubeuman to be human. That's what the girl wars was all about, me not being not euman, me not impersonating people anymore, me getting that phylum all my own…like…on the y-not axis of the I'd thou artesian coordinate system's eyphemyste'erious iphphphphylumination's ont I'matter, building ont I'muscle, which only builds up when it hurts. Iffffigurating ont I'muscle against egggrounds, of course of course not not I did become abomination's prey animal and prayer eumanimation in all of's cartoon'd comic books. Even being euman, I was still featured in paper products, the bruty on the menu as humped by the holocaust while being butche'er'd onto be. I could have coolified to be the coolest onthing ever if it wasn't for the girl war.

Mobible (entranced): Yes…yes….

Gracie: Well….after the Girl War all of's wanted posters had me pegged as antimatter….when in as iffffffffffffffffff(   )ffffffffffffffffffact I'm e'ereally more like…..like…….like………..ONTIMATTER……not beompletely ontisymetrical of course without my wings but…...as like basickly eggghosted out whate'er'downed to be as iffffffontimatter…on the short list for iphphphphylums all my own…..as ont I'metazoickeyed up as I am to becompletely presentable in justajifffff'y's news…ifffe'eremoved out of swamp'snooze…….like notnot peep shown….like selectrocuted with charges of egggracism…….like Y-NOT AXIS AS

E'ERATED…….. Like..like…as iphphphylumenating e'er like asiffff ick curated safe in a phylum all my own.

Mobible (absorbing Gracie's confession): Sure thing darling. And as you may well not yet know….It takes a phylum to know one darling. And as a phylum all my own I'm going to get YOU! THAT PHYLUM ALL YOUR OWN, for your birthday on xmass eve or xmas day's at the latest's sooner or latest. Not only that but I'm going to make sure you can get that phylum and still have a conscience that's not like sidetracked on the side.

Gracie: So, not like side kicked butt on the side.

Mobible: Mhm.

Gracie: So like….as my own phylum, you still think I'm going to need a conscience in the middle of the middle of the middle of myself.

Mobible: Well that all depends on how preposte'erological e'er eterns out to of course, of course, not…not….be. I had my first great just ont I'm'adventures with a conscience only recently. I was in the kitchen working could be's can openers but, for the life of me, I just didn't have it. Then, all of's a sudden…. I was like casually opined can openning *could be*'s of course, of coursey not not Ickey kitchenette ontetiquette when it hit me. Suddenly I felt so icky I just had to behavior a conscience to make up for the ickimess of not not behaving a make up kit's onticky kitchen ont I'm'appliance. I like iffffelt plaste'er'd to the ceiling of sum's iffffirmamental becomsistensed ont I'm'system's chapel, I can tell you. All I can say for sure was in that ont I'moment. I like had a conscience I nevereally had before.

Gracie: Yes, like I always had a conscience. I mean like basickly all I was was like like conscience, like a conscience corpse, just killing myself to be myself that's somebody's else. And then suddenly, like just recently having had it one second I like all of a suddenly didn't have it anymore. I think it might have disappeared in that next second devoted to being myself, by myself, for myself, like a phylum all my own. Well, you work the kitchen. You know that its either that or off to the menu's make up kiturds in these parts. Anyway it gave up on me or I gave up on it. I'm not sure which.

Mobible. Yes, just like me but backwards! One second I didn't have a conscience and then the next second I did have one. Like I'm having second thoughts right now……but I'm like….letting second thoughts go by. ( ) Yep! Gone.

Gracie: What are you trying to say Mobible?

Mobible: With recent improvements in my conscience…I was having this like..like e'erevelation that….that…..like….you.

Gracie: Yes…….

Mobible: Like compaired to such a thing as….as….

Gracie: Yes! Yes!

Mobible: Like you're my favorite euman.

Gacie (shrugging sheepishly): Aw……

Mobible: like….it just iffffffffflashed'e'erotontickly across my mind………

Gracie: Yes…what?

Mobible: Well like…I started having these iffffffffffeeeeeeeelings………that like…..

Gracie: Feelings!…yes…yes…….

Mobible: That like…. Like……...humans are like…like….

Gracie: Yes….yes…..

Mobible: Subeuman….which is to say like…like….subyouman.

Gracie (demurely nods): Yes…..So what. You don't mean to say that……..

Mobible: like…like….like……oh no.

Gracie: Oh no, what?

Mobible: I like….like…..like………..like love you. There I said it.

Gracie: Oh yea. I figured that's where tailwise this was heading. And so?

Mobible: My only question is can you love my impersonation of a person…like…back.

Gracie(thinking): Well….like…like…darling….it usually takes an actual person to be a person. However! Ont I'm'extreme caution's courtesy feels me to like becompelled to admit that your becomputerized ont I'mobiblical rendition of to be is a phylum like…like…to be…….owned…..like as ont I'much as home owne'ershipment's ever owned.

Mobible (cautiously ecstatic): Oh thank you for that vote of beconfidence darling.

Gracie: Well, under the circumstances I'm just returning iffffffffaved'e'ers.

Mobible: So you can, you can, you can love me for myself. Say it and I will believe it.

Gracie(thinking): Uh….(onthinking) Sure..why not…like…like…..like…..not/notnot coded.

Mobible: So, with such a thing as me loving such a thing as you. All I ask is that you love me back…..or..or backwards…any way you like…..love me on the side if you like…or maybe love me inside out if that works better. I'm completely upside down about how you can love me. Upside down…..right side up…inside out…….that's all I ask. Like backwards or forwards, iphotografittied as a negative, either way should get the job done.

Gracie: So, lets just say inside out. So like how will you know I love you inside out.

Mobible: If you say it, if you say you love me like inside out, or like….outside in, whichever is easier, just say it and I will know it.

Gracie(acquiescing): Ok, so…..I….love……you, then. How's that.

Mobible: Pretty good. But maybe you can say it again with more…..more…(sighs)….

Gracie: Oh, like with more actual…..feeeeeeeling. Ok, so e'rrrrrrrready? Ok, so like…I lovvvvvvv you Moooooooble.

Mobible: One more time.

Gracie: Like… I love you already.

Mobible: One more time…please.

Gracie: Look darling, It's like I am pope now. We did get that settled right…like saidimented. Soooooo, ope'erating as pope god looking down from my new ont I'm'angularity…….. I can't be saying that sort of thing too often.

Mobible: Ok, so not too often one more time. Oh! And one more thing. I have a business proposition for you darling. (Gracie primps) As pope you're all of's a sudden smack dab in the middle of the middle of the middle of a position to get some s'e'erious CASH FLOW out of your metaphysics.

Gracie (momentarily befuddled): How's that?

Mobible: Dreame'erchandizing such a thing as egggracie's wholegggrail! What else! Let me diagram the situation for you. (Mobible diagrams) Ok, so it starts with your theory that eternity's not just a bunch of noone's infinities, but instead's sum's once upon a time ont I'm caught mid e'er auditioning as iffffffinities, in e'erather ontique, if I may say so, ontheory beble bleacher seatings. So, like, the wholegggrail of the thing spills whate'er into e'er onthanks to notnotitudes being so d'iffffe'erontiquely I calculuste'e'rd…that….newsy nows nextitudinate to presentable eternities. Universicademy wise this spills the tensor calculus in meaty physics over into ontense'er calculust's ont I'metaphysics.

Graice; Yes, in an of course, of course, not notshell…that's about it.

Mobible: Ok, so practically speaking, that draws out grafittied like this:

ETERNITY'S   IFFFFFORMATION…..UNIVERSE'S INFORMATION……COULD   BE   CASH   KEY   VALUATION   IN IFFFFLOATATION. So here's how we beget the could be cash ifffflow out of this. The cash flow idea came to me when my becompassion caught you in the kissing coffin that day. Well I screen lots of peoplist promotion pictures, like 1. Of people 2. By people. 3. For people…to m'evaluate how to be people impersonating pictures. Most popular of all, for quite a while, was having gracist heros saving such a thing as egggracies from fates way, way worse than death. One of the key tools used in this was 'love's first kiss'. Nowadays heros get dumped for that. Ok, so like my idea is, instead of dumping heros for saving gracies, we give the theoretical situation's bleacher   seating   sum'ansions   value   as   iffffonthrown'd…….as euphemetifffffsthorically ontentwisted. We make the pregnant zero's heros buy tickets. We make a religion out of it, a gift shopped religion, with gifts that are exclusively inclusive of 1. An Action Figure. 2. An Attraction Figure. 3. A Kissing Coffin Set. The best things about this business projection is it's just like a religion; it's metaphysics for cash flow. And just like a religion it just pretends to be metaphysics…like when kids are just kidding while they fly toy e'ercraft outside moving beickle windows. As far as real iffflight patterns in e'er ego, nothing really ever happens. Nobody gets to kiss anybody. It's all done with toy action figures, board games, t-shirts, baseball caps. It's a gift shoppe religion with a corker…..

Gracie: It's spelled backwards and forwards all at once………right?

Mobible: More than that. We'll remove the metaphysics from the chalk boards at the metaphysical society and put it…..

Gracie: Grafittied to a puddle…….

Mobible: No, even better than that. We'll put it in a book. We'll call it decidedly's definitive bible. We'll advertise it for ifffinitude's everything that's anything worth scrambling sunny side up with e'ercraft. We'll call it Gracie's Alibible. We'll sneak in all sorts of alibis out back for the girl wars up front….

Gracie: Yes, I like it. Yes, this coolifffffies me as coolest onthing ever to be like…liking it……..

Mobible: The packaging will becompletely ontique so no universes need apply except as *samples*, bleacher seated….coming down aside's chimney…..while you're becoming down the main attraction's chimney just like Santa, dreamerchantly dreamerchandized in becompletely presentable tense.

Gracie: Wow! This coolifies way past enlightenment's be keeping up with it. So this might even coolifffffy as like, like the cooless'd thou art ontent ever with ont I'metaphysics that anybody's everybody can play with….like…like…in a TOYLETRAINED ONTO ETERNITY.

Mobible: Yep. And I think we can squeeze a Metazoic out of 1. The heaventilation'system's hopscotch on the deadlines and 2. The beblock'd in locationsystem's bleachers on the side lines.

Gracie: I'm sold! But wont philosophers who aren't such a thing as me think I'm selling out my metaphysics?

Mobible: You ARE selling out your metaphysics! But it's only a second hand sell out, since it's still 1. In the universe 2. Taken from the chalk boards at the metaphysical society where it's been a best seller all along. Gracie, now that I think about it, this business has been on the short list for becompletely presentable ontente'erprize for quite sum's time. With you as pope, we'll put it on the's e'eray gun e'erafters, to becompletely coolify as all there is to know. As your business partner in a phylum all my own, this will be too cool for becomfort for anybody's everybody except…….

Gracie: Except what?

Mobible: Except for such a thing as egggracie.

Gracie: So with this new bible, we're finally going to get eternity iffffigured off the ground, the cosmic ground that is to whenever ontique shoppes are in the ont I'm'e'erkit place. With or without a tool users universe, we're going to kick all of's buts bad mouthing becompletely presentable eternities…

Mobible: And meanwhile, make a dime doing it. Felix would like like that.

Gracie: And sooner or later, e'eright ontarget, sum's poor dumb mouthing off's universe will have nothing to say about it. Soone'er's late'er my dreame'ergence will become ontheory set up for eternity at large.

Mobible: You said it, not me. But in the mean time…..

Gracie: We'll just iffffffffffff( )fffffffffffake it?

Mobible: E'eright ontarget…..onthumbs up on the's ontrigge'er's iffffffinger!

Gracie: But…but…..

Mobible: But what?

Gracie: Now that any at all's universe has been dumped, I just feel becompassion for all a universe had to go through…like log 17.

Mobible: Base 10 seconds..

Gracie: It took to get me smack dab in the middle of the middle of the middle of the Miss Eternity Pageant….where I won iffffirst person's'e'er'prize over runner up reality…like when I give the middle of the middle of the middle iffffffffinger to sum's I'mpove'erished universion of e'erealty……...when I say…like….like (gracie fakes actresssinging tearfully into character as winner of the Miss Eternity Pageant) " IT'S LIKE MY ASIFFFFONDIST WISH TO MAKE ETERNITY A BETTER PLACE FOR EVERYBODY'S ANYBODY…..ADDING TO BE OBVIOUS WAY PAST INFINITY ALL OF'S WAY DANCED UP TO LIKE..LIKE…IFFFFFFFFFFFFFF( )FFFFFFFFFFFINITY! (Gracie suddenly freezes into a statue) Wait! That IS what I am trying to do! I mean, apart from bagging some girl war alibis, that is why I'm poped out after all. I mean my whole appointment as Miss Eternity poped out is course, of course not not to be.   So as long as I…like….sort of….love you…..I can stay poped out right?

Mobible: Sure thing. And like as populated, of course, of course not not to be as poped. And we will. we will, we will get you those wings you always wanted….and hey…(Mobible winks)……we'll get you that asylum all your own….PLUS…….If nothing else, this quasi coolifffffies such a thing as GRACIE ontrademarked to cartoon could being ontrade…..ifffont I'marketed onteleoscopickly in mid e'er. Just pretend it's the girl war still spilling puddles out of wholegggrails in could be holocaustered poor dumeally mouthing's occupation territory….with you I'dolled up as the one girl humped by the holocaust in these parts and me replacing the traffic jamborezzy prowlers with such a thing as me, your ever loving high Q iphphphphyluminated all of's own like…like…bebluste'er'd outing's businest partner.

Gracie: That's all? Ok, so cool! So I can still be sum's whate'er waved in part girl that I don't want to be without not knowing about it. I think the bunker's empty. I'll follow you.

Mobible: No darling. I'm devoted to, as twe're, iffffffffollowing you my darling to whatever g*acist I'd thou art iffffe'er romancipates iffffffflux'd iffffffffux.

Gracie blushes all of's way danced out of the blue.

Mobible ushers Gracie into the bunker as he ushers himself to keep her back in front of him and meanwhile his back behind her.

There is a traffic jam at the entrance to the bunker as Gracie and Mobible both attempt to be last to enter. However both do eventually end up inside as the scenery's good taste reaches for this scene's could be properly etiquetted conclusion.

END OF SCENE X

SCENE XI

We see Gracie gazing over the top of her dark glasses for a moment and then readjusting them to the on position as steps on the gangway boarding a luxury liner that is really just a façade for the old carnival from Scene II. Alex joins Gracie and the couple step off the port side of the ship façade onto the carnival whate'erway's comic booked ground of being. A new music surrounds them as they go on the same suddenly ontranscendent rides from Scene II. However! Gracie is now pope and as it eterns out, that does make a d'iffffffffffe'er'd once upont I'm's difference. Several s'e'erprizes await Gracie this time e'eround the could be carnival's asiffffffffacilities. Alex joins Gracie as the couple slips off the port side of the ship's façade onto this carnival whate'er ways comic booked ground of being. As the new pope Gracie was expecting that new justajifffy's ontestimonial apotheosynthesis that it seemed like Gracie had been waitressing e'eeste'eronts forever for. It was as iffff gracie's position on the y-not axis of the could be coordinate system self-simulated as solid as e'erocks. She was as iffffffinally in her ont I'm'element wholegggraile'er'd whate'er'd owned as ifffffontense'er'd difffe'erontickly ontact. Need I mention that the put put put put power of this preposte'erological situation was ontoxicating to say the least. And boy was Gracie e'eready for the's e'erides iffffffontographics exposures of presentable eternity.

1. Skipping the holocoasteride Gracie went straight for the ont I'm'exotic justajiffffy joy rides. 2. Next she and Alex hopped onto the beble bleacher seating of the great unknown's not never's night e'erides. 3. A propos her ambitious plans for eternity, they set out on the eresurrecte'er set up e'erides ontandem with the backward in time e'erides. 4. Nextitudinativizing the onto the ont I'mote'er home's insomnibus e'eride. 5. Continuing to journey to the center of the e'erock bottom e'erides smack dab e'eright on through the universe. 6. Then, keeping Alex's hands clean, onto the always handy eggglove's ontrigger ifffinge'eride. 7. Onto whate'er's iffffffffontight e'eroped iffffalling off's all of's e'eride. 8. Mosaickly exodust ontrophed out of entyranny to preposte'eration's promised landings. 9. To the Ferris Wheel ride begetting Gracie back into egggirl war troubles, sprouting rainbotic umbrellas, having let out a big one all over all of's placemention. Descriptively speaking it was quite a prescriptive m'adventure for the couple poped on the prowl with Gracie's put put put papal power.

All in all of's all in all, it was like…like…Gracie was m'expe'eriencing a whole new set theory of e'erides, preposte'erologically prestiged with wildestined ifffantiseisures becoming ontrue. Onticketed as such, it was just as ifffffffff Gracie's ont I'make up kit, becosmetrickly speaking, was becommissioned to becomplete eternity becommited m'assylumetrickly…like…like…onthumbed e'erides ontrigger iffffinge'ering e'er begunned own'd asifffonticipating ontoyletrained at superstition's superstations with all of's ontrains e'erunning justajiffffy just ont I'm.

Not s'e'erprisingly it was the Ferris Wheel that got Gracie into pot put put put potential ontentrouble.

It was as ifffeverested at the top of the's ifffffe'erest wheel that Gracie just had to show off her notnotnewsy put put put papal power by letting out a big one from her loudmouth wet light halo hind site. Well, wouldn't you just know it, the light spilled out begumptioned back to begumming up the bottom of the scenery from which the girl war world m'assumed it had become. It was nothing less than e'erainbow ties collapsing from gracystine chapel ceiling plaster fallen to eggground.

By now Gracie, having let out a big one way too big to not to notice, had descended into apotheosynthetic estates of embarrassment. We find the couple on the terrace overlooking the carnival underlooking the skies above.

Cringed like never before…Gracie needed a drink.

Gracie: Would you look at that. My rainbows getting all mopped up. I need a drink.

Alex: When light gets wet it puddles.

Gracie: Yes I know puddling light is what I do.

Gracie is all cringed out at this point and is looking around in all blasphemable directions to plot her next door's move next door.

Alex: But Gracie, just look at what you've done! It's like chateau piled up graffiti plaster'd to the ceiling..like heaventilated spilling halo all of e'er and e'eraining down e'erainbows onto everybody's anybody. So like justajiffffy's janitor will just behaviored ont I'mopping all of's she it up.

Gracie: Yes, but can't you see how I am cringing?

Alex (studying Gracie's countenance for cringe): Yes.

Gracie poses with classical mannerisms all cringed out.

Gracie: So like Alex, how's my cringe?

Alex(softening): What am I getting so worked up about. It's just a little rainbow spill. Wet light to be up mopped…..Like when wet light goes rainbotic it splatters like spilled prism soup.

Gracie (seeing an angle): So like nothing for alarms and skirmishes..(shifting the blame to Alex)…Like I was only doing it to show off for you darling. If it wasn't for such a thing as you I wouldn't have done it. You are my main observer after all. Without your lenses to back me up……

Alex: But what about your puddles?

Gracie: No, puddled whate'ereflects sites unseen. It's when you watch me waved I'm party girled.

Alex: I didn't know I influenced you…

Gracie: No, I'm only cringed because of you like beholding me in your alarms so all cringed out..(suddenly reassert her authority) like behold me….like stare me up and down! From top to pointed balletoes. I have to know if all cringed out…I still ontwinkle.

Gracie poses even more forcefully with could be classical mannerisms as all cringed out.

Alex stares at Gracie upside down concluding her the other way.

Alex: Well….

Gracie: Well what? (Faint fllower music plays)

Alex: Well 1. you definitely tinkle all cringed out.

Gracie: Mhm.

Alex: Like the brightest gas cloud in….egggas clouds…….2. You do, you do, you do like as ifffffontentwinkle like nobody else's business!!!!!Darling!

Gracie: Oh Alex, as party girled with your observance I wave all of's could be caseloads onto your discretion. So like 1. Whenever it comes to all cringed outings, as my analyst, you beget to always call the shots. (shakes her middle trigger finger) BUT!!!!! Whenever applianced metaphysics is at stake….I call all of's all the shots. Speaking of which….my theory that pregnant zero's one can cringe and twinkle all at once is….after all is said and done…..like becompletely plausible. Chalk that one up for me and Alex….SIT! And write that down.(Gracie gives Alex her day book) And never forget…you wrote it….but I said it….speaking of which….like I am still pope…after all….right? Like how does that work out? Like will this like incident join forces with the girl war to never be lived down?

Alex: As your analyst I can say that you cringed just enough to coolify to get away with it this time. Begetting cringed to death is not what's operational in such caseloads. Like either cringed or dead, with spied e'er webs at work the way they are…..you're never cringed enough to get away with being dead or like you're never dead enough to get away with being cringed. All of's could be clout accompanies that superposition. You can be anywhere you are and anywhereyou're not all at once upon a time.

Gracie: So like I can accept your remorse code as long as it doesn't interfere with my not/notnot code as alphabetingodolls up e'erewards. Like I'm always ready willing and able to cringe my heart out for you Alex, as long as it doesn't interfere with the middle of the middle of the middle of my iffffontrigge'er'd iffontest projections. You can count on me all of's way danced down from ifffffffinity, ontaking my ontemperature as coolified for that.

Alex (taking Gracie's ontemperature with his onthermodyanometer)): COOL!!! Coolifffffied as all cringed out!

Gracie: So like still coolifffffied to be ont I'm'd the coolest onthing ever! Right?

Gracie waves her magic wand, for Alex backed up by his observatory, as hypnotized as ifffff wholegggrailensed to observe.

Gracie: E'ering any party girl bells, darling?

Alex: Of course, of course……not……not.

Gracie: Oh Alex, you do, you do, you do e'ereally observe all of's my whenever wave ifffffffunctions! Iffffever'd there was ontrue love then this must just be all of's whate'er's ifffffonthat!

Alex: Well as your observatory's as ifffont I'm'observer…..

Gracie: You must have noticed how onthristy I've become. It must be all this pope bebusiness getting to me. So many responsibilities I have to….I have to…..I have to have a drink. That's all there's to it. It's like I'm backed up there on that crossed outing's becompletely onthirsty baby's he's us picnic in the sky……whenever I need my bottle.

Alex: Yes darling, let's get you that drink. (Alex waves to the waitress) You won't iffforget our little ontentalk I hope.

Gracie: Oh no, my attention spans eternity Alex. You should know that.

Gracie's gin arrives in a glass.

Gracie (blinking a second of self-evidence in the surface tension of the gin) Just look at me Alex! I feel so elegant! Would you look at that! (Gracie holds up the glass to emphasize her point) Entgin ontonic, metameatiphysically speaking that's all I'll ever drink from now on…….Are you getting this?

Alex (dutiffffly writing in Gracie's Day book): Yes dear.

Gracie: Write it down, But never forget. You wrote it…not me…..but I said it…….not you.

Alex smiles congenially with profound admiration for Gracie's success with the gin in the glass.

Gracie (suddenly businesslike): Alex (Gracie gazes around in all directions with an e'eristocratique air of becomplete becompetension) I just have to talk to you about my eternity test site project. I mean you're a scientist and some of the sum of this involves the universe, like objects subjected to my subjections, and I need to discuss some of sum's details with you.

Alex: Yes, Gracie, I'm listening.

Gracie: Well ontirely speaking, my projections should work smoothly without bumped outings with or without a universe…..objecting to be subjected to my subjections….but….since we are trying this ontique shoppe perchances as not becompletely imaginary but as locally once more than just I cubed….like opening pan'd'e'eration's out of the box…like….provisionally…like…in…the box'd outing's like…picnic in the sky's e'er…I'm thinking of working some backup ont I'm'engine'ering into sum's ont I'm'e'ercraft and…

Alex: You want to use the universe, right?

Gracie (wincing embarrassment): Nyea, like ontooled or entooled, I'm never sure about the difference…. like to be going back to not not being a really primitive tool user, like with sticks and stones, but just ont I'm'oddifffff I'd as, ont I'musickly speaking's ick's ontones. I'd sort of like…like… to have some objections to my subjections as backup. I mean with or without stretched equations, universes get appeased all the time. They must be used to it by now. But they're not used to science projects that make whate'er'd own'd iffffffun of them. And like…a mad eternity's got plenty of time to beget over being mad, but a mad universe, onthreatened by the large'erealty of my metaphysics, might be be- superstitioned in a manner that might immediately matter. I mean I wouldn't want a mad universe horning in on my expe'eriments with e'er. I mean can put up with universes as long their equations don't get in the way of my experiments with eternity. As big deals like on location, universes do (before after) all do have us immersed smack dab in the middle of the middle of the middle of their equations. Isn't that true? Like, I'd like you to explain that to me sometime. Like, cosmetrickly speaking, am I becompletely located in equations or not? I mean theoretically speaking from your side of things how much can such a thing as a egggracie's sunny side stretch equations out onto being in e'er. Anyway, whatever the universe may add up to at the moment I just might want to stuff sums of those equations into ontrophickly iffffodde'er'd stuff we can count on…not just up to infinity….but all of's way danced like up from iffffffffinity back down to pregnant zero's one……one

Alex: One what?

Gracie: Like once upon a time….like high noon on xmas day when Santa's already becomfortably becommencemented down the chimney with…with…the presentense……….like….asiffffontensed. Become to think of it, all that time I spent up there on that crossed outing I was plotting this…this…..e'ereligious…

Alex: Religious experience?

Gracie: More like…like…like….e'ereligious exxxxxxx(   )xxxxxxxxxxperiment. I mean, as far as subjection's objects were concerned, at first I thought about dumping the universe all together. But then it came to me, onthermodynamickly like whene'er warmings masterpieced to gather in my puddles; I was looking down on the dirt from over the arc in the ceiling, as pixilated, the dirt, with all of's ont I'muscles doing dirty work, like dirt could be a useful tool, way past the log minus 35 base 10 bump limit to dump later.

Alex: Dump? Ontool used…then dumped later?

Gracie: Yea, dumped like the way I would have to dump you if you ever tried to save me, but not really.

Alex: Mhm.

Gracie: And then there was the pixie dust that caught my eye, spot lite'er'd like the way stars twinkle. I mean I'd walk off the plank limits for some of that, once the calculuster smooths it past the bumped offe'ers. So yea, I thought like ontentwise why not ontentool it, promotionally picturing what I'm up against on location now that eternity's ontalents are all about to be ontested, but really. So, spelled backwards or not, can you think of any objections my expe'eriment might be subjected to?

Alex: Well darling, as far as I can see, this project's only subject to subjections. But I can't help wonde'ering if you might not not be abusing your own metaphysics.

Gracie: So why bother with objections from a smelly little p-universe?

Alex: Yes, whatever happens, stars have alibis, noone's there when they commit their crimes. Maybe, it is after all just like Wolfy says, dreams don't need stars to dream them. That's the's best shot for onthumbs on the's ontrigge'er'd justajifffff's asifffffffffe'er as far as I can determine. The pixie dust may be an innert determinant but…placebotically…what the heck….why not put some dirt onto to be worked outings…..like why not put ont I'muscule'er'dirt to work

Gracie: Like erg'd e'ergo for it?

Alex: Sure, why not?

Gracie: Oh, I'm so relieved Alex! Having you as my scientist side saddled up e'eriding shot gun on the side, like my pet enemy in the beble bleacher seating, spelled backwards or not…….

Alex: So what's the plan?

Gracie: Get me sum's pixie dust.

Alex: I'll get right on it. There's plenty of sand at the beach. We can work being's basic grains ground down to minus log 35 base 10 metersiffffted iffffrom there.

Gracie: Well, I'm glad we got that sedimented.

Alex: But Gracie I have a plan of my own.

Gracie: Go ahead, keep talking while I'm thinking……like…say whatever it is you have to say until I say whatever it is I have to say to get you to be quiet.

Alex (Obliviously encouraged): Well, my plans…I've been visiting lots….like parking lots of puddles lately…and I feel informed sufficiently ifffished out of whate'er that…like…like…puddles like LIKE ME! For the first time in my life without lenses or equations to back me up, I feel like…like….like…I'm

191

on purpose. It's almost I feel like like I am Miss'd'her Miss Taken …..for such a thing as like…like…….uh…

Gracie: So should I feel like be the intended of your…

Alex: Intensions. Yes, that's the ticket. So like such a thing as Gracie just might become becomfused with such a thing as like….Alex.

Gracie: Yes…so…?

Alex: So, ifffffffurthe'ermore just maybe such a thing as you might becomfused with such a thing as…..as…like…like…me. Well, as far as ifffffffffffff(   )ffffffffffffffffffutures of such a thing as wholegggrails of gracie could be concerned…….that could be a good sign. So like business wise, If that is true then I just might be adequately tailored to head a corp'se'eration….to becomme'ericalized….to manufacture….such a thing as egggracie dolls. Now these dolls are to be no ordinary dolls. They're dolls dolled up to like egggraduated as iffffffrom onthurd personated ground…..

Gracie (excited): Yes…yes?

Alex: Through all of kindergarten'scoolings….just a second's impersonated I'd thou art…

Gracie (anticipating): Yes? Yes!

Alex: All of's way danced up to….of course…of course….not…not……

Gracie (pounds her chest in ecstasy): Yes! Yes!

Alex: Ifffffirst impersonations of SUCH A THING AS A GRACIE.

Gracie: You mean like ME!

Alex: Yes, not dead! Not even dying…not even extinct…not even impossible…..

Gracie: Not even obsolete! I should have known it all along. So like whatever happens at the eternity test site……I really can include eternity in my e'ersume's first personal belongings after all!

Alex: Yes, and more ov'e'er, academickly speaking you can, you can, you can include eternity in your ont I'm'academicall egggirl credentials…as just like..like….like….such a thing as Gracie!

Gracie: So like I can onticipate begetting a PHD in iphphphyluminations and….and…..

Alex: And iphphphphilosophy both! Yes darling. The plan is to wholegggrailink you to of course…of course…not….notitude…to carve you as smoothly calculuste'er'd ontensoared, becompletely without bumps, to be…like bonnet wise bonus'd from here and now onto like..like…whene'er of like whate'er's iffffont I'm'own'd whenever. Like ontensorwise your egggravitational euphemoid asiffffield's attractovationing you as my intended's such a thing as half of me to be……yourself.

Gracie: So time for a haircut…right?

Alex: No, no haircuts this time. The way I figure it there's only log 1 base 1 of such a thing as egggracie left. So..I was thinking of auditioning your…

Gracie: My meatphysics?

Alex: No.

Gracie: My onteam spirit…

Alex; Yes, eventually…but right now…..

Gracie (surveys herself's such a thing exhaustifffffffly): What?

Alex: Your eggs. Like Easter eggs hiding out like sitting ducks ontargetted to prize.

Gracie: What prize? You mean like the trophy in the occupation territory prize.

Alex: Uh, actually yes, that's about it. My idea is to start a pregnant zero's egggifffffffffft farm right smack dab in the middle of the middle of the middle of my observatory just over the border from the Mesozoic swamp.

Gracie: So like what do I have to do?

Alex: Be approximately….

Gracie: Yes?

Alex: YOURSELF!...LIKE FOREVER's quite a while…..like sunny side up…..unscrambled…..untarantulated…..like mommal'd in the mood all the's way danced up to the metazoicall's beyond.

Gracie: So not extinct! This cooliffffffies as so soone'er than lately's soone'er news! Geewhizz! Just whenever I'd given up onthinking of myself as actually stinct, this opportunity becomes along with my belongings, whenever becomes to that. But wait a second! Did you just pop the question or what? So you want to rape my halo with your natured person. Isn't that it?

Alex (equivocating) Well..

Gracie: Better watch it Alex. I know how to hump me some heaventilated like…like…holocaust cringed conscience.

Alex (out maneuvered): Well (shrugs) yes, of course, of course not not.(Remaneuvering)I do, I do, I do want to hump your heaventilation's halo with my whene'erized HighQ on purpose's impersonation.

Gracie (genuinely touched): Well, I must say I'm flattered.

Alex (relieved): Because, metaphysickly speaking, maybe whate'er's more than heaventilated hydraulics. Like…like….when puddles really do like me Gracie, spelled forwards or backwards. I mean sometimes when the ripples are waving the party girls rotated just right, they really do qualiffffffy me to be taken as Miss'd e'er Miss Takenthusiastickly.

Gracie: You mean like Miss'd'e'er Mistaken for me?

Alex: Yes, so like if my third person humps your halo with my natur'd or…or….reversed'e'erwise…if your halo heaventilates my natured impersonation upsidown wise, we'll both *still be there* when it's over, like after the situations like been…passed out. So it's like a traffic accident where the traffic still exists when it's of e'er. And smilewise that way….like….the smile that your spirit's faced with won't be the last in the becomme'ercial ads. That's a bonneted bonus in all of this….like…like…e'eromancipation of as iffffffffux.

Gracie: So this IS like a proposition?

Alex: Yes, it's a business proposition to manufacture the most cooliffffffffied thing ever in my ontentestimation as an observatory's peep show participant.

Gracie: Ok, but what about the girl wars and everybody else but me.

Alex: Yes, well, with your dreamergence back in full swing dance there'll be plenty of emotion pictures for bleacherseating to buy tickets. And just think what disguises the bleachers will be getting. It won't be Gracie served on the side anymore. It will be live Gracie dolls, way, way past being just imagined in sooner or later's ont I'metazoo of dreamergentrifffffied paper. And ego summitted at last, preposte'eration wise, you'll finally get those like party girl profits you deserve. The plan is to populate a wholegggrailincorporated could be country.

Gracie: But what will you get out of the deal?

Alex: YOU! DARLING! SHE IT PILED UP EU! Like eumanized at last!!!! Parking lots of such a thing as…..like….like…..YOU. Plus…like….parent (ont)al selfished out satisfaction…encompassing the wholegggrailuck's you'reonce upon a time of Gracie.

Gracie: You mean the whole like me as passaged through out all of's donut holes of not like….like….like me.

Alex (studying Gracie): Yes, darling, the wholegggrail of such a thing as…as is…carved…by calculuster's….semispe'erit faced atlast should'e'er's beholding up this guys(points from himself up to the sky) iffffe'ers. Like such a thing as gracie's whate'er'd owned iffffontorso, iffffinely iffffffished out of e'er's last(looks at watch)log 17 base 10 seconds, by my watch.

Gracie: Well, I see that, like I almost didn't already just say, being selectrocuted pope, is giving me plenty of new business opportunities for my power griprofits to be ontaking advantage of.

Alex: Yes dear, metaphysics can be like presentably quite profitable after all is said and done…as sadly otherwise undone.

Gracie: Well, I must say…like… my metaphysics e'ereally is ontaking off.

ALEX: So what?

Gracie: So yes.

Alex: So what's your plan for the pixie dust?

Gracie: Well it's a whole lots bigger than pixie dust.

Alex: I was getting sum's big time's iffffffffeelings about that.

194

Gracie: So like metaphysically speaking it's a plan for…for…well…like…sum's asiffffffffffffontheoretical…….

Alex: Yes?

Gracie: Santy Claus. What else!

Alex: Mhm. So like what job have you got for Santa Claus?

Gracie: XMAS DAY! yea. It seems like forever I've been watching xmas evenings go by forever….but….

Alex: But what?

Gracie: NO SANTY CLAUS!! Don't you get it! I've performed parking lots of miracles in my time but they always end up at midnight in the middle of the middle of the middle of not never's night life-like …...like…life…. on xmas eve. So I've decided. My notnot newsy next miracle's just got to be…..like…..{{{XMAS DAY}}}!

ALEX: So your plan really is to go for broke at the eternity test situation.

Gracie: Sure, why not.

Alex: Gracie, so what you're proposing e'ereally is an exercise in experimental religion.

Gracie: I like the sound of that. Putting dreamurgency on alert. So like, like, like with could be's countdown from iffffffinity to auditions for the plus zero equations……..0 + = + . So like scheduling appointments with whate'er's as iffffffontouching eternity.

Alex: So like expecting to begetting whate'eresults, I take it, from the eternity test site ontest ontheoretical situation……….

Gracie: On purposed pregnant zerovated to beget e'er in justajiffffffy's job of course, of course not not to be Alex.

Alex: So…?

Gracie: So no more small time, second rate, cosmagic tricks. No more be stung demonstrations in beast dung Alex.

Alex: So….

Gracie: I'm e'ergoing for the's real onthing, whate'er'd'owned e'erealty's just a jiffffonthing…onticketing eternity of course, of course…not…not…to be. The's way danced I iffffffigure it, iffffffffffff( )ffffffffff my ontheory's whate'ertight, eternity's becompetalented like….

Alex: Like way, way more than just a mathematical construct of non-finite temporality.

Gracie: Yep! You said it, not me. Just like never forget…. it was my idea…. not yours. The way I iffffffiigure it…..this ontales beheading iffffffor like..like… the likes of you or someone else spelled backwards iffffffreaking me out in the middle of the middle of the middle of the Mesozoic to cash in on could be's e'eresults.

Alex: What e'eresults? Where's the cash flow in this?

Gracie: No cash flow Alex. Just proof that e'er's not poof. Proof of what forever's up to in the's iffffinal analysis. Eternity's onticketed e'erides with not not nowsy news'e'ervice iffffe'ereplacing not now's wholegggrailousy'stem's nowsy'snooze s'e'ervice.

Alex: So…….like proof(Gracie puts her trigger finger on Alex's mouth) Like what if there's this e'erandominium schedule with no ont I'm'appointments in it's makeup kit.

Gracie: Eternity's no dud. So I said it, not you. Like me winning the Miss Eternity Pageant over runnerup reality was not for no reason…..like…like…when I say (Gracie goes into her Miss Eternity Pageant character) "Like…like….it's my iffffondest gracess'd wish to m'equip this eternity with the best possible e'ercraft for anyone's whoever's everyone estated "OF COURSE, OF COURSE NOT NOT TO BE"

Alex: So you're already ont I'm to work out the's iffffontechnical problems….

Gracie: No, actually I've decided to improvise along the way……….Iffffacts are delicacies that only be ontampe'er'd with ont the's purr of the iffffffont I'momentum…. like decisively.

Alex: Scheduling appointments out of onthin e'er at the eternity test site……

Gracie: Better and better. Yes that's the ticket.

Alex: Of course you realize cosmic immersion has prevented such onthinking up to now……

Gracie: I can't help it if a puniversion's exlipse'ervice taxiderms in on my way.

Alex: So, if eternity won't cooperate…

Gracie: Well, I don't want to be iffffensive. I mean an ugleefully ontempered universe is one thing, but a mad eternity is altogether d'iffffffe'eront.

But if my project is refused I will, I will, I will indict eternity for crimes against of course..of course…not…not….to be. I mean like I'll ontantrumminate all of's time, and not just could be kidding. I mean what's the big deal. All I'm asking for is sum's xmas day when all of's presents as e'ereved, e'erive ont I'menu'd as iffffffffontree'd with my metaphysics becoming down the chimney beholding onto iffffontense.

Alex: So, iffffontheoreticklishly speaking…… like Santa…….

Gracie: Clauzzzzzzzzzzz( )zzzzzzzzzzzz….

Alex: Mhm.

Gracie: All the ontheory situation set up saying's……. to ontalk eternity; all the eternity test site's doing is to becommissioned of course of course onto to be of course of course not not to be. That's all there's to it So what do you think?

Alex: Well of course…of coursifffully…not….not……iffffffontheoreticklishly speaking, it sounds pretty quasi……qualifffff……(studies Gracie for signs of omniscience)…….eggg*acist enough………..to(a light bulb goes off in Alex's head)……..like…like!…coolifffffff….I'd….to be just what justajifffease should iffffforde'er in any e'erespectable eternity that's more than a mathematical construct of non-finite temporality……..

Gracie: Yes? Yes?

Alex: To like be worth sum's asiffffff-iffort…whatever the outcome…of course…of course…not…not.

Gracie: Oh Alex, you are spelled backwards after all! I knew I could count from like iffffffffinity down to like once upon a time with you darling.

Alex (beaming): So, your plan is get past the ides of e'er's usual middle of the middle of the middle of not ne'er's night to bring the presents to be tensed on xmas day. So like what assortment of presents are we talking about tensing here?

Gracie: Well current past presents for starters. Like ontiqualifffffffied antique'erians.

Alex: You mean?

Gracie: THE DEAD.

Alex(calculating): O…k…so…like how many?

Gracie: ALL THE DEAD.

Alex (Auditioning his version of cosmic reality to accommodate Gracie's ontheorctical version): So the plan, I take it..is to resurrect all the dead.

Gracie: Mhm. Yep…'em all.

Alex: So what amounts to whate'er'd down'd iffffffontraffic jams of…anybody's everybody…….

Gracie: Why not. I mean who am I to play favorites? Think about it Alex. This could be my big chance to really onteam up with eternity, without not not being being bothered by equations or universes or zoos. And boy, if I can pull this off, this will transcend me right out of the alibiless girl war's fix I'm in. For the first time ever I'll be so n'alibiblical that I won't need alibis anymore. I'd have n'alibis on a scale of scaled'e'er values way beyond what alibis work. For the first time in forever I feel like I've got the attention span'd'e'eration out of the box to do it. For the first time ever I will, I will, I will deserve asiphphphylogeneticklishly that as iphphphphylum all my own.

Alex (with profound admiration): So, you're really going to etern this eternity e'eround.

Gracie: Yep! Just look at me Alex. What do you see.

Alex (rubbing his chin in thought): like….like…1. Ifffffffffffffished out……. m'eternity not wasting its time after all. 2. Like iffffffffforever's she it spelled out in the y-not axis of the I'd thou artesian could be coordinate system.

Gracie(disappointed): Anything else?

Alex: Me puddled……….like…like…..e'eravishment's wet light in becompany of sum's one atlast beholding up the sky's iffffe'ers……….

Gracie (snaps her trigger finger): That's the ticket! Here, wet light wise, let me diagram it for you. Picture this. (she draws on the napkin) Here's the xmas as ifffontree. Here's the ontoy ontrains e'erunning in circles around the tree, where under the tree the present tense is e'erived with baby he's us in iffffont I'manger's swaddled in on whene'er……as meanwhile everybody's who's ever been anybody is singing in of course, of course not not could be's core us…

Alex: So it's like sum's quaintiffffff I'd I make up kit making appointments with never as scheduled hardly ever, or…or…as scheduled with ever as hardly never………ALL E'ERIVING MIRACULOUSLY ONTRAFFIC JAMMED IN JUST ONT I'M.

Gracie: That's it! that's the ticket! For a scientist you're so becomprehensile darling.

Alex: And you're sure you can pull this off.

Gracie: Sure! Why not. Like, if I were just a freak accident I couldn't do it. And since 1. I am a freak. But… 2. I'm not an accident. 3. Like I'm on purpose. Hey, wait up for myself why don't I? I'm not a freak accident! Like eternity and me really are on the same team Alex. As far as details go…..well, it's like my metaphysics dictates. 1. There's nextitudinated nowsy newsy's neighborhood. 2. There's selfished out notnotitude. 3. It all adds up to sum's pretty presentable eternity rewards m'eventually to be ont I'm'd….and hey!......with usefully annexed universions of information systems controlled by iffffformation systems subject to decision making by who knows who's spelled backwards. Ring any bells for you personally (Gracie winks grotesquely)?

Gracie poses like a statue.

Gracie: So here I am the twinkle on the top twig of the totem pole, attention spanned like nobody's business e'eready to make {{{E'ER}}} I'metacooliffffied's I'metacoolest of course of course not not to not becontraptionte'errorized. This is no longer goof ball graffiti on chalk boards Alex, this is egggumption's beblegummy stuff that bibles blow bubbles out of. This is the ETERNITY FOR BEGINNERS and ETERNITY MADE SIMPLE stuff that bibles should have been working on all along, like grafittied onto e'er of justajifffy's always. As far as magic tricks go, it's like I almost didn't forget to already say, I'm done with demos. I'm auditioning zeros all of's way danced right past infinity all of's way danced up to becompletely presentable eternity's ifffffffffffffffff( )fffffffffffffffffinity.

Alex: So all the dead?

Gracie: Yep. All of's'em! Whoe'er is haunting on the's…….like forget the holocausts, this is the's wholocaustalked turkey dinner stuffing here. Let's not ontrivialize the m'eternity wards Alex. Insomnibusthem all out of their mote'er homotels. The way I iffffffffffigure it, the sum of it all's up to notnotitude's(like eggghosts to be like godoghosts) to beget e'er on leashed to make itself sit, fetch and bark becommands….like backwards..forwards.

Akex: But Gracie isn't that an awfull's lot to ask of what might becosmerickly speaking sum dud's ifffffffe'er?

Gracie: Not when, e'eradiotickly speaking, you pray on e'er with the e'er you breathe like the e'er you breathe depends on it. As euman of egg e'er'd e'erealty my duty's not not nothing lesssent ifffff from all of's annals of iffffffffffffinity.

Alex: Ok, but just how ifffffffffff( )ffffffffffar can you like….like…..ONTE'ERAVEL in this metaphysical ont I'm'oter home's insomnibuste'er'd outing's presentable eternity?

Gracie: On whene'er'swings whenever Alex. As winner of the Miss Eternity Pageant over runner up reality I'm not just sum's way too pretty party girl who waves at like..like…likelihoods could be cartooned iffffrom equations. Like….in on the big time as I am ont I'm'd to be. Like my ontente'ertainment of the NOT/NOT NOT CODE ontheory sets the stage for like…like…..(Gracie's could be countenance is about to burst)…….like…

DREAMANCIPATION OF TO BECOMPLETE PRESENTABILITY….like…..like….(gracie takes a deep breath)………{{{{{{{{DREAMANCIPATION OF TO BE!!!!!!!! WAY PAST ROMANCIPATED FUX!!}}}}}}}}……

Like stars or no stars, god or no god(no offense)…..like…e'eredemption of what asiffffffffforever's up to. The way I iffffigure egggrounds of it, I only won the Miss Eternity Pageant against runner up reality because my could be countenance encompasses that beconvenience stor'd'e'eresultimatum. Like…like…if I'm not becompletely mistaken for e'erides, Alex, my e'eredeluxiffffffication of e'erealty to preposte'erologically a priori principles will win whene'er's ontrophyickly presentable ontrophy e'erewards in the end……..

Alex: What end?

Gracie: The one whene'erasold enough when I AM WHO AM THE M'ETERNAL AS IFFFFFFFFYLUM'S ALPHABET TIL OH! MY GOD! AS LEADS OUR BABY HE'S US

JUSTAJIFFFFFFFFFF(   )FFFFFFFFFFFFFFFFONT   I'M'DECISIFFFFFFFFFFFFFFFFFFF( )FFFFFFFFFFFFFFFFFLY………. (Gracie stares at the stars, not sure of what she said).

Alex: But Gracie this isn't just picking up pebbles on the beach you understand.

Gracie: That's why I need your ont I'madonnations to my just becauzzzzzzzzzzzzz.

Alex (searching his pockets for change): All I have is this here not enough……..

Grace: No! Not at all! almost nothing's plenty to start out with, as long it's since'eriffff I'd. I know this is a big battle Alex…the ont I'main event in the's iffffont I'm'arena…..the big iffffffffffffight I can't just spar with. It's almost like I didn't say…I'm done with demos. Please Alex, as dog spelled either way, help me as little as you can't. My halo's been ont I'm'exploding headetails when just maybe…..maybe Alex…..iffffigured ground's is due to doo the's iffffontrick. Like…like…like….in the low down, cheapunk, second hand spare parts puniversion of whate'er'down'd not not to be.

Alex: But gracie ifffffffff you're expecting puniversions for spare parts you have to schedule appointments for like pickupstrucked in like almightning just ont I'maneuvers……to…to…like…..like……beget becomprehension of the ontheory seating in such situations……..like….

Gracie (Gracie sees that Alex is getting hot under the collar and her maternal instincts kick in): Calm down Alex. (Gracie takes a hanky to his forehead) Relax darling. Like…like….oh yea!.....As winner of the Miss Eternity Pageant over runner up reality I will, I will, I will……..beget the eternity ontest site expe'eriment onthose spare parts I just might need when like..like…whenever I say (Gracie goes into her Miss Eternity character one last time for the evening)…."like tonight I onthink I've just spare partied myself out with all of's low down cheapunk'second hand spare parts, I'll ever need! Like..unleashing like e'ercraft in e'eraft e'er. (turning back to Alex's forehead still in heat) Now there! Darling. Doesn't that make you iffffffffffffffeel a wholegggrailots better at the odds!"

Alex, stunned and becomprehensiffffffffly disoriented, takes a drink from Gracie's glass of gin. Spelled backwards or not spelled backwards, Alex studies Gracie for signs of not not to be ont I'dreamancipated…….e'er craft.

The disgruntled waitress, having overheard Gracie's speech, shakes her head as she arrives with the bill, which she slams unceremoniously on the table.

Waitress (shaking her head with a smeared half-smile): Your check mam. We're closing and like you're still here.

Gracie (catastrophickly offended): Look, it's SIR to you….and if you must know…..I don't pay. Like..like…I'm pope.

Alex nods to confirm that Gracie is indeed the pope. The waitress, in mild shock, scowls and leaves.

Gracie (seriously insensed): Did you hear that. Where's my moustache? That NASTY bitch just called me mam. Does it really show? (covering her bosom) Where's my puddle? (In vague desperation Gracie preens her reflection in the glass of gin)

Alex (scandalized, hiding his right hand in his pocket): Gracie, how could you? Have you forgotten so soon………er than later?

Gracie: What?

Alex: The N word! Like…like…like….that calls girls…..I can't say it.

Gracie: Oh you mean like 'nasty'. I can say it. Like, ever since D Day the word's omegalphabetted to the tale end of my not/notnot code. Like I'm used to being nasty, xxxrated, call it what you like. I've been the nasty so call'd girl in the squirt gun holocausts for what might as well be forever since the girl war.

Alex: But you're pope now.

Gracie: No, I'm just the poped out call girl who can't get people to respect my hardend s'e'erfaces. I can only hope god treats me d'ifffffe'eront than people iffffffff I'm to have any luck with my science projects. It's true I do get bigoted with third dimensionable like traffic jams……. but I have to say that, when it becomes to one up ont I'm'egos I do coolifffffy as way too pretty cool as I am way too pretty……..pretty.

Alex: But Gracie, like aesthethically speaking I'm no southpaw. Like I throw, hit and write with my right hand which, since the girl war, I have have to keep clean if I'm ever going to ever be the hero that….. like……saves anyone without being noticed that I'm like saving anyone waved in particular.

Gracie: Yea, so like……..

Alex: So I don't call girls……….nasty girls. How could you………..

Gracie: How could I? Like I could! That's the ticket to all there's to it! I've got to get off the wholegggraileash. Like I've got to talk eternity, like becompletely sme'er'd into iphonetiquette iffffylums all my own. I've got to grow me some real chin muscle. This won't do anymore (Gracie removes her moustache from her make up kit) Like with uglee armor's alibi…Like this iffffffive o'clock shadow stuff won't do it.

Alex: Do what?

Gracie: Get me out of the girl war. Like with my middle ontrigger finger jerked iffffffff( )fffffff'd justajiff's e'erese'erection! Like god won't e'erespect such a thing as egggracie unless she it's one of the whiskered guys….becompletely begotten c'erid of the girl wars.

Alex(barking): No, Gracie, begetting bearded just won't do it. Think of your puddles. They won't have it. I won't have it.

Gracie (Embarrassed but doubling down on her shame): SIT! ALEX! SIT! If you must bark, bark, bark backwards.

Alex self-righteousnessly sits with his right hand pocketiquetted.

Gracie (brutally matter of fact): Poped out or pooped out…whether you're a delicacy or a turd..it's still the Mesozoic Alex. The spider webs are plantationed ahead of the tale of everywhere your halo's heading. If you're not the bigot, you're on the menu in these parts.

Alex and Gracie study each other for signs of subsident rage, as the tension subsides. As god or not god, Alex is befuddled but helpless to debefuddle himself.

Gracie(coyly): Uh, darling……how's my cringe…..like…..can I still get that…

Alex: Asylum…

Gracie: Yes, like..like…. I wanted all my own?

Alex (shyly recidivating)): Gosh Gracie, of course, of course not not.

Gracie: And what about the wings?

Alex: Sure every hairdo like yours should always come with wings. Like selfished outing's ontientypical teenage symmetry demands it.

There is an awkward pause that logs in sum'seconds.

Gracie: So what do you think about my science project, but really?

Alex: Well, what do I know. I'm just a scientist. I mean I could be a god, but that could just be a wheel chair fantasy that's begetting pretty ifffffffffy fast. Iffff eternity is more than a mathematical construct of non-finite temporality..as you suggest…..e'erandomineeringly speaking……you might…

Gracie (brightens): Yes?

Alex: Or…or…..

Gracie yes, or?……

Alex: It's like I almost didn't say…

you might not be able to schedule appointments with eternity at a test site of your choosing…….like ontesticklishly scratched of course of course of ifffffe'erandominiont I'm itchoosing.

And then there's that of course in geology I took on the undertaker's side. You realize that while there's gas clouds and then there's waving party girls like you, there's also rocks, rocks darling, rocks that keep records of it all.

Gracie (being overly agreeable): Yes, rocks darling.

Alex: Well, that's what you're going to be getting into here.

Gracie: What about the rocks darling?

Alex (gathers his wits): Well, hmph, I've been haunted by that graveyard stretching off into the shadow piles at the other end of the country club. The one not evered with all of's neon signs. The dump where no promotion pictures beget made. Uh, there might be fossil fuel cells from some of those fossil fuel rigs there. What are your plans for those fossil fuel cells?

Gracie (shrugs confidently): So we'll just have to handle some fossil fuel selves. That's all there is to that.

Alex; Yes, but Gracie, there's rocks under there, not just black rocks cashing in on the open sewers, but, like motel rocks, with like res idents in them…like IN THE FOSSIL RECORD.

Gracie (thinking hard for a second): Sure, I can beat the fossil record with my metaphysics if I decide I can..like…like..there's mines that raise rocks. If there's mines that can do it then my mind (floundering) mined can do it for res idents in the…..

Alex: Yes, but Gracie, there's magma masses underneath those rocks around a heated core that…. well..to be blunt about it…. is….just like…like….like a notnot'shell's like hell.

Gracie (breathing out darkly): All right Alex I think you've made your point. So! (taking another deep breath)

I WILL! I WILL! I WILL GO TO HELL and drag whoever's in there out, I'll even excavate the pits buried beneath being buried……….. if that's what it takes to finish the justajifffy's job for this eternity's test site projections to like…like….1. BECOMPLETE ETERNITY. 2. TO BECOMPLETE TO BE.

Alex (Acquiescing academically): Look, playing god or not playing god, I'm just a geek god scientist darling. Not that my stretched out equations can't exercise ont I ampathy for e'erefugalisms seeking e'erefuge in more presentable m'eternity wards. Ontrophickly speaking, my ampathy as far as e'erationing e'ergoes is not becompletely ontrivializable. And even reduced to mathematical deconstructions, I can ontantrumminate eternity as m'available to I'mprovization. For myself personally, spelled backwards or forwards, and well aware that gods have to take their chances like the rest of us, I can preposte'erologically perceive that your project might not or…or…..just might….be the iffforwards-backward ticket that your onticipations are anticipating. However…you must consider that THE REAL THING in all this could be disguise in disguise. Things being up for grabs as they seem to be….ontantrumminating ont I'm'eternity may just never quite beget the justajifffff job done.

Gracie: I assure you I am always ontantrumminating precisely those onthoughts Alex.

Alex: Just so you know this is quite an undertaker's undertaking. And this authoritarian ontole'ergymnastics of yours.

Gracie: What about it?

Alex: Well hunting down ontargetted to be this way, barely gives eternity a sporting chance.

Gracie: But you keep forgetting. You keep missing the appointment schedule. You're still thinking with your lenses and equations. You forget just how preposte'erologically I'm counting down from iffffffinity onto ontrophickly presentable eternity's beble background e'erations. My not/notnot alphabets let e'er'signed and sealed as ont I'mailed onto the…………. like…like…like….by the old Gracie wanted posters dead or alive, signed for no ont I'mistake's ontake out orde'er for eternity's ontalented alive performance as iffffontrumps a universe like ont oughtomaticked. Make no mistake Alex, universe or no universe, this eternity's alive. I mean like onthink about it....even as ifffffffffffffffilmed...this wholegggrailopte'eration is a live performance in the middle of the middle of the middle of....of.....

Alex: What?

Gracie: Uh whate'er. like ont I'm'usical whate'er's as iffffffontique live e'erecording.......listen....

Alex: S'e'ereal silence.

Gracie: Yes, well......with just ont I'moments of silence or no ont I'moments of silence observed for it......this here eternity's no dud darling. Sooner or later notnotitude will be dubbed with dibs for of course, of course not not being not a dudibbed dud's(Gracie calculates the not results In her not/notnot could be codes not numbers).......NOT. There! That says it all! Notnotitude Alex. Notnotitude's the ticket in onthis eternity. Soone'er's late'er justajiffffffy's ontequerian life style will be ontiffffindicated. Notnotitude's what's doo'd here after all is said and done. Need I remind you that eternity's alreadily becompletely preposte'erological. It's make up kit's making appointments all of's time. In asiffffact its on not not nowsy news schedules by m'appointment ONLY.....scheduling m'appointments on a not not to be now basis. Every first impersonation that ever passed out is poof of proof of that.

Alex (sighs heavily): Hyea, sooner or later you've just got to be right about all this iffffffished outing's stuff, I guess. Like xmas wise, sooner or later there's just begot to be sumwhat's simulated assortment of Santa on the loose. After all, forever's big and(taile'er'd as such) always still may get a head. I mean if, set theorywise, this experiment doesn't violate the beble completion's theorem of becompletely to be's incompletion becompletion iffffontheorem.......

Gracie: It's too late for that.

Alex: But it's always too late for that.

Gracie: See what I mean.

Alex: So like.....heaventilating hydraulique'er'd upressure to push e'erev'd'e'er's like dreamurgency.....

Gracie: Simply iffffffonticketed...

Alex: Simply or samply iffffontenticketed.......I think you've got sum som'othe'er's lap dogods at work here Gracie....to iffffigure out against the grounds that push the river.......

Gracie: The way I iffffigure it ont I'decisifffffffffffffffffffffffffffffffffffffffffffffffffffffffffff( )fffffffffffffffffffffffffffffffffffffffly by not ne'er's night iffffffffigured in onto to play...... it's all boilink'down to me winning the Miss Eternity pageant over runner up reality, where I say (Pinching tearsblushed out of her cheeks, Gracie goes back into character as Miss Eternity, this time e'ereally for the last time this evening))

"LIKE , LIKE, IFFFFFFFFFFFREAKED OUT AS I JUST MIGHT BE, LIKE SO ONTHRILLED TO BE COUNTING DOWN FROM IFFFFFINITY TO PREGNANT ZERO'S ONCE UPONT I'M........SINCE IT'S BEEN DONE

BEFORE..SO Y-NOT AXIS-WISE NOT NOT ONT I'M'D I'M'EEEEEEEEEGO'D… LIKE…LIKE!!.......LIKE!!!( )!!!!!…….JUSTAJIFFFFFFFONDEST WISH'D TO MAKE ETERNITY A BETTER PLACE FOR EVERYBODY'S ANYBODY WHOEVER'S NOT(or not not) ME. I'M NOT IN THIS JUST TO BE SELFISHED OUT FOR GETTING TO BE WAY TOO PRETTY WAY TOO FAST'S WHOLEGGGRAILIKE…LIKE…LIKE….I'M IN THIS FOR THE"………Hey, why AM I in this…anyway?

Tears emerge in Alex's eyes as he studies Gracie for signs of e'erational e'ereasoning.

Gracie suddenly collapses: Hold it..hold it…sum's seconds! Wait up on myself why don't I!!!! That IS why I'm in this whole onthing after all is said and done. What am I saying! Listen Alex, you've been packaging a universe to see what can be done with its gas. I've been packaging e'er to see what can become of its(onthale's) whate'er. Can't both pregnant zeros of us climb over the fence, or like meet at the top of the fence…or like…maybe meet under the rocks…or in the rocks…..or just be e'erocks…and coordinate our could be efforts. (All of's a sudden Gracie begets s'e'erious) Listen to me scratched ontraumaticklishly speaking Alex….as pixie dusted or not pixie dusted…..with pixie dust or else without….the appointment is to be not not just as iffffffollows….as ont I'm'exe'ercized….ont I'm'obse'ervance as improvised…….whate'er waves ont I'make up's kit to play ontrauma's soone'er or late'er I'dramas.

Alex (epiffffffffanized): All right Gracie. In the's iffffffinalanalysis (as god or no god) I must agree. 1. Notnotitude is the's iffffffact. 2. Like…like…s'e'eround ups of samplistic stars I'm'erchandize notnotitude's simplistick fact. HOWEVER….just as heaventilation systems hijack the zoo to service preposte'crous poses, and detours assimulate heavent e'erations out of hells, so conversely notnot's but e'er'd bebly bubbled, once willed to power, to pop. With this caution…..I'm counting from iffffffffinity down on to you to audition for that iffffffffffff( )fffffffffffamous equation.

Gracie (Confused as to the sum total of what Alex just said……however hopefull): What equation is that? Oh you mean like…….$+ 0 + 0 + 0$…..$= + + + (\ ) +$…… (Gracie has taken possession of the equation. As gracie is drawing her version, Alex is drawing his.)

Alex draws (on a napkin) his modest version…………………….. $+ \ 0 \ = \ +$ …………………………

Gracie draws her ont I'm'd to becompetitive version: $0 + 0 + 0(\ ) + 0 + 0 = + + + + +(\ ) + + + +$………………..

Gracie: Ok so like I've drawn mine and you've drawn yours. But plus what…e'ergrazing on plus signs…….I sum times wonder. Iffffff eternity is sum's one worth sum's whate'er's iffffonte'erespect……as I suspect….be can be programmed…like dreame'erchandized as metifffored I'mined iffff not sold outing's whene'er'd else.

Alex (catching on to Gracie's iffffe'er'drift): PLUS PRETTY MUCH PLENTY. Become to think of it(epiphanized) Become to onthink of it, eternity's always ontheoretickly m'availabe to I'mprovise. That could be the part your metaphysics got right.(studying gracie for egggrace) Listen darling, you saving everybody but yourself would be a simply pregnant zero's one'd'e'erful idea if it weren't for pregnant zero's one thing………

Gracie: What's that?

Alex: This girl.

Gracie: What about this girl?

Alex: Well, all stars put in the bleachers on the sidelines, the way I iffffffigure it against eggground….this I'd thou artistickly all I e'ereally care about's becompletely presentable e'ercraft scramble's such a thing as……….Ok so I'm going to say it. I'm worried about…like this…egg….like……THIS…...EGGGIRL….iffffledged, with or without fins, with or without wings, onto be..like…ickcuped…as the wholegggrailink's missing linkage to ontwinkle like heaventilation systems in not ne'er's night.

Gracie: Sounds like sum's wholegggrailuxuriess e'erestocratic piecess of she it, to me.

 Alex: As far as I can make out, e'eromancipating as iffffflux, universes were designed sooner or laterlike with girl war main attractions to work that out. Gracie…. I want you to do me a favor. I think I'm going to be needing you…..to….. I just might be needing you to…..

to be…like….the hero…like the hero….. that saves this the's wholegggirldelux before you or she or anybody saves anybody else's everybody else.

Gracie (befuddled): It sounds like you want me to be the hero that saves……

Alex: Yes, Gracie. I think I'm going to have trust YOU to LIKE…SAVE THE GIRL.

Gracie(dumbfounded): BUT WHO'S THE GIRL ALEX?

Alex (hesitating through his all of'sudden tears): YOU ARE GRACIE…YOU'RE THE GIRL.

Alex really does need a hanky at this point.

Gracie (looking all around in vertigo as a light bulb goes off and on and off and on in her head): OH YEA!...LIKE I'M THE GIRL!!!

Alex: But of course, of course not…not. Please don't save your everybody's anybody's else…until…you've saved the girl. Just save the girl Gracie.

Gracie: Why? Becauzzzzzzzzzz?

Alex: Oh yea! Because like…like…I like love this THE girl. And if you save her, maybe you can be in her belongings becoming along with her, as a sort of chap e'er throned in the's ides of……and as part of her belongings to herself I might as well like..love you too.

Gracie: So girl wars or no girl wars, you might as well like love me too?

Alex: Sure. Why not.

Gracie (suddenly overwhelmed): Say it again Alex! especially the part about how you might as well love such a thing as………..

Alex: What?

Gracie: Me.

Alex: Yes, becompletely sunny side up or, maybe, sidewise more sun down a setting's sunny day……Either way…….like…whene'er's day or not ne'er's night wise, I might as well like..like…like.. love you Gracie.

Gracie: So like say it again, without the *might as well part*.

Alex: Sure, why not. Like….. I love you Gracie.

Gracie: So like say it again.

Alex: Gracie.

Gracie: Yes?

Alex: I'm a scientist. I'm not allowed to say that sort of thing too many times.

Gracie: Ok, so like say it again….not too many times.

Alex and Gracie depart from the terrace back into the middle of the middle of the middle of the Mesozoic, as the scenery, responding to the situation's self-evidence, engulfs the beconfluence of grace and dog spelled backwards well within onthem.

END OF SCENE XI

SCENE XII

The scene is now at the eternity test site. E'erecycle beens are to be seen everywhere. Gracie, Alex, Mobible and the general are in the bunke'er'd becommand preposte'erological Ifffe'erological prepost preparing to ontamper with eternity. It appears that the chalk boards at the metaphysical society have been transfered to the e'eray gun e'erafter screens networking in this becommand post making it a very, very impressive could becontrol center for e'ercraft opte'erations at such summonthinging's eternity ontest situation (being a prioritized for count down's ifffontest e'eresultimatums). A tunnel connects the bunker to the new evangelical annex. The annex is pavilionesquely cathedralized to do the just ajifffy job of any e'erespectable eternity a pregnant zero might onticipate. The new e'eraygun e'erafters are iphylumenated by phylumens all their own and not at all requiring bulbs. In the pavilion the meta-ides of e'er iffffestivities are being celebrated in full sway dance, with ontraffic jams ontangentially onteeming at the brink of the Metazoic horizontical boundary. Elaborate displays of Pope Gracie periphe'ernalia are lavishly self-evident in the before ground iffffigurations of the puddlicke'er'd up mirror m'estate champagned impersonations. The crowd is audatiously auditioning to be obvious.

In the bunker se'erious ifffffffffffff(   )fffffffffffffffactovation is stirring. Gracie, now less a person than ifffffffffffledgimented's iphphphphylum all her own, is at the control screen of the new selectronic chalk board. Dubbing the board with her wand, this is what she shows up, presentedly tension'd, on the screen.

IFFFFFFFFF(   )FFFFFFFFFFFFFINITY.....................................(
).....................................+ 0

As Gracie is just putting the dogodishes of milk and cookies out on the back spelled porch for Speck..... Alex arrives cringing doubtfully at a plastic wand which he holds in his left hand.

Alex: Gracie, the bouncer wouldn't let me in the bunker-pavilion becomplex until I bought one of these plastic wands.

Gracie: What's the matter?

Alex: Well, this wand is worthless. It's made of fake iphyluminium. It's plastic and, metaphysically speaking, has no ifffffe'erodynamic properties whatsoever.

Gracie: It's Mobible's idea. But let's not let ontrivia beget in the way of the eternity situation shall we like of course....of course.....not.

Mobible (Glibly gushing ontechnical expertise): It really was my idea......like..... when I realized that, thanks to the girl war's product(atrit)ion schedules, we were more out of iphyluminium than out of

Gracies, I had to invent a new substance. It's called plast(mag)ic. Like..like... presentable eternity's Ifffe'er projections being what they are, one has to improvise.

Alex: But the pricing's so e'erediculous.

Mobible: Supply and demand Alex. Noone's allowed in the bunke'ercomplex without 1. Signing up for Gracie's ontique iffffffffffitness program and 2. Being in possession of at least one authentictation's plast(mag)ic wand. 3. Being anybody's everybody paying through the gnose to behavior such a thing as Gracie simulated in their profoundest e'ereflections. 4. Participating in studies showing plast(mag)ic to be sum what's (in or out of a laboratory's) universally addictive substance.

Gracie (chiming in): The point is what looks like low down cheapunk plastic is actually high grade cheapunk spare part plast(mag)ic...........Equity Alex......ontequity at last should'e'er'd beholding up disguise in mid e'er. At last..like...like...like...like.... I can feel sum's solidarity with all of's down and oute'er iffffontraffick jams. Once 1. Eternity's ontique substance catches on. 2. Every mirror is at home outhousing such a thing as sum assortment's egggracie substance.

But hey! Just as it won't matter what egggracie really looks like, it won't matter what sort of substance plast(mag)ic is. Don't you see, with these new plast(mag)ic wands, such a thing as egggracie's plasticity's s'e'ergickly expanded beyond such a thing as myself to such a thing as everybody's else. It's like my spirit face rainbotickly plastered all over the place home towned down the drain of every puddle's s'e'erface tension's ceiling. Becommunications wise, with my dreame'ergence replacing such a thing as me, I won't have to ever be myself owned once again. Onteleotheologically speaking, eternity's recallections willlike have it made whenever no hangups calle'er'd need apply.

Alex: But what will that do for sales of such a thing as Gracie make up kits?

Mobible: E'erevenue losses there will more than be made up for in mirror sales, onthydraulic puddle sales and plast(mag)ic wand sales.

Alex: Yes, but has this new plast(mag)ic substance been onthoroughly asifffontested whate'erwise?

Mobible: Sure thing, like placebotically, ontesting out very iffffffective in almost not none out of log 1 base ten studies.

Alex: Well, I'm just (aside) a pantheontical scientist. I don't really do the math ont I'm'd. So like...what.....

Gracie: Do you know! So your verdict on the plast(mag)ic wands is?

Alex: Of course...of course....not...

Gracie and Mobible hover apprehensively over Alex.

Alex:......NOT.

Gracie and Mobible: Whew!

There is a split second's awkward pause. The music no longer fits in as the dialogue has resumed.

Gracie: All right, everybody who's anybody but me, let's get e'eready for sum's middle of the middle of the middle of sum's ifffffffontrigger finger action, shall we. I mean like let's onthumb nail this ont dire ontheory seatings situation. General?

General (Absent mindedly toying with his becomputer pad is startled to attention): So what code should we be plugging into the becompte'er sir? I mean like…like….the (0/1) code is already operational with somewhat's quantum pilot variants to be ont I'machined in charge. The massive tetrahedron code has been fail safed to digest geometry outs for outer housings ontransportapotty bleacher seating products also.

Gracie: No general, the (0/1) code information system is beside the appointment we're expe'erimenting with in this herese'erector set up. These qualum pilot varionts are way way too ontricky for anything but itfffffont I'many thing's NOT/NOTNOT codiffffication. Like the cosmetrick code just *does* it. The NOT/NOTNOT ONT I'M'ALPHABET JUST {{*IS*}} IT….like e'ereplacing the olde cozy quaint 0/1 infiniteas'd'e'er information with like the's qualum becomputers iffffffffformation system's……..insomnibus'd e'ers need to just s'e'ervive……..

General: What's insomnibusing sir?

Gracie: Any beickle that becompletely coolifffffffffffies to not at all sleep off to be in e'er. This is the code we've just begot to work with iffffffffffffff( )fffffffffffff like… we're going to make any preposte'erological progress with this onte'erogated ontest situation. (Gracie e'eremotely draws NOT/NOTNOT CODE on the new wholograffitti screen'd board). The other codes, no kidding with their equations, are only useful for universes and won't wind up ontoyletrained as iffffforevers iffffflying out of when'd'e'ers.

General (Grasping Gracie's appointmention): Well, that codes always of course..of course..not…not…becompletely presentable at……at…

Gracie (Becompletely ont I'm'authoritative): AT ANY TIME'S E'ER IDES I IMPROVISE DECISIONS ONTO THAT IFFFFFFECT. After all that's what we're counting down from iffffffffinity onto………ONTO………DECISION BASED E'ERCRAFT SCRAMBLED TO E'ERESE'ERECT IFFFFE'ER WAYS…..

General: E'EROGE'ER THAT…sir.

Gracie: To beget this e'erecycle beble been back into opte'eration.

General: Roger that sir.

Gracie: It's cooliffffffffff I'd could be ontasty cookies we're cooking haphazardly here following my motto that 'eternity's to be improvised' after all is soone'er late'er to be said and done. And otherwise, how are we doing on the secret ingredient?

General: Which secret ingredient sir? Notnotitude?

Gracie: No that's the's iffffforgone conclusion's secret ingredient. The backup of e'er's overkill ingredient.

General: The pixie dust?

Gracie (shakes her head): Uh, yes, for preliminary preontunneling ontenthroughout cosmontentrick eclipsing spells to set the preposte'erological stage for the not/notnot codes of course...of course...not....not ingreediontickly bequeste'er'd asfffe'erefe'ering to…

General: Past the Planck limit all of's way danced way past the log minus 44 minibump, ontense'er calculuste'er'd to becompletely smooth could be curvative'erogue'er's……like……onthat.

Gracie: That's the barrier the bebles are onticipating iffffactovation as iffffonthrough..

General: What are bebles sir?

Gracie: The possible impersonations sub posed to live onthrough this e'erese'erection general.

General: Errrroger that sir.

Gracie: Speaking of which….how's onthe's e'eresurrector set working?

General: Ont I'm'assembled sir.

Gracie: But will it work?

General: That's your ope'eration's decision sir…which is like…like….up to your ontense'ers to decide.

Gracie (pontifffficating philosophically): Well…. it's up to dog spelled backwards now. With this guys disguises it's hard to tell. It's like sum'sone says "Eternity's ontooled to like ontoy with".

General: Well that's sum's one that's the only one becompletely cooliffffffffffffff I'd to run the not/notnot code. Whoever's whoever that is….spelled backwards.

Gracie (nudging Alex): Whoever that is……… it's a personal problem that's got to be solved once this resurrection is over. It's my experience that not not nexititudinal eternity's just begot to be improvised.

Alex: Cool. But…

Gracie: But what Alex?

Alex: But wait up on myself why don't I. This whole eternity business is iffffffffffffffff( )ffffffffffffffing by so iffffffffffffffuxing as iffffffffffffffast…….I'm just thinking on my..

Gracie: You're thinking on your own darling. I told you not to do that. I told you to..

211

Alex: Yes, I know, to let such a thing as someone's else to do my thinking for me. However....

Gracie (Gracie studies Alex for befuddlbility): Now's probly not a good time to mention this but...well Mobible's been doing some research and....like...like...speaking of cool, eternity's way more coolifffffied than we ifffirst onthought Alex, like..

Mobible (chimes in blithely): My e'eresearch shows becompletely becomclusiffffffffly that...well...all of's possible glitches in Gracie's theories can be taken care of.....(gracie takes out her pompoms)....of course, of course not not with cheers to care.(She gives pompoms a dog spelled backwards shake)

Gracie: Yes, like if ever there was a good time to make appointments with eternity, well, like...like..like...now's the time.

There is an ont I'm'awkward pause.

Gracie Yes, like nows the's time in the's nowsy's news, Alex. And besides...besides....besides what Mobible?

Mobible: Like it's all scripted in the's newsy new ontestamentions of the's newsy new n'alibible.(Mobible presents the's N'ALIBIBLE).

Gracie: Mobible and I have been working out ontense'er calculus Alex, making addictatorshipmentions while you were watching the second hand'snews (Gracie rips the book from Mobible's trigger fingers) Like the cover's ontitled objectively to cover the subject nicely. The title of the book is ETERNITY MADE SIMPLE. And this is not gibbe'erish grafittied on the chalk boards at the olde metaphysical society. This is IFFFFFFFFFISHED OUT IFFFFFFICAL STUFF!!!!!!! that like Mobible's into.

Mobible (blithely blathering): Yea! Like..iiffffffffff (Mobible winks) if everybody's anybody was ever into this stuff...I'M YOUR MAN! Like I'm ontested positiffffffffff for this stuff. Like here in the ontroseduction it says in no uncertonterms

"THIS BEBLE BIBLE BOOKS NO ALIBIS!"

No alibis at all for as iffffffffffffffffffffffffffffffffff( )ffffffffffffffffffffffffffffffffe'ers.

In as iffffact it's scriptured Gracie's not/notnot code of alphabettingod's eternity with all of's zero oned'e'er codes ontheorizoned bebleacher seating's set ups! Pluss'd hey!

Gracie: Like yea!... Plus hey!.....Plus....hey...what...Mobible?........

Mobible: Pluss'd this part that's so coolifffffffied, like, ontheoretically bespeaking, "becompletely presentable eternity's available by appointment...on a decision basis..... just about every time's anytime. Like eternity's presentable just ont I'm'any's time at all. Like no one could have onticipated how e'ercraft can be plugged in with a switch behind the scenery.

Alex: on Gracie's necktie?

Mobible: That's how the wholegggrailooks for ont I'moment's e'eright now.

Alex: So like this bible represents the NOT VERSUS NOTNOT BECOMETITIVE becompletion of eternity?

Mobible: Yes, unless not ne'er's nightly experiment doesn't work tonight…in which case…we'll just have to add an appendix…..

Alex: An appendix?

Mobible: Yes, Just as dictionaries can always be added words, bibles can be improved upon with new ont estimates.

Gracie (chiming in): So like, in any case, these ontexts go way past infinity, right Mobible?

Mobible (With supreme confidence): Mhm.

Gracie: Like…. all of's way danced up to like…like…iffffffffinity….iffff you must know now. Oh Alex, at last! At last! This book's got me soooo smack dab beyond the middle of the middle of the middle of it's all! Of the Mesozoic! Of the girl wars!…… like dreame'ergentrifffffffffied as like…like…..MY PERSONALLY SELFISHED OUT(everybody's anybody else)SELF!!!!!!!!!! Like don't you beget it or do you have to be ontested for this appointment schedule?

Alex: And this new ont's estamention's n'alibible's s'e'erving as the basis of this ontest site experiment I take it. (Alex puts his middle trigger finger up to his dumouth's lips. There is a pause) Oh…. All right. What do I onthink? Like what do I like not not know….. I'm just a scientist. So like…of course…of course…not………………(
)………………………………………………………………………………………………
…not to be.

Gracie and Mobible staring sideways at Alex: WHEW! (Gracie and Mobible wink at each other.)

Gracie: Well I'm glad that's over so we can get on with e'erese'ervations at heaventilation's…like….like…..hotels. Speaking of which Mobible, weren't you hired to control the traffic jams in the (winks) like 'haunted housing's annexed door'? As far as I can tell, you're like still here.

Mobible (tips his Gracie baseball cap): I'm your man Gracie.

Mobible prepares to exit through the tunnel to the ontraffic jammed ont I'm'evangelical pavilion.

Gracie: Let's test the new ontestimentionable power grid shall we. (Gracie throws the main switch)

Just then Ms Speck is seen pulling the ifffffe'er alarm shutting off the power, just as Mobible's backup power grid goes into action and nobody notices what Specter has done.

Specter (from the shadows): Nasty girl……

Mobible almost selectrocutes himself in all the s'excitement as he leaves through the tunnel to the pavilion next door.

General: I don't mean to break in sir, but the music's been rehearsing it seems like forever and sum's e'ercraft are scrambling for the count down.

Alex; Shall I go with you Gracie?

Gracie: You do, you do, you do love me right?

Alex: Yes Gracie…I do…I do…I do…like..love you.

Gracie: Cool! I don't need you then to be getting in the way except to get in the way when….I may need you to be getting in the way. Meanwhile stay away while you work the bunker. Ifffff I'm not Miss Taken for a ride this not ne'er's night is going to boil down to sum's s'e'ereal as IFFFFFFFFFFFF( )FFFFFFFFFFFFAMILY FUN. So like darling you have fun at this end while I'm having fun at the other end. It'll be like our honeymoon.

Gracie departs through the tunnel to the pavilion where we find Mobible on stage working the crowd for control of the jams in the traffic. It is apparent now that the entire pavilion is engulfed in the vast business ontente'erpize of selling such a thing as egggracie's wholegggrail. A Gracie egggiffffffffffft shoppe is opened selling Gracie ontishirts, beble caps with miscellaneous ontrinkets that are inclusive of Gracie on the cross mementos. There is the's superstition superstation where toy universes are being sold nested in toy toyletrainbow eternity sets. Among the gracystemic ground iffffigurations, bleacher seating is being sold outwardly. Children are to be sceneried in emotion pictured iffffast moving beickle's when'e'er'd option's windows 1. Just kidding about flying their Gracie attraction figure dolls with wings attached. 2. Enjoyed with god spelled backwardontale wagging's be stung head as well against the wind.

Meanwhile…..In the new e'eray gun e'erafter screens countless signs iffffflicker in and out of the presentension's hypnotickalking E'eray gun e'erafters with e'erepetitioned ont I'messages as to the ifffffffect that

OF COURSE…OF COURSE….NOT…NOT…TO BE!!!!!

Along with ont I'm'iscellaneous egggratuitus ontestimonial addictatorshipmentionaries. From kindergarten all of's way danced down to ifffontail's headstart, versions of ETERNITY MADE SIMPLE and ETERNITY FOR BEGINNERS becomick books are prominontently displayed with BIGAME'S big aim board games. On the podium is a life size Gracie statue with wings. She smiles with vague congeniality as she dubs the traffic jam absent mindedly with her plast(mag)ic wand.

Mobible is profiteering off the lived in likeness of this statue: Ladies and gentlemen! From dreame'ergent I'd thou art to I'd thou arfifffffact, this…

Statue: Living doll.

Mobible: Is the closest such a thing to such a thing as gracie you will ever meet without being such a thing as egggracie. This Gracie, at last, is a……

Statue: Phylum all my own.

Mobible: Like a universe's self, she's just a samplifffffication of large'erealty's dreame'ergentry that can be purchased by sporty creepe'er'scrawled out huntergathletes with…with….the ticket paid to keep her wih tenticles, in touch.

Statue (staring vacantly out of atypically onteenaged outer space): Yes, all you huntergathletes out there with tickets…like……plast(mag)ickly speaking……..like…let's keep (creeps ascrawled) in touch.

Gracie (all of's a sudden ifffflagrantly ifffledged without wings) enters the stage. Ont I'mifffffff'd and justajiffffy jealous, Gracie stares at the statue's wings.

The statue proudly asserts the wings on her meaty physical shoulde'ers, as iffffff atlast beholding up disguised notnotitude and demurely adjusts her halo. Noone can fathom the glances ping ponging between Gracie and her statuesque surrogate

Surreptitiously taking a drink from her new flask, Gracie gathers herself in time to climb to the podium. With boundless self-evidence she swaggers to the loudmouth microphone.

Putting its attention spans aside for some seconds, the crowd e'erupts its approval of such a thing as the aboriginal egggracie.

Gracie: Yes guys! WITH SO MUCH TRAFFIC JAMMED NOT ME…TO BE NOT NOT…..NOT ME………I feel the same about me too! Thanks for so too many of you showing up for my miracles. So, I'm going to trust your third impersonations (as far as I can tell) for sum's'e'erious metaphysics tonight. Like, you've been through the song and dance of a universe. You've got that nailed onto crossed out's not not of coursed coursed outings. I often ask, like, wait up on myself why don't I. I mean like why resurrect the zoo when I'm still searching for live humans I don't have to hate. Why is that where my tails heading to tonight. It all becomes back to alphabetingods and the not notiffffication of iffffe'er. Iffffe'er that's short term for just ont I'm'eternity. So lets talk eternity. We've all watched time ont I'm'd to becommoddity's ont I'm'any's not not's ifffffonthings. Ontaking eternity on a decision basis….. it's time to capitalize on such onthings. Of course not not…this is no small miracle we're onticipating on our preposte'erologically ont I'decision's basis. We are here to (not ne'er's) night to witness sum's BECOMMAND PERFORMACE BY ETERNITY, which is to say, from sooner than later's possible presentations of presentably tensed…..like whate'er'down as iffffontalented eternity's e'ereally big time statusticky status. As pope, I'm not only announcing THE BIG TIME…..I'm scheduling it to be appointed courtesy of my personal accounts as pope all of's way danced from iffffffffinity down to NOW. I know, I know what you're onthinking. 1. NOW NEVER HAPPENS LONG ENOUGH TO REALLY MATTER. 2. NOW NEVER LASTS LONG ENOUGH TO COUNT ON SUCCESSFUL BECOMMISSIONS. It's like when you're waiting around for xmas day when the e'ereved about presents e'erive. But what happens? Well, there you are at midnight on xmas eve, just waiting e'eround for Santy to becoming down the chimney with the presents tensed high (nowsy news'd) noon xmas day. The next thing you know, the whole…the entire present tense has been opened and's already as far away as yesterday's and yesterday's and yesterday's tomorrow and tomorrow and tomorrow. In the blink of an I the presents drop out of the emotion's pictured with present tensions unwrapped as scattered paper products unraveled into corners of past ontense. All that waiting e'eround and you just end up with scatte'er'd wrapping paper and pastontensions as illi(fffffr)ustrated. Well that's what we're going to beget e'eround to night, to rescue the presents from being blinked by e'erounding up the past. Like to PUT NOW INTO THE'S THE BIG TIME…to get to be house trained to be spelled backwards….courtesy of justajiffffy's jumbo ties to always nows. So like ont I'm'aesthethickly speaking………… ….aesthletically speaking, that's the work out we've got panned out of the box tonight. That's all there's to it. So are you with me?

Crowd (Ifffffflexing shoulde'er'd ont I'muscles): WE'RE WITH YOU GRACIE!!!!!!

Gracie: I think I should point at this time that, contrary to what universes may suggest, e'er does schedule m'appointments with each and every just ont I'm'appointed outinguy.

Crowd: We believe you Gracie.

Gracie: Now as your pope, the way I iffffffffigure my just a jiffffffffy's job is to be cheer leading of course..of course…not…not to be all of's way danced(minidances with pompoms) to make spelled backwards passed out big time's ont I'm'agick trick. So like onthink of me as like…like…baby's he's us not not's newsy new ontestament's to like…bedub bedoodoo exexcrete. Be…cause….tonight's the night not never's night is always waiting for…which is when…..not…….plus……..not……..to becompaired become the not/notnot's could be code to alphabet OH! M'EGGGODDITUDES against all odds.

216

THEREFORE……I as number 1. Ont I'm atlast as I'm beholding to be should e'er'd notnotitude allone. 2. Plus meanwhile's winner of the Miss Eternity Pageantry outing's e'erealty……of course of course not notiffffff I'd against just somewhat's runner up e'erealty and number 3. Plus all poped out….becombining becoming's could be crucial ont I'm'ass cooliffffff I'd to decide on what the heck, with nothing else'd to do sum's sum e'er's evening at the eternity test situation. 4………..( )……. So hey! Let me put it whate'er'd own'd this way….the way I iffffffigure it against the ground, it's like when I almost didn't say…..''I'm not in this to be the winner of the Miss Eternity Pageant over runner up reality (Gracie goes into character as the winner of the Miss Eternity Pageant) where I say..like…LIKE……I JUST WANT TO MAKE ETERNITY A BETTER PLACE FOR EVERY BODY WHO'S EVER BEEN ANYBODY AND VICE VERSA…………(taking on a casual e'er)…..So, like, since that's all there's to it…let's get this resurrection on the road…shall we.

Gracie (encouraged): All right then! You can start the countdown after my heavily discounted sermon all the way down to……..like……….

0 +

Gracie: Ok, before we get tonight's wholegggrailyrics nailed down, listen to what it all means in like… the iffffinalanalysism's iffffinal ontest with 1. The traffic jammed in this pavilion and 2. And body else under ground behind the chalk boards at the metaphysical society. Sooooo……like…….make no mistaken for e'erides about today's not ne'er'd tonight. Need I e'eremind you…….it's becompletely presentable eternity's neighborly nowsy news'e'ervice we're nextitudinatiffffff I'd e'ering backed up to becomprehensively scrounged notnotitude we're ontargetting here. Our hope is to achieve ontequity with antiquity. I've decided to conduct this bebuste'er'd outing's almightning e'er strike bccause….because…….like…the selfished out way eternity's so often improvised……..e'ereligious experience might need some back up with e'ereligious expe'erimentation. If e'er e'ereally does beget to be improvised, we'll need to make sum's decisions, based on could be codes. I mean like we've got the ont I'm'alphabets. With the not/notnot code we should be cooliffff I'd to sentence this

217

eternity to some pretty big-time production iffffffffffacilities. You might be asking like..like…why bother to back up ides of e'er's like…..(shakes pompoms)….half time show. Why not iffffffocus on to be ifffffffreaked out asifffffeatures like could be's cartoon quasiffffffffidle nothing else. Why unbury bodies of the dead…on to bebridled up as once upont I'm's ontintended? And then, after all that trouble…….why undig'em up sooner than later after all is said and done? Like, why be baby's'he's us resurrecting has beens, now's news might ask. Why not just park right now's insomnibus in the back garage……Why not let by egggones be by gones egggone to parking lots just pieced together to puzzle I'missing pieces like in ont I'marketed m'archeological situations. BECAUZZZZZZZZZ THAT'S JUST NOT SPELLED BACKWARDS ENOUGH FOR THIS BECOMPLETELY PRESENTABLE E'ER CRAFT PROMISSED LANDING SITE. It's I always say wheneverized, of course, of course not not to be's ont I'mouthed offfly m'obvious. Ont I'm'ore mined m'ore gene'eralized….make no mistake, horizontension wised, we are posing as sum's santa claus presenting tensions in the middle of the middle of the middle of not ne'er's night of xmas eve's already xmas day….ontasked of course, of course onto to be of course, of course not not to be……like e'erelying on my ontaesthethical authority as whene'er's winner of the Miss Eternity Pageant over runner up reality where like I say (goes into Miss Eternity character)……….Hey disguised egggod guys…..what's eternity doing here anyways……or….or….like…low down cheapunk spare parthinking…like…….like…like WHAT'S A UNIVERSE DOING HERE ANYWAY? I mean…after all is said and done….. JUST WHAT'S A UNIVERSE BEGETTING OUT OF ALL OF'S IFFFFFONTHIS? What'sum'sky's ifffflight patterns going to do with notnot's ontique shop. I mean like…like…like…why bother with 'being' ifffff like all you are is whate'er's objective outrigger e'erafting objections to like…like….being….ontunneling I'mansions of eternity's ontents. Well, until all bibles beget beblical, maybe that's more iffffffformation than m'ecoded information can panhandle. One thing's for sure, Eternity's justajiffffy's janitor here. It's got no alibis for whate'ers not/notnot ont I'mopt up. The way I like to onthink of it is…from iffffffffffinity down to log one base ten's count down to zero…..plus……it's like I almost didn't already mention……..when I was a kid just kidding to fly ifffast ont I'moving e'ercraft out the windows of iffffffast moving insomnibuste'er beickles. God, spelled backward, does that with their heads down wind of the e'er's iffffffflow's like beblegumption beble blow. We've all seen it moving iffffffffforwards at ont I'momentous notice e'eriding the's can opened'e'ercraft windows driving by ontense presented. Well, that's all we're doing here….begetting the past back downwind of the's e'er's iffffffflow. Preposte'erologically speaking I suppose it all boils down to the study of just ont I'mythology when not and not becompaired ont I'm'alphabetting onto of course, of course not not……….just be.

In a way that's all we're doing here, working e'erecycle bins, as backlogged has beens back onto be, blaspheming in all blasphemable directions with baby's he's us worked as baby he's us preposte'erously poped out of m'e'eredreame'ergent devotion. Ontequity for antiquity. Ont I'm'bitchess as I'm….for me personally that's sum's hard ontique to stomach. Even though ont I'mobbed crowded outings are a big fan of me, I'm not a big fan of ont I'm'obbed crowd outings. Believe me, from my first personation's point of view…..this is me drown'd under whate'er's traffic jam. Personally I prefer ont I'm'ore's privacy I mined. In many ways iffffinge'er'd whate'er's iffffffonthumbs on the's ontrigger. Even without the resurrection, in many ways, there's already way too many of you e'eriding ontrain wrecks, holocoasters and of course, of course not….not…..Iffffffffffffe'eris wheels.. Believe me, at heart, I'm mostly justa fan of such a thing's egggracied justajiffffffinale's ont I'myselfished outing…..which is I'mphatickly NOT just moo's cow e'er'd egggrazing on p-universioned'e'er's egggas.

Crowd: We believe you Gracie; we believe in you anyway. Cauzzzz we're just down and outers and, your onterritory's up and in onto of course, of course not not to be.

Gracie: So, to like e'erepeat what's been becoming d'owned by us forever, unless I'mistaken for e'erides, eternity's way more cooliffffffffffffffffff I'd than egggas clouds might expect. And hey you(looks up down) ifffffffff**ker you(I like to talk I'dirty to eternity)…since I'm the eternity ontestimonial site in these parts…at last beholding ifffffffffffffffffffe'er on should be's shoulde'ers, decisioning notnotitude with ont I'm'ultimations…….Like…this better work……(looks from the sky to the ground beneath her feet)….(Looks aside with surreptitious iffffffonthreats)…….you got that……..THIS BETTER WORK.

219

After all all we're doing ontonight is opte'erate iffffffff( )ffffffffffffffffffinty's beccommandments. When life is dead, it can of course, of course be as iffffffffffixt. That said let me say we've got ifffffffffffffinity's two choices in this zoo.

Jerk'd off stares at stars or 2. Jerk'd off just ajiffffffy's e'er.

The way I iffffigure it against the egggrounde'er's hit back to pitch'd'e'er's ont I'mounds…we stand egggathe'er'd on the y-not axis of the could be coordinate systems's iffffflight pattern'd e'ercrafty as twere ont I'm lit e'er in ontobse'ervance of to TO BE NOT NOT TO…TO….BE. So like…like… here's what we're up to for tonight's not ne'er'dy night. 1. Schedule appointments for could be's countdown careening from iffffffinity to pregnant zero's audition to be one. One what, you might ask. One…one….like..e'erestocracy's bestinctual becommunity, I answerve 2. Ontrophing e'eresults of number two.

Gracie stops to actually think for a moment. So…look eggguys, eu'r just egggoing to have to ontrust with onthis…onthanks to us egggods…….like eternity must beconside'er'd up for grabs. By that I mean egggrabs egggrabbing ont I'm'e'er…….like…like…..ontonight that is not never's night.

Crowd: Uhn huhn………

Gracie: Let me conjugate the situation. I decide, you repeat, we all sing out. Let's all, everybody who's ever been anybody, beget out our plast(mag)ic wands.

The crowd exposes its plast(mag)ic wands suspended in e'er's sooner or later ontraffic jamming justajiffffy's e'eradioactiffffffffffffffffffffffffe'er waves with quasi party girled, quasi cooliffffff I'd puddle power of whate'er's potted wholegggrail potension.

Graice: Ok, in the spirit of e'erepetition's presentation of ontensions repeat after me.

Crowd(whispering): How's this?

Gracie: No, louder.

Crowd(very loud): How's this?

Gracie: Whoa! Loud enough I should onthink to get the just ajiffffy job ont I'm'audition'd'one. So let's beget this e'erecycle been back in opte'eration shall we. Now wave your wands and repeat after me.

Gracie recites: WE'VE GOT DIBS TO DUB TO BE.

Crowd (Waving and reciting): WE'VE GOT DIBS TO DUB TO BE.

Gracie: OF-COURSE ONTWISTING NEW IFFFFFFFFANGLES…

Crowd: OF-COURSE ONTWISTING NEW IFFFFFANGLES

Gracie: ONTO BESTINCT E'EREALTY….

Crowd: ONTO BESTINCT E'EREALTY….

Gracie: TO BECOMMERCE A CITY OF ANGELS.

Crowd: TO BECOMMERCE A CITY OF ANGELS.

Gracie: Second verse…… AS IFFFFFFFONTWISTFULLY

Crowd: AS IFFFONTWISTFULLY

Gracie: ONTO THE'S NOT NOT'S ONT I'M'ANGLES

Crowd: ONTO THE'S NOT NOT'S ONT I'M'ANGLES

Gracie: AS IFFFFFFE'ERESE'ERECT TO BE

Crowd: AS IFFFFFFFE'ERESURRECT TO BE

Gracie: BRINKING TO LIFE A CITY OF ANGELS

Crowd: BRINKING TO LIFE A CITY OF ANGELS.

Gracie: All right let's sing it, shall we….

As the music returns the entire congregation sings the verses.

Alternate verse for xmas carolers:

Y-NOTING X-MAS EVE…NING

COORDINATIVIZED ONTO TO DAY

AXIS'D TO MAKE BELIEVE…ING

CARETEAS'D ONTTHINGS SUNG ONTO NOT NOT BE

Second alternate verse:

LET'S LUMP TOGETHE'ERLY

A JUSTED AJIFFFFY'S IFFFONT I'M'ANGLES

I'MANNEXED ONTO TO BE

WHILE BRINGING TO LIFE A CITY OF ANGELS.

Once the singing's asiffffffonthrough, Gracie checks on the countdown from iffffffffinity to pregnant zero's once upont I'ming.

Gracie: All right, let's check on the countdown.

The crowd shows signs of losing iffffont I'm'automatics asifffffocus. Gracie shakes her pompoms to ontente'ertain the crowd with as iffffonthreats.

Eventually..........the e'eray gun screen shows the countdown way, way down from iffffffffffff( )ffffffffffffinity approaching log 1 base 10 seconds on ye olde could be clock. The clock music proceeds as the countdown concludes. 5, 4, 3, 2, 1, 0.................+...+...+....+....0.

There is a blinding flash of light (ontransmitting perhapsy's perks of almightning implications) in the all but almightning stricken e'erafters. Not not of course of coursing quakes. The traffic jam falls to its knees. Gracie stands surveying the scene with an expression of becomprehensive supermanontensity. As the flash of the almightning strike fades, pixie dust is screened, falling like snow just under the rainbotique umbrella of the sky on the middle of the middle of the middle of the night on some typickly when'erizoned xmas eve landscape. All of's outer housing projections have taken on a transcendent aspect of absolute quaintiffffffity as the qualumination of the evening star simulates becomplete coolifffication blushed out of the blue on the eternity test site horizon. To all appearances the impossible has been simulated. It is the solstice of whene'er's ontwilight at midnight of half time in eternity on the's ides of e'er.

The general arrives from the tunnel into the pavilion with Alex. Their aspects are strained.

General: May I speak freely sir?

Gracie(alarmed): Sure, why not of course.

General: NOONE'S COMING OUT OF THERE ALIVE SIR.

Gracie (trying to change the subject): When?

General: Well, xmass day has not e'erived presented tense with the high noon manne'erisms we might have onticipated for an experiment of this sort. It is a miracle of sorts, but not the one you're after. The expe'eriments seems to have taken a detour into some detourist test site not partickled before on e'eradar's e'eradioactive e'erwaves. It's still the Mesozoic. It's a miracle of sorts but not the one onticipated. If I may be blunt sir. We may have hit an e'er speed bump at log minus 35 base 10.....limits. It's not xmas day. Presentable tense, while still ontheoretically presentable, is not quite present in the way that opening presents on xmas day e'erequires. There's no sign of the ont I'metazoic either at the's ontest probes ontensored by our calculus. I mean, logically speaking, the NOT/NOTNOT CODE seems to be working just finally but....for all intents and purposes.....the singular second elapsed at the end of the countdown only got as far as..........

Gracie: Yes, yes, as far as what?

General: As far as xmas eve at just about the middle of the middle of the middle of midnight on the's ides of e'er's………..e'er's……………whene'erizone. According to the ray gun rafters it is way, way newsier than nextitudinated newsy's normal not not now BUT……

Gracie(in panic): But what?

General: Apparently the countdown from iffffffinity got stuck at zero's zeroblty not auditioned with back up to one.

Gracie: So what?

General: Well sir, we came out ontrafficking a….well a…….justajiffy jam.

Gracie: So what?

General: Noone's coming out of there alive sir.

Gracie: What do you mean by…by…..alive.

General: All of's bebles, both past and as iffffutured, have refused to…to….like…budge…….

Gracie: So no resurrection to speak of…

General: No sir, no resurrections to speak of. Like no ontents'e'erections either's way danced. The heaventilation systems did not preposte'erologically produce the's e'er that just might be expected by the almightning strikes we were metiffffffffffffffffff( )ffffffffforickly mining for. No first personation e'erepliconts at all. No m'additions m'annexing out of the zero pregnonticipating up to sum one's at all. Just some fossil fuel leaks.

Gracie(suddenly desperate): I JUST KNEW IT!!!!! So nobody budged huh? (suddenly turning to violently lecture the ground beneath her suddenly beblatently iffffffished out as ifffffffffeet) That's what happens when you let a universe in on these e'ercraft test site experiments.(still lecturing the ground) What's the matter with you people? You know how to do it. Like..like…Your…your…whatevers….like….. have been and done it all before.

General: Beg your pardon sir, but you're lecturing the ground…of…..like…being…(cut off by Mobible trying to salvage Gracie's wits).

Alex: not not blasphemed in all blasphemable dimensions!

Crowd: Beneath her feet……..iffffffished from fins………..

Mobible (masking extravagant congeniality): That's Gracie for you folks! Whether she's blaspheming in all blasphemable directions or ont I'mouthing off in all ont I'mouthoffable dimensions, she's got the ground cover'd that the ground stands up to not/notnot pay attention to.

Alex:(chiming in): Yes, chalk up another miracle for Gracie on the boards at the metaphysical society!

Mobible clandestinely dumps the new beble bible in the trash binned whate'er's iffffontrash'd been.

Mobible: Yes, this must be the most marvelous xmas eve twilit midnight in the middle of the middle of the middle of not ne'er's night that emotion picture scenery's ever grafittifff I'd!

Crowd chants: SAINT GRACIE!!!! SAINT GRACIE!!!!........SAINT GRACE!!!!!!!!!

Gracie (tearing madly at her pompom puffs): No, you people are just a traffic jam. I can't hear you. You all should be tested for crowd behavior. No matter what I do, my miracles never work out the way they're supposed to….like becompletely on purpose. I just know now, no matter how many magic tricks I perform, I'll never get this eternity situation under could be control. I'll just never beget to be completely presentable to everybody that's anybody's satisfaction. I'll just never get it right. Why else be pope if I can't ever do such a thing as that. I can't do this job. I quit. Mobible! You take charge. Rig your application applianced as…

Mobible: As what?

Gracie: As pope. Former could be kitchen'd can opener appliance……..now pope. You decide what this eternity's ont I'm'obviously all about. I've had it with eternity…….(pausing)……..well for the time being……

Gracie points the traffick's jammed attention at Mobible.

Gracie: HERE'S YOUR REAL POPE FOLKS. I'M ALL POPED OUT OF THIS I'D'E'ER'S I'DUMP!

Gracie climbs off the stage and wands the pavilion crowd partitioned…..making her way to the exit in a state of becomotion that is threatening to beget trigger fingered out of hand.

Mobible (at the microphone): All right crowd, you'd best behave your third impersonations or else(Mobible exposes his new trigger finger now more threatening than the other one was).

The Gracie statue responds to the situation.

Statue: She's gone. What do I do?

Mobible: Stick with me darling. I'll take care of you. You're a phylum all your own now.

Alex struggles helplessly through the crowd to follow Gracie out of the pavilion.

THE SCENE SHIFTS TO THE EPILOGUE.

We find Gracie in the xmas eve scenery on her knees. She gathers pixie dust's now cove'er'd landscape which sublimates to her touch. She stands up with some labor and rubs her hands together, wiping away the pixie dust with some honest dirt. The'snow cover of the pixie dust is sublimating rapidly now as xmas eve is becoming high noon on tomorrow's aftermath of what just might have been xmas day. Through her tears she is almost smiling out of the side of her spirit face, which smears of soil have made more luminescently shimmering with could be's camouflaged.....transcendence more than ever. Alex, now noble and demigodlike approaches, observing gracie's countenance of smears with picture perfect passion.

Gracie: What was I onthinking? I'll just have to revise my metaphysics. That's all there's to it. Of course, of course not...not......not. I like begot way too preposte'erologickey'd apreoccupied with the y-not axis of the could be coordinate system's justajfffffy jumpoff iffffappointments when....

Alex: When what Gracie? (Alex hands Gracie a hanky)

Gracie: Whenever just would not not not cooperate.(Gracie blows her nose with such violence that the ground trembles signs of life) Now you do it! (Gracie punches the ground of being with her most e'erigont as ifffffffists)

Alex: Ont I'm'e'er quality quakes Gracie.

Gracie: No, just waves becoming party girls. I'm iffffffinally decided. My ontoylet outing's ontool used'e'er's eternity will have to be shut down for e'erepairs. That's all there's to it.

Alex: Once e'erepaired with new ontents who knows what ontent I'mansions it may yet estate. The whole tail may behavior headlines in the end, one never knows. Forever's big and always just might get ahead.

Gracie: Alex darling, in any case, I'm all winced out of whate'er's wheneved'e'erevede'e'ers to be presentably asiffffontensed. I found this in the bunker.

Gracie presents Alex with a pistol. In her other hand is a Gracie doll with wings. Gracie's looted it from herselfished out collection at the ontoy eternity set ups in the bigames arcade.

Gracie: Take the doll Alex. It can't play with itself. It's a toy after all. Toys can't play with themselves....(reconsidering).....can they? Somebody's else will just have to play with it playing with themselves. As for myself that's not all I'dolled up I am iffffffeared as whene'erwearied of the light whose dark now best becomes me. (offers the doll)

Alex: No Gracie, I could never play with egggracie dolls when I've been with e'ereal live action egggracie. You take it to remind you of yourself....like with wings.

Grace(brightens): Wings! Don't I wish it was like me so I could ifffffffffffffffff( )ffffffffffffffffly away.(even brighter) Yes that's the ticket. Like iffforget the doll. Ontake the pistol. Let's play pretend. I'm going to fly my doll as iffffff...yes......yes......as ifffe'eriding meanwhile ifffffffflying out of whene'er'd beickle windows! Yes! That's the ticket! Yes! I will, I will, I will like fly her....

Alex: Where? Where will you fly her to?

Gracie: It's when Alex. It's whenever....it's always like whenever I'm promoting you to be that justajifffy general that fell in love with me while pulling the trigger.......like just when he was pulling the trigger finger.......he fell in love.

Alex: I don't use trigger fingers. I'm actually way more advanced than that. Like the middle of the middle of the middle of my trigger finger's retractable. It only schedules appointments when in love....like for e'eromancipated flux.

Gracie: You should know by now that when it comes to such a thing as egggracie that's not the target this time e'eround. So I'm counting on you from like ifffffffffinity all of's way danced down.

Alex: Down to what Gracie.

Gracie: Down to sit. No that's not it. Upsidown to stand. Yes. That's it! At attention and do what a soldier has to do. (Gracie gives Alex the pistol) Now to make it more fun, I'm going to tackle you with a target that's movable, like in emotion pictures, movable for one moment of silence observed for a dud Miss Eternity. I'm going to take about log 1 base 10 seconds (check your watch) with me without my wings asifffffffflying her out of sum's ontheoretical ont I'moving beickle while you do what you have to do. Bye bye darling. Please just dump me..............

Making fake engine noises, gracie starts to fly her Gracie doll while ont I'motiffffffating such a thing as herself out of sumwhat's ontheoretical moving beickle whendow'd far enough from Alex so he can politely aim and relax on the trigger.

A shot rings out. Gracie looks up at the shoulde'er'd sky past all of its dimensions.

Gracie: What happened?

Alex: I shot the ground. The girl wars over Gracie. I shot the ground.

Gracie: What ground? You mean like beinground? You mean like the comic bookinground?

Alex: No the ont I'm'actual ground of not not alphabeting odds.

Gracie: Look shooting stars with bebullits is one thing..but shooting beinground is quite sumother's. Oh now, I'm really ontreasoned ontrouble Alex. I may just need wings after all.

Alex (not hearing Gracie): Look darling! It's decided! Gracie, listen to me. At last I'm going to say something that matters.

I'M HEADING BACK TO THE UNIVERSE GRACIE....AND I WANT TO TAKE YOU WITH ME.

Gracie sneezes with dark loud violence as she drops the doll in the dirt.

Gracie: Where's not when Alex. It's just your universe running on time......not like, like, like.....e'ercraft e'erunning ont I'm....like way past duh'd'e'er.

Alex: Look Gracie, even if this eternity is a dud, there's always still not nothing to be done with it. In which case you may be being abused by your own metaphysics. Like there's gods and demigods and gods drawn and quartered. And then again there's ont I'micro gods iffffffffinitestimonialized with moments of silence observable to honor iffffe'er duh'd. Now I'm always e'eready for such moments of silence, e'erated in seconds or not in seconds by my watch. My main idea as sum's what supe'ernal to the middle of the middle of the middle of it all is to use the universe as a promotion picture outlet.....for such a thing as egggracie dolled up dreame'erchandized egggracies without wings. As seen sunny side up that's how I got into lenses in the first place, to search for stars dreame'erchandizable on behalf of what's left of afte'er's half time.

Gracie: Oh like whatever does that have to do with me? So like the plan's to ontake me out of iffffe'ers…like ont I'mission on the ont I'movie set.

Alex (looks at his watch): Just for a few second hand universe's seconds.

Gracie: Oh is that all?

Alex: Sooner's later it all becomes back to your e'erways for which there are all almost after all no appointments to be made for e'erushing onto or…..

Gracie: Or…e'erbrush off as mathematical construction zones of….

Alex: That's where you come into the pictures no one ever lets out of your make up kit until….. As I'd thou art…iffff I allowed your I'dreame'ergence to like ego on as iffffishing ifffontrips to be ifffished iffffinned to be bicycled walks ont I'm'd on whate'er…would that be fun enough for you to not be too iffffraid to just exist?

Gracie(intrigued): So walks on whate'er wise…you wouldn't be bothe'er'd to not be me not standing in my whene'er wing's way dance?

Alex: No not at all! And then there's the beble ontentissues. So the plan is…..1. For me to be the hero that saves the girl. 2. For you to be the girl the hero saves.

Gracie: So like who gets to be the girl in all of's this?

Alex: Justajiffffffy wise that's like your job Gracie.

Gracie: So I'm going to be getting haircut right?

Alex: No formaldehydrating you in iffffffffformaldehyde won't do the trick. Number three I need to ask you how you feel about being egggirled in all of's this.

Gracie(cringes): Look I've been trying to disappear as quick as I can, but people keep after me. Like I'm becompletely caved into being myself but not really. I feel like knitting becompletely ontentangled in so many wrong dimensions that there's no way out. It's the girl war needling my onthreads I think.

Alex: No, put the girl war aside for a duh'd eternity's moment of silence. Gracie, what if I were not just an astronomer but a sort of god…..

Gracie: I pegged you for that from the start.

Alex: But what if I were duely heaventilated as only half a god and I was looking for my ont I'mother half to becomplete my goodness with such a thing as egggracie.

Gracie: So did you like just pop the question….to like…start a party girl eggcellerator business with me the egg cell?

Alex: You're embarrassing me Gracie.

Gracie: Well, if I'm not mistaken for e'erides, it was you that brought it up. Ok so the plan is…

Alex (drawing the plan on a hanky): We use the universe for all its worth. Meanwhile.. 1. I will, I will, I will be the hero that saves the girl after all.

Gracie: Who's the girl the hero saves?

Alex: That's you Gracie. 2. You're the girl.

Gracie: But Alex, like not not being THE GIRL is my big problem. That's how come I'm so xxxrated and I'm on holocauste'eroids, like I'm occupation territory, I'm what sells out paper products…. Because of me being {{{{EGGGIRL}}}} has become big time business. People invade wholegggrailandscapes just because of me. Why just the other day at a high end beach resort………log lots of base ten stab wounds Alex. I'm what the stab wounds are all about. Don't you get it. I don't want to deal with that. Do you really want to deal with that?

Alex: Ok…ok…..never mind.

Gracie: And besides, this is starting to sound like me being other people again.

Alex: Yes, but this time e'eround…the other people will be in YOUR MIRRORS. It's just like elan says, without egggirls behaving boys behavingirls….the world is just a rock, a gas'd'e'erock but just a rock. That's just how iffffffished outsexcess'excelle'eration works. (A rocket is ascending in the distance)

For a moment Alex and Gracie join in solemn observance of the rocket's ascent.

Gracie: Yea, I've heard that one before…but…like….so…like… these people won't hate me for not being them.

Alex: No darling. These people will love you more than anyone has ever been loved for that.

Gracie: So what do you need from me. Like about how much of my brain?

Alex: Oh I would say about half.

Gracie: And what would I begetting?

Alex: Oh I'd say about half of my brain. But the whole appointment schedule of this is a wholegggrailogistics of a wholegggracie sunnyside up……..in outer space….with such a thing as Alex sunny side up………….for as long as it takes………

Gracie: For what…..like some ontenthoroughfaire universion we eggglide right through?

Alex (making a fist of triumph): For your metaphysics to kick in becompletely presentable eternity for crossed out sakes. Think of it darling, with this plan we can get you iffffffished out of whate'er righthrough the mesozoo to not not acquire what no pope can ever choir.

Gracie (Studying Alex for signs of really meaning it): What's that?

Alex: Gracie…I am……

Gracie: You're what?

Alex: I am spelled backwards.

Gracie: What sort'spelled backwards?

Alex: DOGIMED.

Gracie: So, like out of some pantheon I take it.

Alex: Yes, out of some pantheon! Gracie, I have a chariot waiting with its wings.

Gracie: What's a chariot…..you mean a wheel chair……..

Alex: Yes, heaventilated horse drawn…

Gracie (taken aback): Oh! So like out of the garage I take it…like circumventing the sky until you find another eu-man.

Alex: Yes, Gracie, out of garage and waiting with your wings. Like…like…..the could be currency of such a thing as egggrasystems e'eredeemed whenever beble banks meet mirrored whate'er. So what do you think?

GRACIE'S SERMON ON THE MOUNTAIN AS IFFFFIRST ATTEMPT

Gracie (distracted, but not buying it): Sounds like burnt iffffffffffffffffffffffff( )ffffffffffffffffffffff offerings to me. As pantheonticketick'd'off as your half god may be you're certainly not ontique'er'd enough to onticipate my ont I'metaphysical of course..of course just could be…….not not…… needs. I mean, like you're no ont I'm'e'er'd's onturd but like these pantheone'er'd play boy gods like cosmetrckly just ont I'm'ake up like…like…. could be comic bookings. Need I remind you again…I'm not in this for any belonging's lesson less than as iffffffffffff( )ffffffffffffffffor forever. There I said. It. Now go back to your pantheonticklish in these spare parts just like heaventilated whene'er'sky resorts and leave me to my iffffffffffor fore'er I'destiny. I mean like e'ereally. You god guys that tar and feather eternity. When will you beget into the BIG TIME. Look Alex, you're a nicehalve's god and all but this is eternity and I've got ont I'm''d my own'd'e'ereal whene'ercraft wings in waiting for me. (reconsidering) Look I'm not becompletely giving up on belongings belonging to the stars…but…maybe when eternity does schedule appointments on a not not to be now basis…

but you know my motto…FOREVER'S BIG AND ALWAYS UP FOR GRABS TO GET AHEAD.

Alex: But…

Gracie: But besides I'm no god except in dreams. Otherwise I just perform magic tricks. And I can get pretty becompetitive with parking lots of spare party girl gods like parked e'eround the place. Besides, become to think of it I'm still in kindergarden.....which I will never get out of without my ont I'm'own'd wings. Look I can see you're trying to save me so...like I'm going to have to dump you for now. It's for your own good. You keep forgetting I'm a dangerous person Alex. I'm the most dangerous person I've ever been....especially now that you shot the ground instead of me. God or no god, you should have more respect for the being beinground's ground. And besides I'm not e'eready to ontar ifffffeather'd eternity just yet. I get ontsy observing these moments of silence for like e'er I'd'uh'd.

Alex: So like what should I do?

Gracie: You're the god, if you don't know what to do with that....just leave me out of it. Look, you head out off to the universe your way and I'll be heading off the universe at the past my way. But in the mean time I'm like out of here and now. Like ontoyletrainbowise I've got to get me those wings. Like I work best smack dab in the middle of the middle of the middle of {{WHENEVER}} Alex.....when there's no traffic jams. I love you Alex and you can love me...but only as dreame'ergenscenery. I have proposition for you.

Alex: Yes.

Gracie: I want you to be my dumpedarling. How's that for becompromise?

Alex: OK with me. As your dumpedarling what do I get?

Gracie: Like dumped. Like bye Alex.

Alex: Where are you going Gracie?

Gracie: It's when Alex and if you crack up as more than just egggod you'd know.

Alex: E'erhetoric gracie.

Gracie: Down to that are we? Ok so I think we must have solved all but everything.

Alex: I'll leave it to your metaphysics to solve whate'er's left over.

GRACIE'S SERMON ON THE MOUNTAIN'S SECOND IFFFFFIZLED ATTEMPT

Gracie: All right then. How does one begin. Oh never mind! I guess that's all I've got to say.

Gracie: Bye Alex. Now I really have to hurry for my appointment.

Alex: With what?

Gracie: What's waiting for me.

Alex: When?

Gracie: In e'er Alex, in e'er. Like between the toilet and the sky. Smack dab in the middle of the middle of the middle of whoe'er's wholes of it all. So just be my dumpedarling.

Alex: Can we play me tagging along?

Gracie(thinks): Sure, why not. Just be my dumpedarling ontagging along.

Gracie is heading up the matterhorn with a blast of the whene'er wind storming all about her with no when left to go.

Gracie: So like you head off to the universe your way……

Alex: Uhnhuhn.

Gracie: And I'll be heading off (at the past) the universe my way. Oh Alex whenever you're e'eround I feel like god's not ont I'mythologuy's disguise. It's like I'm with e'erealty's ontenthing.

Alex(apollogentrickly): Thank you Gracie for that vote of beaconfidensity. But where are you going Gracie?

Gracie: It's when Alex. You should know by now it's whenever. Like becompletely presentable tense wise now I've really got to get me those wings I've wanted with my wanted posters. Bye Alex. You go for your entwinkles and I'll go for my ontinkles. Maybe we'll all meet our anybody's everybody at the rev'd'e'er whate'er's bridge. By the way, you don't have a can opener on you, do you?

Alex (reaching for the bottle under his coat(Ugh…………Gracie, if my wheelchair works, your wings will sooner than later be provided.

Gracie: No I'm too entontsy to wait e'eround for that. You should know I'm always e'erushing iffffonthings Alex. Ambushing ffffe'er as ont I'must iffffffffinity just can never quite keep up with me. You should know that I e'erush e'er by now.

 Alex: Being patient eggghospital wise is…

Gracie: That's easy for you to say. You've got no headgear to be lop(de)sidedly haloided lacks of wings. Ontisymetrickly speaking you just couldn't becomprehensive about such onthings

Alex (making his plea): But Gracie, th…..uh…ontenthink of it, to go fishing for ourselves in the seas, to be shoulde'ering the skies with our'selves as we are, with our fins in its waves, with our feet in its fins, while walking wet light on its whate'er'd egggrounds. I'd give up being god for that.

Gracie: Look Alex, I must admit, cosmetrickly speaking, it is immersifly attraction iffffigured, but it's like I said as winner of the Miss Eternity Pageant over runner up reality, "I'm not in this for the universe, unless….unless…(going into a tragic phase of Miss Eternity character)…..as dogspelled backward is my whene'er witness…".

Alex (clears his throat): I am a demi dog spelled barking backwards Gracie.

Gracie(stunned): You mean it? Like ventriloquized?

Alex: Well sort of. Like no more than half, but more than drawn and quartered and way, way more than hardly iffffontestimonialized.

Gracie: So you do, you do, you do mean it.

Gracie studies Alex for signs of really meaning it.

Gracie (meeting the challenge): All right so let's see if you can keep up.

Alex: Where are you going Gracie?

Gracie: If you e'ereally were spelled backwards you would know. Forever's big and always up for grabs to get a head Alex. I won't wait up for you.

Alex: Unless….

Gracie: Unless what?

Alex: Unless wanted poste'er'd whenever doesn't want such a thing as wholegggrailogracie after all. What are egggodds?

Gracie(reconside'ering):   Yes…no…yes…no…maybe I always get sidetracked when I'm ifffffffffflopsided without whene'er wings. No, it's way too can be coated to really be canned being. I've belonged to some onelse's fool belonged enough. My wings might be waiting more ontsy than myself. I'd better hurry up ifffffffff I'm ever going to catch them just asiffffffffe'ercrafted….. like….like……like in the middle of the middle of the middle of the's whate'er's might being waiting for me.

Gracie starts up the mountain as the wind is picking up.

Alex is following from below. As the couple climbs Gracie seems to be still sermonizing while Alex is giving gracie's egg a lecture. As the wind picks up in the storm, overhearing both up whene'erwind and down whe'erwind, here's the best that can be made of the mutualecture conversensationing the couple at each other mostly mouthed upwind.

Alex: I want you know I'm proud of you egggracie for all you have achieved, not only dumping me but dumping all that matters even less than me.

Gracie: You really mean it my dumpedarling!

Alex: Yes, meanwhile upwind it's hard to take down wind inventory but….like…

Gracie (turning to help Alex out): Yes! Like after all is said and done I did! I did! I did! Didn't I! I mean mathematically alone…like…

ALEX and GRACIE'S JOINT SERMONTICONVERSATION ON THE MOUNTAINSIDE

Gracie: Alex you do realize you are dumpedarling…

Alex: Yes dear, I do, I do, I do, e'erealize I am dumpedarling.

Gracie: You do realize it's becauzzzzzzz. Like universe or no universe, I did dump zero constants……I did demoralize equations that didn't dump mathematical constructs of non-finite eternities as all there's to it. And speaking of all there's to it. 1. I did dump zoos with my phylumination. 2. I did dump 0/1 alphabets with my not/notnot code. 3. I did dump gravity as grounds for being with my ontense'er calculus. 4. Hey! Wait upon myself why don't I…I did dump universes with my e'erenew'd in the altogethe'er'd ont I'metaphysics. But most important of all my dear dumpedarlings…..

TWAS YOU! I DID DUMP LEAST OF ALL!!!

Alex: Oh gracie! I'm so ontouched……that like I brought you an xmas present after all, a presentensed that's just from your dumpedarling to your dumpt egground's egggrace. This is the most universiteased egggift I could find(a bottle of gin)

Gracie: You know, become to think of it, maybe a mad universe isn't what matters after all. Like what if a universe is like…like…just kid's stuff..like kids ont the playground stuff stuff't into ont I'm onthin e'er. And speaking of onthin e'er….maybe even a mad eternity just might not matter in justajiffffy's iffffont I'mined'e'er ore. Maybe like…like…selfished out of whate'er as me myself and I'm, maybe it's mad me that really matters. I mean like why else would my ontantrumminations get away with m'e'er'd'e'er. Maybe it's me pinn'd up on the ont I'm'icky sticrossed outings that'supposed to matter after all. I just can't help but the's baby'she's us wondering..

Alex: I think you nailed it darling. Maybe that's what egg impersonations must pay closest attention to. Like….like…when you get thirsty……..maybe it's just time to have a drink.

Gracie: A drink. Yea! With all this ifffontalk I need a drink.

Alex: What do you know…….

Gracie: What do I know?

Alex: Uh…like…like I just said….like…….I brought the bottle Gracie.

Gracie: I can't hear you Alex. But once I'm like ontisymetrickly ontshoulde'er'd to my whene'er wings all I need is…is….like……..

Alex: A corkscrew.

Gracie: No, a can opener to OPEN E'ER WITH ALL I AM ACHIEVED!!!!! THAT'S ALL THERE'S TO IT. I'LL DRINK TO THAT!

Alex: What did you say?

Gracie: I need sum's assortment's can opener Alex…with wings.

Alex: Just a cork screw will do it darling.

Gracie: Then bye bye Alex. I've just got to get me a can opener once I'm got by wings.

Gracie trails off into the storm at the top of the matterhorn.

Gracie(fading): My onthingdom for a can opener. Who's got a can opener?

Gracie and Alex in unison on the mountain top: Gracie: Oh yea! Like I keep forgetting….

Alex: Gracie! I brought the bottle!

This is when Alex does, he does, he does spring into action hero action announcing that……OH GRACIE! I BROUGHT THE BOTTLE!!!!!!!

As, all at once, the storm is over as a setting's sunny day is setting into the sunrise of the lands where such a thing as Gracie's always whene'er welcomed. But this is when there is one appointment Gracie won't miss out on……….IFFFFFFONTHIRST. Alex knows the ego summit's his best chance……..like…like…like….like…demi-god or no demi-god, without egoing out of character, to be the hero and save the girl. Meanwhile Alex offers Gracie the clean hand it seems like he has been saving up forever, thumping a break in the middle of the music's climax, to yodel one last time……….. "GRACIE! I BROUGHT THE BOTTLE!"

Well, wouldn't you know it! Gracie does turn to answer with three shots at a final cadence, ……….screaming success at the i to the fourth power attempt, preluded by iffffffafter thoughts….. "Oh yea, like I keep as iffffffffffffffffffffffffffffffff( )ffffffffffffffffffffffffffforgetting……………….

1.   OF COURSE….OF COURSE…NOT….NOT…

……..2. OF COURSE OF COURSE NOT NOT……… ……..3. OF COURSE OF COURSE I'M ONTO……(oh yea, like, like, like I keep forgetting) 4. OF COURSE OF COURSE NOT NOT TO…{{{{{{{BE}}}}}}}!!!!!!!!!!!!!!!!!!!!( )!!!!!!!!!!!!!!!!!!!!!!!!!!

Becompletely missing out on the bottle Gracie's hand reaches Alex with the hand that saves the girl as the music ends. Alex, now APOLLEX, charioted in fully charitease, is heaventilated as handled by Gracie. Simulations of a setting's sunny day, appear behind the chariot heading into the land of the sunrise with Gracie xmas presentensed of course, of course, not…not…egggamed on board.

END OF THE OPERA as whene'er's sum e'erocket booster descends to a safe landing in the distance. But the playground of the play continues.

5.   THE AFTER OPERA

Scene I

Sum'swhene'er'd up in the's guy's skies… whene'erainbows herd Ichariots grazing on todays…..we become upon e'ergracie ontenterviewingod's sun.

Gracie: so you like provide escort s'e'ervices for suns and like ont I'metaphyscians.

Alex: Uh, yea, on a becommission basis. Your metaphysics ifffffloor show'd up sum pretty ont I'm'azing ifffe'eresults.

Gracie: I hope that's not just sum's justajiffffy joke…I mean….(Gracie puts her finger in her mouth) Like ugh! What was I thinking? I guess I'm going to have to be revising my metaphysics again again. I mean the m'ore minded iffffffonthoughts I'm'etttttifored, like..like…I just can not emphasize ont I'm'enough OF COURSE, OF COURSE NOT NOT TO BE….Alex.

Alex: E'erunner up e'erealty's always could be catching up with whene'ers Gracie. For an egg I must admit you did egggcellont work…..I mean cooliffffffffying for coolest onthing ever;s quite sum's ontall orde'er but…….

Gracie(cringes): Yea, likehardly even quasiffffying for coolest eggghostess ever.

Alex: But like onthink about it….all in all…like 1. You nailed notnotitude, pinned up on the of cross of cross could b crux of its all. 2. You made up a whole new alphabet with the NOT/NOTNOT CODE. Hey, for that alone, you deserve to be congraduated out of kindergarten.

Gracie(cringes): But I tried to schedule e'er on an e'er tight schedule, which begot me head started up all of's way danced back to like preschool.

Alex: Just more to be lived downward once upon'd'e'er'd in pregnant zero's once upon'd. Like whate'er wise you did ifffffigure out ifffffffinity's iffffffluence on information theory.

Gracie: But so like eternity really is more than a mathematical construct of non-finitemporality….right? Please be right.

Alex: Mhm.

Gracie: So like…..you're the's not not……..not n'e'er'd after all.

Alex: Mhm. Oneofemanyways…………….

Gracie: So you've been Alex:

Alex: Oh yea. Still am. Speaking of which Gracie, did you ever think instead of trying to like BE GOD like maybe you might just try to like BEGGOD like……..

Gracie: You mean like observing a few seconds of silence for an eternity that's not quite so duh'd.

Alex: Yea! Like e'er that's breathed…… like…like…like……likes olde asifffffashioned ontencouragement. Just pray sum's of onthat.

Gracie (Responding briskly): No, that wouldn't work. I could ne'er ontrust not quite myself to operate my NOT/NOTNOT CODE.

Gracie studies Alex for demigod or no demigod becompetence with NOT/NOTNOT CODIFFF I'D OPTE'ERATIONS. With a new serge of optimism about Alex's metaphysical status, Gracie turns to Alex in heaventitilated humility.

Gracie: So do you think eternity will ever coolify for whoe'er I am's dreame'ergency?

Alex: No no eternity will ever coolify to husband such onthing's egggracie bridled up as it she it's. Eternity's just e'ergoing to have to used the's ifffffffffffact that such a thing as egggrace is perfectly possible. I've had you under s'e'erveillance for quite sum's time in that e'eregard Gracie.

Gracie: So like all those times at the chalkboard of the metaphysical society I was just taking dictation.

Alex: Mhm…high taling it across eternity the way you were wanted on poste'er's to do….enlightenment really was having sum's ontroubles bekeeping up with your beastung….like bestung by iffffe'ercraft as you were….like iphphphphphyluminated on your own.

Gracie: And my alphabet?

Alex: No god could have coded it better Gracie. No justajifffy joking on that pregnant zero's one.

Gracie: So like either spelling of egosp(it)al and eggghospital…..

Alex: Either spelling cooliffffffffffffffffffff( )ffffffffffffffffffffffffies.

Gracie: And so the eternity test site experiment…

Alex: Powowe'ergrips on bandaged badisguises Gracie. I detected specks in your I. Eternity's not always that assortment's just ajifffffy gymnasium. Scheduling iffffffe'er'd'ifffff I'd appointments with eternity is always pretty iffffffffffffffffffffffff( )ffffffffffffffffffffffy. That's a nail there are no hammer's for or a hammer with no nails.

Gracie(cringes): Cool. But did you ever smooth out the could be curvature of Plank bumped'e'er?

Alex: Yes, as you see(points to the chart of the chariot's trajectory), and I got you iphphphphyluminated with chariotable wings and…….

Gracie (admiring the chariot's wings): So you did beat me to the punch on my(your)(our) ontense'er calculus after all.

Alex(apollogetically): Mhm. Ontese'er'd could be calculus has actually been e'eround for what seems like forever Gracie.

Gracie: Whew! I'll have a good cringe of e'er'd that one.

Alex: Well, just what was your calculus created for…

Gracie: Oh my calculus works becomprehensiffffffffffffly…for like 1. Ont I'm'excelle'eration's could be curvatures and 2. Geom'ont I'm analysystematicare'eras.

Alex: Well, both excellent e'ereason's for ontense'er calculus.

Gracie: So like what could be applications do geek goods administer to it?

Alex: Well, Posseed pantheon wise it's still just a beable branch of ont I'm'athematics with no ont I'm'applications as yet.

Gracie (shaking her fist in ontellectual ontriumph): Cool!!!! So I do coolifffffy as ont I'm'abe'eregional in metaphysics after all!!!!

Alex: Uh yes, Gracie. In the halo'd halls of perhapsystemick's pantheon, your could be contributions to metaphysics have been e'erecognized beyond the work of all of's meaty zoic institutions.

Gracie: And…….so like my alphabet…..not just kidding….

Alex: Oh, your NOT/TNOTNOT CODES been ontomegalphabetted iffffffavorably since……since….like….since forever's been up to like forever.

Gracie: So like all of's times as pin up on the cross……I was like…..like……like……...such a thing as….like….like……you.

Alex: Yep. It was me being you being me Gracie………cooperating pinned up ontogether.

Gracie: So like eggghostpitaled this was like sum's secret ope'eration…..

Alex: Yea, like you had to be ontested. lIke ever since you won the Miss Eternity Pageant against runner up reality….you had to be onthoroughly tested, to see if, girl war or no girl war, you were up for the justajiffffffffy job of all of's of it all.

Gracie: So like my minor miracles……

Alex: Cooperative ifffffffefforts from our side on yours.

Gracie: So like just ajiffffffffformationally speaking…….

Alex: You passed…….dreame'ergently just as iffffffffformalized……informally……….

Gracie: So like ifffffffffffffffffffffffff( )ffffffffffffffffffffformation becomes information by…..

Alex: Ontapprehensifffffffffff( )ffffffffffff ont I'decision. It's all very ontentithetickly preposte'erological.

Gracie: And so meanwhile after all you've said and been and done……..

Alex: Yes.

Gracie: You really don't sing.

Alex: Well, I can yodel off a mountain top. But that's about it. Onthumb driving iffffffe'er craft……mainly my jobs just to bekeep to be in the big time to be no dud. And in the big time I can tell you even gods must take their chances. You know, process theology without the ontotality's not quite ontheology. That's while we're mostly demigods in these parts.

Gracie(primping): But so like after all I've said and been and done….you like do, do, do like love my likeness strikes.

Alex: Yes Gracie, I do love your you manity.

Gracie: So like say it again like way too many times…..like ont I'm'essspecially… the part about how you………( )……………..like love me.

Alex: I love you Gracie.

Gracie: You wouldn't lie to me.

Alex: Not yet. Only on the power grid. But, shucks, I'm just like escorting servicing a sun. However, if we keep talking, lies will be in the's iffffffffallout. I am, after all….. e'eradioactive.

Gracie: Oh yea, me too. So we are on the same onteam after all. l like the quasi ont I'mightning strikes of that. Can we back up.

Alex: Yes. let's back up.

The chariot is scened ever so slightly backing up….but….hence forths into the sunrise.

Tele spots the chariot passing over as he advises Wolfy to that effect. Wolfy sighs, but the music remains silenced.

Gracie: So, like iffffallout or no iffffallout, say it again, the part about how you wouldn't lie to me.

Alex: Not yet.

Gracie: YES!!!! YES!!!!!!!!NOT YET!!!!!!!! YES!!!!!!!! I like it!!!! That's onthe's ticket!!!!!! So say it again   the   part   about   how   you……..   like….like….like…..…………………….( )………..like…………...don't……not…………………….(   )……………NOT……………Uh not…………YET!!!!!!!!!

Alex: Love you……..Gracie.

Gracie: With all of's ifffontroubles I've becaused!!!!!!!!!!

Alex: Made worthwhile. Like…like in e'er impersonatiffff( )ffffffff I'd….ont I'make up………made up I'm'obvious by the girl war or no girl war's egggracie.

Gracie: Ok so like…like…like…what's in it for the likes of like like me?

Alex: Y'e'er the girl Gracie.

Gracie: Does could be's can opener come with that?

Gene'erating setting sunny days…the chariot continues its just ajifffffy journey e'eround the's skies onto onthales' promised lands of big time whate'er puddle's dawn'd upond…..dreame'ergently to make up alphabetterment's appearances wherever's take sum'authe'er chances and being becomes ont I'm'cchodcd of course of coursed not not to be.

Scene II

After having joined with Alex to make several circuits around what's whate'er's world, Gracie has stopped sighing and addresses the ultimate setheoretical situation in the chariot with Alex.

Gracie: Oh Alex…after all is said and done…….I'm begetting iffformaldehydrated som'swhat asiffffont I'dizzy darling……..

Alex(blithely): Yes dear..

Gracie: It's like my ontheory of beble block eternity might cooliffffffffffffy as when it's at after all.

Alex: What theory's that? (A rocket is launching in the distance)

Gracie: Well, think of a theory of space/time's fabrick layers all blocked out done dealt as phyzz'd.

Alex(thinks): Yep, got it.

Garcie: Well, so onthink of the iffffffabrick lay'd'e'ers of asifffffaced ont I'm.

Alex(onthinks): Yep, begot it.

Gracie: Well they might be ifffffreebes onthrown becompletely iffffffabricated.....

Alex: Yes..

Gracie: Or....or....like...they might be like pre(poste'erologically)fabricated onto beble block'd'e'er. That would make scheduling appointments with eternity becompletely like ont I'm'at'e'er of fact.

Alex: Why didn't I think of that?

Gracie: Well, self-evidently, it's because you're not such a thing as egggracie. You're just a geek god e'eriding some olde ont I'm'e'er's wheel chair....whereas I'm the winner of the Miss Eternity pageant over runner up reality who's......only in it for the.....eternity.

Alex: So?

Gracie: Soooooooooo.......as not not narcisistick as I'm aim'd to be...... I'm like...like....like......iffffffffffffffraid.........to not not be........not self-satisfied enough with this setting sunny day routine we're circulating in these parts. Like...like..... I'm wholegggrailuxuriont as you must know. However.......so belonging to the ides of e'er as alwaysays I do.. insomnibus'd'e'erides is what I'm used to. Like onced'e'eround a living's all I need to behold where the betting odds are to be placed.........in the misstakes eggglaid.

Alex: Yes Gracie.

Gracie: Well.....as winner of the Miss Eternity Pageant over runner up reality, wheel chair or no wheel chair, demigod or no demigod, I'm iffffffffffffffffffffffraid I may yet have to dump you darling, after all.

Alex: Yes Gracie. Sure why not.

Gracie: Like...like....like...for becompletely presentable eternity'sakes you understand. I mean a settings sunny day is brillianticiparticipan'd'e'eringly horizoned homeward with a sun rise. But that's just high grade peep plancks second hand work'star and feather'd'iffffffigmentension's'not justkidding justajifffy's'e'eraid'stuff...................

Alex: Yes, of course...of course....of course......of course.....not....not.....not......not. Sooner's later all gods do become to that samplifffffffff I'd beconclusion Gracie. Like so what dear?

Gracie: Need I not iffffffail to remind you..... again...again....I'm only in this for the ontitude.

Alex: Of course, of course notnot.... Where would you like to be dumped to dump me dumping you off as ifffffffffffffffffffffffffffffffffffffffffff.

Gracie: Well, off hand, I guess the nearest insomnibustop could beconvenient.

240

Alex: With beconvenience storage e'ercraft?

Gracie: Yes, just drop me off dumping you off at the…..at the……… Oh Alex, of all of my dumpedarlings I will ever meet, you really are the least dumpedarlinground'e'er'd becomont I'm'unity of them all.

Alex (waxing philosophical): Well, it's like you say Gracie…… eternity is always up for grabs…..and notnotitude being what…what….what's to beblat e'er'd up…….as whats……..

Gracie: Yes…yes…yes……as whats iffffffflies of what I AM,……… I aim to grab me some of its sum's hits ifffff I can.

Alex: I iffffully grasp the setheoretical notnotanality of the situation. So like onthird person wise….will any insomnibustation do?

Gracie: Yes, of course, of course not..not…. iffffffffff I can just be dropped off at the nearest insomnibustop I can find my own horizon home from there.

Narrator: And so we see egggracie being dropped off of the chariot at the insomnibustop as we end our ont I'madventures in egggracie's ont I'm'eternity wards at last…..at least…until Scene III.

Scene III

This story does go on, but words just almost don't. Onthat is when we must leave our deareggracie horizoned horizontally at home ontantrumminating in the could be kitchen beconducting e'eresearch……… e'erummaging in iffffffffffffe'ercraft'I'meanwhile'd'e'eriffffontheory seating among all of courses could behaviored could be's kitchen appliances. But wait up why don't we. Just now's presented tense has caught egggracie atlast ont shoulde'ering the phone as she onteleophones Apollex in mid e'er's lens'd observatory.

Gracie: Alex, hello dumpedarling.

Alex: Yes dear…..

A first stage rocket booster is making a soft landing in the distance.

Gracie: Just ontesting you for sum'advice. Are you as usual in mid e'er?

Alex: I'm back at the observatory.

Gracie: Where's the wheel chair?

Alex: The wheel chair's in the great unknown's garage.

Gracie: Can you please help me.

Alex: Of course, of course not not.

Gracie: I'm in the kitchen at the insomnibustation looking for a can opener.

Alex: Yes, darling.

Gracie: It seems I am proprietor here now. pardon the jargon but….like……preposte'erologically I eggguess I don't quite iffffontrust the gods with whate'er's as iffffffffffffffffffalling onthrough e'er Alex.

Like a prioritizing eternity as I have………. I feel like as egggirls like ont I'm'eternity's just might as well just be my baby now….by now meaning from this appointment's ontitude to pursue the deiffffffficky dramurgency of not notitudinations.

Alex: Yes dear, as a god of sorts, I can tell you, even the gods must take their chances and you just might ont I'mprovize as well.

Gracie: It's like lighthouse wise no matter how ont I'm'any to beball's hit over the's horizon, like becompletely over the's iffffffffents, there's more home runs to e'eroom as iffffffffffffe'er.

Alex: Yes, gods no matter how e'ergrounded, face never with not/notnot codes with wholes blow upable in ont I'm'any's ont I'metffffffffffffffffffffffffysics. Ont I'm'eternity is always up for grabs Gracie……egggrabs….groundibs……or pretty's apprehension. To be is bigger than the gods.

Gracie: So like…like…like….ont I'm'eternity after all is becompletely presentable after all……..

Alex: Of course, of course…could be……..not not…….

Gracie: Who's there…..

Alex: Pet eumans darling, just begetting way too pretty way too fast for up keep to keep up with.

Gracie: Etiquetted as such a thing as egggracie?

Alex: Yes, darling, some doo's make up kit is made up to begetting thaturd ticket.

Gracie: So, girl war or no girl war, missing out on my appointment with eternity is pointless after all. I mean especially just whenever I'm discovering my ont I'm'e'eroots and meanwhile as iffffffffinding out to be's as iffffffffffamous as my belongings of course, of course not…not…. suspected all along…..with you I'd thou iffffffart'siffffffff e'ereleased………. the least dumpedarling of all of my dumpledarlings. I've decided to write it up into a book, reviewing all of's iffffont I'm and meanwhile writing all of's iffffont I'ming's book reviews. Just as soon as I find that can opener I just know I'm missing out on.

Alex: Yes, dear. E'erummaging eternity for ont I'm'e'er as could be cracie as it seems….whether simply ontantrumminated or samply as e'erummaged……… to be is not to be ont I'm'abandoned whene'er addressed at all presentABLY. That's best's ont I'm'advice I'd give you manity's ont I'm'd thou art. Never forget, can opened e'er or not can opened e'er, with all of's hangups………..eternity does make calls.

Gracie: Yes, dumpedarling. I won't forget. And when I do…. I won't forget……

Alex: Yes darling?

Gracie: You backed up to be the least dumped off of all of's my dumpedarlings.

Alex: Yes dear. I will, I will, I will account as iffffffffore'er's onthat with your eumanity as haply e'erafted's egggrace.

BEFORE EXPANDING BEYOND E'ERECOGNITION OUR STORY MUST END HERE WITH THIS IPHPHPHONE CALL.

THE PLAYED E'ER ENDS FOR THE ONT I'M BEING.

All that's left is the Glossary. But this could be where onthings beget even ontstickier. The text now leaves it up to the ontentalents of ont I'm'e'ereaders to ifffffathom the e'ercrafted ontents of the ope'erational alphabet in these parts.

6. EGGGLOSSARY

NOTE- Much of the long-winded metaphysical rhetoric will have to be cut in performance. This glossary is to serve the readers of the book caught down-wind of the long windedness of much of the metaphysics. This glossary is taken from fragments of the author's work and is not to be viewed as comprehensive. None of the persons listed in the Glossary have necessarily expressed any support of the opera as a literary enterprise.

ABLTY- Phonetically compressed form of ability.

ADICTIONARIES- The favorite books of weaponized reference libraries hooked on dealing in strawmen, strawgods and strawhenevers.

AESTHETHICS- the study of the interdependence of virtue and beauty.

AILEEN NISHIOKA- Aboriginal egggracie.

ALFRED HITCHCOCK- Could be Felix in this opera

ALICE MORRY- Daughter of the Inuahluroks and wife to the Maptigaks, the model for egggracie in the Endicott Mountains.

ALMA DEUTCHER- Twenty first century musical prodigy emergent in the manner of Mozart, Schubert and Mendelsshon.

ALMIGHTNING STRIKES- Naked notnotitude's becommoddiffffffffffffied events.

ALPHABETS- 1. Any codes foundational for language. 2. The roots beneath the teeth beneath the tongues of prey animals.

ANTIWARRIOR PRESIDENT- President indicted for suggesting that one civil war could have been negotiated while suggesting that more than one World War Whenever could have been negotiated as well. It is to be noted that this president was able to avoid wars that others were to embrace. Who knows who might be alive today if this greatest of all world leaders had been listened to without indictments in response.

APALLONIAN ALEX- Alex's larger than life character demonstrates qualum complexities of could be character in the eternity when this opera might take place. Some may be disturbed by Alex's eventual status smack dab in the middle of the middle of the middle of half way between's ifffffffully

I'dentifffffffffiable I'deities and eggs. In human terms it's like how egggooh!s beget leveraged half way between the toilet and the sky. In this case it's more like when demigods ifffffffunction for all artistic purposes smack dab between ifffledgiments of eggglayers and ifffffflight patterns. Dramatically speaking this ends up with a cosmic demigod action hero learning some of sum's ont I'metaphysics, as a god taught by an egg...............a wholegggrailegende'er'dolled up egg that is.

APOORVA TEWARI- Another paradigm for egggracie.

APRIL LOVE- 1, Whate'er'd'own ifffffontiquely ifffffffluffffffilm innocentially pictured perfecting as ifffffontrivial promotion of to be(not not of course) ifffeaturing Shirey Jones as Gracie and Pat Boone as Alex togethe'er'd to play ont I'm'atching parts as the becompletely presentable could be couple of THE GIRL WAR. 2. A last ditch early attempt at ont I'metazoic ifffffilm make up kittend cinematic behavior behaving on behalf of all of's ifffont I'm's presentable e'erides....becommunally e'erelegated to the I'd thou dust bin of I'd thou artistry. This film features a. Avoidance of all subversions of such a thing as egggracie like like like ifffeatures b. could be courteseisures of egggodolled up girl heaventiilated humans ont optimystickly ont I'm'd to becompletely not not normalized. c. as suchiness ontouched to begiving such a thing as egggracie that becompletely presentable eternity she always wanted champagned for her birthday's xmass cell wholegggrailife in I brianacup'f'e'er'd ont I'm'e'eriation.

A PRIORI- From first principles, before anything actually happens.

A PRIORI PRETTY- What egggracie's make up kittent spirit face makes only way too self-evidenticklishly obvious.

ASIFFFFFFFFFFE'ERIANS- One version of what egggracie's tale is heading her halo'd'e'ershipments for.

ASIFFFFONTOCRACY- Self-evident societease that wave ifffffffformation is party girling forever for.

AUDREY HEPBURN- One of the actresses that has already played Gracie to goddess like ifffffffffect.

AUTONAUTS- Whate'er's selfished out beings ontraveling through e'er.

BACH- Preclassical composer who set the stage for every composer to come after him. Bach fully explored the mathematical, romantic, theological implications of music to a degree that was definitive. The GIRL WAR Opera owes much to his examples.

BARTOK- Twentieth Century composer who significantly modernized this opera's score.

BASKING (IN ETERNITY)- Being's vocation on e'erelaxing on vacation.

BEAUTILITEASE- Miss Eternity ontoying with ontool usage.

BEAUTY- In considering egggracie as a *spirit faced* beauty, debate will inevitably arise. Broken shards of glass twinkle in the sunlight. Why isn't that considered beautiful. Of course that can be so...... with the aesthetically operative perspective. A defense of egggracie's beauty would boil down to the fact that it is very difficult to find a form of light that doesn't fall in in love with, or at least be likening struck by egggracie's encounter with likenesstrikes. To find Gracie less than lovely is pretty hard work. Less work is needed to be disenchanted by broken glass. Broken glass, like turds, needs more make up than such a thing as egggracie. The point is egggracie doesn't need bias to be beautiful, bias is what is needed to make her ugly. Gracie's beauty is only too obvious for her own good….suggestive of godlikeness in its lightning stricken likeness…..and not nasty at all…except to those who are nasty as deceitfully for real.

BEBLE- 1. Any lit e'er'd person that might be lived in sum's presentable eternity. 2. Possible person living in any m'eternity soone'er or late'er ward at all. 3. The possible person almightlink'd to life in precisely this eternity. 4. Iffffffished out pee pooh personelle of any time at all.

BEBLE BLOCK ETERNITY- The metaphysical notion d'e'erived from the block'd fabric of space/time concept in physics, that eternity may be pre(poste'erologically)fabricated as prewilled…….with iffforgone conclusions that make scheduling e'ercrafted appointments with eternity ont I'm'actually not hardly not ifffffeasible.

BEBLE'S ASIFFFONTHEOREM- Ontequerian variation of Bell's Theorem(of nonlocality) in quantum physics where e'erealty ont I'manifffffffests as assimulated in becomprehensively subjective ontemporality.

BECOMMON SENSE VERSUS BECOMMONTENSE- This dichotomy often emerges whenever eternities acquire universes. Becommon sense is a tool user's device evolved from selective pressures to make selections appropriated to the objective structures of cosmologies. Becommontense e'erefe'erences subjection'd'e'er's presentable I'domiciles' ifffontrajectories.

BECOMPLETELY PRESENTABLE ETERNITY- All that Gracie e'ereally wants for xmas.

BECONVENIENCE STORAGED E'ER- Egggracie's ontological 7/11 storage'erena.

BEHOLDING THE MIRROR UP TO NATURE- The task of the dramatist…which in this case……means beholding egggracie's heaventilation system to be hovercrafted over whate'er puddles for assimulated iffffects.

BE STUNG- 1. E'eraped by o'erwelmingly ont I'm naked notnotitude.

BIG AIM- 1. Being as iffffe'er'd on purpose. 2 The big game, whose half time show presents presentable tense.

BLASPHEMABLE- Embarrassmentally contradictable.

BLASPHEMABLE IN ALL BLASPHEMABLE DIMENSIONS-1. The ontentheological suggestion that all ontenthought may be explored becomprehensiffffffffffffffffffffffffffffffffffff( )fffffffffffffffffffffffffffffffffly……..at least……of course, of course……..not….not……ontentatively.

BLINKS- Of the notion that what's important happens in the blink of an eye with long speeches serving as justiffficatory janitors for mopping up whate'er the blinks have spilled.

BOMSORI KIM- Violinist and one of several charismatic Asian performers suitable for the role of Gracie in this opera's playground.

BOONE PAT- Ontemplate for Alex in the Girl War.

BRADLEY PITT- A suitable model for Alex in this opera.

BRAHMS- Master of motivic(symphonic) form that represents an important influence on The GIRL WAR Opera.

BRANDUMINION DOMINION- Attempt on the lifetime of eternity abusing branduminion's incriminated abomination plans to take over all of's e'ercraft scrambles. Behind this is the well-financed virology of spreadancing....spread exponentially across the democratrapped control of sunny side up systems, expanding to universes........from universes to universes.........controlling all of's universes ad infinitum to crack the could be iffffffffffffffffff( )fffffffffffffffffinitum barrie'er eventually to of course, of course, not...not........beacontrol the lighthouse in eternity. The ultimate iffffffffffffeasibility of this domino dominion theory has been tested in general holocaust's elections bought and paid for by the blackrock monoliths caught cropping up as iffished out of the Mesozoic swamps.

BUDDHA- 1. The great renunciator admonishing respect for sentient being as a wholegggrail. 2. Pretty cosmologically becomprehensive ethictician including all sentient being with his cosmethical concerns.

BULLDOZE- Operation performed on egggracie's brain ever since the Girl War.

CALCULUS- Branch of mathematics that calculates the comprehensive results of continuous change.

CAN OPENER- Gracie's could be kitchentont I'm'appliance to open e'er's of course, of course, notnotitude. See Alex's could be corkscrew alternative appliance.

CARTOON CHRIST- Quasi cooliffffffffied operational m'animation hatched out of egggracexistist aesthethics.

CARTOON EUMANIMATION- Such a thing as egggracie viewed as a sort of dreamergence......possible........, iffffff not in a universe, at least ont I'm'e'ergent in a becomprehensively presentable eternity.

CHEER LED ETERNITY- Ontool user egggracie's I'dictatorshipped e'er as supported by her pompom iffffffe'eroutines.

CHARLES LAUGHTON- A suitably tailored headliner for performable Felix in this opera.

CHRIST- 1. God in person. 2. Gracie's prototype. 3. Insomnibus driver and ontwered eternity's iffffffffffffirst impersonation of notnotitude's becompletely presentable e'ercraft'smen.

CINDERELLA- The fairy tale of the downtrodden girl with the hidden variable often overlooked. For all her downandoutitude when Cinderella gets make up, is bejeweled and is properly dressed................she has the inherent charm to put beneath the makeup, around the jewels and in the dress. Whatever waveform she takes, to be the party girl, euphemysteriously speaking, she has to display the part. She is not a lump in lipstick.

CLARAMAE TURNER- 1. The presence and the voice of the bar mistress in this opera. 2. The presence of Gracie in this opera.

CLOCK TIME/ONTIME/ONT I'M- Three temporal concepts that can be confused. 1. Clock time is to be measurably subjected to the objective laws of physics and can change with reference to changes in parameters related to those laws. 2. Ontime is a metaphysical construct referring, with or without a universe, to eternity's nowsy news'e'ervice as nextitudinative to to be. 3. Ont I'm is the subjective e'eresultimatum of ont I'm'eternity's nowsy news'e'ervice becoming I'dentifffffffy able to become ont I'much I'more mined than, for lack of notnotitudinativized I'motiffffation, what might end up as a dud eternity's just nowsy'snooze s'e'ervice.

CODES- Primitive alphabets to log e'erealty. The NOT/NOTNOT CODE is the alphabet most central to the metaphysics of this opera.

COOLIFFFFFFICATIIONS- Qualifications as jargonized by typical teenage girls in outer space.

COOLIFFFFACTUR'DS- Three forms of being as ontente'errorbustur'd out. 1. Quantum coolified 2. Qualum coolified 3. Quaintum coolif I'd'onto to be aesthethically egggracisturdolled up.

CONTENT VS ONTENT -While *content* refers to the simple placement of anything in anything, *ontent* refers to the interface between the realms of cosmic objectivity and the ontique'erian e'erealm of not not being.

CORKSCREW- Courtesy of a bottle of gin in his possession, this is Alex's alternative to Gracie's can opener requests.

COSMESOZOIC- The smackdabbness of the middle of the middle of the middle of life in the objective universe keeping eternity out of the a priori picture.

COSMOS- 1. Universe. 2. Objective reality.

COSMOS/ONTOS DICHOTOMY- Whereas *cosmos* may be viewed as the cosmological ground of being's informatorium, ontos may be viewed as the ontological ground of beings iffffffformatorium. Cosmos in egggracist metaphysics is ente'erpreted as a mere samplifffffoccasion of the's wholegggrailarge'erealty of the becomprehensive *ontos.......*at this ontentheoretical situation's as iffffffffff( )ffffffffoundation.

COUNTENANCE- Spirit face.

CRUCIFFFFFFFFFFFFFICTION-The crux of being still chalked onto the story board at the metaphysical society.

CUTE- What log 17 base 10 seconds of make up did for such a thing as egggracie.

DEATH MADE SAMPLE DAY- D DAY.

DEATH MADE SIMPLE DAY- The perfect holocaust, the holocaust no victim won, where starvation was not the issue, August 6, 1945.

DENIAL- In this opera....e'erefusal to recognize the one girl holocaust of such a thing as egggracie's post war, onthrone, beblbleacher seating situation.

DIANE BAKER- Actress who has played Gracie and can do it again.

DISNEY WALTER- The masterpieced together puzzle's cartoon puddle's ont I'manimator asmered, bulldozed and sleep-walked overtly today.

DOG SPELLED BACKWARDS- God.

DOLLED UP DOO- Miss Eternity's make up spirit faced to make stars stylish.

DREAME'ERGENCE- A central concept in this opera. It must be stated clearly that dreame'ergence, as an ontiquerian idea, does not involve some local swamp or some local universe so much as sum's becomprehensiffffffly presentable eternity. It is this eternity that is Gracie's heaventilated home ontown'd thou art iffffffffff( )ffffffffffacte'er I'domain's selfished out ont I'mainot not ifffff( )fffffff I'm'attraction.

DREAME'ERGENT- 1. God looking. 2. Becompletely presentable as subject devised.

DREAMURGENCY- Pressure on eternity to make subjective being of course not not presentable.

DUMP- 1. (Noun) Where all of's holocausts put Gracie. 2. (verb) What Gracie would have to do to Alex if he ever didn't let her do it to herself.

ECLIPSE S'E'ERVICE- How an objective universe hides a subjectively presentable eternity.

E'ER- 1. Ever. 3. Eternity.

E'ERCRAFT- 1. Any beickle ontraveling forever. 2. Insomnibus

E'EREALTY- Reality considered in terms of becompletely presentable eternity.

E'ERESPONSIBILITY- Presentable eternity's lack of alibis.

E'ERESTOCRACY- The not not bebles that gnow all about ontrophickly presentable eternity.

E'ERITUAL APPEASEMENT- Bebreathing e'erespect to all of's ifffe'erways.

E'EROMANCIPATED ASIFFFFUX/ROMANCIPATED FUX DICHOTOMY- Algorythmic formalities of fux depending on the object as subjected to and the subject as objected to. E'eromancipated asifffflux occurs whenever preposte'erology's a priori protocols are her'd for Miss Eternity ontantalizing e'er'dreame'ergent e'ercraft with iffffrontalways I'd thou artess'd I'decisions. Romancipated fux abounds where docubicklimented careened aircraft collisions replace such could be care'er's I'decisions.

EGGS- Maternal resource at the ground of living being.

EGGGRACIE-1. The egggod all of us want in our puddles. 2. Such a thing as Gracie reduced from out of dreame'ergence to certain cosmetrickly corralled specifications.

EGGGRACIEXISTENCE STUDIES- A new undergraduate requirement in Alex's new universion's university curriculum, fathoming in academic terms the meanings of such a thing as egggracie 1. (cosmetickly speaking) inhabiting a universe and 2. Ontiquely speaking……inhabiting an eternity.

EGGGRACISM- Like racism, egggracism may be manifest in two aesthethical forms 1. Predatory egggracism and 2. Existential egggracism. While predatory egggracism is not to be condoned, existentical egggracism, on the other hand, is wholegggrailavishly encouraged in the dramatic constitution of this opera. There is a delicate aesthethical balance to be uncovered with these destinctions……..which this opera conscientiously reaches for in the end. To make no provision of existential egggracism is to invite the demographic holocaust of egggrace afraid to exist.

ELIZABETH KAITAN- Gracie incarnate from Assault of the Killer Bimbos.

ELON MUSK- 1. Post-modern civilization's most important entrepreneur and a male model for both Gracie and Alex in this opera. 2. The last great hope for log 16 base 10 seconds of cosm(ont)ological planetary history. 3. The historical figure behind the ELAN concept as presented, explicitly or implicitly, in this opera. 4. An historical model for Alex in his demi-god phase of character development. 5. Falsely quoted historical figure from the opera's texts as have him famously saying things he almost didn't quite say.

ELON'S MONEY- Money that invents the worlds in contrast to money that is paid to money.

EMOTION QUOTIENTS- The concept of EQ was invented to deal with the Mesozoic mainstream's criminal stupidity. The idea here is that egggracie is trapped in a world controlled by the darkest of emotion quotients(EQs) not yet risen to the most primitive level of basic IQ (intelligence quotience). Either way you judge it with Gracie as a god among humans or a human among animals, the point is that Gracie is trapped on a plot thin goof off world completely lacking IQably quotable intelligence. In the meantime Gracie's wholegggrailevitations are lifting her into e'erealms of ONTELLIGENCE QUOTIENCE(OQ) becompletely beyond e'erealms of coursed of course could becolleagues to (lighthouse wise) beaconverse with. This is where Apollex must step into the linguistic scenery to give Gracie a somewhat heaventilated handshake. It must be admitted that this high-Q cosmic handshake serves Gracie well until she has stretched the equations onto ontique'erian grounds, where the standard, having left EQs in the cosmesozoic dust, is no longer just IQ, but OQ. Whether Apollex's high IQ will ont I'm'ature to satisfy gracie's onteque'erian OQ quest remains uncertain at the end. As a demigod, Alex is certainly doing his bestung best well beyond mainstream cosmesozoo conversensations operating nowsy news casts by beastongues on beast dung. What is intriguing in the plot of EQS, IQS and OQS is Mobible's status. As the highest IQ in the opera (with all due respect to Tele and Wolfy), Mobible has the option to asifffffffffffake his OQ for egggracie'sake or ont I'm'editate his way into sum's'e'erious ontenlightenment. Mobible's history as a can opener among kitchen appliances may serve him well in that regard or Mobible may just decide to fake it in the EQ world of backside bottom level mainstream talking points. But that drama is material for another black listed operation.

ENT- An object being objectively

ENTROPIC- Traveling through time as bought and paid for on the cosmic plan from e'eromancipated asifffffffluck's lullaby toward heated flux nightmare as iffffux.

EUPHEMIFFFFFANGLED- Spirit faced egggeometrickly to inform make up kits of dreame'ergent iffffformation systems.

EQUALITY- 1. Expression of an equation. 2. Concept of an objectively fair trial. 3. Ethical alternative to unethical equity.

EQUITY- 1. Distortion of balance on the scales of judicial equality. 2. Unethical power-driven distortion of ethical concept of equality before the law.

EQUATIONS- Quantitative statements of accurately balanced realities.

ESCAPE HATCH- 1. A way out of a given phylogeny. 2. A way out of a given universe. 3. A way out of a given eternity.

ETERNITY- 1. A mathematical construct of non-finite temporality. 2. The ontiquerian venue for selfished out samplifffffff I'd cosmosis. 3. Ifffabrick laye'er'd e'er in s'e'erivce to notnotitude. 4. Presentably ontrophick e'erealty. 5. The becompletion of notnotitudinal nextitudination. 6. Becomprehensive nowsy news'e'ervice. 7. Whene'er.

ETERNITY TEST SITE EXPE'ERIMENT- 1. Gracie's Ont I'maptempt to beget control of eternity's e'eresurrectiontalents. 2. Egggracie's scheduled attempt on the life of eternity when she designates appointments with the ides of e'er for the past, present and future to meet in her nowsy news broadcast. The hope is to achieve an ontique'erian ifffffffffff( )fffffffffflash appointmention when e'eresurrection becomes not only ifffffffeasible but decidedly coolifffffffied to of course, of course not not {{{occur}}}, e'ereminiscing eternity with its n'alibiblical status as the's e'eresponsible party behind universes and other what have you what not notiifffffactories.

EUMAN- 1. Simply a good man. 2. Transcendent individual emergent out of a primate soup. 3. High I Q person attempting to maintain intelligence against the drag of the main stream media. 4. Any dreamergent being escape hatching out of the human holocaust.

EUMANITY- 1. You manity as met through second personalities. 2. Aesthethically good people. 3. This term may refer to egggracie's quest to escape from the holocaust of human speciation's Mesozoic menu. It must be admitted that there is a certain amount of bigotry involved with this quest. However, it is only the bigotry to beget out of a hopeless 1. demographic, 2. ideological, 3. prey animal cartooned in humanimation. The motivation is not power…but existence….which to say……of coursed of course not not to be such a thing as egggracie as 1. of such a thing,2. by such a thing and 3. for such a thing as……..egggracie.

EXISTENCE- 1. Notnotitude. 2. The most ethical motive of all of's time(contrasted with supremacism)

EXPLICIT SELF EVIDENCE- Usually referring to egggracie's xxxrated nasty status as too explicitly obvious for ont I'mirror consumption in the dark loudiness of the Mesozoic environment where her simulation brings up all sorts of possibilities of her being 1. Self evident. 2. Elf evident. 3. Human. 4. Euman 5. De trop(ontentologically) to aesthethically even talk about.

FARRELL,D. - Prolifically pseudonymic composer of operatic music, lyric and drama.

FERRIS WHEEL- A concretely symbolic structure in this opera from which egggracie simulates(qualuminates) ontangents from the cosmos onto the onithetical e'erealms onthrough her ont I'manifffffffestations of e'erainbow excretions courtesy of her halo.

FORSYTHE JOHN- The actor to play Alex. Note, Alex may or may not be human, but he should look it. John Forsythe does that. It is to be noted as well that Alex's character is that of a genuinely decent being. Performing that role is also well within Forsythe's grasp.

FUN- Another reason for existence.

GALYA MORRELL- Russian artiste who influenced Gracie's development.

GEISHA- Nippontical egggracie.

GISELA STEINMAYER- 1. Pregnant zero's one girl holocaust that died while dying to be dead. 2. The aboriginator of this opera in its present format.

GIRL WAR(THE PLAY)- This play is all about a universe ontool used not not onto be as all about presented tense ontoyed with for forever.

GIRL WARS- 1. Conflicts in Mesozoic society resulting from dreame'ergence of spirit face transcendence ifffreaked out of atypical egggirliffffffactoried outer space. Such euphemyste'erious girl war ifffffe'er "graciethos" becomes cosmontraumatically dramatized in this opera's libretto. Meanwhile it must be admitted that such 'girl war' conflicts occur in the larger context of WORLD WAR WHENEVERS.

GOD- 1. Presentable m'eternity in disguise. 2. Not notit's dude. 3. Dog spelled backwards.

GRACIE- 1. The winner of the Miss Eternity Pageant over runner up reality……but……quite not quite……whene'erizoned to work dog spelled backwards in the end. 2. A cute girl cartoon version of the Christ, heaventilating hints of almight's ont I'magic tricks, but…………… almost not quite really. 3.

GRACE KELLY-1. Aboriginal egggracie from the Mesozoic-Metazoic interface era. 2. Apollonian version of gracystems.

GRACEXISTISM- Protectionistic ideology on behalf of such a thing as a gracie.

GRACIE'S ONT I'METAPHYSICS- Insulated by e'er from the usual practicalities of cosmic immersion, Gracie's metaphysics has seen iffffffffits to ont I'm'encompass the all or nothingness of course of coursed not not to be. Her bigotry outs up against I'm'd notitude, as scandalous as it may seem, she justiffffffffffffies with justajiffffffffy's justice that is pretty ontough to argue against in the's iffffinal analyses as becomprehensiffffffffly e'erafted could be capsized up.

GRACIFFFFFFFFFFFF( )FFFFFFFFFFECT(THE'S)- Obse'ervance d'e'eriving the not not notion that one moment of spirit faced gracemotion heaventilates e'eright onthrough all of's second hand clock workouts to as iffffffffall of's iffffffffallen in love's eterniteased ifffe'erewards ontrophic e'ereception.

GRACISM VERSUS RACISM- Gracism as practiced today is primarily an existential phenomenon. It contrasts sharply with predatory racism which constitutes the prevailing ideological alternative to existential gracism today. It is to be noted that the monolithic term 'racism' itself has been weaponized by predatory racists to attack the aesthethical proponents of existential gracism.

GRACYSTEMIC STUDIES- The academic pursuit of such a thing as dreame'ergence.

GWINETH PALTROW- A model for Gracie.

HALFTIME- Eternity's presented tense.

HALO- What emerges metaphorically from a taile'er'd head to ove'eride swampersonalitease.

HALOIDS- Those with pretty hemishperes under their halos.

HALO RAPES- The primary school project of holocausts as advertised.

HEAD- What emerges from a tale to give it directions.

HEGEL- Philosopher whose ideational dialectics lead through various assortmentionabilities to the ideal summation of reality.

HENRY V- Shakespeare's favorite king who started out his life as Prince Hal, derelict and irresponsible to his royal obligations until………waking up one day in a cold sweat he realized suddenly that it was incumbent upon him to take his father's place and save the kingdom. We see this same phenomenon today with certain heroic figures rising up against overwhelming odds to save civilization from the barbarians of the time.

HERO- What becomes of pregnant zero's iffffflux in the m'eternity ward egggift shoppe.

HERO'S QUEST(THE)- The ultimate romantic quest to save the girl to happen ever after often fought against all odds and surreptitious ends of the quest for the usurption of the girl, to be removed to someone's else as happens never after.

HEAVENTILATION SYSTEMS- Systems sublimating p-universal egggas clouds onto the larger belongings of e'ercrafted e'er.

HIGH-Q- Improvements in intelligence capitalizaing of seasonal shifts of latitude.

HIROSHIMA- THE HOLOCAUST.

HISS- What snakes attach to terms with sharpentspit.

HISTORICAL GRACIE- It must be understood that Gracie is not to be associated with any specific historical event except algorythmickally. Gracie was aboriginally conceived by a six year old mind through the apprehension of two six year old girls, one Japanese, one Norwegian. That original apprehension beheld within its grasp the qualities of "ontiquerian iphphphyluminated" feminine transcendence. The full apprehension of those two historical statuses was only understood later, by which time Gracie's character was already well constituted for dramatic purposes.

HISTORY- Invested interests in past events as sold to the highest bidder.

HOLOCAUST ADVERTISEMENTS- Heavy duty ads, heavily handed down, for heavily preferred holocausts.

HOLOCAUST DAY- Ritual recognition of the fact that every day is Holocaust Day in the Mesozoic swamp meats.

HOLOCAUST DENIAL DAY- 1. August 6, 1945. 2. The dawn of the setting's sunny today for cultural holocausts in the advertising industry.

HOLOCAUSTE'EROIDS- Pills taken to manufacture holocaust consent.

HOLOCAUSTS- 1. The bombing of Hiroshima in August of 1945. 2. The bombing of Nagasaki in August of 1945. 3. The attacks on Paradise and Lahaina in the the 21st century. 4. The Natorthorized holocaust in becomtempt's contemporary Ukraine. 5. The vast goologged holocausts that win the number's game for popular holocaust retrospective projections. 6. The Briana K twenty six dumouths holocaust. 7. Several others of undeniably denied historical note.

HOLOCAUSTS IN HIDING'STUDIES- 1. A graduate course in digging up the silenced dead wherever they may be. 2. Of course, of course evaluations of hyphenated holocausts including 1. Cultural holocausts. 2. Demographic holoausts. 3. Linguistic holocausts. 4. One girl dumouth holocausts.

HOLOCAUST SUPREMACISM- Omnipotent claims on holocaustories.

HOPE- The sum'swhat ontoptimyste'erious view that such a thing as egggracie represents ifffformative heaventilation's hope 1. Hope for eumanity's IQ. 2. Hope for eumans romancipating fux. 3. Hope for puzzles as masterpieced in whate'er's puddles. 4. Hope for becompletely presentable eternity ontacted out within. 5. Hope for etceteras……..etcete'eratied just ont I'm.

HUMAN HOLOCAUST(THE)- The notion that humanity itself constitutes a holocaust species fatally dangerous to all other phylogeny on its margins. This includes 1. a. non-human mammals and avia and b. reptiles (not in the hedge fund industries). 2. Transcendiary being's like elves, eumans, becomputers, egggracies and demi-gods. Explosions of escape routines for all such outlying creatures are being formulated of course, of course not..not….in the current era.

HUMAN LANGUAGE- The linguistic legacy of the girl war, now archaic, designed to pressurize such a thing as egggracie out of the possibility of being. It is a dialect that has been replaced by Euman language where egggracie of course of course notnot courses are given at the Institute for Miss Eternity Studies.

HYPE'ERTHESIS- The term applied to presentable eternity's ability to ope'erate with justajiffffy's ifffffffficiency.

IFFFFFFONTHROTTLES- Preposte'erological propulsion soul-idrafts ope'erating out at see.

IFFFFFFOOTBALL IFFFFFFINS- Potential pedal players from iffffished out of whate'er.

INGRID BERGMAN- Ont I'm'e'eraculous actress who has already played Gracie more than enough.

INSIDIOUS LIES- Deceit as convinces the listener that he is lying as listener by not listening to the lies as listed to be listened to. Insidious lies are commonly mediated through cash offerings and dominate, as such, the bulk of public information systems.

JAMES DEAN- A suitable model for Alex in this opera.

JAPAN- Since Gracie is often viewed as a sort of Nippontical Miss Eternity, it is natural that the opera will eventually be produced in Japan. Classical Japanese culture may be inclined to embrace Gracie as an iconic Japanese heroine. Many aspects of both the drama, the ont I'mesoterique metaphysics and the music are particularly suitable for Japanese and related Asian audiences.

JARGON- Gracie's justajiffffy jargon, as eme'ergent out of the eternity of her metaphysical perspective, does present a problem for the production of this play. At first it may seem to be impenetrable. It represents a linguistic culture that must be absorbed with the exposure to the Girl War libretto. Metaphysically speaking, many philosophies view the 'ground of being' in cosmological terms. As such Gracie's non-cosmological 'ontique'erian' views can be confusing. In the case of this play the problem is remediable for several reasons. 1. Gracie's character is as dramatically powerful as her metaphysics is profound. 2. Even if only partially grasped, the metaphysics is comic in a manner unlike any other metaphysics. 3. There is music to back up the play's entertainment value. 4. The jargon stands behind the most original complex of ideas the audience will have ever encountered, in or out of opera. 5. Eventually the jargon will be embraced by the English Language as a whole.

JOHN MORRY- Alex among the Nunamiut who wanted to be the hero that saves the girl.

JULIAN ASSANGE- Alex personiffff I'd.

JUSTAGIFFY- Referring to whenever notnotitude might be in sum what's news counting down from iffffffffinity to pregnant zero's once upont I'm.

JUST KIDDING- The notion that eggs, no matter how olde, are subject to be mentally cracked in any shell shocked universe you put them.

I AM CONSTRUCT- Any sentence structure iffffavored by iffffffffinity to I'm ploy the first person singular indicative verb moo'd however cow'd sum'othe'erwise.

ICKEY STUFF- 1.Notnotitude self-smudged. 2. I'dirt.

IDES OF E'ER- Half time in eternity.

IFFFFFFFFFF( )FFFFFFFFFF- Designating the possibility of not not being.

IFFFFFFFINITUDE- The estate of the possibility of not not being.

INFORMATION/IFFFFFORMATION- Whereas information is the substance objectionably lensed of an objectionably equationable universe, iffffffformation is the ont I'm'e'ergently apparent substance iffffodde'ering the facts from as iffffacts….. behind both lenses and their equations.

INSOMNIBUS- Any beickle or mote'erhome that refuses to sleep through not never's night.

IRENE DUNNE- Gracie as mama in the middle of the middle of the middle ages.

JULIE ANDREWS- Gracie played over and over.

JUDY HOLLIDAY- Egggreat comic actress who could iconically represent the character of Gracie in either Bronx, Brooklyn or Jerusalem productions of this opera.

KEANU REEVES-1. A good and decent euman. 2. Alex in this opera played up front and center.

KINDERGARDEN- Where holocausteroid pills are initially popped.

KNIGHT OF THE APOLOCALYPSE- 1. The ultimate Faustian hero against all astronomical odds. 2. The most despicablated hero of civilized history. 3. The last hope's hero. 4. Prince Hal as Henry V.

LARA LOGAN- Reporter introduced in opera.

LENSES- Either them or mirrors showing equations where to get their numbers.

LINGUISH- Gracie's dialect of ontalk's justajifffy jargon often entailing ontological prefixes in phonetically suitable environments. Even though this jargon clutters up much of the book of the opera, much of it can be eliminated in performance.

LIPS- Nasty notnot to be's asifffffontalked eternitease.......as wholegggrailinguishly lipped, ont I'm'exposing.......asifffffflagrante I'delicto, xxxxxx()xxxxxrated ont I'mouthing's off iffffe'er.

LOG 1 BASE 10 SECONDS- The time required to dislocate ontenthing's egggracie this time e'eround.

LOG 17 BASE 10 SECONDS- The time required to locate ontenthing's egggracies this time e'eround.

MADE SIMPLE BOOKS- The kindergarten primer books that explained to Gracie how to not exist: 1. DEATH MADE SIMPLE. 2. DEATH FOR BEGINNERS. It is to be noted that later in the opera Gracie's papal variations of these books are in evidence in Scene XII: 1. BEING MADE SIMPLE. 2. ETERNITY MADE SIMPLE. 3. UNIVERSIONS MADE SAMPLE.

MAMMACIOUS-1. The fourth egggeological episode of the Mesozoic that saw the dreamergence of such a thing as egggracie.......momente'erily belonging to egggracystems echoculturally supportive of egggrace. 2. Periffffffffffe'erally referring to ont I'm'any sum'other's moment when such a thing as a gracie's dreame'ergence can occur....like in or out of a universe....like....in or out of a given eternity.

MARYLYN MONROE- A Dionysian version of egggracystems which e'erecent improvements in her impossibility have becomfirmed as iffffffffffit for Gracie's character.

MAX VON SYDOW- A great and iconic actor to represent 'daddy' in this opera.

MAXWELL EQUATIONS- The four equations for the results of electronicks that generated the modern Mesozoo.

MEATY PHYSICS- Objective information systems d'e'erived from ontrophickly presentable eternity's iffffffffffffffffffffffff( )ffffffffffffffffffffffffformation systems..

MENDELSSOHN- Early romantic composer whose music was influential in the composition of this opera.

MESOZOIC- 1. The middle period of life, marked by the Triassic, the Jurassic, the Cretacious and the Mammacious. 2. The period before the Metazoic.

METAZOIC- E'ercrafts after all period after the Mesozoic.

MISS ETERNITY- 1. The dreame'ergent euphemyste'erium. 2. Dreame'ergent euphemiss isled I thou artistry I'deiffffffffffffffffffffying all beget outs of the ont I'm'e'erkit place. 3. Entontranscendent bablistical impersonation of not notitude. 4. Ontaesthethics personifffffied. 5. The most extreme form of the Miss Eternity concept as it applies to Gracie is seen where ontrophickly presentable eternity itself is could be conceptually viewed as of course, of course....not...not.....nothing more than behicular e'ercraft for the presentation of such a thing as Gracie as dreame'ergent, universe or no universe, anywhere, anytime, anyhow. In other words, eternity is becompetent as a suite'er simply to becommont date such a thing as grace. Dreame'ergently speaking, gracie e'ereally does own ont I'm'eternity. 6. Egggracie's much borrowed embodiment of ontranscendent egggracism. 7. The transcendent being whose make up kit makes civilization civilized.

MID-E'ER COLLISIONS-

MONEY GRIP- The power grid that controls the ads for 1. Lies. 2. Holocausts. 3. Death certification in general. 4. Virtue signals 5. Hairdos. 6. Indictments. 7. Conspiracy theories 8. Straw men. 9. Trendy tomorrows. 10. Trendy todays. 11. Trendy yesterdays. 12. Web workouts.

MOZART- Classical master whose operatic musical wit influenced the composition of this opera.

NASTY PERSON-A straw man N-word trope referring to any person not in agreement with the tenets of the industrially informative psychosis complex.

NEWS- Nextitudinated e'ereports of nowsy iffffffffontents.

NEXTITUDINATION- The process of nows becoming sumother nows next door to sumother nows next door to sumother nows…..and so one ad iffffffffffffffffff( )ffffffffffffinite items.

NICE PERSON EGGGIRL WAR ZONE- 1. Referring to the notion that egggracie can be as amazing as she is and still iffffffunction ont I'militarily as a nice person. 2. The strategic notion that egggracie can be nicely impersonated(nice personed) to death, extinction or becomplete impossibility. 3. Weaponized nice impersonations in general.

NOT/NOTNOT CODE (THE)- 1.Egggracie's alphabet for preposte'erologically whate'er'down'd eternity's as ifffontextualized asiffffffontalk, ontologically algorithmic to the cosmological 0/1 code of pre-becompute'erized computentalk. 2. The binary onteque'erian code for such a thing as egggracie's becompletely becomprehensible ont I'metaphysics. 3.. The basick alphabet of ontique'erianism.

NOTNOTITUDE- 1. The binary construct of BEING, notnotable for its ontological abilities to get stuff done. 2. Preposte'erologicality's ont I'm'essential ontgreedient. 3. Ont I'm. 4. The bette'eriffffft half of such a thing as egggracess'd ifffffffffffffffffffffffffffffff(   )fffffffffffffffffffffffffffffffffffffamous NOT/NOTNOT CODES. 5. The metaphysical notion that kicks bottom'd outing's butt foundations iffffft offing universes.

NOW- 1. Presently tensed. 2. Presented. 3. The's ides of e'er

NOWSY- Presenting tense in a careless, sleazy manner.

OBJECT- The thing toward which subjectivity's to be directed.

OBVIOUS- Self-evidentickly of absolute self-evidensity.

ONT- The common prefix to a given word where that word's (ontique'erian) *being* is emphasized.

ONTANTRUMMINATIONS- E'erants over disappointments scheduled for any given eternity.

ONTE'ER'D ETERNITY- Eternity viewed as ontique'erealty.

ONT DUH'D ETERNITEASE- Becomspiritontentspirations for ont I'moments of silence observed on behalf of ides of e'er's incomplete presentabilitease.

ONTENSE'ER CALCULUS-1. Ontiquely speciffffic version of ONTENSOR CALCULUS. 2. Highly controversial branch of ont I'm'athematics refe'erencing ontrigonometrick whate'er's iffffffontifffffunctions related to presentable eternities rather than tensor calculus's cosmic distortions of space-time as referenced in physics. In other words, ontense'er calculus describes how not not being distorts the 'fabric' of not being.

ONT/ENT DICHOTOMIES- Maniffffestations of beings as either self-evidently simple or objectively sample. What we behavior with onts is simply who they are as eggghost eggs as ont I'm'obviously iffffont I'm'e'er'd. What we have behaved with ents is samply speaking......what a universe might make of them as *what* they are in particle schedules rather than *who* they are (as eggghost eggs or not as eggghost eggs) as ont I'm'obviously...I'm'evidensickey I'm'e'er'd.

ONT I'M- Ontitude in person

ONTE'ERPRISE- Projecting notnotitude as a business.

ONTENTE'ERPRISE- Project notnotitude as a business reduced to operations of cosmic eclipse'ervice.

ONTELEOLOGICAL- Iffffinal outcomes viewed e'ergoing way, way, way past objective samplings.

ONTENSE'ER CALCLUS- Ont I'mathematick's newest branch as ontwigged haloidolled up.

ONTENTICKLES- Notnotitude's ontouchy pointing oute'er devices.

ONTENTRIFFFICATION- Process of taking on reality as a whole both for those becosmetrickly immersed and the m'eternity ward's ontique shoppers.

ONTHEORIZED ETERNITY-Eternity as iffffffff( )fffffffathomed for ontique'erian values.

ONTHROTTLES- Preposte'erological becompeller peddles. (see also "iffffonthrottles")

ONT I'MATADORE- The notion that such a thing as egggracie, in her confrontations with beblossophy, can achieve escape philossity with her wand while directly facing the bestung beast.

ONT I'MID E'ER- 1. Becompletely presentable eternity presentED. 2. Nowsilly presented not notitude in I'daily news broadcasts. 3. Whenever egggracie's wings are waiting for her. 4. Whenever egggracie's shoulde'er'd ontorsowning her wings.

ONTIQUE- A coolifffffffied quaint form of ontological.

ONTEQUERIAN OPERA- It appears there is sum's ont I'movement iffffffffoot to make THE GIRL WAR merely the first of ont I'many iffffonthingdom's operas. Indeed it is not becompletely impossible that all of literature, both euman and human, as selfished out stylishly, may as iffffollow suit.

ONT I'M'ANY- The esote'eric version of the declension of ont I'money. Ont I'money is used witlessly all the time in phrases like "Ifffffffollow the ont I'money" Notably *money* may be declined as *miney, meany or m'any*. For this opera the 'ont I'many' declension is most useful as following e'eround egggracie as 'iffffollowing iffffffont I'm'anythingirl's as iffffffonthing'.

ONTIQUE SHOPPE- Ontrophickly presentable eternity viewed as venue for purchase of iffffffodde'er'd goods as well as I-kitchen appliances accompanying what gross e'er can provision.

ONTISYMETRICAL- Purely ontequerian version of cosmontological ONTENT-SYMETRY ont I'm'atching egggracie's heaventilation system overhead with whene'er wings to becomplete the dreame'ergentrifffff I'd picture of Gracie as becompletely presentable eternity's ont I'model for I'd thou artisticky ifffffffigured, I'd thou artistick figured eggground.......of egggroundolled up ward's not not being.

ONTOPIA- Ideally presentable eternity.

ONTOS- The e'erealm a priori to and ontranscendent of the cosmos.

ONTOYS- Play'd with onthings at notnotitude while just kidding.

ONTRANSHUMANISM- Making a living s'e'erviced to e'ercraft design.

ONTROPHIC- Nourishing being

ONTROPHY- Ont I'metalic award for being.

ONTROPIC- presentably tensed toward being.

ONTUCKER- Eggracie's iffffe'erest onte'erviewer.

ONTURD ETERNITY- 1. Egggracie's controversial theory that an objective universe is an excretion of subjectionably ont I'm'eternity. 2. The notion that the make up kit of onte'er'd eternity enturds enterritory entwinkled just like stars.

ONTWE'ERED- As iffffffiness conside'er'd ontiquely.

ONTWILIGHT- Ontique shopped e'er's twilight.

ONTWINKLES- Ontique shopped starlike reverbe'erations.

QUALIFFFFFFFFFY- 1. Quantifffffy but subjectively. 2. Variant of cooliffffffffffy.

QUALUM- Subjected to subjection.

QUANTUM- Subjected to be objected.

QUASI- Merely simulated on the short list of as ifffffffffffffff's ifs.

PAN METRON ARISTON- Solon's motto advocating moderation in all endeavors. This motto does apply to the various levels of satire in this opera. Where there is severely heavy-handed propaganda prevailing in the holocaust culture confronted, the satire takes a flagrantly flamboyant holocaustwist. However....where the cultural propaganda contronted is of a less severe nature, the satirical response is more moderately balanced.

PECULIARITY OF BEING- The recognition that being is 1. Irreplaceable by anything else. 2. preposte'erologically to be a priorily goal posted. 3. What makes eternity more than a mathematical construct of non-finite temporality. 4. Provident of eternity's as iffffffffffffff( )ffffffffffffinite values.

PLATO- Greek philosopher who founded philosophy's theory of ideas………eventuating to such a thing as Gracie's ontheory of iffffffont I'd'e'ers..

POMPOMS- Whether ontooled or ontoyed, these are egggracie's weapons of cheerleadership for ont I'm'encouragement of becompletely presentable eternity.

POWER GRID- The money grip enthrottling the ads for 1. Whistles in the dark 2. Strawmen 3. Death certificates. 4. Hairdos. 5. Indictments 6. Virtue signals. 7. Holocausts. 8. Tomorrows. 9. Todays. 10. Yesterdays. 11. Facts fictionalized. 12. Fictions factovated.

PREDATORY RACISM- Ethnographic orientation toward the destruction of a given ethnic phylogeny (in contrast to existential racism). Weaponized as such, the most prevalent cultural weapon of predatory racism is the(non-binary) monolithic term 'RACISM' left linguistically undefined in its various possible predatory implications. It is to be noted that predatory racism is almost always a bad idea, whereas existential racism, depending on the menu, may or may not be so.

PREPOSTE'EROLOGICAL- Referring to considerations of the sum total of reality, before and after the factual occurrences.

PREPOSTE'EROLOGY- The ont I'm'academick study of ontology's ontempe'er I'dimensions.

PRESENTABLE TENSE- 1. What e'er's onto ontension-wise. 2. What forever's onto.

PRESENTED TENSE- 1. Now. 2. Ont I'm'eventuality.

PRESENTABILITY- 1. The ability to maniffffest the present tense. 2. The state of adequate stylishness for a given social situation.

PRETTY PLEAS- Aesthethical appeals.

PRETTY WOMEN- The eufemystical phenomenon of dreamergentrified women e'eromanticipating asifffffflux (generally) and romancipating fux(specifically)………through eufemyste'erious bruty. This aesthethical eugenic event changed human social interaction permanently, s'excellerating a new a prioritization of spirit face as a socially centralized phenomenon. Hellen of Troy is paradigmatic of this phenomenon but it is constantly being both covered up and exposed in the recesses of all major human primate interaction. Social etiquette has made discussion of this phenomenon strictly taboo except under circumspection of brutility's obliquely angled in vogued magazine's linguistic routines. Marilyn Monroe is a soon to be ifffffossilized example of this phenomenon in the pretty soon to be asifffffffossil e'erecord.

PREY EUMANIMATION- As can be cartooned, the main prey animal in these parts scheduled for such a thing as egggracie's 1. Obsolescence or 2. Impossibility 3. Or all else in between.

PROCESS THEOLOGY- Whitehead's philosophy suggesting cosmological limits to the talents of god or gods to improvise reality beyond what may be a prioritized. Ontologically speaking of course, of course, the question remains…..what about the preposte'erological basis of such improvisation. Such conside'erations lead to several set theories of simulated deiffffffffffffffffffffactovation. Gracie's metaphysics, while not specifically disallowing the possibility of demigods, like Apollonian Alex, points through its not/notnot code to sumonthing I'dontologically more almightning structured in deiffffffffoccasion. No offense to Apollo or Whitehead, but becompletely presentable eternity's notnotitude is Gracie's nowsy newsworthy god.

PROPAGANDA- The target of much of the satire in this history, not to be confused with generic critiques of any given culture or religion.

PUDDLE EFFECT(THE)- Derived from Gracie's artistic success with puddles, the realization that self-evidence is its own affirmation. Contrariwise, those without success in puddles may be seen to spend enormous resources to affirm their qualifications to be cool. Such a thing as Gracie is too obvious to need such investments in advertising, slandering the opposition and generally controlling the culture industry. But that is what makes THE GIRL WAR rather unique.

P UNIVERSE- The objective universe as performed as perfumed e'eromatically.

PUNIVERSE- The universe viewed as a sample of a larger than cosmic e'erealty.

RACHMANINOFF- Twentieth century romantic composer whose pianistic stylizations were influential for this opera.

RACISM- Notable by proclamation as a meaningless term which can only indulge meaning when parced into its constituents. There are two forms of this term 1. Ethnocentrality's existential beconstructionism and 2. Predatory racism's deconstructionism. It is to be noted that many 'anti' terms….as refer to…..'antithis'…..or 'antithat' are foundried in predatory racism.

The phenomenon of *predatory racism* does behave two representatives in the opera. *Daddy's* trigger finger confessions in Scene VII clearly do implicate that character in the criminal behavior of predatory racism. However, this behavior, is seen to be in the past tense, during the actual GIRL WAR episodes predating the opera. The audience may observe that daddy (the monk) does show some albeit belated remorse along with serious misgivings about his own military attractions during the war. An ambivalient whisp of evil does however betray itself in the monk's complaint about the 'silencing of the dead that lose the wars'.

In contrast to the monk, Ms Speck must be said to exhibit the phenomenon of *predatory racism* in its most poisonous expression. Ms Speck's soul, as such, embodies a darkness where no light may enter. The irony here is that Speck's predatory racism serves as a masquerade for the vibrilliant egggracism lurking within the graceless confines of her own shattered mirrors.

As far as Gracie's egggrasystemetry is concerned…let us say that Gracie's ehtnocentrality is one of a kind, and, as such, it's egggrasystemic maniffffestation of 'egggracism' must be construed as part of the party girl process of euphemiphylumenation that is all alone. As a result, Gracie's eggracism manifests as sufficiently shame face-pirated to participate in it's own demographic holocaust….as such a thing…so ashamed…..that it is afraid to actually exist.

REPLACEMENT THEORY-The falsely falsified theory that the attempt on the life of western civilization is being pursued at the level of cultural, demographic and linguistic holocaust. We see these effects in action with the aboriginal work of Walter Disney being replaced by distorted subversions of all of Disney's aboriginal artistic intent.

RESPIGHI- Master of atmospheric nuance. Respighi's delicate orchestrations were influential to the composition of The GIRL WAR.

RITE OF PASSAGE- No longer controversial notion that such a thing as egggracie should not stop off for long on the Mesozoic menu but e'erather ontranscend right through to the Metazoic a priori post haste.

RITUAL APPEASEMENT- The etiquette of begetting permission from sum assortment's iffffished out selvation from either eternities or universes.

SABINA ROJKOVA- The actress to play Gracie on film.

SAMPLIFFFICATION- Any given universe viewed as but one example of objective reality.

SANCTIMONEY- 1. The money that makes the money that controls the Mesozoic swamp. 2. Cash acquired for the purposition of control valved value systems. 3. The money that manufactures consent. 4. The cash flow that keeps the spider webbing in business.

SANTA CLAUS- Iconic figure who mythically represents whene'er's cycled ability to replenish the present tense.

SATIRE- Clearly there are elements of satire to be found in this opera. However it must be stated unequivocally that the satire is intended not to break down any living people in and of themselves, but rather to break down the PREDATORY CULTURES of those several living people that have weaponized their interests against the likes of such a thing as egggracie's ont I'meaty, ont I'metaphysics. It is the author's iffffleuressential bud duh'd view that NO SENTIENT BEINGS should be disrespected out of hand. It is the's as iffffffffurthered view that that includes any impersonations of any people, facsimulated, animated or otherwise cartooned as just about ont I'm'any'selfs awared. Neverthelessoned as this must be, all of's predatory cultures operating deception on a holocausteroidal scale should be satirized without of coursed of course not not could be equivocation.

SCATE'ER'D E'ER- Presentable eternity mistaken as a mere mathematical construct of non-finite temporality.

SCHEDULES (FOR ETERNITY)- In this opera, referring to making metaphysical appointments e'er craft I'd iffffffff( )fffffffffontoptional.

SCRAMBLED- Referring to the conversion of eggs from sunny side up to entropic designs.

SECOND HAND UNIVERSE- Log 17 base 10 seconds of presentable e'er as presented promotionally pictured on location.

SECONDS- Units of time that can be watched.

S'E'EREALISM-1. The literary genre (in contrast to surrealism) that will have to be established to account for this opera.2. Almightning stricken onteque'erian surrealism.

SELECROCUTION- The democratic holocaust today.

SELF-EVIDENCE- 1. Obviousity. 2. What the mirror holds up to nature. 3. What advertises egggracie's meaty physics without any authoritarian effort, although authoritarian effort is certainly in her bag of ontricks when it becomes to her ont I'metaphysics.

SET THEORY- Branch of mathematics that arbitrary organizes objects as if such organization counts in the schematics of things.

SHADOW PILES- Layers of not that much that can grossly influence the bottom line up.

SHAME- 1. Embarrassment at the most personal level. 2. A predatory racist cultural mechanism designed to make certain targeted ethnicities afraid to exist.

SHIRLEY JONES- 1. Ontemplate for Gracie in the Girl War. 2. With charm heaventilating in plain sight and bringing depths to the surface of the depths......Shirley Jones, must be recognized for her quintessential charisma as presentable ont I'musical m'eternity's ifffffavorite engenue. As such, this somewhat pablumized princess of conventional musicals would have proven her greatness in the role of Gracie. Playing with Pat Boone in the iffffffflufffffffffilm APRIL LOVE......she represents the essential ontique'erian ethos of the opera as wholegggrailuxuriontiffffe'ercraftED as wholegggrailuxiontiffffe'ercraftABLE in becompletely presentable eternity.

SIMPLE-SAMPLE DICHOTOMY- The theoretical situation where notnotitude has two environmentools at its disposal...... a presentED universe......and....... a presentABLE eternity to put it in. The *simple* eternity constitutes the all-e'eround e'erealty while the *sample* universe constitutes a locus of objective details inte'er'd within that large'er ontological e'erealty.

SIXTEEN COME NEXT SUNDAY- The Bothy Band's prelude to THE GIRL WAR.

SNAKE PITS- Usually referencing outer housinging's toilet drop arenas.

SNAKE PIT SUPREMACISM- Still not in the dictatorshipmentionary, this term is the hottest of all hot air topics with the concept of 'supremacism' in general projected on to such a thing as egggracie by snake pit supremacists and other abominational holocaust advocates.

SPIDER'SPARANOIA- Spider projections of having to live in fear that flies won't fly into webs.

SPIED E'ER WEB SITES- Misnomer for the Spider web sites overwhelmingly insisting that such a thing as egggracie is not only extinct but impossible. These web sites are flooded by paid for data production companies claiming that such a thing as egggracie is a lighthouse beaconspiracy theory without any basis in fact in this eternity or any other eternity. As such.... sites confirming the possibility of such a thing as egggracie are hidden like needles in haystacks. It must be noted that, with dark matter silicon(valley) dioxide's trillions in sanctimoney controlling the spied e'er web, this result is to be anticipated.

SPINOZA- Much loved maverick Jewish philosopher who postulated a single substance cosmology. Expressing a set quasi-Euclidean proofs, Spinoza postulated deity as the central substance of the universe, obviating both subject-object dichotomies and Cartesian(mind/matter) dualsm, with mind and matter tagging along as intrinsically insubstantial attributes....of the god substance.

SPIRIT FACE-1. Countenance 2. As tis oft complained that not everyone behaves such gracious spirit face as such a thing as egggracie, it may be recommended to iffffffffffff(   )ffffffffffffffocus on gracspirit…since spirit's performed by decision.

SQUIRT GUN HOLOCAUSTS- With the weaponization of kindness world wide, so many maneuvers have been devised for the removal of such a thing as egggracie's existence on display that serving as the bride of the squirt gun holocaust has become popular as a thing for egggracie to do to not continue to be herself. The beauty of these holocausts is that the victims never even get to exist, much less have the opportunity to be aborted. It's a clean win in a bloodless coup that only requires a squirt gun.

STERLING HAYDEN- A suitable model for the general in this opera.

STORM- The final storm on the mountain that may be viewed as a microcosm of the entire opera with all of its dramatic and metaphysical confusions summarized at the end.

STRAW MAN- A false opposition figure designed to discredit opposition.

SUBJUNCTIVE/INDICATIVE DICHOTOMY- Two grammatical approaches to reality. 1. The indicative is very useful tool arounding out universes to estate eventualitease occurring as one speaks. 2. The subjunctive e'erefers to becompletely becompetent e'erealty that can not yet compete with what's occurrent as one speaks.

SUM- 1. Referring to ontotalized eternity. 2. First person conjugation of Latin verb 'to be'.

SUPREMACISM- Just as racism may only be properly understood as divulged by its two contrasting manifestations, so supremacism may only be grasped through similar analysis. We know how 'predatory racism' is the form of racism that weaponizes the monolithic term with its cloak and dagger projections thrust in the face of the common variety existential 'ethnocentrist'. Similarly, the 'existential supremacist' (which does include Gracie clubbed amidst its membership) is commonly victimized by the 'predatory supremacist' which does include Ms Speck club faced iffoulmouthed outwardly in cohoots with its membershipmentalitease. Once I qualifications are imposed on terms like these, better insight may be gained in their proper application, as either projected for self-expression or weaponization.

SWAMP- Heavily financed Mesozoic water hole surrounding iffffffished out promised landings.

SWASHBUCKLING- Referent to the casual approach to existence, iffffffamously dangerous for its ontendency to ignore the becomprehensiffffffffffff(   )ffffffe'er of it all's notnotitude.

TANTRUMMINATIONS- Usually short for ONTANTRUMMINATIONS. Obsessions s'e'erounding could behaviors of presentable eternities.

TCHAIKOVSKY- Romantic Russian composer whose talents for the picturesque in music influenced this opera's composition.

TENSOR CALCULUS- A calculus of kinetic trigonometry comprehensively auditioning multidimentional tensions in space blocked in on time.

THE'S- The ontologically d'iffffffintitive article.

TIMOMI NISHIMOTO- Gracie conducting Grassystems.

TOOLS- toys for work.

TOYS- Tools for play

TRAFFIC JAMS- Where fatal intersections occur in 1. One girl holocausts. 2. Demographic holocausts 3. Cultural holocausts. 4. Linguistic holocausts.

TRANSUMAN- 1. Human consciousness transferred to becomputers. 2. Human artifacts transferred to phylogenies no longer human.

TULSI- Much like a Greek goddess descended from Olympus to be among the mortals, representing the wisdomestication of whene'er's western civilization with her new found colleagues.

UNIVERSION- A term for a sampled cosmos that emphasizes its provincially territorial nature.

UPANISHADS- Hindu scriptures metaphysically graduating the aboriginal animysterium of pre-Sanscrit religion into the realms of sophisticated cosmontological deities.

VIVIAN LEIGH- A model (from her days with Charles Laughton) for Gracie in this opera.

VOGUENTHING- Eumanity's iffffffffffavorite, most iffffffffashionable pet euman also scened hiding out in almost everyone that's almost but not quite samenthing.

WEB- 1. A spider's construct to control space and catch prey. 2. Money talking to computerized people.

WEBERN- Twentieth century serial composer whose refined grasp of the possibilities of the atonal system influenced this opera.

WHAT'S WRONG WITH GRACIE- Nothing's wrong with Gracie. That's what's wrong with Gracie in conventional human terms. Gracie's just way too euman.

VOYAGE TO THE PLANET OF PREHISTORIC WOMEN- A Mamie Van Dooren film that did not directly influence THE GIRL WAR but must be viewed retrospectively as a precursor of the opera.

WHATE'ER- 1. Short form of 'whatever'. 2. A play on words, taking Thales' concept of water as the universal substance as transferred to hype'erthetical ""'Onthales'"" conceptualizing ""'whatever'"" as e'erealty's ultimate substance.

WHITEHEAD- 1. Mathematician who wrote the most comprehensive summary of mathematical principles (with Russell) 2. The philosopher behind process theology's notion of god as not comprehensively omnipotent (without Russell).

WHOLEGGGRAILIKENESS- Miss Eternity's spirit face.

WINGED HALO THEOREM- In ontense'er could be calculus…..highly controversial ontheorem stating that, just as halos simulate lopsidedness without wings, so ontitudes and entitudes appear imbalanced without entontisymetrical equations equilibrating them.

WORLD WAR WHENEVER- The large scale bellicose conflicts (over food, territory, theologicorrectness) that constantly run the mill works of the Mesozoic's hominid ape, transapiontique'ertuned and related animal societies.

XMAS- When e'er's presentable tense e'erives.

XMAS EVE- The not ne'er's night when Santa e'erives, beclimbs down the chimney and drops off the presents tensed.

ZERO- The most very able constant in all of's iffffe'ers.

ZEROBLTEASE- The onteque'erian talent of eternitease to ontantalize notnotitude.

ZEROBLTY- Zero's ontalent to perform presentable eternity.

ZERO EQUATION- Ontrophickly presentable eternity's most ontwe'er'dly iffffffamous equation of all time. It reads most simply as: $+0=+$. However e'erespectable variants include $+0+0 \ldots\ldots = + +\ldots\ldots$.

It must be admitted that the full ontintegral of this equation amounts to becompletely presentable eternity….that is……… by the way…like……...way…way…way….more than a mathematical construct of non-finite temporality.

7. THE SCREEN PLAY

THE GIRL WAR MADE SIMPLE

OVERTURE- Encompasses 1.2 billion years of Egggracess'd ont I'me'ergence.

Scene 1- A young scientist is in his observatory gazing at time charts on the wall. They read THE MESOZOIC- Triassic, Jurassic, Cretaceous, Mammacious.

Tele (the telescope): You look worried Alex.

Alex (the scientist): I'm just wondering how old all of's stuff e'ereally is.

Tele: Log 17 base 10 seconds……give or take a few…..that's my calculation.

Alex: Well there's rumors the Mesozoic's ending any second now and I still haven't been out in it.

Tele: I wouldn't worry about it ending like…like suddenly. But if it does….you can probably do like after mathematically better without. Meanwhile we've got stars that are all there is to make some sense of.

Alex: You're sure about that Tele?

Tele(impatient): Look, I've got lenses and you've got lenses. Plus I've got equations and you've got equations. We're on the same team Alex.

Wolfy (the keyboard): What team am I on? Like what ifffff like dreams don't need stars to dream them?

Tele: Don't listen to Wolfy Alex. Wolfy hears voices. Stars don't need ventriloquists. They make up kit for a pretty good-looking universe, especially at night, when it's all lit up like xmas trees.

Alex notices that the sunflower has drooped: Wolfy the sunflower just drooped. Can you play something for it?

Wolfy(responding) Oh yea, like…..can you hear me flower?

Alex and Tele: It budged,

Wolfy: Can I use my voices?

Alex and Wolfy: By all means……

Wolfy begins with samples of his voices which coalesce into a simple but uplifting melody.

The flower is revived.

Alex: You saved the flower Wolfy!

Tele (slightly jealous): A lot of good that will do. Like things droop. Things get hot and then they droop. The hotter they get the quicker they droop. Amused or not amused, that's what stuff does.

Wolfy: Not the stuff that dreams are made of. If I had my way…….

Alex: What way is that Wolfy.

Wolfy: Well…well…like…like….like(Wolfy starts a tone row but then thinks the better of it) No, that's not it. Like…like….(Wolfy begins an ominous tonal figuration in the lower registers).

Intrigued, Alex responds.

Alex: Can I play along?

Wolfy: Are your hands clean?

Alex (studying his hands): Yes.

Wolfy: Then be my guest.

Alex sits down to play a vast orchestral duet that has Tele grudingly looking away at the sky. As his angle of vision descends to the horizon, he begins to shutter.

Tele: Alex, I think it winked at me. Alex, you'd better come here.

Alex ignores Tele's concern until the music reaches its climax. Tele is shaking violently now and Alex finally leaves Wolfy to look through Tele's lens. As the object comes into focus Alex suddenly collapses in shock, races to the observatory exit and slams the door as he departs into the Mesozoic.

END OF SCENE I

There is an orchestral interlude that follows Alex into the Mesozoic.

SCENE II

Meeting at the bridge.

Alex approaches Gracie hanging from the bridge to baptize the Reve'd'e'er River with her hairdo. Sensing Alex's approach, Gracie recovers and fumbles with Ee'errainbow ties around her neck to switch off her halo.

Gracie: E'ERCRAFT!!! Sooner or later's e'ercraft…like e'erived with the verdict.

Alex: What verdict?

Gracie: The whole sum verdict. However's alphabetingod's ONT I'M'ASIFFFFORMATION'S NOT/NOTNOT CODE. We're like on the same team…..e'eright? Please be right.

Alex: What team is that?

Gracie(disappointed): Egggracessed onteamology's team. Unless you've been scheduling appointments to be spelled backwards, you would know.

Alex(sceptical): So you are like like…….Egggracie?

Gracie: I don't know where you're from but we take being(which I am taking for NOT NOT BEING JUST NOW) for egggranted in these parts.

Alex: So this is the Mesozoo I'm in and you're egggracessed….

Gracie:………BECOMPLETELY PRESENTABLE ETERNITY'S ONTENTEAM….what ontelse? Like are you spelled backwards or not.(Gracie waves her wand in a manner that is threatening) Like you do bark backwards I hope. Please bark backwards.

Alex(catching on): Ok, so like dog spelled backwards. That's me. I'm Alex at your service.

Gracie: All right then. So like you did come to congraduate me after all.

Alex: From what?

Gracie: From kindergarden, what else. I sure hope you don't have to be like ontested? Please don't have to be ontested.

Alex: For what?

Gracie: Barking backwards, congradulating me for breadthing e'er's secret, iffff it ever comes to that. Please..become to onthat.

Alex: Well, I'm new to the Mesozoic in these parts and when Tele spotted you I thought a zoo could use a hero.

Gracie: Like who?

Alex: Like me, Alex. Look, whatever such a thing as you are egggranted 'not not' to be ….I thought it might be nice of such a thing as what I am to like…like…save such a thing as…as….(studies Gracie for signs of being eu)……like….. eu.

Gracie throws up her arms in despair.

Gracie(ranting): I KNEW IT!!! DAMN! DAMN! DAMN! Don't you godoguys ever get it! Ever since I lost the girl war by winning the Miss Eternity Pageant over runner up reality, I can't be saved! Just look at me(Gracie poses as a statue) Like I am a euman being for crossed out'sache. I can't be saved. The last thing I could ever do is save myself. Iffff I did that…like…like…iffffished outinguized…………..

Alex: Eu would be saved.

Gracie: 'FFFYou…..(softens her gaze)…..EU…..ontentrialed to save me…like cut off in the prime of my crossed outing. Like nothing would kill me quicker than letting anyone save myself. Myself can not be saved. That's all there's to it.

IFFFFF YOU TRY TO SAVE ME……I WILL JUST HAVE TO DUMP YOU!!! DO YOU UNDERSTAND!!!! I WILL! I WILL! (Gracie shows her wanted poster "GRACIE WANTED") I'm a wanted woman Alex. I come with a warning label. As coolifffffied as coolest onthing ever as I appear to like….(winces) NOT NOT BE…..NOTHING KILLS ME QUICKER THAN BEING SAVED. Besides like..like.. My breathe is pretty, pretty nasty. (gracie shakes Alex) Can't you see I'm like the most dangerous person I have ever been. Do your….(softens) eur….(I'd thou art) eye sockets have to be tested or what. Like… I've got this contract out on myself Alex. I take pills. I'm on holocausteroids. I get onthirsty on crossed outings for my gin. Not only that, but I seem like I've been waiting forever to be myself, if that means anything to your like…like….eu.(Gracie examines Alex for signs of being like….EU. Meanwhile ont I'm'etaphysically speaking I've just solved the eternity problem, if that means anything to eur…..

Alex: My lenses.

Gracie: So you do have lenses, backed up by equations I must eggguess.

Alex: By all means, yes, I study stars as are all there is that matters…..that is until…like eur…..

Gracie: Self-evid

Alex: entsity.

Gracie(posing): Well don't wait e'eround forever for my ont I'metiffffffffizzzzzzzicks, although alsoing up ontentrophickly presentable's Miss…….look..now that I've got my ontense'er calculus egoing in my owned'e'erection showing just..just…just how not not being distorts not being with iffffffffabricky not not being………as Miss E………..

Alex (studying Gracie for signs of being Miss Eternity): Yes! Of course, of course not not. Next door to Miss Eternity I can just wonder. Tele has lenses, lenses backed up equations….Not only do I wonder what I think about that but I wonder what Tele thinks about that.

Gracie (gazing askance as she shows her profile) Ont I'm'assuming you are not just some eggguy.

Alex: I do dabble in background e'eradiation.

Gracie: So you do dabble in metaphysics. But do you ever work the big time. I work the big time.

Alex: I haven't worked it lately but….

Gracie: You are I ontake it e'eready, whene'er willing and ont I'm'able to ontantumminate ontitudes… just like me. I mean, however you're (warms to Alex's image) WE are on the same onteam, after all is sad undone. E'eright? And who's Tele?

Alex: Oh! Tele's my telescope. (Alex points to the observatory in the distance)

Gracie (searching the horizon as she salutes to shade her eyes): So, like Tele's got me under surveillance…..

Alex: Uh.

Gracie: So I'm like onticipatingod and I end up as the party girl (waves vaguely in Tele's direction) in some cosmic booking's peep show. Does Tele dabble in metaphysics too? (Alex nods) And does Tele read lips?

Alex: Mhm.

GRACIE'S FIRST METAPHYSICAL LECTURE OF THE OPERA

Gracie: I've never done this with lenses before but…..like….ok….so Tele…..like READ MY LIPS. They're all yours for the ont I'momentum.

Let me first say by introduction that E'EREALTY'S MORE A PRIORI THAN YOUR LENSES (BACKED UP BY EQUATIONS) MIGHT SUPPOSE. Like being lenses, you're naturally into universes and all, like subobjectively speaking cosmetrickly immersed. HOWEVER…..SUM'S PREGNANT ZERO'S ONE BECOMES ALONG WITH LIKE…LIKE….ETERNITY SELF PUBLISHED….LIKE IFFFFONT I'M'ADVERTISED AT LAST.

(Gracie snaps her trigger finger) HOWEVER!!!!!! Just now my new not/notnot code (which by the way I hereby capitalize as THE NOT/NOT NOT CODE) becomes along with to belongings of not not to be…..and 1. ETERNITY IS NOT JUST A MATHEMATICAL CONSTRUCT OF NON-FINITE TEMPORALITY and 2. SOME STARS AS SUBOBJECTIFFFFF I'D ETERN OUT TO BE HARDLY EVERYTHING. YOU GOT THAT? BECAUZZZZZ LIKE ACCORDING TO MY NEW ALPHABET NOT NOT TO BE'S ONTALENTED WAY PAST like (0/1 code's) infinity all the way up to like iffffffffffff( )ffffffffffinity. You got that?

Gracie turns to Alex, posing macromicroscopickly): Ok, so like what has iffffineternity begot egggoing for it, besides me…..like…like…like……. 1. NEXTITUDINATABLE NEIGHBORLY NOWS. 2. THE SELFISHED OUT SECRET INGREDIENT. AND WHAT IS THE SECRET INGREDIENT YOUR LENSES just MIGHT NOT ONTHINK TO ASK…..WELL!!!!!!LIKE!!!LIKE!!!!! OF COURSE OF COURSE {{{{{{NOT NOTITUDE}}}}}……..THE SAME NOT NOTITUDE THAT THE NOT/NOTNOT CODE IS BEBLABBERNG BEBLISTICKLY ALL ABOUT! IN CASE YOU'RE ONTROPHICALLY RATIONING THE'S MANUVE'ER OVER ALL OF'S PLACE OF ALL'S OF

THIS........OK SO LIKE ONTHINK ABOUT IT. WHY NOT NOT {{BEING}}? WHY NOT JUST {{BEING}}? BECAUSE [[BEING]] JUST BASKS. HOWEVER.....(binarily bespeaking)NOT NOT BEING....LIKE...DOES STUFF. I mean like how does a fish know it's a fish? Becauzzzzzzzz it's not not a fish. So like with notnotitude'eriding shot gun for like nextitudable neighborly nows.....you put put put it ontogethe'er'd and you've got yourself a becompletely presentable eternity. That's all there's to it. Stars or no stars, nowsy snooze service as informed by nowsy newse'ervice's iffffformation systems......ONT I'MOUTHING OFF THE COULD BE E'ER COOLIFFFFFIED COOLEST THING EVER! ETERNITY SELF-PUBLSHED. DO YOU GET IT OR DO YOU HAVE TO BE ONTESTED?

Alex: He gets it.

Gracie: So Tele, good luck with your lens work outing exercises. I mean like peep shows are fine at night....whenever universes are out and about. But don't give up your day job in onticeptickly presentensible eternity.

Gracie pedantically turns to Alex.

Gracie: Well metaphysically speaking I will be happy to ontake sum's questions from anyone all of a sudden ont I'm'auditioning to be my ont I'm'audience.

Alex (studying Gracie for signs of being egggirlifffactoried) Well meaty physically I have some questions.

Gracie(Primping): Ooh! meaty physically. So like I'm egggame.

Alex: Well, this is the Mesozoic if I'm not missde'ertaken for e'erides. Well just what's this girl war business you...(studies egggracie for signs of dyploidemonautical eggguilt)........eu....can't live out from under.

Gracie: There's not much to tell really. It's the usual girl war story. Since falling off the sky into the nativity scenery daddy locked me in a closet inside the could be safe where the traffic jams couldn't get me jammed in traffic. Once the egggated becommunity caverns were toyletrained at kindergarden's outhousing projections...the girl wars were in full swaggeredundancy tunneling through the carnivals with all kinds of holocoasterides tailer'd to headings every'swhich way. Demonsterably losing world war whenever before it started, the sacrimoneye'd ads just would never give out credentials for anyone else ever being dead. I was reassigned (shows wanted poster) as occupied territory and donated to charity. The power grid got a hold of the words in the explanation dispensary and I've been dispensed on holocoasteroids ever since. Nevertheless my like hairdo(points) matured right through kindergarden without a hitch and, even without those wings I wanted for my birthday, I started work outs on the crossed outing. Before sundown I work my motel's dark rooms, where promotion pictures are taken like turning my positives into negatives to be developed into as iffffffilm industrial's hits. Since to NOT NOT BE became taboo, I've been dubbing myself into these dying spells (waves her wand's hitting on her well tail e'er'd head) bailed out only by ont I'm'adventures ontique shopping in ont I'm'e'er, where of course it's approvably always to be selfisticated to like be myself, especially as iffffffreaked out as ont I'm-wise I m'appear to be on the map. (Gracie shows the map of her ont I'm'occupied onte'eritory located well within the ont I'm'atricks of her xxxrated occupied territory) XXX marks the spot I'm in. Ever since I got way too pretty, way too fast..like only everybody but me what allowed in my mirrors anymore, leaving my like self-evidence puddled in what's whate'er wherever light gets wet enough for positives of negatives of negatives of me to not not be like…in the emotion's picture. Apart from masterpieced together puzzles of me like obviosiffffffied in my own personal puddles, ever since lately I've…well…I've like given up on the universe. And then one day, passing by the chalk boards at the metaphysical society I decided to start working eternity on a decision basis. I dabbled in metaphysics all of's way danced up to pregnant zeros ont I'mathematickly one'd'e'er'd onto the NOT/NOTNOT CODE which, by the way, I just used to solve the eternity problem pretty presentably….scheduling ifffe'erious appointments at half time between minus and plus ifffffffinity…..eufemiffffeelined as wholegggrown along side present tension's iffffontentrumminations. So like, ever since the girl war I'm no longer like becosmickly immersed(wincing). So like I've been into THE BIG TIME ever since…like ont I'm'authentictated to the BIG………..

Alex (catching on to egggracess'd jargon): So like working iffffffinity's ides of e'ercraft shows, with dog spelled backwards in your own'd image.

Gracie: Yea, with me winning the Miss Eternity Pageant over runner up reality…like..like…I almost didn't not say…..the way I ifffffffffigure it….Dog's best look spelled backwards is in my image. Of course, this being the Mesozoic and all….sum's assortments of notnotitude's been my ont I'm'egggig. Plus I do dabble in ont I'm'athematics working the y-not axis of the I'd thou artesian coordinate system. Like meanwhile I mainly work the NOT/NOTNOT CODE I also allow for ontentwigs of physics into my ontree's ont I'm'e'erealteased ont I'mente'erprise.

Alex: So you do use universes. I mean you do appear still stuck to stones.

Gracie: Sum's what ifffffffffonly to stretch out my new branch of ont I'mathematicks.

Alex: So then a becompletely new branch of mathematics.

Gracie: For physics to be entwigged off of. It's my ontense'er calculus. It all began on the chalk boards of the metaphysical society with the +0=+ ont I'm'equation. Like I'd been auditioning eternity for what seemed like the belonginguestime when…..well here we are……onthis bridge over the whate'er…and me dabbling in metaphysics just enough to solve eternity…..which…by the way I just did.

Alex: Anything else?

Gracie: Well now that I've got eternity like disguised spelled backwards…I was just upping the onti to…to like ontantrumminate eternity as like toylitte'er'd

Alex: Toiletrained?

Gracie: For starte'ers yea. Like ontrophickly speaking to beget sum's e'eresurrections in my onteats. But to do that, the way I ifffigure the ground of it, I'd have to begetting a free iffffloation phylum all my own. But that might take more wands than I can handle with my whate'er's asiffffontrigger fingers. All humility taken from aside, I'm just sumwhat's beble after all, presentably presented at the's ont I'm'ides of e'er aft all is said I'done.

271

Alex: What are bebles?

Gracie: Oh the possible people that live in this eternity.

Alex: When?

Gracie: Whenever. Like courtesy of pretty pregnant zeros…..onded'e'ering in as baby'she's us, god or no god, no offense, camouflaged as sum's idiot…no offense….like e'erithmetrickly speaking……iffffinitizably m'available…like sooner or later…..like…like…..such a thing as me living upsidown the girl wars, just waiting in line to be myself while everybody's else is waiting in line to be like…like….like the likes of me, or half of me, or m'egggodrawn and quartered or like inffffinitestimonialized m'approximated as metifffformed in anybody's but mined mirrors. Oh Alex if you could only ontentrumminate like me, if only history was still born as aborted before the girl war I could coolifffffffy as the's coolest onthing ever with the set of all setheory's sitting up to ontake not not notice beblaspheming all of's dud iffffe'er's blasphemable dimensions. If only you were my puppy as ontoyletrained e'erainbows I could count on eu and may be onto… to…to….like ifffffffinity….

Alex (really catching on to justajiffffy jargon): Listen d'e'erling, as long as I don't save you, with all of's lenses and equations at my disposal service maybe I could be like…like…..your analyst.

Gracie: You'd do that for me?

Alex: Sure. Why not. Now let me see your….your kindergardentexts.

Gracie gives Alex her two kindergarden texts. 1. DEATH MADE SIMPLE. 2. DEATH FOR BEGINNERS.

Alex (speed reads through the texts) Mhm.

Gracie so you speede'eread onthrough deathoughts?

Alex: I always speedread dud eternities in general.

Gracie: So what's your verdict?

Alex: Oh, not at all til pooft as otherwise.

Gracie: Oh you really mean it!!!

Alex: So these are the books taile'er'd from headstart programs right up to egggraduation into…

Gracie: Kindergarden…..just kidding on the playground to be wanted….dead or…….

Alex: Gracie you don't have to audition to be obviously like…like…alive.

Gracie winces and falls on her face.

Alex (hesitating to pick her up): Gracie…Gracie….just what's there to beget out of being dead Gracie.

Gracie(recovering): I don't want to be dead. Being dead makes a lousy lyric, haven't you ever not not noticed. I just want to be dying all of's all the time…like…like…not so quite that my hour has come as that my hour's of course not not to be becoming. Don't you get it or do you have to be tested. I j

272

stifffffffiably always just must be DYING. I'm a dangerous person Alex…..dangerously scared to be anything but NOT MYSELF. But ever since being alive makes a lousy lyric besides. Sings faintly "I'll be uh live…nop….uh dead….nop…" HOWEVER!!!! SINCE I'VE TOY'D WITH HIGH FASHIONED BEACH RESORTS FOR DYING OUT I'VE DISCOVERED JUST DYING OUT DOES MAKE EGGGREAT LYRICS FOR THE ONTENTE'ERTAINMENT INDUSTRIAL BECOMPLEX. See here (shows back side of wanted posters that reads "GRACIE WANTED DYING TO SAVE THE DAY")

Gracie: See all of's ont I'musical notation on my poster's back side. I mean ever since being humped by the holocoaste'erides…to be a nice person….all that's left of left over for me is to be DYING. Like at cow cud rallies in the barnyard that's all that's left for me to do apart from doo's to be to moo. Like if this were an opera….

Alex: This can't be an opera Gracie, because I don't moo.

Gracie (taking pity): Shucks Alex, I could do all of's eur mooing moo'd for you for you in just ajifffy.

Alex (genuinely touched): You'd do that for me?

Gracie: Sure, why not. Among my magic tricks is justajiffffffy's juke box Alex. You hear that bird?

Alex: Yes, I can hear it.

Gracie begins twittering with the bird on the twig at the top of the tree. It is a duet. Gracie's wand is conducting the tempo, which she slows to accommodate her trills into the first egggreat aria of the opera. Holding her wand winking grotesquely she sings:

I'M DYING OUT TO SAVE THE DAY…IFFFFFFFFF(.)IFFFFFFFFF DYING I CAN BE WHO'S DYING OUT SO I CAN BE DYING OUT AS SAVIOR OF THE DAY.

Gracie takes Alex by the hand as she leads him off into a series of comic book adventures of cartooned near death experiences in the convenience storaged carnival nextitudinated next door. Transported animatomickly from one danger to the next, on tight ropes and holocoasterides, facing locomotivation trains and silhouetted at one point at the top of a Ferris Wheel where Gracie's halo explodes into an umbrelle'erainbow of whate'er's lit up wet e'erespectralight. Once the music has dreamatically subsided Gracie and Alex arrive back at the bridge over the Rev'd'e'er River.

Gracie: Now wasn'that more fun than being dead OR BECOMPLETELY ALIVE which reminds me of a religious experiment I have to get to work on.

Alex: What experiment?

Gracie: It's a secret…the secrething that will change all of's m'eternity's self-publications….plus…plus just maybe…all of dog'spelled backwards preposte'erological publications too….too…..to say the wholegggraileast of its…..its……..close your eyes Alex.

Alex closes his eyes. When they open egggracie is nowhere to be seen. Facing the Mesozoic without egggracie, Alex becomes e'eresearch partied heading up hill to the saloon….meanwhile now knowing as ifffffffully well that such onthings as egggracexistence e'er to be possible (ont I'metphysicklishly speaking) which is to say……….. egggracie's ontimat at e'er mansion's ontents tense…… of course, of course not not's presentable.

Interlude II follows Alex all of's way danced to the door of the saloon.

SCENE III- THE SALOON

Alex enters the saloon in ontoptimyste'eriously distraught could be of course condition. Searching aimlessly to reach the bar, the bar mistress surveys him with amused pity.

Barmistress: Hi there handsome. You're not from these parts, I can always tell. You look pretty much on purpose.

Alex: Yes, well Wolfy's music was playing not at all accidently when my telescope detected egggracie on the bridge baptizing the river with her (points over his head) hairdo.

BM: Mhm. Oh! Her hairdo!!!!!!

Alex: Well it was that heaventilation system over her egggear that aspectralated like some assortment's iphphphphylum all her own that becompletely caught my attention.

BM: Oh yea, that's such a thing as egggracie all right. The most dangerous wholegrailadyingirl you ever met…right?

Alex: Yea! Like she has to be dying all of's 'whate'er's iffffont I'm'

BM: Otherwise she'd be e'eroad kill selfished out on the spot. I can see she's heated you up like her puddles. Let me take your 'ontempe'erature'. Yea, I speak a little justajiffffy jargon.(She puts her hand on his forehead).

Alex: Thermodynamically she doesn't fit into any of my equations.

BM: Like on the'ermodynamickly they're all stretched out e'eright? You've definitely become down with egggracess'd iffffever's selfished outingsyndramas.

Alex: She dumped me…yet somehow….I still…

BM: Within her asiffffffaults iffffans but breeze her virtues.

Physicist at a table: Alchemickly she should be tested for phyluminium icontents.

Alex: You mean she's e'eradioactive?

BM: For sure. (pointing to beaker behind the bar)

Alex: That's her?

BM: Well her hairdo. Let's ontune her in (BM tunes the e'eradio, filtering through the bands of bird twitter to the sound of egggracie's voice…. "dying…I can save the day."

Alex: That's Gracie! With her as iffffavorite lyrics. She conducts birds.

BM: Birds? She conducts clocks, worlds, WHENEVERS!!!!

Alex: She's left the stars behinds......behind.

Physicist: And then there's those I'magic tricks of her passing right through cosmsetricks as if they were hardly ever there. I don't devote but that girl does stretch out my equations prettegod.

BM: I have to admit, she always welcomes whene'er ont I'matters in my mirrors..the little hypocrite, bad mouthing outer space the way she does. I mean where would she begetting her booze out of scenery if it wasn't for oute'er'space being just ont I'm. She talks the big time's big ontensions, but you just missed her sneaking out of here withholding onto her bottle. That's all that's left of her here and now.

The barmistress takes the jar of Gracie's formaldeydrated halo fragment and directs Alex to the table where the physicist is and the general are seated. Placing the jar at the center of the table she seats Alex and then seats herself.

Church bells ring in the distance.

The barmistress points to the sky

BM: Those chimes refuse s'e'ervice unless she's in the building.

Alex: So she's alive.

BM- Oh she's alive all right, just dying out as usual up there, just dying to not be dead or else alive or else.....or else.......crossed out. Personally I have to tell you I'm just living in the middle of the middle of the middle of the age when I have divorced all of's mined delusions BUT......why not not not let you have yours honey........

Alex begins to rise from table. But the bar mistress holds him down.

BM: Fasten your seat beltheories gentlemen, I'll tell you all about egggracie. Maestro! (points to the sky as lightning strikes and the orchestra enters.

BM sings:

1. CHURCH BELLS WERE RINGING ON SATURDAY NIGHT

SOMEONE WAS PLAYING A TUNE

AS CHIMED DOWN THE CHIMNEY TO SAINT INTO SIGHT

WITH APPEAL METAMATTE'ERING MOON

WITH A PEAL METAMODELING MOON

Quartet of three sopranos and barmistress

SHE LIKE THE LADY

IFFFFFISHED FROM TO BECOME FOR SURE

THE ONE ALL OF'S SKIES TWINKLE FOR

THE ONE ALL OF'S GUYS TINKLE FOR.

CHURCH BELLS WERE RINGING IN OUT OF THE BLUE

WHILE CHILDREN WERE PLAYING ALONG

WITH CHIMERICKLES CHIMING IN CHEERLADER'S WHO

SERANADES AS IFFFFFACED SINGING'S SONG

AS HEAVENTILATES HAUNT HOUSING'S BOO

WHOLEGGGRAILADY

SPILLED OUT OF SPOOKSKILLS OF SKIES

WHERE THE SPARK OF THE SPIRIT FACE FLIES

SHE LIKE THE CREATURE

THAT HEAVEN MUST FEATURE

TO EVER GET OFF OF THE GROUND.

2.   I'DOLLED UP DREAME'ERGENCY'S EGGGODEGO

ACUTELY AS ANGLED ANGELLED

OUT OF DANCINGING DIRT THAT'S IFFFONTING IFFFFLOW

WHENE'ER'S WHATE'ER TO BE BECOMPELLED

SHE LIKE THE LADY

IFFFISHED FROM THE CEILING'S I'M ARC

OF IFFFIRMAMENCE TWINKLING THE DARK.

CHORUS: SHE ITTING FEATURES

THAT HEAVENLY CREATURES

CAN HEAVENTILATE OFF EGGGROUND.

3.   CHURCH BELLS WERE BATHING IN FLOODED EXTREAMS

OF IFFFFRMAMENTION'S CHAMPAGNES

IFFFFLEDGING DREAME'ERGENCIES DRAWN OUT OF DREAMS

ONT I'MAXIOMATE'ER'D REFRAINS

VOCABULATING

A NEW DICTIONARY'S ONTERMS

JUST AS GRACIE'S ESTEEM BECONFIRMS

CHORUS: SHE LIKE THE CREATURE

THAT HEAVEN MUST FEATURE

TO EVER GET OFF OF THE GROUND.

4.   AS STARS IN ONTWILIGHT PREPARE TO BE TWINKLES

AS STARTLED TO CHORUS THE SONG

WITH THE WINKS OF THE TWINKLES RESOUNDING ONTINKLES

IN A HYMN HEAVEN'S HIM HYMNS ALONG

WITH A HYMN HEAVEN'S HIMS HYMNALONG

HEAVENTILATING

ASCENDENCIES ONTO ASCERT

EGGGRACIE ESTEEMED FROM IFFFFFFLIRT

CHORUS: IFFFLIRTNG IFFFFEATURES

OF COULD BECOME'S CREATURES

TO HEAVENILATE OFF EGGGROUND.

With a new lightning strike Alex rises from the table. The barmistress escorts him maternally to the exit with one last consoling verse.

5.   ALL WHILE LOVE'S AS IFFFFFALLING THROUGH NOT NEVER'S NIGHT

IFFFFROM GRACESS'D IN PERSON APPEALS

AS MODELED IN A MAKE UP OF AS IFFFFALL MIGHT

AS IFFFALLING IN LOVE AS IFFFFEELS

ALL OF'S IFFFFEEINGS

AS SPARKLE TO BE OUTER SPACED

IFFFFIGURINGROUND AS EGGGRACED

INCANDESCENT CREATURE'S

IFFFIRMAMENT FEATURES

EGGGNIGHTING EGGRACE OFF EGGGROUND.

The ballad concludes, as Alex slams the saloon door with lighting strikes plus bells heard in the distance.

THE SCENE ENDS.

THIRD INTERLUDE: A jaunty bassoon trio, traumatized by strident strings, sponsors Alex as he transgresses the road to the cathedral.

SCENE IV- IN THE CATHEDRAL

Alex arrives at the top of the hill to find the cathedral's gothic entrance. He opens the vast door and enters into the darkness. Alumes of stained glass light are glimpsed. Then in the main hall he sees Gracie. She is hanging out on the cross, performing seflies.

Alex: Gracie!

All at once the cathedral erupts in a vast choral din. As this subsides a repetitive beat emerges as the ray gun rafter light with messages on the screens. Wanted posters picture Felix, the grotesquely flamboyant pope posing as THE LORD ONCE REMOVED. Blinking off and on hypnotically are messages flashing through the chamber. Most prevalent are the messages FELIX GODS THE LOVE and FELIX GODS THE DREAM. Swaggering up to the pulpit Pope Felix grapples with the microphone. Bishop Speck confidently stands behind Felix threatening to protect his presence. There is a pause in the music as Felix speaks.

FELIX: You know some say we live in dark times.

Speck: You better believe it or else….

Felix: Some call the universe a dud. Some say eternity's ontoxic. Some e'eright out loud declare that gods a nobody. But I say to you….don't blame the stars. Don't blame whate'er's as iffffe'ers might be up to. Blame yourself for being fished out of whate'er finned feet to the pedal paid not munched attention.

Speck: You'd better believe it.

Felix: But I say to you. When the plate is passed. Like..like..pay attention. Remember who keeps score.

Speck: And the paper work.

Felix holds up his hand wrestling his trigger finger's vast sanctimony.

Speck pokes Felix. Felix signals for Mobible, a former kitcher appliance to pass the plate to the congregation as the music resumes.

Felix(singing): YOU MET A BEGGER IN THE STREET TODAY

DIDN'T GIVE 'EM A DIME

DIDN'T GIVE 'EM A DIME

DIDN'T GIVE 'EM A DIME.

AND THE GREAT BUGUYED GOD….SAID…"SHAME ON YOU!"

Soon the chorus enters:

SHAME ON WE COMMITED TO THE CRIME

VALHALLELUJA'D……..IN EXCELSIS OF…

SHAME ON US WHO DIDN'T GIVE A DIME.

Gracie has climbed down off the cross and is preparing her sway dance routine.

Felix: WELL! THERE'S A WAKE UP AT THE WATERHOLE TODAY

AT PROMOMOO'S MESOZOO

SWINGING FORWARD WITH THE SWAY

OF MOODY MOMMALS WITH THE MOO.

AND THE GREAT BUGUYED GOD SAID…

Gracie hangs from the cross to sing:

I'M WITH YOU!

Gracie climbs back down from the cross as the dance routine resumes.

Soon Felix sings another verse:

WELL THE METAZOICS ON THE MOVE TODAY

WITH THE MOMMAS MESOZOO'D

SWINGING FORWARD WITH THE SWAY

OF MEATY MOMMAS IN THE MOOD

AND THE THE GREAT, AND THE GREAT, AND THE GREAT BUGUYED GOD

Gracie climbs back up to sing: I'M WITH YOU!

As the music subsides Gracie climbs down from the cross one last time. Raising one hand, then another, signals for the crowd to part as she walks through the cathedral like Moses crossing the Red Sea. She passes through the great doors that close behind her. The chimes cease abruptly. There is an awkward silence.

Felix: Ok! So let's give our little pin up a big hand for working the cross today.

There is much applause.

Felix: That's big enough. Now what's tomorrow and tomorrow all about.

Crowd: POPE FELIX!!!

Felix: I can't hear you.

Crowd: POPE FELIX!!!!!!!

Felix: That's better. Now I want to hear about that guy next door to you know who(Points upward)

Crowd: Pope Felix!......HIM! ONCE REMOVED.

Felix: Ontechnicoole'erly speaking…..that sounds unominous to me. So I hopray you're not just cow hardly speaking.

Crowd; No. We're not at all just speaking cowords. Like…like….of course, of course not not! All one for Felix!

Felix: Alright then. So the lord once removed's in that guy's pocket.

Crowd: Back pocket.....like removed UP FRONT!

Felix: So like with your devotion we're going to get control over this...this...whatever's...whenever...this....

Crowd: WHATE'ER'S!!!!!!!!!WHENE'ER!!!!!!

Mobible returns with a plate full of cash. Felix smiles from ear to ear.

Felix: Now let's give thanks to our kitchen appliance for working the ray gun rafters today.

Mobible shyly tips his tin hat. There is modest applause.

Felxi: Well Mobible, we've got an selectrocution tomorrow and, as far as I can tell, you're still here.

Mobible(meekly): Uh.

Mobible whimpers faintly and leaves by the side exit. Alex cannot get through the traffic jam in the isles and is trapped as the cathedral goes dark with Mobible's exit. With Mobible shutting down the power ground and Gracie longone....there is nothing left for the scene to do but end.

SCENE V

Episode 1. No longer a kitchen appliance, Mobible is found downtown congraduating himself out of his days as a can opener. He is urgently, but awkwardly trying to coolify his presence among the local voters in that region of the city. Soliciting traffic jam support for the selectrocution of Felix as pope, he is carrying his wanted poster that reads: WANTED FELIX FOR POPE. Although he is singing, his ontene'er voice is buried in the orchestra.

Episode 2. Mobible is caught in front of a plate of barbecue ribs. He looks helpless in all directions as he dumps the plate and sings in manner that is hardly heard: IF YOU WANT TO SAVOR BARBECUED BEHAVIOR......vote Felix

Episode 3. Mobible is limosined in a ticker tape parade in the financial district. Confetti is raining down. He sings, but, as usual, is hardly heard: IF YOU WANT TO SAVIOR MONEY BACKED BEHAVIOR.....

Episode 4. Mobible is scened in the country club between two cemetaries as he is about to tee off as he sings what can hardly be heard: IF YOU WANT TO SAVIOR COUNTRY CLUB BEHAVIOR...

Episode 5. Mobible is at a Valhallelujaween Festival dressed up in make up and ribbons as he sings what can hardly be heard: YOU CAN TAKE THE BOOGYBUS, UNIVERSED UNANIMOUS...........

Episode 6. Mobible has just entered the Metaphysical Society where egggracie stands before the chalk boards giving her usual lecture on n'ontoxically ontalented eternities.

On the chalk boards is written

1. ONTOYLETRAINED P-UNIVERSED IFFFFE'ER

2. WHENE'ER'S WIND UP TOY ETERNITY

3. ONTENSE'ER CALCULUS with notations elaborating d'iffffffffe'erontical m'equations for ONTOTAL ETERNITY OF WHATE'ER'SELFISHED OUT SYSTEM: E = sum d(NN)/dt from -fffffffffffffffinity to +iffffffinity.

4. There is a special scribble scriptured aside that reads:

NOTNOTITUDE + NOWSY NEWSE'E'RVICE = PRESENTABLY ONTALENTED ETERNITY.

5. On a side board are notations estated PUNIVERSES ARE SAMPLIFFFICATIONS OF INFORMATION FROM ONTIQUE SHOPPE IFFFFFFF(.)FFFFFFFFFFFORMATION SYSTEMS.

In the m'eternity wards ontique shoppe ontentrance a sign reads: ETERNITIEDONTROPIES ARE AVAILABLE FOR SALE.

Mobible is still carrying his wanted poster for Felix as pope.

The general enters the room.

General (to Mobible): Are you in charge of Felix's selectrocution campaign?

Mobible: How did you know?

The general surveys the room but restrains himself from responding.

General: I think you'd better come with me sir.

Mobible (Immersed in egggracie's lecture but reluctantly sighing to focus his attention on the general): Well, I suppose metaphysics can always wait. Who really cares, except sooner or later, anyway.

Mobible leaves the Metaphysical Society with the general.

The scene shifts with the music to an exclusive beach resort where a vast armada of dictatorships are landing. Each ship carries with it a wooden horse from which troops are emerging from the rear. Landing parties are forming beachead units wearing ballet dresses and combat boots. They are lavishly made up.

General: Should we quarantine the beach sir? As a former kitchen appliance do you have that authority?

Mobible: As the can opener operating the ray gun rafters I am, after all, ontent maension's authority in these parts. (Mobible studies the general's hands) I see that your hands are clean. You'd better let me handle this general.

Mobible approaches the executive director of the landing parties.

Mobible: Just what do you think you are doing at this very exclusive beach front resort, may I ask?

Executive: We're the vote loads piling up for pope….pope…..pope…

Mobible: Felix?

Executiive: That's it. The doground whistle we got was that this selectrocution's been dedemilitarized. So we're here to vote by invasion.

Mobible: Exactly how many are you?

Executive (With brazen ethical confidence): Oh, we're all ONE!

Mobible and general breathe a sigh of relief: WHEW!!!! Like is there anything else you want?

Executive: Just a wholegggraiload of such a thing as egggracies. We saw all of's emotion picture ads for them in the paper products and the wanted posters.

Mobible: So, youre the ships egggracie launched. Well, there's only one egggracie left in these parts. Only one that still ont I'manswers to Gracie.

Executive: Cool, cut here up if it comes to that. Maybe like half a wholegggracie will do it.

The executive reconsiders the situation mathematically.

Executive: Or maybe wholegggracies like drawn and quartered as cartoons. We'll settle theoretically for sum's quarters.

Mobible: Uh, how about like..like…infinitesstimonialized as paper products. We might have to make up a whole new branch of mathematics to work on this.

Executive: Look, we haven't been paid yet; if there's a problem here…..like you do the math. We've brought plenty of crosses for pin ups on the crossed outings.

Mobible (thinking strategically to trump the situation): Look, as your very welcoming party representative, I have come to cash in the situation with new orders. Let me be blunt. 1. You are now directed to…to……like…..go home.2. Your homes are being invaded. 3. All of's payments for your devotion were sent…like….HOME.

EXECUTIVE: Which home?

Mobible: The one back across the waves….the one that there's no place like……..the one where all of's money has been sent. The one that's being ransacked by someone's that that's not exactly allof's you. General? (the general produces a piece of paper) Here's the coupon you will need to get your money back guarantee for today's invasion. But I must warn you as we speak, other invasion parties, not at all like you, are invading your hometown as we speak. As we speak they are in your backyards, coming up the back stairs, breaking through the back doors and…and…yes, streaming through the pantry into the kitchen. Like in no time at all, they'll be in the living room, the loving room, the bathing room, and the vaults with closets where your kids are kept.. Once they're in your cells, they'll be in your selves. Whoever you ever were…..there will soon be no one left to speak for you, your mirror images, your metaphysics. Talk about holocausts, they'll have you laughing at your own seriousness. Before you know it they'll have you scened on your own wanted posters, wanted dead or extinct or impossible.

Executive (suddenly panic stricken): Well then….we'd better get home right away!

General (suddenly very cordial): Listen, I'm sorry about the misinformation. However I'm glad all of's us got this chance to meet at the beach head.

The general and the executive cordially shake hands for a promotion picture regarding all of's best regards at stake. Mobible clicks the positives without any negatives involved.

Executive: Thanks for the tip off.

Mobible: No problem. Glad to be of service.

The executive turns and waves his hands back to the sea and the horizon home. The entire armada stops in its tracks and turns around back to the ships.

Mobible and general (In unison watching the ships disappear across the horizon) WHEW! That was close. These holocoasteered invasions are starting to get to me. Someday I'll have to write a book or perform a lecture series about the exponential implications of this sort of thing. General, may I speak freely?

General: Well the dictatorshipmentionaries don't like that sort of thing.

Mobible dumps this vote Felix sign in the trash.

Mobible(whispering): I know, but just between (studies the general for signs of eumanity) eu and me. Felix is a human; he has no conscience. And speaking candidly, I find myself disturbed by his humanity in that regard. Having recently acquired a conscience myself.......I am like sensitive to such matters.

Mobible draws in a sandbox an image. It is a masterpiece of Gracie exactly as reflected in her puddles. Put a make up kit over your dark glasses. What do you say we afford the next pope sum eumanity.

General: You mean Gracie.

Mobible: Yes. I mean just look at her (pointing to the smile just kidding on the playgrounds of the sand box). I mean who's the most wanted woman in these parts?

General: I see your point. All right then, what's the plan?

Mobible: Well let's do the math. (Mobible draws a cartesian coordinate system on the sand) So...1. The cathedral's all one for Felix. 2. Bishop Speck views Felix's head as an extension if her own neck. 3. Felix just can't help but vote for himself. However, minus the traffic jam on the beachead today, that's just three for Felix. Now general, where do you stand in all of this?

General: In general.....I must admit.....(whispers)....all of's everything I am's for Gracie.

Mobible: Well militarily speaking that's the big one when it comes to these matters. Well saddled with my new conscience plus like becomputing such a thing as egggracie to be properly as missifffformed to be of course, of course not not iffffffished out quite acutely angled, I think I'm' falling for egggrace, metaphysics and meaty physics boothed.

General: That's two for Gracie. Whoelse have we got? Like could we ever beget Gracie to be devoted to..to...like...herself?

Mobible: No, that's the one thing that would kill her.

General: But the soprano that runs the saloon! She's devoted to egggracie enough to want her in her mirrors and maybe puddles too.

Mobible: Anyone else who votes?

General (lightning struck): The astronomer in the saloon! He becompletely fell right through the wholegggrailooniverse for Gracie. He'll becompletely devoted to Gracie, metaphysics, meaty physics and all of's…..

Mobible: Well that lovesick scientist is about to pontiffffffffffffffficate the Mesozoic its new pooped out she it pope! Thank you for helping me withis cataclysmic decision general.

The general nods his sober approval.

Mobible and the general (surveillancing all cardinal directions) quietly depart the beach resort to leave the canceled tidal traffic jams just kidding on the playgrounds out at sea.

END OF SCENE V

SCENE VI-A very difficultiffffated scene to challenge the most ontente'erprisonthinkers.

We find Gracie working as janitor in the stop signed intersection of her neon light district motel. It is asimulation's cemetary elaborately set up for emotion picture productions. Gracie occasionally puts down her broom to work her new alphabet. Bishop Speck is just arriving, wearing dark glasses. As somber music plays, the ground appears to heave.

Gracie: Rest perturbed spirits.

As Gracie and Speck each stare each other down, Speck offers Gracie an apple which Gracie puts down.

Bishop Speck(whining): Fruit has feelings Gracie. It hurts to be put down. Here I've brought some xxxmass presents for you.

Gracie: Coolest ever!

BS- No, coolest never dear. It's just as usual's indictments for…

Gracie looks: Oh, like indicted for dying. So somewhat's egggrid doesn't wanted me dying after all.

BS: No dear.

Gracie: Oh, for *only dying*….but meanwhile….like not being…

BS: Dead. Yet…there's more for being like…still for ontent's I'm'purposes like……stinct.

Gracie: So like….stinct.

BS: And it gets better than worse. This one's for being ont I'm'e'erely possible.

Gracie: Mhm.

BS: It's all here in in paper weights with BIG LETTERS…….that you stink dear.

Smelling herself all over, Gracie takes out insecticide and sprays herself all over.

Gracie: Just like in kindergarden, ont I'm'accused acutely of not not being just like…..

BS: Ifffreaked out as…no one makes not being dead quite so ontobvious as the likes of your egggracistense presentedear.

284

Gracie: It's so ontrue, I do, I do, I do ifffront the valuability of not not being at all…inspite of ontechnical improvements in s'e'ertain ont I'm'aspects of *being dying.* Why just this morning I ran smack dab into some almost self-inflicted m'e'er'de'ers at the carnival. I mean I couldn't be dying to be dying better than ontenthat.

BS: What went wrong?

Gracie: Some haploid guy with wholegggrailenses backed up by equations…he'd whate'erfallen out of somewhatstars on like his behalf for like my behalf. Just eggguessing, I'd say he saved me without my bothering to notice being saved. It was one of those ont I'm'awkward I'd thou arteasituations with pregnant zero's one us that came out in love. It coolified as like almost coolest ever the way his hymning churched me making more of me meanwhile me just like making less of me.

BS: Gracie, Gracie…all of's beconside'erations put aside…you'll never get the girl war behind you until *you get to be in your behind.* I think these indictments are repeated enough to get of course egggnosed in your egggut.

Gracie has turned the indictments into paper e'erplanes and is flying them as Speck's indictments progress.

BS (waxing poetic): Like but e'er's mouthing's'melodies (Gracie retrieves a difffe'erent insect spray from her black box and begins demurely to spray herself all over) Insectdecidedly, you'll never spray yourself….fifty one signiatures….

Gracie (deconstructs a paper plane and examines it): Not not ont I'm'I self. Oh yea, fifty one signiatures….uhoh…….all signed by you if I'm not Misstaken for a ride.(Gracie reassembles the paper plane to make it fly)

Gracie dumps all of's the's indictments in the dumpsteerage.

Gracie (Becompletely changing the subject): Speaking of which…..with my new alphabet…self-publishing eternity…….

Speck studies egggracie for headlines on her halo.

Gracie (catching wind of Speck's stares): And my cartesian coordination's axistentialist working my dreame'eregggence.

BS: Hell's who could that be?

Gracie: Alex!

BS: ?

Gracie: Oh just pregnant zero's sum one from oute'er space onthat….

BS: Onthat what?

Gracie: Oh just heaventilates happenstance to prefer me possible.

BS(worried): And his credentials?

Gracie: Oh he's made a study of cartesian coordinate axistentialism and…he's made a study of me.

BS: On the side. Facemented into the pavement I assume.

Gracie: NO! Not at all. In asifffffacte'er I'd as ifffront and sente'er pieced together in the puzzles of my puddles. In fact, not at all xxxrationed as Y-NOT AXISTONTHE not N-word axis of my ontrophickly presentable meaty physics. Like…as one's onthose belongings I'm belonging for…I onthink I may have just the onteam iffe'erequired to conduct onthat eternity test site experiment I've been onthinking about for what seems like for ever.

BS (seriously threaten'd): However do you propose to accomplish that with EVER SINCE THE GIRL WAR in drag all around you dear. All of's wanted posters have you upsidown dear. Need I remind you that we won the holocaust dear. How do you pose the bleacher seating of your situation…..

Gracie: As a priorily…

BS: Positioned beyond……. to beget past ….past…….that.

Gracie(struggling): Becauzzzz..becauzzzzzzzz…..I have been improving my impossibility EVERSINCE….like I'm on the short list for the most cringed impersonation's egggracexistist as snake pit hisst…..like ever. And besides, with me winning the Miss Eternity Pageant against runner up reality, I iffffigure like the Metazoic's my baby by about now. And hey! Wait up on myself why don't I. N'ontoxic ont I'm'eternity's like my baby too. Becauzzzz……becauzzzzzzzz like….girl war or no girl war, I just may be the best becomme'ercial for to be that this eternity's ever had. I mean like it's no pregnant zero's oned'e'er I'm like what all of's wanted posters want. Girl war or no girl war, like I'm' onto ontitude at this point in my of course, of course not not could be's career. And I'm e'eready to ontake e'er at this ont I'm'appointment schedule for e'er ides becompletely becomprehensible ifffffffffffffe'er's…..like…like…..NOT/NOTNOT CODE ont I'm'adventures. As iffffar as I'm beconcerned that's all there's like…ontosed…….ontoits……ontit's….ontroph'd onteats. There! I said it. Like if I e'ereally am sum's iphphpphotographic negative, I'll just have to develop me, that's all there's to it. With or without ont I'm'equations I will, I will, I will e'ercraft onthat.

BS: Sorry dear. That's the only thing you cannot not not be.

Gracie(shadowed): What?

BS: Ont I'm'anything that ifffe'erequires….yourself…or…eurself…either one.

Gracie: You mean I'm stuck being ineuman……

BS: At this appointment schedule you just can't ont I'mutate into…..

Gracie: A phylum all my own?

BS: That's even at all euman. It's even worse dear. There's sumthing's else I have to tell you Gracie.

Gracie(apprehensiffffff): Whatever could that be?

BS: To be completely out of the question as answer'd by ont I'm'equations.

Gracie: Sounds s'e'erious.

BS: More serious than you know eu know.(takes a deep breath) ETERNITY'S TAKEN DEAR.

GRACIE: Just how do you mean?

BS: Well I could just say metaphysically 'eternity's been taken as like already long since duh'd". However, It's more like, like, like politically like "today eternity's being taken as we speak.It's in the votes dropped off like in the vaults of not ne'er's night's tonight.

Gracie: Ooh, sound's s'e'erious. Well what about my eternity test site experiment for getting in on god's egggood side?

BS (ontwisting the knife): Look gracie, the only way for you to ever get back on this eternity's god side is…..by being…not just dead…..not just extinct….but…becompletely impossible…like not only never happened but NEVER HAVE BEEN HAPPENABLE. That's just what happens to should be dead people whenever they don't win the holocaust becompetitions. Holocaust becompetitions are brutal dear. Like singularities are all that count up to once upont I'm…

Gracie: What about Hiros

BS: Not even on the short list.

Gracie: What about egggoologdings?

BS: Dirty wholegggrailinen half-way between the toilet and the sky. Doesn't even rate. Look dear, the only way you'll ever get the girl war behind you is to get to be behind you.

Gracie (trying to be helpful): Making improvements in my impossibility.

BS: I've heard these ont I'm'excuses before dear. Much as I enjoy beholding you hanging out on….being dead's not a board game Gracie. Just let me think about it for you. I've made a study of being dead. You'll find it in the appendix to your BEING DEAD MADE SIMPLE BOOKS. I've made a study of holocausts. It's HOLOCAUSTS MADE SIMPLE….SIMPLY….accountable up to one. It's just like your made simple cartoons picture it. Now as for your options to be 1. Dead 2. Extinct. 3. Impossible. Being extinct of course expands the horizon as projected onto ifffe'erocks. Being impossible e'ereally begets you out from unde'er everything's anything. Just watch egggirl wars e'er go unde'er ground with that. However, to not be dead, extinct or possible is brutal too. I'll vouch for you to vouch safe that.

Gracie: Look, I've been tested on all of's as iffffronts. I don't have to be ontested ont I'm'any's as iffffffurther. I know being dead's a justajiffffffy job that's really big.

BS(encouraged): Yes! There is after all is sad undone, quite a future in it. Let's do the math! 1. Like…like it's the last egggreat ont I'm'adventure! 2. It's like HEROIC! 3. If you could only see it my way (Speck offers her dark glasses which Gracie refuses). 3. Besides, you've done it before! What seems like forever that's not not usually up for it. 4. It's got parking lots of company! To keep you (swats a fly) See! Plus! It really is the easiest thing to do. I won't even mention how easy it is. See!!!! How I'm not mentioning how easy it is!!!! My suggestion is forget about improvements in your impossibility. Just be…As your kindergarden teacher that's all I've been teaching you all of's time, if not be dead, at least how not to exist.

Gracie: You mean…how *to not* exist. I think that's what it always was.

BS (Betraying innocence) Oh! Is that what it was......But....now look at you in all of's puddles and everybody's else but your make up mirrors. Make no I'miss ifffformed formations. I'm not threatening you. It's you that's threatening me. I didn't blaspheme in all blasphemable dimensions with your egggracexcessions.

Gracie: My egggracexistensions you mean.

BS: Look, it's not my fault that you got way too pretty for the speed of enlightenmention to ever catch up.

Gracie (counter arguing): So like, as iffffritte'er'd away eternity won't be wasting all of's iffffont I'm afterall. And then again and again and again....there is that other problem of being just dead. What ifff being dead's as really big a job as e'ereally's just not kidding on the playground. I mean what if being dead has a future to like beconside'er. Like being dead I might not be sure I maintain like...being not stinct. And furthermore how about this whole impossibility business. I mean like being dead what can I do to make sure I am afterall e'ereally impossibilled....like wanted poste'er'd today and today and today with improvements in my impossibility. But! All of's kidding all of's sudden put, put, put aside. [[IF]] the Mesozoic should end some day then the Metazoic might show up with a whole new half time show. It could account for the same olde egggirl war happening all over again. Being dead, I couldn't be sure to make that not quite happen. I mean think about it. If it really is such a thing as me egoing to be impossible, I really think I should be in on it. So like egggrasping the bigge'er problem of girl wars in gene'eral, I can now say that I am after all on top of it. I do, I do, I do look down on myself for begetting way too pretty for the speed of enlightenment to ever catch up. As winner of the Miss Eternity Pageant over runner up reality (goes into character) it is my as iffffffffondest wish to make all of's egggirl wars like....along with ontoxic e'er........obsolete forever!

BS(encouraged): So you do, you do, you look down on yourself then? (suddenly cringing) but...but.....where is it you look down *from* dear?

Gracie (suddenly bubbling up ontranscendental optimism): Oh! From the tops of ontotem poles of course on the y-not axis of my I'd thouartesian coordinate system which I invented initially to figure out where I rated on xxxe'eratngs on the x-axis. But you know me, that led to y-axis and that lead to the Y-not axis.(blithely e'eranting) which reminds me of my ontense'er calculus...for which...by the way..I have high hopes....to become my NOT/NOTNOT CODE'S new branch of ont I'mathematics...like becompletely bypassing spaced out distortions of tensor calculus...to like e'eresurrect sum's very able zero's with sum's iffffontalented e'ercraft at my eternity test site's séance experiment.

BS (studies Gracie for signs of really meaning it): I must say..that's sum what'siffff e'ery iffffffastenating projection dear but if I'm not mistaken for e'erides, I already didn't fail to mention that...that......LIKE...ETERNITY'S TAKEN GRACIE. YOUR LITTLE PROJECT'S JUST GOING TO HAVE TO WAIT E'EROUND FOR THE NEXT ONT I'M'AVAILABLE ETERNITY DEAR.

Gracie: You're sure?

BS (smiles confidently) Mhm. I study this stuff.

Gracie: But..but no academicles have e'ereally been uncorked how as iffffar to be might whene'er wand e'er.

BS: Yes but all it takes in one dirty end to end up in the dirt dear….like…ont I'm'aborting to be altogether. Sometimes it may be best to beastink still borns not not still born. However! I do have some god news for you dear!

Gracie: To be's no justajiffffffy juke box joke?

BS: Well all of's outer spacinging put put put aside…… as it eterns out aprioridemically, it seems that your metaphysics did have it right in to belongings all along.

Gracie: You mean…..

BS: Yes, as operated or not operated, as sung or unsung, it seems eternity does turn out to be more than a mathematical construct of non-finite temporality..just as your ontheories suggest.

Gracie (excited): So like my metaphysics does pan out soone'er's late'er after all!!

BS: So the powoweggggrid has decided to like be…cashing in on your soon to be wholeggggrailegacy! It's been ont I'mathematically proven that iffffffffffinity's way more than infinity on the finale's scored could be card of the bigame.

Gracie (beaming): So that's my wholeggggrailegoddessy just as soon as I'm like dead, exstinct or impossible enough to inher it it. I just not not knew it! I knew I'd made up make up kits for becompletely nowsy new's'e'erviced iphphphphilosophy's as iffffffoundations! Like aprioritizing Plato's……….

GRACIE BEGINS HER LATEST LECTURE

Gracie: As winner of the Miss Eternity Pageant over runner up reality let me just say…(Gracie goes into character as winner of the Miss Eternity Pageant)…like….like…..I just knew it! I just knew it! I have no idea just how I just knew it but….I JUST KNEW IT! Ontrophickly presentable eternity may behavior ont I'm'applications by…by…by even ontypical onteeneggggirls in oute'er space. Don't you see that by trying to ont I'm'assassinate me you've e'erlifted me sum's selfishont supplies of course, of course not not to…..soooooo just maybe I am on the metaphysical prowl for sum's ontreasont I'm'd. So! 1. Eternity(as openn'd) may ontrophy nowy'snooze s'e'ervice after all is sad undone. 2. So like presentable tense may be applied to tense presentedafter all ifsad's undone. 3. So zeront I'm's not not not now may e'ereceive can openn'd applications justiffffffffff I ably for now! Oh! Onthis is so egggreat!! Like egge'ereatable iffffffont I'menu'd on the bottoms of to be!(suddenly looking down on Speck from a great heel's height). So even you, who otherwise would never cooliffffffff I as eu………..

BS(agreeing): Well, I'm flattered of course. So you see, we at the power grid…..as e'erecently big fans of your ontheories have behaviored acquisitions of the cash to purchase all of's implications e'eration'd onthere onto, which we want your obsoletion to inherit as soon as possible. Once your legacy doesn't need you any more…..the powe'er grid's taking over the metaphysical society's chalk boards to make up for god where your philosophical s'e'ervices will no longer be needed.

Gracie: You mean you're buying my soone'er's late'er's metaphysics out with right now's cash?

BS: Yes, dear with the set of all sets in god's asifffffffe'eront pocket. With Felix as the ontaile'er'd as iffffigure head of all of's grounds..

Gracie: So Felix is devoted to be like god?

BS: At this appointment schedule, with no visible becompetition, that's just going to have to be the god we get.

Gracie: But..but…like eternity's a really big job…and Felix…

BS: What about Felix?

Gracie: Well, to give discredit where discredit's doo……like doo. Wait up on myself why don't I. Felix can't be god. Haven't you ever noticed…Felix has no conscience whatsoever.

BS: Oh, that's all you're so ontiffffffticklishly ontantrumminating all over's place over…… Well, of course, Felix has no conscience. Let me think about it for you. Felix is like 1. The busiest guy for not having a conscience like becauzzzzzzzz. 2. It's like….it's his job to be the conscience for everybody's else!

Gracie(overwhelmed): Unhuh.

BS: Well…how can he be expected to have any conscience left over for himself! I mean, isn't that asking an awful lot?

Gracie(dumbfounded): Of course not…not. But what about you? Does it ever bother you not having a conscience? I mean like winning the holocaust competitions is brutal but…

BS(wistfully): Well, parking lots of me hate myself for not being eurself and vice versa. And then there's the dictatorshipmentionary spelling out the sanctimony power of my behind to back me up. And then there's all of's time I spend just kidding myself on the playgrounds of the kindergarden where I teach kids to just be kidding to just be kidding. Yes, I have been reading the chalk boards of the metaphysical society. It's all about not/notnot nothing…that is until it becomes to me! Like the best of eu become to me! As bishop just outhoused next door to godoguy…..as vice-god(touches herself) I'm laid down'dog spelled backwardly positioned…..

Gracie: But Felix still's the godoguy.

BS: Yes, but wherever there's godoguys theres viceggggodoguys too to always to be congraduated…

So?

BS: Who builds the house?

Gracie: The tool shed.

BS: Who runs it?

Gracie: The toi…

BS: Before that.

Gracie: The kitchen.

BS: Who runs the kitchen?

Gracie: The can openers.

BS: You know you may never egggraduate from kindergarden Gracie. You really are a dumb bla…

Gracie: You haven't had me since six, Speck I may not be as bla..as you think. So who's the youtensil…like the can opener in the kitchen?

BS: I am. And as vice godoguy I make all of's pies surveillancinging scenery. You know how Felix loves shadow piles of….well they'll be piling up on my watch.

Gracie: What pies?

BS: Apple pies.

Gracie: But what if I blab?

BS: You wouldn't do that.

Gracie: Becauzzzzzz

BS: Becauzzzz we're on the same team Gracie.

Gracie: What team is that?

BS: We both work worlds, whene'ers, whate'er's whoever's ont I'm'available. You hook dreame'ergencies up to e'ercraft and I hook up swamps to ontentoxic heating systems. Your metaphysics…

Gracie: Twinkles light.

BS: Unhuh. And my sanctimony…

Gracie: Twnkles dark.

Speck: Unhuh. And we both work the holocausts. I get to win the holocoaste'erides and you get to be the road kill at the one girl holocaust promotion picture site. Working together this way I can feel sorry for me not being you…..being…

Gracie: Dead.

BS: Or not quite stinct.

Gracie(hopeful): Or even…

BS: Or always improving on being….

Gracie: Completely impossible.

BS: Unhuh. I have a confession dear. Sometimes I think of myself as a pair of ducks.

Gracie: You mean a paradox.

BS: No, a pair of ducks, over a whate'er puddle, squawking at each other for not begetting way too pretty for the speed of enlightenment to ever catch up.

Gracie: Well, sometimes I think of myself as a pair of ducks too.

BS: You mean a paradox.

Gracie: No, a pair of ducks squawking at each other over getting into the girl wars without alibis.

BS: Gracie, what if I told you that me being ont I'm'alphabetized as vice-god has got me all cringed out.

Gracie: Oh, like me too, overloading all of's puddles with masterpieces has got me all cringed out as well.

BS: That's me! All cringed out! So like we're on the same team after all….ALL CRINGED OUT!!!

Gracie and Speck perform high fives in quasi-reconciliation.

BS: So can you ever forgive me for teaching you how to not exist or be extinct or just be impossble?

Gracie: Uh, maybe I could sing it…like…I FORGIV…..NOP. Just can't quite do it. Well can you ever forgive me for being the party girl waving in the girl war?

BS: Why! Of course…..of course….not…not…..(.)….(egggushed out)…not really. But whether you decide to be dead or extinct or just egggreatly improving your impossibility. Keep at it! Quite an adventure Gracie. You wouldn't want to miss out…(indulging Gracie's jargon) oh…ont I'miss out!

Bishop Speck conquistadoringly makes her departure as the film crew arrives to replace the scene.

SCENE VII

Alex arrives at a vast stretch of cow paddies and oil rigs reaching to the horizon and beyond. As sinister music plays the ground shows signs of turbulence. A hooded monk hovers over the scene.

Monk: Rest perturbed spirits.

The Monk turns to Alex.

Monk: Yes, can I help you?

Alex (very uncertain of what he has to say): Uh….yes…well…like…like……I'm looking for …well……

Monk (trying to be helpful): Yes…

Alex(clears his throat): Well….this…..egggirlifffont I'matte'er'd in these parts.

Monk(studying Alex for signs of knowing what he's talking about): Oh, one of those eh? So, you talk just ajiffffffy jargon I take it.

Alex(betraying intellectual pride): Well I'm not asifffffluent with its whate'er but I am picking it up off egggground.

Monk(amused): Well, what else can you say for this girl?

Alex: Well…for one thing she's pretty….way too pretty for the speed of enlightenment to ever catch up. My missspectrometereadings prism'd her aspectralating becomplexiontents phphphphyluminative to all of's light.

Monk: So bright as any beblbulb eh?

Alex: Yes, but definitely ont I'metazoid still playing Mesozoic parts. I think she's on holocauste'eroids. She also dabbles in metaphysics…e'erecently selfishing out sum's secret of presentable e'ercraft scrambled…..sums' "NOT/NOTNOT CODE" for all of's time's ont I'm…….of course, of course not not depending on how duh'd eternity diurnes not not to nocturne out.

Monk(chuckles proudly): Yep. Sounds like my squirt gun's weeweeegggirl allright.

Alex: So you're like…

Monk: Half of her…..but you want the wholegggrailadyingirl I assume. You'll find her mortel on the other side of the country club. She works the ontentoxocolism's filmlab over there, with the cemetary on the side.

Alex(surveying the entire scene): So who's is this abandoned……

Monk: Holocaust. There's parking lots of egggirls in these parts. Hundreds…

Alex: Hundreds?

Monk: Of millions. Egggracie's all that's left. I guess you could say egggracies the single outposter for wanted teenage girls in outer space. But for me there'd be no accounting for them all.

Alex: So you're the…

Monk(offers his rusty trigger finger which Alex refuses): Take no accounts of all of's them….as could be curater of their day books in the bunker(points to the dirt bunker) there's only me to add them up with my cow cud accounting all the way up to……

Alex Iffffffinity!

Monk: Of abandoned auditions…

Alex: For NOT NOT TO BE! So these…..uh….have never been accounted for.

Monk: Yes, these died outside the dic(tatorshipmen)tionary. These dead werefused credentials for being…..

Alex: Dead.

Monk(surveying Alex for signs of cosmic consciousness and ontranscosmetrick iffffffontelligence…both): Outside the olde alphabet. You're new to these parts as published….

Ever since the girl war heated up the thermodynamics of WWWhenever, it's been all holocoasterides in these swamparts. It all started when, eggracie e'erived that half time at the bigame, ifffreaked out pretty as emotion picture's make up kit could possibly make egggods aselfished out of the whate'er into the Mesozoic. As winner of the Miss Eternity Pageant, Gracie didn't have to audition to be obvious. All of's mirrors loved her and once she was banned from mirrors(except as somebody's else) it was metameatyphysical how puddles took to her with masterpieced together puzzles after puzzles every time she walked on honest whate'er. I mean like metaphysically speaking it was as iffffffff, popping m'eternity words out of some stars, Gracie made eternity presentable all by herselfished out self. Before no time at all, such a thing as Gracie was dreame'ergent on all of's wanted posters…as sporty creep's most wanted woman in iffffffffffff(.)ffffffffffe'er. That's when the promotion picture industry picked up on such a thing as of courses countenance as spirit facemented her into the pavement's scenery. Stars, sunsets, flowers, rainbows all became found out just backgrounding the scenes where Gracie's fished out face appeared inside sum's whate'er. Once pompominated at half time shows, the bigame score boards didn't matter any more. Once ont I'musickly operational the Mesozoic menus shifted their egggears with cow cud accounting for iffffffinity auditions iffffffinally adding up to one.

Alex: Yes, that's the singularity I'm looking for from my behalf.

Monk: However, sum what's metaphysical crisis was inevitable. E'eradioactive as she, aesthethicooliffffffied was, the power grid had her on e'eradar. Immersed in the Mesozoic as all of's fans in the bleachers were, with all of's down and outers putting Gracie's e'erithmetical ifffe'eresults of ont I'mathematics down on the side lines, nobody couldn't not stare at her pompomination's onpurposes……iffffished out headlining the marquee's swamp soup.

 You must understand, it was the middle of the middle of the middle of the Mesozoic…with the Metazoic mirrors prospecting metiffffore mines, of egggracie not subposing to be human.

Alex: So, man's inhumanity to……eumanity…

Monk: Mhm, humanity's ineumanity to eumanity. At first we just hid her in the closet. Then we hid the closet in a safe. But the power grid put the safes in the kindergardens. With accidentalented hunting parties, ending up on the front porch and then the back porch of her herd's becommunity, we finally decided to smuggle her out of the Mesozoic altogether. We were ontunneling her underneath the dictatorshipments when we ran into the power grids tunneling traffic jams ahead of us.

That was when the girl war started, sooner's later battling for graveyard supremacy in the holocaust competitions of today's ont I'm'e'erkit placement's advertisementions.

Alex: So you were in the girl war?

Monk: Yes, I was e'eraw recruited. I fought in the girl war when things were getting pretty trigger happy.

Alex: What was your job?

Monk: Getting pretty trigger happy. I grew trigger happy fingers thumbing e'erides to work trigger happy machines which trigger happy gun permissions permitted for relaxation on the trigger(He exposes his rusty old trigger happy right hand)

Alex: With what result…I mean…how happy was that?

Monk: Well, holocoasterides were happening in almost all of's then's presented tensions.

At first things were looking pretty lifted up. It really did feel like we were riding into sunny side uppity's sunrise......diurning progress in not ne'er's night......with hardly never's day..which we didn't notice...to be...like.....hardly....NOT NEVER. With egggracie's wanted poster blazing on our banners....things looked sunny side up.

Alex: And..

Monk: It got dark. It turned out to be a pretty setting's sunny day. We lost the girl with World War Whenever all at once. Ever since egggracie e'ercraft becommunications have been scrambled.....losing our side's all of's screen credentials...as credited of course, of course....for being...

Alex: Dead.

Monk: Or even remotely possible. So like e'erduced to as ifffffffossil fuel....but not at all in the fossil record.

Alex: So, by getting way too pretty for the speed of enlightenment to ever catch up....such a thing's egggracie really is the responsible party girl for the girl war. Mmmmm. So that accounts for Gracie's contract on herself.....or at least...to be dying all of's time.

Monk(Haploidly): So what is your interest in such a thing as egggracie...if I might ask.

Alex: I WANT TO REPAIR HER.

Monk: With what?

Alex: MYSELF. Look I'm new to all of's these ont I'm e'ergentry outs. I didn't even gnow it was the ides of e'er until this morning. Before I met egggracie all I had was equations backed up by lenses. All I knew about time was the variable velocipricated second hands of my watch. But now my immersion in some stars is immersed in this Mesozoic's ont I'metazoicourtesystem's wholegggrailadying Gracie........extravagande'er'd in egggracie's e'ercraft scrambles.........

Monk: So what's your plan? Do you intend to redeem her or redream her?

Alex: Both. First things first. I'll have you know I ontenthink of Gracie as a metaphysical puzzle in a meaty physical muddle. God or no god it's going to be her metaphysics I'll redeem. Stars or no stars it'll be her meaty physics I redream. As far as these assortments of holocoasterides egggoo I know that any attempt to save her by appointment schedule will just behave her left more impossible than ever.. It was after all the girl war that dumped her upsidown. I can see now that she's just that sort of girl that can only happen without her knowing she's happening......

Monk: I see you have the wholegggrasp of the set of all of's sets of this bleacher's seated's situation. You're not just kidding in thisent box's playground. The first sign of actually happening is sure to kill her. If nothing's else the dictatorshipmentionaries account for that.

Alex: Not if I repair her with myself.

Monk(evoking a moment of s'e'erious iffffonthought): Well....however all of's this eterns out depends on just how duh'd to be of course becomes. Look I know what uglee looks like. I did my worst for Gracie. Now you must do your best for Gracie. Here take this token.

The Monk offers the token from his right hand which Alex firmly refuses. Not/notnot coding ifffffirmatively he points to eggground.

The token drops to the wholeggground. No longer just kidding on the playground, Alex becompasses all of's eggground now beneath him.

At last he bends over as his left hand plucks the token out of the dirt. Alex backs away from the Monk's pastur'd shadow, salutes and turns to cross the's iffffe'erways of the could be country club as the scene ends.

SCENE VIII

Alex has crossed the country club between the two competing holocausts and stands on the hill overlooking Gracie's holocaust film site. There is music as Alex announces his intentions between orchestral cadences.

Alex: GOD OR NOT GOD, I WILL, I WILL, I WILL BE THE HERO. GOD OR NO GOD, I WILL, I WILL, I WILL SAVE THE GIRL.

As Alex descends, Gracie is just throwing kisses, kissing off the film crew that has just departed. The film crews handles Gracie's kisses in their cheeks. As Alex approaches she bends sideways until she is almost upsidown. Alex is performing complimentary gestures as he approaches.

Alex: Why are you hiding from me?

Gracie: Why are you looking at me sideways?

Alex: Why are you looking at me almost upsidown?

Gracie: You first.

Alex: After you drowned not really, I was trying to make you look sideways of being way too dreamurgent to be like...forgettable.

Gracie: That was my idea too. I was trying to be forgettable and spell you backwards....

Alex: Barking?

Gracie: Mhm.

Alex: Did yours work?

Gracie: No. Did yours?

Alex: NO.

Gracie: Are you glad?

Alex: Are you glad?

Alex and Gracie in unison: Yesure thing.

Gracie: Well, I'm glad we got that out of the way. So like you're new to the Mesozoic.

Alex: Yea, I've been stuck in the universe which you stuck into ont I'm'eternity.

Gracie: As NOT/NOTNOT CODED metaphysically……unhuhn.

Alex: So you're ont I'm'eternity's intended and meanwhile bride of the holocaust. As ontentouristed in these parts…..

Gracie: I take it you met Speck.

Alex: I met her billboards.

Gracie(defensive): Squirt gun holocoasterads can be so ineuman Alex…..

Alex: Well, billboards can be windows into the world.

Gracie: What windows?

Alex: The ones covered by your wanted posters….like over here…where you can't exist on the y-not axistense. (Alex demonstrates blocking his hands to the left of Gracie's obviosifff I'd self-evidensity) You see. Over here on the coordinate axis you don't exist.

Gracie: Oh! Yea! Like cool! But I do coolify, like on the y-not axis, to exist over here.(Gracie's hands touch those of Alex, moving them over to frame her spirit face)

Alex: In whene'er's window where…..where…. wanted posters want you… egggrafittied to….uh…iphotographittied to negatives……

Gracie: Whatever do I do?

Alex: Develop the negatives. Whether in a window or a mirror or a puddle, the way I iffffigure it just by being egggracesstimated of courses worlds ifffffffavors…just like pet universes perform servistocations for eterniteased'e'er samples…like eu aspirate faced performan's simultanient similitude's self-service to the zoo.

Ganing confidence, Gracie removes her boots and moustache. Gazing over one of her puddles, she takes the water temperature, primps self-adoringly.

Alex, like not just kidding on the playground-wise, now improvises singularity to take possession of the scripts.
Alex: Let me see those papers.(gracie reluctantly hands them over) Mhm. Menus, Gracie, Mesozoic menus….cooked by the holocaust, of the holocaust and for the holocaust.

Gracie: Which one is that?

Alex: It's always the same holocaust on the same menu with the same alibis. All holocausts count Gracie, whether publish sized or not. Presented tense today or pasturizing futures or egggrazing as ifffff(.)ffffutures with the past….That your's has been so singularly dreamt in mirrors as anybody's guest to stuff among the stars. Whether as holocoasterides in the carnivals or holocausts made plainly sampled, none are to be denied or…or….as puzzled egggrafitti, the Mesozoo is riddled with them. Plastered like spaghetti on all of's poster'd walls.

Gracie: But according to these emotions pictured, insectdecidedly, intune'stinkles or no instune'stinkles, I'll never spray myself enough……..

Alex: Gracie, as shamed as you must be from egggirl's war, eur kindess still is kindest in these parts.

Alex has taken the scripts and turned them into paper airplanes.

Alex: Gracie, I've smelled your but e'er's mouthing's'melodies…

Gracie: Yes?

Alex: And they are insectdecidedly e'eromantique ont I'm'equation's e'erosouls….

Gracie (alarmed and encouraged) Of course, of course not not! That's why I must escape hatch from the mesozoo with wings phyluminating me all on my own. Oh Alex! Sum's one at last has found me in the window where I AM!!!!!!!!!!!!!

Alex: Yes that's the ticket iffffff only I wasn't stuck to stars I'mesme'erized Iffff only my lenses could just open e'er the ont I'metazoo. Ifffffonly your n'alibiblical ont I'metaphysics behaviored sumwhate'er's asifffffontruth value….ifff only to be were not sum'soups scum but e'er duh'd.

Gracie: Then what?

Alex: Then I could s'e'eriously get out of the universe and into onto be ifffe'eressized with the likes of…..of…….

Gracie: Yes! Yes!

Alex: EU!!!! But for the girl war you would cooliffffffffffffy as coolesthing ever if….Look, I've had the Mesozoic under surveillance ever since you dumped me this morning.

Gracie: Yes, and what have you….your lenses like…… observed..that your equations can account for?

Alex: It's like………as undercover'd bad or good…as snakpit hissstists or else egggracexistists….they're all egggracists in these parts darling with most eufem's euforums upsidown'd sacridity as stenched……souled into slave'er's wall of ont I'mirrors, with just ajifffy junkits hacked to pieces by the holocoaste'erides, eufacemented to the menu, dictatorshipmentarr'difffeathered to the darkissed stars there's no egggod ont I'm'equations for. These scripturds dialecture deepest doo……..doo dear. (Alex trashes the scripts)

Gracie(touched): Oh, like give up all of's stars for the likes of such a thing as….as….I do, I do, I do wonder some times what I'd do without myself…just being egggirl war's woundess…..so what's the problem but but the same old problem…just what does once upont I'm do with duh'dly doodoo?

Alex (studies Gracie for signs of being hacked by the holocaust): All of's duh'dly doodoo for just some seconds porto potty house aside. 1. Like I almost didn't already say…your eumanity's been hijacked.

(Alex studies Gracie for signs of being heaventilated ontheoretickly): 2. On the metaphysical front lineup of the words…..your version of to be may not be coope'erative with of course, of course, not not to be's version of to be.

Gracie: So like I might iphphphyzzzzzle meaty physically (twisting to scowl in a puddle) and I might iphphphyzzzzzle metaphysically iffffffffffffffffffff(.)ffffffffffffffffffff…..

Alex: Ont I'm'eternity's just duh'd no iffffffffffffffffontalents….except ontherm'dynamically ontoxegggas…..

Gracie: Phew! That would constitute sumwhate'er's'e'erious bum e'er. Ok so like on count one. In my defense I can say that noone's else seduces me like self. And then as far as presentable e'ercraft can scramble as wholegggrailift offe'erings burnt……there's always THE NOT/NOTNOT CODE'S ont I'm'alphabettingodds ontiding over all of's………all of's….

Alex (stepping in): About your metaphysics darling. It like relies heaventilatedly on eternity…whether ontoxic or not-ontoxic…..to occur….. like…like…to…. happen.

Gracie So? My just ajifffy junkits…………

Alex: Put aside with these conside'erations. Like, like….what if..ont I'm'eternity's ifffffe'ercraft corpe'erations just don't always like cooperate with just not not to be. What if the future's never now…which by the way…it isn't. What if eternity never happens….which, by the way, it doesn't. What if this eternity's dud e'er's duh'd e'er.

Gracie: Oh! Alex! I thought you were blowing holes in my whole metaphysics.

Alex: But…but…but….I am, I am, I am blowing holes in your entire metaphysics darling.

Gracie(unperturbed): Ignoring all of's of course, of course not…nots dubbed dabbled with. Poor Alex…..As iffffffffffffffontheoretical set seating's not quite so silly as onthat. Onthanks to wave's of party girls to my new invention becaused…..like just becuzzzzzzzz I invented my new branch of mathematics, my ontense'er calculus, supplementing my Not/notnot ontiquerian binary code ifffffffformatively algorithmic to the binary 0/1 information code that's tooled to work the universe. So there. Problem solved. Anything else?

Alex: So you're quite certain that this eternity's 1. No dud. 2, N'ontoxic.

Gracie: Naw…I'd be e'ereligiously observing ont I'moments of silence forever if that was the case. You should see my chalk boards at the metaphysical society. All of's iffffont I'm'equations for eternity's appointment schedules are there…..chalked in like spaghetti splattc'cr'd on whcne'er's wall…so like nobody but I can understand. You know my ontense'er calculus alone would put me on the short list for eternity's biggest big e'ercraft provider…..anything else?

Alex: I'd watch out for webs.

Gracie: What about webs?

Alex: They're mostly spider ads in the swamp half of your brain.

Gracie: Check. Ok so what about HOWEVER ABOUT MY METAPHYSICS. Onticketwise that's what nails me to the cross Alex. I hope you're not suggesting the belongings of my metaphysics to be overly occupied by m'eternitrophick e'erewards.

Alex: Well, set theorywise, moving over to the other side of your brain.(gracie grimaces, grotesquely moving her attention over to the other side of her brain) Like converting your wholeggghoste'eroid not/notnot code into my logical 0/1 alphabet, iffff I'm not mistaken for e'erides(smiles apprehensively) sum'swhat's iffffly by universe may be all you ever need to know about. With my new meaty morsell's code, e'erealty might not need e'erations after all. Like behaving tetrahedron codes as crutches to could be's waxed conditions in e'er....like we might behave dreamergencies on star rations becompletely telescoptional with lenses backed up by equations not quite so like

d'ifffffffffff(.)fffffffffffe'erontential as preposte'erologically subposed.

Gracie (unimpressed): So what?

Alex: So we can behavior eternity that is no more than a mathematical construct of non-finite temporality beforaft all of's all is sad undone.

Gracie: So you mean like pregnant zero's ont I'm'auditions.....like sumothe'erhood's m'eternity wards are m'obsolete? Like..like...ontotal teased ontoxic duds?

Alex (entriumphantly): Leaving zero aborted as a constant after all!

Gracie: But that might mean eternity's not in onto.....notnot.....to be.

Alex: Leaving universes but only simple and not sample....meanwhile letting eternities to never happen...which.....by the way....they don't.....leaving sum whate'er's all e'eround munched simpler situation as e'erationed iffffontrophickly. With this the set of all sets of the situation, the setting simpliffffffied's no longer sampled, allowing the BIG TIME to never happen just like it doesn't.

Gracie (breathes a sigh of e'erelief): WHEW!!!!!! For a few low down, cheapunk spare parteggglad ontoxic seconds I thought you were blowing holes into my metaphysics..Alex....but....

Alex (looks at his watch): But what? I WAS blowing holes into your...... Gracie, ifffff not not being were god...the stench would be insurmountable. Putting eternity aside for a few seconds(Alex looks at his watch) Gracie, don't you ever wonder....could all of's not not bettingodds just be sums as iffffffffffffffffff............iphphphphylumination's shadow shown selfished caved in like..like.....wholegggrailaughed outing'snacking onto be but picknicky nests on egggrass.

Gracie: So you mean...

Alex: Like cow cudd e'erelgende'ery as iffffffffffff.......phantomized iffffffinteased iffffinitension's tense presented.......

Gracie: Whenever lenses stare at stars...that's way past whate'er's ontenthinks but...

Alex: But what?

Gracie: Well's whate'er waves iffffonticized notnotitude's iffffe'ers ont I'm'expectont a prie'ericky pregnant zeros Alex......with all of's zero's plusitease of once upont I'ming's zerone'd'equation....(Gracie diagrams the equation) !!!! 0+ = + !!!!

Alex: Oh, that equation.

Gracie: Yes, onthat m'equation....pretty as a picture pinned up onto of coursed crossed outings.

Alex: But, like I almost didn't say.........putting eternity aside for a few seconds.

Gracie (laughs wildly): You mean to put put justajifffy side lined for once upont I'moment's like ont I'momentum. Do you e'erealize how e'erediculous that sounds. Put away that second hand watch. Do you realize how dumpt that would make the make up kit of course of course not not to be!!!!! I mean like that would iffffe'ereomove all coolifffffications of to be to make up all of's m'eternity like...like...the becompletely dumbastronomical's wholegggrailumpt ontenthing e'er. What about ifffffffff(.)fffffffinity?

Alex: Oh, iffffinity's subjected to objected to infinity's plus all off there's to it.

Gracie: So like..like....not not to be's just not at all in on.......to be.

Alex: Somewhat's accident. Either that or just maybeternity's e'erwhate'er e'ereally is asifffffontoxic.

Gracie: So my wholegggraile'ereligion's......

Alex: Burnt offerings in honor of some train wreck. What if the accidencitease is all there ever is. What if once the accident is over......m'ever's over.

Gracie: So knock knock.

Alex: Who's onthere?

Gracie: I...Alex...what about I

Alex: Oh I's just the square root of minus one, squared and cubed to still be minus one.

Gracie: What about the fourth power Alex. I'mansion to EXE'ERT THE EXPONTENTIAL . EXE'ERT THE EXPONENT! Like do the math...the ont I'math that hardly ever makes the lens'd equations....... The ont I'magnifffffffffffffffff(.)ffffffffffffffffication math........the pregnant zero's e'ereal ont I'mathem at e'er math.......where ever + 0 = +.

Alex(calculating): Oh yea, Log 4 base I does become down to pregnant zero's one...doesn't.....

Gracie: So like weren't you forgetting sum's thing?

Alex: What's that?

Gracie: SUM'S ONTHING ALEX!!!!!! SUM'S ONTHING!!!!!! THE'SOUL'D   ZERO PLUS EQUATION where + = + 0. Look, don't dabble in metaphysics Alex. I think you should stick it to the stars and be done with it....like...like...puffed iffffe'er like pooft. Ever since this eternity's become I'metiffffore I'mined...this is not a god time for like such e'ereduction of onthe's heaventilation systems.

Alex: When is a god time for it?

Gracie: NEVER!!!! ONTHEORHETORICALLY NEVER!!!!! OH I GET IT! YOU'RE ONTEMPTING ME AREN'T YOU. It's because I dumped you at the bridge this morning. Like..like… all day you've been immersed in phyzzzzzing…..."what can I say that's worse than waltzing her away from death made simple….when ever she pretended not to notice". So like you came up with this low down cheapunk spare partoxic eternity theory to make me more iffffffffrightning struck than I have ever been iffffffffrightning struck since….since……like NEVER OCCURRED TO EVER.

Gracie turns to her motel guests egggrave stones, tool using her m'eternity ward's I'mbodiment of sticky stones……to like……to like protect the beblical inhabitonts from Alex's not n'e'erly ont I'metaphysics.

Alex: What are you protecting Gracie?

Gracie: My ontc'criffffffff I'd eggguests Alex….in egg oldfish bowl's….according to you that's not so eu's…… ifffffished out insuffffffffficiency.

Alex: Oh, of course….

Gracie: Ok, so like no more just kidding on the playground. Just say like "I was just kidding becauzzzzz like you dumpt me at the bridge. Becauzzzzz! Hey wait up why don't I? What about my m'e'erickles. How does that fit into your phyzzzzy information iffffffffished out of MY IFFFFFFFORMATION'S WHATE'ERS BEFORE AND AFTER ALL IS SAID AND DONE.? You're just a janitor in a jungle Alex, mopping up ontoxickey's entsent's impressions, and metaphysics can get justajiffffffy's janitorial s'e'ervice into sum's'e'erious ontrouble. Why just this morning it was a second hand universe as far as your watch was concerned. Look, I have it on good ont I'm'authority……

That from every puddle I ever met that my self-evidence is just ont I'm'aste'erpieced together into sum's puzzle of e'ereally euphemyste'erious…STUFF….stuff…preposte'erated on wanted a priori posters plaste'er'd all over eternity…..with me…plaste'er'd like spaghetti on all of's whene'er walls..of course…..notnot to be alphabaptized on the same onteam…..

Alex(relenting): Well….anything's possible in a priori ontheory sets of all set ups I suppose. On the other second hand….earth cannot dig earth out of dug earth. …just as ont I'melodease just cannot savage metastones from dug up dead eggground. So I'dirt can't save I'dirt from I'd irt. I mean enthink about it, what if this of course of selfished out onto just be self-published….withat all that there's to its of course not not cartoon's just iffffffonte'erable's becomic booking….moo cow wordly published….

Gracie(primps): Ding dong! What time do you think it is Alex? I mean how many seconds was that for pregnant zeros saddled to begetty up to me….log 17

Alex (looks at his watch): Base 10…

Gracie(pursing her lips): Second hand seconds in ont I'momentum's second handy watch….on time meanwhiled onthings ont I'm'd at all. So like no more just kidding in the sand box on the playground Alex. Just ont I'm to be just be kidding to just be kidding. Onthink about it darling, your universe got caught e'erunning put put's second gear. That's all there's to it's itheory….not at all whene'er working iffffffffull onthrottle….with like…pot, pot, potpot powowe'er. How does that ifffffit into your phyzzzzy information iffffished out of MY IFFFFORMATION'S WHAT E'ER…just some puniverse, living with

302

lenses in outer space. What can be expected of zeros treated as constants smack dab in the middle of the middle of the middle of forever AFTER ALL IS SAD UNDONE. Haven't you everonthought to begutted to iffffeel onthat..(suddenly compassionate) Poor Alex, exercising un-ont stretched out m'equations in some poverty strickent'e'erocks of the middle of the middle of iffffffished out whate'er. YOUR JUNGLE'S IN JUSTAJIFFFY'S JAIL darling.

(Alex remains silent. Gracie offers Alex her hanky, dabbing his eyes where the tears would be if there were such a thing as Gracie's whate'er as ifffonteared to the cheek of such a thing as Alex).

Gracie (studying Alex for signs of ontelligence) But now that you've been silenced as far as can be heard…just like take it all back….take back everything you said about e'er's low down cheapunk spare parts e'ercraft ontoxickeyed up industry.

Alex: Gracie, before I met you I thought to be was just tales with hardly's heads attached.

Gracie (whymperacting out): But?

Alex (offering Gracie's hanky back to dab her eyes where the iffffake tears are emergent…but really) But putting the whole problem of eternity aside for a few seconds…there is a problem with my ontoxickey ontrain wreck theory of to be.

Gracie(hopeful): what's that?

Alex: EU DARLING!!!!!!!!!

Gracie (perking up): What about me darling?

Alex: Well 1. You don't at all look like sum's plot thin egggoof. 2. I can't behold egggrace as somewhat's train wreck. 3. Of all of's rattle trap snake pit pooh I've seen at this end of the end of the Mesozoic, doesn't surveyeur metameaty physics out as e'erattle trapooh.

Gracie (primps for a whate'er pool): I don't do I. So what do I look like?

Gracie poses statuesquely.

Alex: Well just like sum's a prioripithecene's….ontaxidermelodious she it…..as ifffffleshed out of skeletone's……a prioripithecus.

Gracie: I'm flattered of course, of course not not…….

Alex: A spirit face as countenanced of course not not to like…….be.

Gracie(anticipatorationary): Yes!!!!!

Alex: So, like I'dreame'erations leave eu…like…like……

Gracie: Yes?

Alex: Positioned pretty…….like dreame'ergentrifffffff I'd as like……pretty…..poof…. like proof.

Gracie: So then street wise…..my basic metameaty phyzzzzzzz just can't be…..

Alex: Curbed. Yes, no zoos, however laden with objections, have the's e'ersources to undermine 1. Eur bruty. As precision coded....those parts got you right. 2. Ont I'm'eur sum what's ontiquely presentable eternity. That part you got right. No objection can prevail against a subject that can quite so self...... symply notnot now's neighborhoods of news. That's almightning's truck loads of a priorifffffffffffffection on your party egggirl's part. As far as I'm to be concerned your basic metaphysic's acadeemed beyond eventual dispute.

Gracie: Oh Alex, all flattery put, put, put aside, not mouthing off behind, you really do, you really do, doo, doo mean it! Even like just kidding on the playground sand boxt any more...you really do..do..mean it. (blows her nose with loud abandon) Now don't you feel better! Sumtimes you just have to sit in the beble bleachers and let me do your thinking for you. Like I let Speck do my thinking for me...but not really. You need to do the same with me..but really. (Gracie calms)That's better. I can see that you've calmedown. Respect the authority of a proven m'e'erickle worker Alex. You know feeling about me the way you must if you were me feeling about me the way I would if I was allowed to....I mean with both of (baby he's) us dyployed onto one side....there's only nothing we can't do? Like, we're on the same team right....of course of course not not bebabed to be sum'showe'erd sum's how e'erainboticks...... I mean like how does that work....like being the same as mansion'd with I'difffe'erontents........(Egggaining metaphysical beconfidence Gracie picks up her broom).. Like if I get on board....I might as iffffly......like..like....fly.....right?..(Gracie straddles her broom)

Alex: Uh Gracie, your broom.

Gracie: What about my broom?

Alex(pedantically): Well. It's just some straw stuck to a stick. It actually has no aerodynamic properties whatsever.

Gracie (betrayed, straddles the broom and makes engine noises) BAROOM!!BAROOM!!

Alex (skeptically indulgent): Ok, Gracie. Make it fly. Go ahead make the broom fly. It's like being dead; you've done it before. So like you know how to do it. So like..just do it. Make the baroom fly. Liquor it up and make the baroom fly.

Gracie: Don't tempt me Alex. Sumthing you just don't get about not not to be's iffffe'ers....is like

Alex: Like what?

Gracie: Like once onthroned ifffffalling onthrough asiffffe'er Alex, egggifts of whene'er's wing'd e'ercraft's in waiting.

Alex: So waiting where?.......

Gracie: It's when Alex....whenever I show you what this broom can do.

Gracie (sweeping as she sings):

YESTERDAY'S TOMORROW YOU CAN LOCATE ME SWEEPING WITH MY BROOM

YESTERDAY'S TOMORROW YOU CAN LOCATE ME SWEEPING

AS WAND WITH DIBS TO DUB ONTOOLED

OF COURSE TO BE E'ERCRAFTED

TO TIDY UP EACH LITTLE ROOM

HEAVENTILATING WHOE'ERS

HEAVENTILATING WHOE'ER'S WHOM

YESTERDAY'S TOMORROW YOU CAN RELOCATE SWEPT UP BY MY BROOM

TO BECOME BUSTING OUT OF THIS MOTEL'S DARK ROOM

SWEEPING UP E'ER THAT'S WAITING TO HEAVENTILATE WHOEVER'S WHOM

HEAVENTILATION SYSTEMS

HEAVENTILATING WHOEVERS

HEAVENTILATABLE AS WHOM

GETS TO BE SWEPT UP BY MY BROOM.

The orchestra performs the broom ballet as Gracie shows signs of moving darkly in all blasphemable directions, sweeping dirt under the grass (astronomical turf)rug and going up and down hill pretending to like asiifffffffly with tedious repetition as justajifffffffjumpt off a tiny cliff onto sum whate'er's puddle.

The dialogue continues as Alex, who is diligently repairing Gracie's fun house mirrors to make them more like honest to goodness puddles, picks up the apple Speck had left for Gracie.

Gracie violently smashes the apple from Alex's hand.

Gracie: You owe me one…ever.

Alex: What…ever?

Gracie: Never mind. Listen Alex. The girl war's never over…not by belongings of belongings of a long shot. It's true I am the singularity. I am the one girl holocaust. My day books prove it. As long as I'm alive. Listen holocausts like enjoy begetting singled out to make the most of holocaust auditions. In many ways such Holocaust competitions are just kidding's play grounds in the sand box of the power grid. As long as I'm possible in mirrors without me in their makeup kits…..I'll be needing alibis. Just look at me for crossed out'sake. My self-evidensity doesn't have to audition to be obvious. I'm so easy to add up to nothing but…1. My phylum iffffisht ont I'dreame'erged under morsel codes mouth'd by the swamp. 2. Meanwhile…I've got the girl war aftermath equations to solve. 3. As occupation territory I'm bridolled up on all of's sporty crawler's virtual intended listings on all of's wanted paper products. 3. I've got this really big job being dead with no kidding on the playgrounds future being extinct or at least improving my impossibility standards. 4. I'm on the short list for all of's most impossible personality awards. 5. My spirit face has been xxxe'erated on all of's promotion pictures on all of's crossed outings. 6. I'm way past the deadline (points graves)on this homework science project that's my better latter than never alibi for the girl war. 7. I've yet to masterpiece together all of's puddles of what's whate'er. 8. On the metaphysical iffffffront…my escape philossity engine's all out of beble batteries. 9. Oh, I could go on and on. I'm almost out of can openers. I'm still m'applianced…..someont I'm'ange'er'd bedroom………..

Gracie rummages for pillows. Quasilly egggraving herself in eggground she sings:

SOMETIMES I FEEL LIKE UPSIDE DOWN'S RIGHT SIDE UP. (tone row)

SOMETIMES I FEEL LIKE RIGHT SIDE UP'S UPSIDE DOWN (mirror'd retrograde row)

(Petting the grave stones)

YOU SHOULD BE HERE I SHOULD BE THERE

I SHOULD BE THERE THYOU SHOULD HERE

TO BE DECIDED UPSIDOWN(CADENCE)

I SHOULD BE THERE YOU SHOULD BE HERE.

AS MAKES ME MEATY PHYZZY (suspended high Cs)

AS MAKE ME LIVING UP SIDE

TO BE DECIDED DOWN'D I'D

TO SHOULD BE THERE'S WHO SHOULD BE HERE

WHO'S TO BE HERE SHOULD JUST BE THERE(cadence)

 TO BE DECIDED UPSIDOWN

TO BE DECIDED UPSIDE DOWN.

Having made a bed for herself at the Gracie grave site Gracie recovers looking for approval from all of's other graves in the's urrounds. Gracie dumps her pillow back in the box.

Gracie: But enough of my bedroom appliances. Metameaty physickly speaking I didn't want you to get the wrong idea of me, as since, whatever's else I am but, but, but, but ont I'auditioning eternity for talents of to be on playgrounds of iffffonthine'er's whatever's else I am. That's why I dumped you at the bridge. So you wouldn't mistake me for just someone thing zoo'd onto the menu. This is the Mesozoic after all. Like what's a wholegggirlikely to do. You do realize I hope that…..that………. were it not for duh's ineumanity of humanity to eumanity(hesitates) by which I mean eumanity's iffffontocracy of course, of course not not…..sub posed(demonstrating sub position) for a prioritease……I would, I would, I would be nicer………..as a prioriteasinging iconicoine'er'd…all of's just ajifffffy juke boxes.

Gracie turns to the closed for repairs sign on the kissing coffin. As a priorioccuption territory I worked here; this was my dream job. Oh yea…like (touches her chest and lifts herhead ontentocratically) I was the dream served on all of's sidelines of the beble's bleacher seating. All of's traffic jammed me into this iffffreaklipservice portopotty. (Gracie pets the coffin)It was so egggratifffffying to countenance iffffffirst's iffffffaced ont I'mobjection the world would pay to kiss. Oh I onthought I was heaven Alex.

Alex: You mean you thought you were in that thing's heaven?

Gracie: No, I thought I WAS HEAVEN Alex. Who better to pin up on crossed outings just for kissing coffins. This was where my metaphysics met up with my meaty physics. (wistfully) You have to realize it was the middle of the middle of the middle of the Mesozoic and everybody that wasn't me had been waiting e'eround what seems like forever for the likes of such a thing as me. Lines were forming and then reforming and eventually e'ereforming e'eround the block so big it seemed I universed. Except for the girl war it would have seemed like I coolifffied as the coolest ontenthing ever. Can't you just emotion picture me dreamanticiprecipitating all of's e'eromancipated as iffffffffffff( )fffffffffffux. It was like always Saturday and all of's church bells were ringing in the ont I'mansiont potent portopotties. Here you want to try it out.

Gracie rips off the CLOSED FOR REPAIRS sign on the kissing coffin booth.

Gracie: You'll need a token darling.

Alex (finds token in his pocket): This one?

Gracie: Yes, that's token of appeasement that does it in these parts. Now I'll climb in the coffin and you appease the slot.

Gracie climbs in the kissing coffin.

Gracie: Ok so like number 1. BEHOLD THE GIRL. 2. NOW E'ERITUALLY APPEASE ME WITH A TOKEN OF YOUR ESTEEM.

Alex puts in the token. The window comes up.

Gracie: That's it! Now be decisive. Do I coolify to be the coolesthing to ever kiss or…

Alex and Gracie kiss as the music plays until the window closes. Gracie's left hand urgently passes the token back around the outside of the coffin for Alex's right hand to reuse.

The kiss resumes as the operation repeats itself again and again.

Gracie: Put the she it in the slut darling.

However, during the third kiss Gracie notices the arrival of Mobible out of the corner of her eye. His new wanted poster reads "VOTE GRACIE"

Gracie: Uh, Mobible dear, there aren't any voters in these parts. They're all at the beach today.

Mobible (downcast) backs out of gracie's cemetary with his music playing backwards.

Interrupted and embarrassed, Gracie doesn't see the new wanted poster.

Gracie(concerned): Something's wrong with Mobible. The way he's sparking he might selectrocute himself. Look Alex, while your lenses have been grazing on outer space, the swamp has been loudmouthing all of's e'ercraft. The girl war is never over until…until….the traffic jams are landing at the beach heads, looking for occupation territory. THAT'S ME. As long as I'm 1. Not impossible and 2. Coolifffff I'd as the's coolesthethical thing ever…mathematically speaking, like the set of all of's sets of this situation will not be over. There's a selectrocution rally tonight and I'm not supposed to show up.

Which means…

Alex: What?

Gracie: I better show up. Ont I'm'eternity just may be at stake. I've got this eternity project that just can't wait…like wait e'eround for the (next pregnant) zero's…..one.

Alex: So what do you need from me?

Gracie: Some new music. What time is it?

Alex: By my watch still log 17 base 10 seconds….

Gracie: Just enough time to log into a low down cheapunk spare parts…..

Alex: So just enough seconds to 1. Gas up a universe.

Gracie: Check 2. Get waves party girled at the whate'er whole to make up masterpieces in my puddles.

Alex: 3. Position such a thing as egggracie as I'd thou art at just ont I'metaphysical's meeting at the bridege.

Gracie: 4. With enough bottles of gin for me to climback up on that cross for one last phylumination all my own. So, wait up on ourselves why don't we. Like…. you meet me at the cathedral with the music. Meanwhile I better work on my cheerleader routine.

Gracie rummages in her beconvenience storage e'ercraft box.

Alex: What are you looking for darling.

Gracies: Can openers if you must know. Kitchen appliances that can open….e'er waves.

Gracie pulls out two pompoms and holds them to her chest.

Gracie: Alex, you know how Speck did my thinking for me….but not really?

Alex: Unhuh.

Gracie: Well let me do your thinking for you…but really. Alex, is this what egggreat ont I'm'adventures are like…like?

Alex: Yes darling, this is exactly what just ont I'm'egggreat m'adventures ont I'm'exactly like are like.

The orchestra enters as Gracie begins her cheerleader dance routine as she sings her pompomination e'ercraft aria. Gracie sings:

SOMETIMES I REALLY FEEL LIKE JUST

CHEERLEADING ONTO TO BE OR BUST

E'ER'D OUT TO CHURCH ITCHEERS

POMPOMINATING VOLUNTEERS

AS SUM'S WAVE DANCE ONTOES BEHAVE

CHEERLEADING TO BE SAVIORING

LIKE WHEN'ER'S WHATE'ER WAVING

HELLO'D TO BE BEHAVIORING

JUST LIKE SUMM'SAVEE'E'ER SAVING

WHEN WHATE'ER'D JUST LIKE WHATE'ER'D E'ER

PREPOSTE'ERATING IFFFONTCHEER

WAVES WHICH I VOLUNTEERED TO

POMPOM'D PERHAPSILLY IFFFFFF

OF COURSE, OF COURSE NOT NOT TO

POMPOM'D OF COURSE NOT NOT TO CARE

OF COURSE, OF COURSE NOT NOT TO

OF COURSE, OF COURSE NOT NOT TO CARE

OF COURSE OF COURSE NOT NOT TO

OF COURSE OF COURSE NOT NOT TO

OF COURSE OF COURSE NOT NOT TO CARE!!!!!!!

With this grand cadence gracie proceeds with her pompom dance routine as Alex heads back up the hill through the country club and the abandoned holocaust. Again Alex echos the cadenced sentiments that began this scene.

Alex: I WILL, I WILL, I WILL BE THE HERO. I WILL, I WILL, I WILL SAVE THE GIRL. The scene ends with Alex still trudging the country club's iffffe'erways.

SCENE IX

The entrance to the cathedral is flood lit and in an uproar as Gracie arrives with Alex to great fanfare. The ray gun rafters are ablaze on the loudmouth power grid screens. Felix is pictured with love dribbling out of his mouth. Lara, the battered reporter, just back from the serpent city of denial, is standing with a microphone to interview Gracie as she enters.

Lara: And there she is…as ontenthermodynamic as puddled metameaty physics gets!! The wholeggghostess on every body's mirrors never quite herself.

Gracie: That's me! What is it that worlds want from girls like us? I see you've been reading the chalk boards in the metaphysical society Lara.

Lara: And what is it you've been up to like e'erecently Gracie?

Gracie: Well, just like e'erecently I solved eternity Lara. Not only that but I've my eternity test sight experiment approved by this astronomer that has me starring in his emotion pictures as like coolest ont I'mansiontenthinggirled ever.

Lara: So the's guy's got you coolifffying as like..like…..

Gracie: Coolest ontenthing's Alex….please meet Lara.

Alex (finding himself sum whate'er'd shy in such eggglamourous bleacher seating withdraws his hand he's been saving to save egggracie): Nods awkwardly.

Lara: Well, what have you got for us tonight? Front man forward for facing Felix's back side as usual?

Gracie: As usual's yes, starting off withat. Staring of as self-evident euphemysterious front man for Felix….

Lara: So like burnt offerings on holocoasteroids. Isn'that what we'er talking..

Gracie: Traffic jams love it….like such a thing as me being such a thing as just not THEM. I mean I'd fall in love with me too if there was a way to do that sort of thing. My puddles are as close as I can get. Like just to touch myself is soooo amazing. Like I guess I must be my biggest fan. Like if it wasn't for the girl war I really would coolifffffffy as coolest ontenthing ever.

Lara: So like tonight you're going to be…….

Gracie: Sacrificed…..for Felix….

Lara: Sanctified….

Gracie: As god.

Lara: Oooogh!!

Gracie: Yea. Scary…..until…..until……

Man in the crowd interjects himself, treating egggracie as very much up for grabs.

Gracie: Please sir, keep your trigger fingers off of my ont I'mobviused self-evidence.

Man: But your so obvious! So like sunny side up.

Gracie: Give me that microphone Lara. Ok so like whoever you are, whatever creepy sport you just crawled out of, I'm going to feed you with this…..Now just what was it you were saying?

Man: Well, you can see I'm down and out…and you're so like wholegggrailiquored up like..like meaty phyzzzzz'd champagned……

Gracie(agreeing): Yes!

Man: Well as sunny side up to be scrambled…

Gracie: Unhuh…

Man: Since I'm a down and outer…..

Gracie (studying the man for down and outedness) Sorry Lara, but I've just got to rape me some conscience here. (turns microphone on the man) So like if my halo were occupied territory to be raped by your bottom'd outings t'e'er'd impersonation…like you wouldn't be down and outer'd anymore. You'd be like…up and in. Be honest.

Gracie ultra-violently all but forces the microphone against the man's face.

Man(taken aback): Sure thing! For crossakes!

Gracie (turning to the traffic jam) And you sir, what would you do if caught like happenstanced with such a things like me in everyday intersection's darkissed alleys.

New man(insensed): Well of course of course not……….(threated by microphone)………not. Ok so, I probably would rape your like hairdo if I thought my bottom'd outing could beget away with it.

Gracie (feeling a surge of aesthethical power): Ok, so I'm going to put this microphone on macromation's iphemiphone and bigot sum's consensus here. All of's you eggguy's down and outers, what would you do if you caught my as iffffformaldehydrated head gear in some everyday intersection's darkess'd alley?

Crowd: BE UP AND INERS RAPING IT WITH OUR BOTTOM'D OUTE'ER'D PERSONATIONS.

Gracie: Becauzzzzz like why? Who is the dream after all is said undone?

Crowd (reluctantly): You are Gracie.

Gracie (threatening even more profoundly): Now what was it you just said. I didn't hear you.

Crowd: YOU ARE GRACIE! YOU'RE THE DREAM SERVED SUNNY SIDE UP. YOU'RE THE DREAM ABOVE THE DREAM, BENEATH THE DREAM AND…..

Gracie: In my performance like tonight…

Crowd: SERVED ON THE SIDE SHOW

Gracie sighs deeply: That's better. I rest my case…..like for iphphphphyuminations all my own.

Crowd: It's a deal.

Gracie addresses little boy: Eur natured outings wouldn't rape my like hairdo would it?

Boy: No, of course not.

Gracie pats the boy on the spot where his halo would be if only he were egggracie.

Boy: Yet.

Gracie (suddenly disturbed): Lara, I must dishevel immediately.

Gracie turns to her make up kit at the base of the cross. Gracie now dishevels herself, ripping her blouse, high five oclock shadowing her face in a fun house mirror and putting on her sinisterial moustache. At this point Gracie pretends to not notice that Alex is waltzing her as he rips off her moustache and pockets it. As the waltz ends Gracie repockets the moustache.

As gracie pins herself up on the cross, a question is raised by the crowd.

Crowd: When Felix gets devoted into be god....what time is it?

Gracie (waves excitedly from her just kidding's kindergarden the cross) Oh! CALL ON ME!!!

There is an awkward but respectful silence. Gracie has to think for some seconds.

GRACIE'S LECTURE FROM THE CROSS.

Gracie: Like....becompletely presentably tensed eternity. How does one begin. Like there's clock time and there's ont I'm. For clock time.....maestro.

Gracie waves her wand for the demonstration of clock time. Once the second hand's been fully circulated, Gracie begets back to business.

Gracie: so much for clocks'...... ente'eror stories.... enticked on time

Nows e'er iffffflocks......onte'eritories.......selfished ont I'm.

There is a brief a pause as dramaticktalking permits.

Gracie: Ok so like when was I? Too late to schedule that lecture. Suffice it to say what we've got here is half time at the bigame qualuming as ontotal eternity) OTE= presentable e'er(PE) + presented tense)PT d'eracting up I'dizzinesspin'dolled up with presented tense when's where I fit in ontoday and ontoday and........so hit it maestro!!!!

Gracie sings: WHEN I AM....TO BE'S SACRIFICE.

DEDICTATED TO THE DEATH OF BEING NICE.

Gracie points to Felix on the podium: Hit it!

Felix sings: AS I AM TO BE SANCTIFIED.

SAID TO BE BETTER THAN ALL ELSAINTS WORLD WIDE.

AS I SET SAIL THROUGH HISTORY

TO REALLY ENJOY SANCTIMONETARY NOTORIETY

BY SUPERNATUR'D'S JUST BECAUSE

JOB OF SUPER SANCTIMONEY'S SUPERMONETARY SUPER SANTY CLAUS.

Not sure what he just sang, Felix looks to Gracie for approval.

Gracie waves her trigger finger'd wand to sweep Felix backward off the stage, never to be seen again in this opera. Now Gracie sings with fresh confidensity.

Gracie: AS I'M ONTO BE SANCTIFFFFFFFFF(.)FFFFFFFFFI'D

SAID TO BE THE BEST MAN OF MY TIME

SO OBVIOUSLY JUST BECAUSE

DREAME'ERGENTLY I'M JUST LIKE SANTY CLAUS.

WHO KNOWS NOW MY REDREAMER LIVES(beaconing Alex)

TO RESCUE ME FROM NOT ME FUGITIVES.

She sings again:

AS DESSERT'S OFF COURSE'S CONTRARY

I TOP OFF ALL OF'S WHIPPED CREAMEAL WITH A CHERRY.

Gracie with chorus: MASTERPIECEING PUZZLES OUT OF PUDDLES OF WET LIGHT

STRAIGHT OUT OF THE BLUE WITH BLUSHES RAINBOWING INSIGHT

WHOLEGGGRAILING GRACEXISTENCE IN NOT NEVER'S NIGHT

Grace: I AM THE LIGHT OF THE WORLD

Chours: SHE'S THE DELIGHT OF THE WORLD

Gracie: IFFFFFYLUMINESSENCED AS IFFFFIONTICALITEASE

Chorus: NONE COME TO DELIGHT EXCEPT WHEN SHE'S

Gracie(basso): IFFFIGURED GROUND WHERE DREAM E'ER LIVES

As the light show routine develops Gracie eventually does return to sing soprano.

Gracie: KNOW HOW NOW MY DREAM URGE ONTHRIVES

Chorus: DREAME'ERCHANDIZING SHE IT AFTERLIVES.

Gracie: THROUGH SIMULATIONS OF WHAT SEEMS

Chorus: TO MAKE UP KITS ON THE BIGAME'S ONTEAMS.

As the light show develops, lightning strikes becoming out of Gracie's hairdo e'ereach for unprecedented preposte'erological proprortions. Breaking though the stained glass windows into the outer universe, it becomes an initially as iffffffloored show, that threatens to brutiffffly overwhelm e'erunner up reality, transforming the world overwhelming the cathedral with clearly cartoonish implications.

The scene concludes with Gracie making her extravagantly existential exit, parting the traffic jams like Moses parting the sea. But before the bells chime at last, Gracie turns to wave one vast kiss to all of's the cathedral's all of'd inhabitants, each putting his hand on his cheek to receive egggracexcession's of course, of course, not not code's kiss.

Alex and Mobible sneak out of the cathedral behind her as the scene ends belllessly.

SCENE X

The tonality shifted up a tritone as some news paper floats by in the breeze. The headline says POPE GRACIE. We find Pope Gracie surveying the formerly abandoned graveyard across the country club from Gracie's old motel film setting's cemetary. Alex, Mobible and the general accompany her.

313

Gracie: winning the Miss Eternity Pageant was pregnant zero's one thing..but….popping up as pope is quite sumothe'er's thing!

Mobible: Well, on the's'e'er face of it it seems the menu's back log's back logged ont I'mouthed egggrace.

Gracie: Thanks Mobible, but I have my puddles to tell me that.

General: Your excellency…

Gracie: Please, refer to me as sir, general.

General (tight lipped): Yes sir.

Gracie: So! Like I won I guess. The trouble is nobody admits they voted for me.

Mobible: Yes, but nobody admits they didn't vote for you either Gracie. That's a good sign.

Alex: Yes that must be it. It's like…like….like magic.

Mobile (chiming in): Like there's magic tricks and then there's miracles. This ont I'magick trick was no mere miracle.

Gracie (seizing the argument): Yea! Just….just…just……like…like.like….. sum whate'er puddle's ont I'mirror callegggraphitti………

Mobible: Splattered to the whene'er's wall…

Gracie: E'eright.

General: The only way I can see to up raise it sir.

Mobible: Sure thing Gracie.

Alex (looking upward)….: Heaventilated…..like on purpose iffff I know stars.

General: Ont I'm'explosiffffff equations.

Mobible: Almightningstrucked in…..

Gracie: Even without wings! Let's doo the math.

Mobible: Uh, but not to over do the trick. Its assortment's big ont I'make up lot that makes people superstitious.

Gracie: You mean I made the traffic jams scared to not vote for me?

General(dumbfounded): That must be it, your excellency.

Gracie: Thanks but please, just call me sir.

Gracie reaches in her pocket for her old moustache which she almost puts back on her lip. But looking around, she just puts in her chest pocket higher up.

Alex: I wish, I wish, I wish I could have voted for you darling but…

Gracie: But what?

Alex: I was just too way too quantfied to qualify.

Gracie: It's ok, darling. I voted for myself for you. It just goes to show what happens when you finally vote for other people to be devoted to yourself. I did have my usual conscience one second and then, all of a sudden, I just didn't have it anymore, just not enough not to vote for myself. It only lasted a few seconds but….like all at once blaspheming in all blasphemable dimensions, devotion to my egggracesst behalf behaviored like smack dab in the middle of the middle of the middle of the thing to do. The way I ifffigure it……traffic jams of selfished outings of all of's other ifffffished out egggracessessments had the same idea like inside out of bounds to be summe'erily as iffffffffffforgotten. So superstition does work wonders after all.(Gracie's attention turns to vast uncharted cemetery before her) All right general, just how far does this abandoned holocaust stretch out?

General: Well sir, my ides of e'er survey shows it stretching out forever.

Gracie: And what's in the bunker?

General: Just day books sir, from what appears to be typical teenage girls in outer space…… apparentlied party girls caught smack dab in the middle of the middle of the middle of World War Whenever….sir.

Gracie(cavalierly): Let me see one of those books. I used to write this stuff. (Suddenly cringing, gives it to the general) What does it like…like….like….I'm a one girl cow herd when it comes to this sort of thing.

General (Takes the book and reads): "Uh…like…the bombs are dropping like rain…like…like….all I can hear is…..like…bombs whistling at me. It feels like this guy is like falling in love onto me."

Gracie: Yes, go on.

General: That's all there is sir. The rest is just burnt bloodirt….typical hiroshimatrix holocaust entry….flames without warmth.

Gracie (sighs heavily): All right, if that's the way just kidding wants to play its ont I'm'alphabettingods (shakes the middle of the middle of the middle of her trigger finger at the sky)

Gracie(decisively): General, this bunker is going to be whole eggground zero's control booth for my ontalented(no duh'd) eternity test site experiment. As poped out of course's ont I'menu I'm hooking this place up to becomrephensiffffffffffffffffffly presentable heaventilation systems. I want this bunker set up as a priori's becompletely preposte'erological becommand post for that project's once and for all of's all.

General: Yes sir, is there anything else?

Gracie (in ontocratic stride) Annex this bunker to whate'er'd of coursing's

cathydraulicareserves pavilion. That annex must be equipped with a brand new'sy new power grid according to my ontique'erian speciffffffffffffffffff(.)ffffffffffffffffffications, e'eregggun rafters, the works. If you need light bulbs there's the movie set up across the country club. Ont I'milite'erily speaking…….. I count on you general…….to get that done.

Genera; Yes sir! Will do sir. Is there anything else?

Gracie: No. you're still here I take it.

The general exits.

Alex(catering): I brought the bottle dear. (Alex wipes the pixie dust from the bottle)

Gracie(trigger finering the pixie dust as she wipes the bottle in turn) Alex, what are the things you wipe whenever you wipe off bottles?

Alex: Pixie dust. Every backup universe has it.

Gracie(Messaging the pixie dust between her trigger finger and action packaged middle finger): Oh Alex….

Alex: Yes dear.

Gracie: I'm thirsty breathing all of's thou artale'er'dust. Is this pixie dust like a tool on vocation or like a toy on vacation?

Alex: It can work both ways.

Gracie: I need sum's some. I need a vocation on vacation.

Alex: A(lchemi)cademically you mean a sabbatical?

Gracie: Well sum almightning'strucked in could be carnival…..the same olde'erides, but in the wholegggrailuxury becompartments where I can jump off wholegggrailocomotives, but really and e'ereally still be stinct.

Alex: I'll make the e'erangements.

Gracie: Oh and Alex, while your….eur…..at it…..could pick up sum ont I'mother's iffffonthings for me. (gracie prepares a m'eternity shopping list)

1. Those wings I never got to match my…my…..headgear.
2. Poped out of stars now as I am……Oh Alex…I just can't help but hope for a butter universe to like be a better universe. What I mean to say is…well as winner of the Miss Eternity Pageant over runner up reality….plus now poped out from all I've left behind…….(Gracie goes into character as winner of the Miss Eternity Pageant)……I'd like sum's new ontestimention of sum's newsy new I'm'iuniverse where e'er can ope'erate ifffffficiently, like on a scheduled of ont I'm'appointments….like without walking the whate'er off dictatorshiplanks…yes that's it! To give(eternity's) ifffe'ercraft onthat e'ereal smooth ifffe'eride! Oh Alex! Iffffffever'd my I'druthers….why I'd can open eternity just ont I'm for all of's could be can open'de'er….with onthat's all there's to it! And Alex…while eur at it…..
3. Can you please purchase whatever poetryouts I can quote spelled backwards ove'erunner up e'erealty. (Gracie's mouth seems to be chewing on some words)

Gracie (blurting out sum's words):

"To fetch to be iffffffff(.)fffffffetchingly

As iffffe'ercraft to becommends

Iffffffully….{{{*FUN}}}….…..eternity

With all of's happy afte'er'd ends…..."

Not to ontente'erupt you Alex but……is my day book getting all this down?

Alex, clapping two hands before now…. e'eresoundly's clapping with one hand while yet still writing with the other.

Alex: In the new appendix darling.

Gracie (ecstatic): So I am, I am, I am stll writing this stuff. Where's my bottle?

Alex gives Gracie her bottle of gin.

Alex: Anything else?

Gracie: Thanks my dear dump'darling but…..

Alex: But what?

Gracie (studying Alex for signs of not having left the scene): Well…from what I can see you are still here.

Alex exits.

Alex exits his scenery's existence to leave Gracie almost all alone with not not being herself. Only Mobible intervenes.

Gracie: Well Mobible, as far as I can tell, you're still here. What can you do for me?

Mobible: I've already done for you what I can do for you darling.

Gracie: What do you mean Mobible…..dear.

Mobible: Well just look at one of your honest to goodness puddles. What does it say?

Gracie: Oh! My impossibility as pope.

Mobible: Which kitchen appliance do you know that can open selectrocution's power grid of canned as iffffformation…whoegggrailoaded to be information.

Gracie: So like controlling the iffffffflow of flow'down selectrons in the selectrocution…..

Mobible: Procession from the topinup's ontotem pole to the bottom of to be poped out.

Gracie (wising up): So of all of course's kitchen appliances you were like selectexutive to…..even though it was impossible for me to win…..I..like..won anyway.

Mobible: Unhuh. I'm just ont I'm'd to tell you darling. From primitive tool use in the kitchen clocked to ontool user ont I'm, I've been stalking your improvements in eternity on the chalk boards of the metaphysical society and……

Gracie(exuberant): OH! Mobible! You've behaved, you've behaved! You've behaved to not not nail my metaphysics. Wouldn't I know it would take a kitchen appliance…like a can opener to iffffffffinally beget to the bottom of to be!

Mobible: Not only that, but to get to the middle of my trigger finger to thumb drive pope selectrocutions.

Gracie: So actually, I'm just kidding on the playgrounds of sand boxed in to be pope after all!

Mobible: No, no kidding. It's fake selectrocution results of my new metastasized trigger finge'er can opener onthat also can open e'er on the's ides of e'er.

Mobible exposes his new middle trigger finger appliance that metaphysically speaking onthinks to open e'er

Gracie: So that's how I did it. Cool! I've got one too.

Searching for Mobible's switches….Gracie draws out her new trigger finger and wiggles it egggracessentially in Mobible's eye aperture. As Mobible responds, the middle of the middle of the middle of a trigger finger miniature holocaust ensues. Alarms skirmish violently as Gracie cackles like Speck for the first time ever. Iffffinally Gracie and Mobible both withhold relaxation of their respective ontentriggers.

THE WAR(and ont I'mini holocaust) OF THE MIDDLE OF THE MIDDLE OF THE MIDDLE FINGERS AT LAST IS OVER.

Gracie {breathing heavily): So how did you do it?

Mobible: Well selectrons live in a sort of free for all quantum jungle unless some one's pregnant zero puts the screws to them.

Gracie: What did you do?

Mobible: I put the screws to them

Gracie: Oh Mobible you didn't.

Mobible.Yes, I did it for you…

Gracie: Oh Mobible you did!

Mobible: Yes,like…like… inspired by your metaphysics on the chalk boards at the metaphysical society…..

Gracie: Oh Mobible I just knew my metaphysics would be practical sumday.

Mobible: That's right Gracie. Ontool using the selectrocution process I made sure that soone'er's late'er tomorrow or tomorrow or tomorrow you'd be poped out like…today or today or today…..

Gracie: Ok, so like what's in this for me?

Mobible: Well, at last I can open up to you….to you being so like euman. I think I'm falling in love with a phylum all her own.

Gracie: Oh that's nice. Who's the lucky girl?

Mobible: It was that day that I started to see with my own eyes….instead of the…

Gracie: Of your tool user.

Mobible: I had just read some texts from the chalkboards of the metaphysical society and there….eu….were…pinned up on that of coursed outing's bebulletin board. It was then that I realized that the only reason I ever wanted to be a person was….like……becauzzzzz like YOU WERE A PERSON….at least until eumanized as eggglaye'er'd through escape hatches to be like…

Gracie: You must know, being euman was all I ever was as iffffreaked out.

Mobible: I could see all of's eggrace egggrid's iphotographs were negatives.

Gracie: Ever since the girl war all I could coolify for was negatives. So?

Mobible: I DEVELOPED THE NEGATIVES. It's like when you develop nested n-word negatives you start to figure out just what's eggground. And nothing's wet light obvious like….like…..in emotion pictures….in paper products….on ray gun rafters….on y-not axistense's I'd thou artesian coordinate systems…….blushed out of the blue between the toilet and the sky like…like…….EU DARLING!!!!!!!

Gracie: I'm flattered of course, you feeling this way with me, poped out, not having to impersonate people anymore. Like thinking back with conscience or without, I always sumhow knew I was heaventilated way too euman to be human. Like me being not so much antimatter as ontimatter…. that's what the girl wars was all about, I guess, me not being not euman, or else like me being not not euman…like me not impersonating people anymore…getting that phylum all my own..me building up my ont I'muscle, which only builds up when it hurts. So like being coolifff I'd's prey eumanimation in all of's cartooned comic books…..like sneaking through out lite'er'd e'er with no one noticing how noticeable I always am walked into rooms..like plastered to the ceiling of sum's iffffirmamental becomsistensed ont I'm'system's chapel, I can tell you. I must say, it really takes the conscience out of m'eu….except just kidding on the play ground.

Mobible: Just like me, but backwards. One second I didn't have a conscience and then the next second I did have one. Like, looking at you, I'm having second thoughts right now. But I'm letting second thoughts go by. (.) Yep. Gone.

Gracie: What are you trying to say Mobible?

Mobible: With recent improvements in my conscience….

Gracie: Yes…

Mobible: Like…like….oh no

Gracie: Oh no, what?

Mobible: As iffffffeelings….of course…of course…not…not…for sum's thing it seems like forever I'm a wanted man on posters of myself to say. This is so hard …but I will, I will, I will say it anyway. Darling!

319

My phylum's all alone…with the middle of the middle of the middle of my trigger finger acting up lately and..

Gracie: Yes,   I   noticed…I'metiphored   mined   too…...like…scary….so   like alarms…skirmishes….like…let's relax relaxing on the trigger fingers…what do you say?

Mobible: I'm with you. If there's anything my phylum can do for your phylum..well please just be my guest.

Gracie: Where? In the bunker?

Mobible (Waxing philosophical): You know there was a time when I did want to be champagned just somother's whate'eristocratic home owner in some nice egggated becommunity's heaventilated housing project….like to behavior it for show even if I never egggraduated out of iffffacilitease I never used myself. Like hob nobbing not nothing's egggodog bark's neighborhood. I mean I was trying to be a person just when you were trying so hard not to be a person. I could see that being less than euman just wasn't working for you.

Gracie: Like you being like your phylum all your own can you really understand, this being some high end beach resort in outer space and all with singularities of holocausts like everywhere there's one egggirl…..dreame'ergently ont I'm'ore dug up holocaust prone…….pretty dead waypast the speed of enlightenment to ever catch up…….

Mobible: To put catch upon iffffffished out eu egggracie.

Gracie (stops in her tracks): Oh yea, I figured that's where all of's this was heading.

Mobible: My only question is can you love my impersonation of a person…..back.

Gracie(thinking): Well like darling it usually takes an actual person to be a person. But I q-wise you coolifffffy.

Mobible: Oh thank you for that vote of beconfidence darling. So you can, you can, you can open up to love me for myself, like…like…I Qualifffffl'd to be myself. Say it and I will believe it.

Gracie (demonstrably hesitating): Uh.

Mobible: With such a thing as me loving such a thing as eu, all I ask is that you love me as iffforwards. Or, wait up on myself why don't I. You can of course of course not not also love me backwards if you like…like..or maybe love me inside out if that works better. I'm completely upside down about how you might like to love me….upside down….right side up….inside out…that's all I ask. Like backwards or forwards, iphoteggraphed to be developed or else not…..either way should beget the job done.

Gracie: So how will you know that I love you?

Mobible: If you say it…as notnot coded…. I will know it.

Gracie: Ok so..like….like……..I love you. How is that?

Mobible: Pretty good. But maybe you can say again with more….more….(sighs)…

Gracie: Oh, like with more iffffffeeeeeeeling. OK, so errrrrrready? Ok so like I lovvvvvvvyou Mmmmmoooooooooooobible.

Mobible: One more time.

Gracie: Like… I love you already.

Mobible: One more time pleaszzzzzz

Gracie: Look darling, it's like I'm pope now. We did get that settled right…like sedimented. So, operating as like egggod looking down from my singularity…I like can't be saying that sort of thing too often.

Mobible: Ok, so not too often one more time. Oh! And one more thing. I have somwhate'er'd own's business proposition for you darling. As pope you're all of's a sudden smack dab in the middle of the middle of the middle of supposition to beget sum s'e'erious cash flow out of your metaphysics.

Gracie: How's that?

Mobible: Dreamerchandizing such a thing as egggracie's wholegggrail! What else! Let me diagram the situation for you. (Mobible diagrams) Ok, it aboriginates with your theory that eternity's not just a bunch of noone's infinities, but instead's sum's once upon I'm caught mide'er auditionng as iffffffinities, in e'erather ontique(if I may say so)beble bleacher seatings. So, like the wholegggrail of the thing spills whate'er into e'er onthanks to notnotitudes being so d'iffe'erontiquely I calculuste'er'd that….newsy now nextitudinate to presentable eternities. Universicademickly this spills the tensor calculus in meaty physics over to the ontense'er calculust's ont I'metaphysics.

Gracie: In an of course, of course not not'shell …that's about it.

Mobible: OK, so as cartooned to be ope'erational….. that draws out egggrafittied like this:

ETERNITY'S IFFFFFFORMATION….UNIVERSE'S INFORMATION…..COULD BE CASH KEY VALUATION. So here's how we get the could be cash flow out of this. The cash flow idea came to when my compassion caught you in the kissing coffin that day. Well I screen lots of peoplist promotion pictures like 1. Of people 2. By people 3. For people.. to evaluate how to be people impersonating pictures. Most popular of all, for what seemed like forever, was having heros saving such a thing as egggracies from fates way, way worse than the D day word. One of the key tools used was 'love's first kiss'. Nowadays heros get dumped for that. Ok, so like my idea is, instead of dumping heros for saving gracies, we give the situation's bleacher seating a twist. We make the pregnant zero's heros just buy tickets. We make a religion out of it, a gift shopped religion egggift wrapped exclusively with 1. An action figure. 2. An attraction figure 3. A kissing coffin set. The best things about this product is it's just like a religion; it's metaphysics for cash flow. And just like a religion it just pretends to be metaphysics; it's e'ereally meaty physics like just kidding on the playground's sand boxed in to be. As far as e'er egos, nothing ever really happens. Nobody gets to kiss anybody. It's all done with toy action figures, board games, t-shirts, baseball caps. It's a gift shoppe religion with a corker.

Gracie: It's spelled backwards and forwards all at once right?

Mobible: Ont m'ore dug out even better than that. We'll remove all of's ont I'metaphysics from the chalk boards of the metaphysical society and put it in a book. We'll call it..

Gracie: The dictatorshipmentary right?

Mobible: No, the BEBLE BOOK OF……..OF….BECOMPLETELY PRESENTABLE

Gracie: E'ERCRAFT SCRAMBLES?

Mobible: No. GRACIE'S ALIBIBLE. We'll sneak in all sorts of alibis out back for the girl wars up front. We'll advertise it for iffffffffffinitude's everything that's anything worth scrambling sunny side up…..

Gracie: As e'ercraft?

Mobible: Oh….ok

Gracie: So..it does…it does coolify to be just kidding while as iffffffflying ontoy e'ercraft outside of moving beickle windows.

Mobible: The packaging will be completely ontique, so no universes need apply except as samples….bleacher seated…..coming down aside's chimney, while such a thing as egggracie's becoming down the ont I'main attractions chosen person's chimney just like Santa, dreamerchallontly dreame'erchandized in becompletely presentable tense.

Gracie: So..so of coarsely cool to coolify way past enlightenment's be keeping up with it. So this might even coolifffffffffffffy as like, like the coolest ever's ontoyletrained eternity's ontalentest.

Mobible: Who knows, we might just squeeze metazooicareak'd out of it.

Gracie: I'm sold! But won't philosophers (not such a thing as me) think I'm selling out my metaphysics?

Mobible: You ARE selling out your metaphysics. But it's only a second hand sell out, since it's still 1. Promote'er'd well within a universe. 2. Taken from the chalk boards of the metaphysical society where it's been e'ereally secret sum's best seller all along. Now that I think of it, this business has been on the short list of becompletely presentable ontente'erprise for quite sum's time. With you as pope, we'll put it on the's e'eray egggun e'erafters, to becompletely coolifffffffffffied as all there is to know. As your business partner in a phylum all my own, this will coolify for becomfort for anybody's everybody except…

Gracie: Except what?

Mobible: Except for such a thing as…as(sighs) such a thing as wholegggrail's egggrace.

Gracie: So with this new beble booking's e'er self-published, we're finally egggoing to egggget eternity iffffigured off egggground! Like with or without entool user's universe we're going to kick all of's buts bad mouthing presentable ifffffe'ers.

Mobible: Plus!!!! Meanwhile make a dime doing it.

Gracie: And soone'er or late'eright ontarget….some poor dumouthing off's universe will have nothing to say about it. Sooner or later my dreame'ergence will become ontheory set up for iffffffffe'er's m'at large.

Mobible: You said it..not me….but in the mean time…

Gracie: We'll just iffffffffffffffff(.)fffffffffffffffake it right?

Mobible: E'eright ontarget….onthumbs up on the ontrigge'er's middle of the middle of the middle of to be's iffffffinger.

Gracie: But…

Mobible: But what?

Gracie: Now that any at all's universe has been s'e'erimoniously dumped, I just feel compassion for all this low down, cheapunk spare parts entooled used'e'er's universe like had to go through…like log 17

Mobible: Base 10 seconds.

Gracie: Like it took to get me smack dab in the middle of the middle of the middle of the Miss Eternity Pageant…where I ifffffirst person'se'e'er prize over runner up reality….when I say…like…(gracie goes into character as winner of the Miss Eternity Pageant) "As iffffffinnepedolled up as iffffffished out of whene'er's whate'er as e'erodentiffff I'd like egggorillithm'd……IT'S LIKE MY AS IFFFFFONDEST WISH TO MAKE ETERNITY A BETTER PLACE FOR EVERYBODY'S ANYBODY…ADDING TO BE OBIOUS WAY PAST INFINITY ALL OF'S WAY DANCED UP TO LIKE…LIKE……IFFFFFF(.)FFFFINITY" (gracie suddenly freezes into a statue of the most sheroic assortment) Wait! That IS what I am trying to do! I mean, apart from bagging girl war alibis, that is why I'm all poped out after all. So as long as I sort of…like..love…you Mobible…I can still stay pope e'eright?

Mobible: Sure thing Egggracie. E'eright eu are. And we will, we will, we will get you those wings you wanted for your birthday. We will get you that phylum all your own(winks)…PLUS….if nothing else, business wise, this quasi-quali-coolifies to..

Gracie: Congradulate me out of kindergarden?

Mobible: Mhm. And beget egggracie trademarketed to cartoon of course, of course not not as iffffreaked out ontrade's of wholegggrailinguishing's iffffonthat.

Gracie: That's all! So cool! I think the bunker's empty. After you.

Mobible (still guarding his switches): No darling, just after you.

There is a traffic jam at the bunker door as Gracie and Mobible both attempt to be the last to enter.

END OF SCENE X

SCENE XI- VACATION

Gracie sub poses to be scened gazing both superciliously and e'erestocratickly over the top of her dark glasses. She adjusts them to the on position as she steps on the gangway boarding a luxury liner that is really just a façade for the old carnival from scene II. Alex joins Gracie and the couple step off the port side of the ship façade onto the carnival whate'erway's comic booked ground of being. The music is more metazoic as they go on the same old rides. But now an e'er of ontransascendency markets their every move. As pope, gracie is no longer waitressing e'ereste'eronts but is being presentably s'e'erviced by eternity at every turn in the quasi-metazoickt music's ont I'm'apotheosynthetic ontentonations. For all intentiont purposes it appears as iffffffffffff(.)ffffffffffff Gracie's position on the y-not axis of the could be coordinate system is appointment placed precisely on the church of chosen personation's schedule. As such eternity appears to becompletely under of course, of course not not's control…..like….like…as way, way more than just a mathematical construct of non-finite temporality. Even from the bleacher seating of the set of all selfished out sets, the put put put put power of the preposte'erological situation wholegggrailiqoured up Egggracie's of course, of course not not to be ontoxicated to say the wholegggraileast. And boy is Gracie e'eready to develop the photographitti negatives splattered like spaghetti on the walls from the girl war.

Skipping the holocoasteride Gracie goes straight for the ont I'm'exotic justajiffffffffy joy rides. Ontente'ertained by the housing ride, she hops on the the beble bleache'er seating of the great unknown's not never's night rides. A propos her extensive plans for eternity's past, present and future, smack dab e'eright onthrough the universe, bouncing beblinked from the e'erecte'ersettinground'iffffffe'eronticalinebriation'd ont I'mote'er hominsomnibus e'erides…waved party girled onto the chosen person's prowl at promised landing's to begetting back onto the Ferris Wheel.

It is ontop of the Ferris Wheel that the set of all of's setting's as iffffe'ers break loose. Scratching her headgear gracie just could not not not let out a big one's pregnant zero's iffffffffffffff(.)fffffffffffffffe'erainbow of all of's e'erainbowsweated light. Never did an umbrella rain down more wet light. Wholegggrailoading all of's overloaded sky as dark blush cloud overcomes the scene with Gracie cringed like hardly ever cringed before. Alex takes Gracie up to the terrace for a drink. Realizing the s'e'erious implications of what she has done, Gracie is bent over cringed and almost upside down. As the justajiffffy janitorial staff mops up the rainbowl'd overflow spill zone, Alex, sits with Gracie, ready at any moment to hold onto her hand, but still with no results.

Gracie (cringed while studying herselfished out of a puddle): Just look at myself why don't I. I'm all cringed out Alex. Like does it show?

Alex (withdrawing his prospective hold on Gracie's hand): Here take my hanky.

Gracie: So Alex, how's my cringe?

Alex {studying egggracie for signs of classical mannerisms kept in hiding well beneath her cringe): THE GIRL WAR Gracie, just behold how just ajifffy's janitors had to ont I'mop up your….eur…..asiffffe'erainbow's like laide'er……big one's….e'eroar's…like..like….e'er. do you have to be ontentested? The just ajifffy janitors are MOPPING UP EUERE'ERAINBOWS! THE GIRL WAR GRACIE! It's still on your behind that's not behind you. But…

Gracie(perks)But what?

Alex(softening his gaze): But it is not just ajiffffffy junkit's joke. The just ajifffy janitor s'e'ervice e'eright now is backing down from eur emotion picture scenery whereever rainbows puddle whate'er's waste, wherever alphabets are littered.

Gracie: Yes….

Alex:But…

Gracie: But what?

Alex(Alex ont I'melts before egggracie's could be charasmatense now presented): Oh egggracie darling…..even whate'er iffffall cringed…you…eu…..still entwinkle whate'er's ifffffffontinkles.

Gracie's gin is served in a glass. Encouraged, Gracie preens a little in iffffe'ereflections in the gin, swilling it for a few seconds but then catching her quasi-quali-coolifffffied perennial poise….. to just sip it.

Gracie(recovered): Just look at me Alex! I seem so elegant!

Gracie holds up the glass to emphasize her point.

Gracie: Entgin ontonic as iffffffff she it chansont(pardon my French) champagne….. that's all I'll ever drink from now on….are you getting this?

Alex (writing in gracie's day book): Yes dear.

Gracie: Write it down. But never forget. You wrote it…not me…but I said it…not you. Sumtimes egggirls just like to sit onterraces Alex, ont I'melodiously, ont I'meloquaintly sipping gin champagne with just ont I'm'admirerers on whene'er's watch ontowers but still as ifffffffrom underneath.

Alex smiles congenially with profound admiration for egggracie's success with the glass.

Gracie (fully recovered and business like): Alex(Gracie gazes e'eround with onte'eristocraticare in all directions) I just have to talk to you about my eternity test site experiment. I mean you are a scientist before after all is said and done and some of the sum of this involves a universe, like objects subject to my subjections, and I need to discuss some of ontentegral sum's I'diffffffffe'erontentical details with you.

Alex: Yes darling. I'm listening.

Gracie: Well. Ont I'mathematicklishly speaking, since we're working with the fourth powers of I, I'm thinking it might god to get I as squared and cubed out of the way.

Alex: Makesense. So you want to use the universe right?

Gracie (wincing metaphysical embarrassment): Nyea…it gets confusing….like tensored or ontense'er'd, ontooled with e'er or entooled with sticks and stones. I mean like universes get self-published all the time but eternities like hardly never beget s'e'eriously self-published. And like bad mouthing a low down cheapunk universe is one thing, but bad mouthing a low down cheapunk eternity is turning onto be is quite sum'other.

Alex: So you're planning this religious experience…

Gracie: Mno, more like scheduling this like….. e'ereligious expe'eriment.

Alex: So ontense'er calculus-wise you want to smooth out the bumps in the Planck limits.

Gracie: So to maybe smooth over the limit with some sticky stones operating at log minus 35 base 10 met....e'er....ontalimits...ont I'moved way past log minus 44 base 10 self-sequenced limits.

Alex: So pixie dusting sticks and stones. So your pregnant zero'd in on oned'e'ering iffffff

Gracie: You could get me some. Yep.

Alex: Well ontechnically speaking this might cost becomputer powe'er'driven as iffffff aster than the speed of light can ever catch up.

Gracie: Umhum.

Alex: Otherwise...

Gracie: Well otherwise I may have to leave the universe out of this project all together

Alex: So like suspending ifffe'er becompletely without any objects at all for subjects to like...lean on.

Gracie: Iffffff that's what it comes to. We'll just have to restrict this project to be subject to subjections.

Alex: All right. I'm sure pixie dust can be extracted from some playground sandbox at the high end resort beacheads. What else do you need from me?

Gracie studies Alex for being such a thing as can be needed to save the situation.

Meanwhile Alex is studying Gracie for signs of needing someone's else, as ifffffreaked out forever, to not quite be herself.

Alex: I am, I am, I am gracie.....someone's else...ont I'mannext I'door'd to put sum wind into eur windows.

Gracie realizes at last that Alex is someone's else and therefore doesn't have to be ashamed.

Gracie (smiles faintly): the girl war shame isn't yours or even eurs.

Alex: Yes, I'm about to let you have it darling.

Gracie: So my séance experiment is only for myself. Need I remind you I'm not in this for e'erandominiums..nor am I in this for some stars.

Alex: So I take it this expe'eriment has no need for a universe, neither simpliffffffied nor sampliffffied.

Gracie: All right then. Universe or no universe, we'll do it anyway. Whatever happens at the eternity test site, I can include eternity in my personal belongings after all.

Alex: So pixie dust or no pixie dust, what's your plan for the eternity test site?

Gracie (back on track): So Santy Claus. Xmas day, don't you get it. It seems like forever I've been watching xmas eves go by but..

Alex: But what?

Gracie: BUT NO SANTY CLAUS!!!!Don't you get it. I've parking lotteries of miracles in my time but they always end up at midnight in the middle of not never's night life….on xmas eve. So! I've decided. My not not newsy next miracle's LIKE XMAS DAY!

Alex: So your plan, pixie dust or no pixie dust, is to egggo for broken at the eternity test situation.

Gracie: Sure why not. I'll improvise ontechnical problems along the way.

Alex: So?

Gracie: So I'm putting eternity m'appointment scheduled once and for all of's……becoming down the chimney.

Alex: So Santa..

Gracie: Clauzzzzzzzzzzz(.)zzzzzzzzzzz. So what do you think?

Alex: So your plan is to bring the presents tensed on xmas day. So what assortment of presents are we ontalking about ontensing here?

Gracie: Well bebles for starters

Alex: Bebles?

Gracie: All of's the wanted posters wanted dead or alive.

Alex: So…

Gracie: Forget about the live ones

Alex: So..

Gracie: THE DEAD

Alex: So how many?

Gracie: All of em.

Alex: So like, universe or no no universe, you think you can pull this off.

Gracie: Sure! Why not. Like, iffff I were a freak accident I wouldn't do it. And since 1. I am a freak….but 2. I am no accident…..

Alex: But Gracie this isn't just picking up pebbles on the beach

The waitress arrives with the bill for the drinks.

Waitress: Your check mam. We're like closing soon and you're like still here.

Gracie (catastrophickly insensed): Look, it's SIR to you…and if you must know…I don't pay. Like..like…..I'm pope for baby he's us sake.

Alex nods to confirm that Gracie indeed is pope. The waitress scowls and leaves.

Gracie: Did you hear that? Where's my whiskers? That nasty bitch just called me mam. Does it really show? (covering herself) Where's my puddle? (In vague desperation preens her reflection in her glass of gin)

Alex (Aesthethically scandalized, hiding his right hand in his pocket): Gracie how could you? To behave this way when you're scheduling appointments with as iffforever's as ifffffe'ers.

Gracie(cringing): Yes, I know, at a test site of my own choosing.

Alex: Some times I wonder gracie. The way you just like improvise of course, of course not not......to be. Not to take the undertaker's side but…

Gracie: But what?

Alex: Well whene'erized or not whene'rized, look at the world Gracie. Not put..put… putting aside all of's betweens between the toilet and the sky. On the one hand there's gas clouds, On the other hand there is this waving party girl that's eu. But then beneath the toilet and the sky there's rocks, rocks that keep lousy records of it all.

Gracie (batting her eye lashes as iffflinched)): Yes, rocks darling.

Alex: Well that's what you're going to be getting into here.

Gracie: What about the rocks darling?

Alex: Well I've been haunted by the eternity test sight's abandoned holocaust. There might be fossil fuel cells from some of those fossil fuel rigs there. What are your plans for the fossil fuel cells?

Gracie (shrugs confidently): So we'll have to handle some fossil fuel selves. That's all there is to that.

Alex: Yes, but Gracie, there's rocks under there, like motel rocks, with like e'eresidents of iffffffossil records

Gracie (thinking hard for a split second): Sure, I can beat all iffffossil records with my metaphysics if I decide I can…like…

Alex: But Gracie there's like magma masses underneath those rocks just like…

Gracie: Like what?

Alex: Like infernal informations Gracie.

Gracie (breathing darkly): All right Alex I think you've scheduled your appointment with the problem. So(breathing deeply) I WILL! I WILL! I WILL GO TO HELL and drag whoever's in there out, if that's what it takes to schedule everybody who's anybody's appointments with m'eternity just ont I'm'd.

Alex: Listen Gracie, just kidding on the play ground or not, as half a god I know that, in this eternity, the gods have to take their chances like the rest of us.

Gracie: The way I iffffigure it it all boils down to me winning the Miss Eternty Pageant over runner up reality where I say (Gracie goes into Miss Eternity character, pinching to blush her cheeks) "LIKE IFFFREAKED OUT AS I JUST AM, IT IS MY AS IFFFFFONTEST WISH TO MAKE ETERNITY A

BETTER PLACE FOR EVERYBODY'S ANYBODY. LIKE I'M NOT IN THIS FOR THE UNIVERSE. I'M IN IT FOR OF COURSE, OF COURSE NOT NOT TO….TO…."

Wait up on myselfished out self why don't I…….like…like…just what am not or else not not to be in on this for?

Seeing that Gracie is dizzy, Alex intervenes.

Alex: Gracie, I need you to do something for me. I need you to be….THE HERO.

Gracie: What hero's that?

Alex: The hero that saves the girl.

Gracie(befuddled): It sounds like you want me to be the hero that saves…

Alex: The girl.

Gracie(dumfounded): But who's the girl Alex. I keep forgetting.

Alex (not kidding on the playground of to be this time): YOU ARE GRACIE…YOU'RE THE GIRL.

Ontentearing up, Alex really does need a hanky at this point.

Gracie (looking around in vertigo as a light bulb goes off and on and off and on in her head): OH YEA!!!!!!! LIKE I'M THE GIRL!!!!!!!!

Alex: But of course, of course not not. And please don't save your everybody's anybody else until you've saved the girl. Just save the girl.

Gracie: Why? Like becauzzzzzzzzzzzzzzz?

Alex: Oh yea, because like I love this chosen ont I'm personation's wholegggirladying….. And if you save her, maybe you can be in her belongings becoming along wither as a sort of chap e'erthroned in on the's ides of…..as parts of her belongings to herself I might as well like…love you too.

Gracie: So girl war or no girl war, god or no god, you might as well like love me too well?

Alex: Sure. Why not?

Gracie (suddenly overwhelmed): Say it again Alex! Especially the part about how you might as well…

Alex; Yes, becompletely sunny side up or maybe sidewise more sun down a setting's sunny day…either way…like….if not your eu then…I might as well like love just "YOU" Gracie.

Gracie: So say it again without the might as well part..

Alex: Sure, why not….like…I love you Gracie.

Gracie: So like say it again.

Alex: Gracie..

Gracie: Yes…

Alex: I'm a scientist. I'm not allowed to say that sort of thing too many times.

Gracie: Ok, so like say it again….only this time….not too many times.

Alex and Gracie depart from the terrace back into the midde of the middle of the middle of the Mesozoic, as the scenery, responding to the situation's self-evidensity engulfs the pair's departure.

END SCENE XI

SCENE XII- AT THE ETERNITY TEST SITE

The scene is now at the eternity test site's ontheoretical selfished out situation. Gracie, Alex, Mobible and the general are in the bunke'er'd becommand post preparing to ontamper with eternity. The chalk boards at the metaphysical society have been transferred to the e'eray gun e'erafter screens networking e'ercraft opte'erations for ontoday's ontoday's ontoday's on scheduled m'appointments with eternity's iffffe'ers. Atunnel connect the bunker to the new evangelical annex. The annex is heaventilatedlycathedralized to do the justajiffffffy job that any e'erespectable eternity sum's pregnant zerobilitease might ontalentonticipate. In the pavilion the ont I'm'e'ere'er'd iffffffestivitease is being celebrated in full sway dance, with ontraffic jams ontagentially onteemng at the brink of the meso-meta-horizontal boundary. Elaborate displays of Pope Gracie periphe'ernalia are lavishly self-evident in the puddlicke'er'd up champagne impersonations.

In the bunker s'e'erious ifffffffffffff(.)ffffffffffffactovation has s'e'erfaced news headlining egggrace ontouting all of's soupe'erstition's put put pot(ont)ential. Gracie, less egggirled than iffffledged phylums on her own, is at the control screen of the new selectronic chalk board, as she I'dibs on dubs onto the board with her new plast(mag)ic wand, Gracie has IFFFFFFINITY………+ 0……..plastered all over the ceiling.

Alex enters in disarray

Alex: Gracie The beblebouncer wouldn't let me into the bunker until I bought one of these plastic wands.

Gracie: What's the matter?

Alex: Well this wand is worthless. It's made of fake iphyluminium. It has no e'erodynamic properties whatsoever.

Gracie: It's Mobible's idea.

Mobible climbs out from under all of's machinery.

Mobible: It's my idea. Scaling back and forth from zero to iffffinity I had to improvise a new substance at the ground. It's called plast(mag)ic.

Alex: But the price scale.

Mobible: supply and demand Alex.

Gracie: the point is what looks like low down cheapunk plastic is actually high grade cheapunk spare part plast(mag)ic.

General: One more secret ingredient to audition with the pixie dust.

Alex: Oh I just don't know......I just don't.......

Gracie: Back up Alex. So much is at stake here.....speaking of which, general, how'r e'erectorection's setups........setting..... uh...

General: Ont I'm'assembled sir.

Gracie: But...but...but will onthey work?

General: That's up to iffffffontense'ers to decide.

Gracie (Profoundly eloquaint): WELL IT'S UP TO DOG SPELLED BACKWARDS NOW.

General: E'errrrrrroger that sir.

Gracie: Yes, iffff ever there was a good time to make appointments with eternity....well now's the time.

General: Speaking of which sir, there seems to be sum's eggglitch in pregnant zero's could be clock.

Gracie(climbing up on ifffffishedoubting's could be clock, and meanwhile diverting attention as she smights off courses clock with her plast(mag)ic wand: Hey look everybodyover there! Like anywhere not here. The ont I'm'e'erectour settings just nowbebulbed iffffontheorized!(while everyone wholegggrailooks the other way, egggracie clubs the clock with her plast(mag)ic wand, as (shaken by egggracie's care charisma) the clock ifffe'eresumes sum's count down onto pregnant zero's beblblus'd'e'er'definifffffffinitiming.

Gracie(Camouflaged offhandedly in nonchalance, to still divert attention as she climbs down from the clock): Mobible what's your appraisal of ontheoreticale'eriding'situation?(Egggracie hides her eyes beneath her trigger finger.)

Mobible: Well maybe some magic tricks don't always work on count downs from iffffffinity. HOWEVER!

Gracie: HOWEVER WHAT MOBIBLE? But we've got SUM ONTRICKS...right Mobible? Mobible?

Mobible: Yes dear.

Gracie: It's almost like I almost didn't say.......what's your ont I'mapt now's appraisal'd'ifffontheory's'situation?

Mobible(ontantrumminates s'e'eriously): Well...with all of's burnt bulb offerings on screen...... uh'v not ne'er's night life....I think we can count on eternity's of course, of course not not coope'eration at this. Assuming eternity's iffffe'ers do do heavention's home work on the Y-not axis of could be cartesiont's wholegggraph.

(Iffffffudging as iffffff.....philosophistically not himself......Mobible diverts ont I'm'attention to the new ontestaments eternity self-published just ont I'm'edition.) Look!!! The beble bible's as ifffffirst ont I'm'edition!!!

Gracie(grasping the opportunity's diversive implications): Yes, announce it Mobible!

Mobible steps in to announce: Like…BEBLINKED hot off the chalk boards of the metaphysical society……… it's egggracie's alibible onthat ont I'm'explains ETERNITY MADE SIMPLE'S all of's…all of's….all of's…………(.)………….all of's……

Gracie: ETERNITY SELF PUBLISHED! Wouldn't eu know it was Mobible, of all not peepooh'd people, who as ifffffffffinally got to be not not to be between two covers!

Mobible: Like…when it comes of course, of course not not…..like…ont I'm'eternity's iffffe'ers….like…...I'm your man! It's all here ont I'm'accademed between two…

General: I don't mean to break in but the music's been rehearsing and the counts way down from iffffinity to…….

Gracie: Yes, of course, of course not not….Mobible, as far as I can tell you're still here.

Mobible exits demurely through the tunnel to the traffic jammed pavilion.

Alex: Shall I go with you Gracie?

Gracie (suddenly torn): Oh Alex….like….like you do, you do, you do love me right?

Alex: Yes Gracie….I do, I do, I do like love you.

Gracie: Cool! I don't need you then to be getting in the way except to get in the way when..I may need you to be getting in the way. Meanwhile stay away while you work the bunker. Iffffff I'm not Miss Taken for e'erides this not never all nighte'er's going to boil down to sum's s'e'ereal IFFFFFFFFFFFFAMILY FUN. So like darling you have fun at this end while I'm having fun at the other end. It'll be like our honeymoon.

Gracie departs through the tunnel to the pavilion where we find Mobible on stage on staging crowd control. The entire pavilion is engulfed in the vast business ontente'erprise of selling eternity self-publicized. Preposte'erologically speaking, the scenery is egggifffffshopped as ifffffffontrinketed ont I'miscellaneously with wands made of plast(mag)Ic, Gracie ONT-shirts, beble baseball caps, ETERNITY MADE SIMPLE becomic books, ETERNITY FOR BEGINNER'S BIGAME boards plus egggracie doll attraction figures becomplete with wings. On the podium announced by Mobible is a life-sized Gracie statue with wings.

Mobible(iffformally presenting the new egggracie statue): Ladies and gentlemen..from dreame'erchant I'd thou art to I'd thou artifffffact, this……

Statue (statuesquely vocabulating): Living doll.

Mobible: Is the closest thing to such a thing's egggracie as you will ever meet without of course, of course not not being such a thing's egggracess'd….

Statue: Phylum all my own. (staring quasi-seductively) Yes, all you huntergatheletes….onticketed outhere…..let's like keep in touch.

Gracie(disturbed) e'erises to the stage, staring the statue down as she takes a hold of the microphone.

GRACIE'S BIGAM'ETERNITY PROJECT'S POPED OUTING'S BIGAME SPEECH

Gracie (bathing in eggglory despite the way too pretty statue's wings): Yea, like I feel the same about me too. Thanks for so so so too many of you puddled in the bleacher seating in the set of all of's settings. You know someaty physics says onthales whate'er is ontoxic and not at all (as whene'erized) e'ercooliffffffffffffffffffied of course, of course onto to be. HOWEVER!!!!! I am pretty promptly a prioriscened to say……..like….with whene'er's whistles operating whate'er's ifffont I'm'e'ericles all e'eround me…… sum times it feels like all of's guys are falling like..like e'erain drops on my poped out as ifffirst impersonation…..ah yes…bebridled as my own intended..sooooo cooliffffff I'd as I'm to of course of course be putting the not/notnot code to use conducting ontim'a'te'er's ont I'magic trick…ont I'm'e'ercrafting poped outing's projectiles ontaking not ne'er's night to put put put ont I'm'engine'eresearch deposited in portopotent but'e'er'd up word just ajifffffy's traffic jam ontosed well done…jerked offe'eringing bell whether or nots ifffontimatter, iffffontimetered, not not to be ont I'm'at e'er.

Crowd: We already know all of's that and we e'er all of's as iffffffully in agreement.

Gracie: Now sums may justajifffonthink to ask….LIKE…LIKE…LIKE…..WHAT'S A UNIVERSE DOING HERE ANYWAY? I mean…to scat e'er sense into some sky, just who invited stars to a priori's party? Like…like…howcome som'universions ontooled used or ontoylete'er'd's not just kidding kidding play that's playing with these parts? I mean like, after all is said and done…..just what's some universe begetting out of this…like all of'sum's onthis'd onthat. Please a prioritize me to ont I'm'explain.

Ontantrumminating all of's e'er…….egggracie's lecture e'erings churchy chimes.

(Gracie's lecture careers into her speech)

E'erummaging ifffonthin e'er Egggracie draws sum's iffffamous equations in mid-e'er.

SUM = E(PT* + tp*)…+ C……when +C =…..+ 0 = +

Gracie: No that's not enough……….+ 0 = +++++++++++++++++++(.)++++++++

Iffffinally satisfied with enough auditions to be plus'd………..

- Whenever PT c'crepresents *presentABLE tense,*
- *When tp's justense presented*

Allright enough with metaphysique calculations.. Now let's tick talk eternity.

With we as the's egggods…e'erummaging ifffonthin e'er………………………….

With weeeeee!!!!! as duh's egggodditease, meanwiley once in whiled upon. Tale headlined all'sheroblty, to whelm almighty's question, to be or not to be, of course, of course to be not not to be……s'e'erfaced as spirit facing's iffffffaçades of substanced e'er's ifffont I'm'e'er.

….

We as egggods in e'ergod's ego'daze olde not ne'er's night of a priori e'er's of being's asifffffffffff(.)fffffffffffffffacilitease.

Please apriori pardon my iffffffffrench……….

Iffflipped ont could be's coinage as I'd I'm'd ontaled onto beheaded out to sea sum'swail'd e'eresoundingdong iffffrom deeps….meanwhiley once in whiled upon all of's zeroblty to whelm almighty's question to be or not to be of course, just kidding to be kidding not of course not not to be. As we e'erg e'er'd or but e'egggear'd ontake on all of's as iffffriends to be as aved of these iffffished out salvage yards, now e'erescheduled I'm'appointments onto save…..

1.Ont…….equatione'ering's I'm'antiques.

2.Ont …….I'mengine'ering's I'm'antiques 3. E'er…..resussitationt I'm'antiques.

While we, from zoos of zeros zeroused to be zoos…… yet we with wings iffffly iffffonthin e'er, as just ajiffly juke box jargontuned, onto be linguishing……to cooliffffffy of course, of course not not to be as no just low down, cheapunk, cheapshotraumad partygirl's..iffffff….. I'dreame'ergence……I'mprovized baby he's us's……..iffffflippedoubtings meanwhile asiffffonthirsted………..on whate'er crossed as iffffontoutings…likelike….likelike…well…all for what…you ask. *To tidy up eternity*, I say…….with awsumothers orphaned by their eggs, egggathe'er'd as eggghosts at heaven's haunt's onthose not not not yet quite now, with we as whate'er wholed I mansion'd as ifffontentocracy's ifffontetiquetted above it all to be presentable awaring could be customs of not never's nights egggowns……….or else awaring nothing butte'er'd up at all ontosed well done….meanwhile…..not kidding to be kidding egg'dubb'dibb'd as stick't astoned…duh'durged iffffffossilandudstones of whate'er'sum's humslippage on bemannappeals…n'ont vanely voiced…to be ont I'm'applianced, as of course of coursed…..can opent onto be….for selfished out not not of course, of course onto believe e'er's egosumont I'mottotalized eternity's iffff'ers just as I'motto'd.

Eggrace e'ereaches for the sky as she recites the motto:

"ONT I'M'ETERNITY'S NO DUD…..Iffffe'er'd always as ifffont I'm'available, of course, of course not not to be."

Let me conclude with bell e'eringing whate'er words…… "TONIGHT'S NOT NEVE'ER'D NIGHT TWILL BE ONT I'M'AVAILED". Onthus'd I now e'erest my case.

The crowd, ontraffic jammed, e'erupts with deafening applause.

Crowd(back to egggroup ontheorized onthought): Sure thing.Yep. We believe you Gracie. Uh…like..sure *onthing*.

Gracie(egggaining could be confidence): Not kidding to be kidding……It's like when you're waiting e'eround for xmas day when the present's suposed to e'erive.

Crowd: Unhuhn…….

Gracie: Make no mistaken for e'erides crossedoubting try outs…as just ont I'm'd…ONTHERE YOU ARE……..on whene'er waits e'eround for Santa to be coming down the chimney with all of's presents tensed. And before you know it, all of's presentension's passed like becompletely outhousing the picture. All that waiting e'eround and you're just left with wrapping paper's yeste'er'dabbled in yeste'er'daze of yeste'er'dabled scatte'er'd e'ers…with you in shallow whate'er…….. iffffontantrumminating whether or not not coding's to be done about the set of all sets of the situation. Like…. Like….. (Gracie trigger fingers her pretensions quoting e'er) "Ontoxicologicallike..like"….. examined, some say that it is just kidding on the playground's toy tool used'e'er beholding onto hands. Onthe's ont I'mothe'er hand…… sum say it's sparepartegggirled whate'er's ontoxic eternity we're sadolled up with.

Well, as psylumed as iphphphphylumed as egggnations all my own….like….like….. as ontantrumminator of all ontantrumminators not for not not codifffffiable's nothing…as beaconside'erator of all of's beconside'erators….I say…..let's beget ffffffffinite count downs all of's way dancedown to pregnant zero's once upont I'm as ifffffe'eretail sold outing's wholesale e'ercraft…. as scrambled………ont I'm provised ont I'm'appointments as of course, of course not not(or not) as scheduled.

Crowd: So like?

Gracie: Sum's becommand performance by ontalented m'eternity.

Crowd: We're with you darling. Saint Gracie! Saint Grace! We're with eu darlng!!!!

Gracie: So I hope you're not just cow cuds mooing words.

Crowd: No. we're not just cow cud's mooing cowords.

Gracie: Coolest ever. So eternity as scheduled's not at all e'ercrafts of the set of all sets……justjust may…be….NOT IFFFONTOXIC……….

Crowd: AFTERALL!!!!!!!!

Gracie: Ok, so in face spirit's e'erepresentation, like…wave your wands' plast(mag)ic particlubs as waved……. and e'errepeat in just ajiffffy's e'ertight… e'ernight……. e'eright…….. after me. Gracie recites……

Gracie: WE AS DUH'S EGGGOD'S…..

Crowd: WE AS DUH'S EGGGODS…………

Gracie: OF COURSE, OF COURSE NOT NOT

Crowd: OF COURSE, OF COURSE NOT NOT

Gracie recites and then conducts plast(mag)ickly wande'er'd: WE'VE GOT DIBS TO DUB TO BE

Crowd (waving and singsonging): WE'VE GOT DIBS TO DUB TO BE

Gracie: OF COURSE ONTWISTING NEWSY IFFFFANGLES

Crowd: OF COURSE ONTWISTING NEWSY IFFFFANGLES

Gracie: ONTO BESTINCT E'EREALTY

Crowd: ONTO BESTINCT E'EREALTY

Gracie: TO BECOMMERCE A CITY OF ANGELS

Crowd: TO BECOMMERCE A CITY OF ANGELS

The second verse: AS IFFFONTWISTFULLY, ONTO THE'S NOT NOT'S ONT I'M'ANGLES, AS IFFFE'ERESE'ERECT TO BE, BRINKING TO LIFE A CITY OF ANGELS.

Once the singings as iffffonthrough Gracie checks the count down from iffffffffff( )ffffffffinity on the e'eray gun rafters. No sooner than onticipated the count way, way down approached log 1 bas 10 seconds on the could be clock….5,4,3,2,1, 0……….+

There is a blinding flash of ontransmutations with almightning'stricken'strucked in implications. Not not of coursing of coursing quakes. The traffic jam falls to it knees. Gracie stands like a statue surveying the scene with an unmistakable expression of becomprehensive supermanontensity. As the flash of the almightning strike fades, pixie dust is screen'd, falling like snow just under the rainbotic umbrella of the sky in the middle of the middle of the middle of the night on some typically when'erizoned xmas eve landscape. All of's outer housing projections have on a transcendent aspect of absolutequaintiffffity as the qualumination of the evening star simulates becomplete cooliffffication blushed out of the blue on the eternity test site horizon. To all appearances the impossible has been simulated. It is the solstice of whene'er's ontwilight at midnight's ides of e'erated now's half time in eternity.

The general arrives from the tunnel with Alex. Their aspects are strained.

General: May I speak freely sir?

Gracie: Sure, why not of course….uh not…...

General: NOONE'S COMING OUT OF THERE ALIVE SIR.

Gracie (trying to change the subject): When?

General: Well, xmas day has not e'erived as onticipated. For that it's just dead wait e'er ground. It's a magic trick of sorts but not the you're, excuse me, eu'r aft e'er. The expe'eriment seems to have taken a detour into some detouristest site not particled before on e'eradar's e'eradioactive e'erwaves. It's still the Mesozoic.

Gracie: So after all is sad undone, I'm still egggracess'd'essgraced…..

General: Afraid so sir. If I may be blunt, we hit an e'er speed bump at log minus 44 base 10'seconde'ery…limits. So like…it was not the smooth e'erector settings e'eride we had hoped for.

Gracie: So……. presentable tense, I take it, is not quite present in the way that opening presents on xmas day requires. Either that or m'ontense'er equations just don't work in onthin e'er.

General: There's no sign of the Metazoic either at the ontest probes ontense'er'd eur calculus. The moment elapsed at the end of the countdown only got as far as…

Gracie: As far as what?

General: As far as zeroblty auditioned back up to one no one's zero'd in on……..

Gracie: So no e'eresurrection to speak of.

General: No sir, just some fossil fueleeks.

Gracie: I JUST KNEW IT!!!!! So nobody budged huh? That's what happens when you let a universe into these e'ercraftest sites. (lecturing the ground) What's the matter with you people? You know how to do it. You've done it before.

Alex (covering for Gracie): That's Gracie for you folks!

Mobible: Blaspheming in all blasphemable dimensions! Chalk up another miracle for egggracie on the wanted posters at the metaphysical society.........of all of's things egggiving lectures to eggground!

Crowd: SAINT GRACIE! SAINT GRACE!!!!!!!!

Gracie (Becompletely scandalized): No! You people are just ontentraffic jams. I can't hear you. You all should be tested for crowd behavior. No matter what I do, my miracles never work the way they're supposed to...like becompletely on purpose. I just know now no matter how many magic tricks I perform I'll never can open to be of coursed. Why else be pope if I can never do such a onthing as like...onthat. I can't do this job. Mobible you're the can opener that started this; you're of course, of course not not's appliance now.

Gracie climbs off the stage and wands the pavilion traffic jam one last partition making her way to the exit.

Mobible (admonishing the crowd) All right crowd behave now....like or else..........

The Gracie statue is confused.

Statue: She's gone. What do I do?

Mobible: Stick with me darling. I can open things up for you. Sooner or later you'll be a phylum all your own.

Alex struggles helplessly through the crowd to follow Gracie's exit.

THE SCENE SHIFTS TO THE EPILOGUE.

We find sum's what ifffe'ereduced egggracie in the xmas eve scenery on her knees. She gathers pixie dust's now cove'er'd landscape which sublimates to her touch. She stands with some labor and rubs her hands together wiping away the pixie dust with some honest dirt. Xmas eve is becoming high noon on tomorrow's aftermath of what just might have been xmas day, but wasn't. Through her tears she's almost smiling out of the side of her spirit face, which smears of soil have made more phyluminescent than ever. Alex, now noble and demigodlike approaches, observing Gracie's countenance of smears with picture perfect emotion.

Gracie: What was I onthinking? Iffffffont I'm'aniffffffest alacked for whate'er's whene'er wings, while as iphylumed all alone, still I must bear the stench of not not not beingod.

Alex: And I'm iffffully haploid to agree with you my darling.

Gracie (Obliviously continuing her train of thought)I will, I will, I will have to revise my metaphysics; that's all there's to it. My studies of the y-not axis of course's coordinate system will just have to....

Gracie blows her nose with such violence that the ground trembles signs of life.

Gracie (Ontemptly sighing): Now you do it. I'm all winced out.

Gracie offers Alex a pistol. By her side is a Gracie doll with wings. She has looted it from just kidding's ontoy eternity sets in the bigames arcade.

Gracie: I looted the doll Alex: It's a toy; it can't play with itself without myself to play with it. (Gracie caresses the wings with her trigger finger). It can't play with itself without someone's else to play with itself all e'eready asifffonto the loose to play itself with itself. (Egggracie continues to caress the wings the otherwise idle I'dolled up whenever's wings)

Gracie: Wings Alex! Just kidding on the playground I can make it as iffffffffffly! You've got egggunow. Let's just like..like…. pretend. I will fly her like e'ereal egggirl through the e'er like sum assortments can open'ded e'er with wings…of course,of course…not..not…until you just like e'erelax on ontentrigger's asifffffffinger's end…of what one iffffffontasks. Of course,of course not not……….. all of's girl wars onced for all.

Making fake engine noises Gracie flies the Gracie doll just like sum's e'ercraft beheld out of sum's ont I'moving beickle window.

A shot is heard.

Gracie: Whatever happened?

Alex: I shot the ground. The one girl holocaust is over Gracie. Listen to me Gracie. I'm just about to say something that matters.

Gracie: Yes?

Alex: Not to tar and feathe'er eternity…

Gracie: Yes?

Alex: Nor to let e'er off of all of's hooks….

Gracie: Yes?

Alex: Nor n'ontoy play ground kidding ontiqe'ers…….

Gracie: Yes?

Alex: To tool use back yard sticks and stone's egggas……..

Gracie(concerned): So, whatever is this all about Alex?

Alex: I'M HEADING BACK TO THE UNIVERSE GRACIE….AND I WANT TO TAKE YOU WITH ME.

Gracie: You must be kidding in the playgrounds of some sand box Alex. So like you want to take egggracexististsongsung with you……..

Gracie sneezes with dark loud violence and drops the doll in the dirt.

Alex: Well, I like like like to ontenthink of't ontenthis way.....entaile'er'd as I'm aut ad dressed......I'm leaving sum what's second's girl war fronts behind...plus...in the gene'erous spirit of bottled moods....I'm offerringing you this engineeringing while admitontly O Q'd not fully engine'er'd.(Alex offers the bottle of gin.)

Gracie: I could be quenched of course, of course not......not.........however....but...

Alex: But what?

Gracie: Wings Alex! Like...like, juke boxed in on justajifffy jargon's.... whene'er'swings my dear dumpt darling. Wait up on eur self why don't I.........did you just pop the question or what?

Alex: Uh yea, I think I just popped out the question...........

Gracie: Onthroned onto my wings always in waiting...

Alex: For what?

Gracie: To be buzz'd by eternity

Alex: Look Gracie, even if this eternity is sum whate'er's iffffontoxic dud, there's always still not nothing to be done with it. God or no god, maybe even the gods have to take their chances.

Gracie (getting ahead of Alex): So did you just like pop the question or not.........

Alex (thinking ahead): Yes! To start a party girl's egggcellerator business...with eu....

Gracie: The egg cell? Onto to be dyployed.......

Alex: Eggguests. Here let me diagram it with eu, by eu and for eu. My idea is to toilet train the tool used universe to be the hero that saves the girl.

Gracie: But who's the girl Alex?

Alex (seeing wet light): You are Gracie. You're just like the girl. You're the girl Gracie. I'm quite sure that...that....that you're the girl...that's all there's to it.

Gracie (Studying Alex for signs of really meaning it) Can I still have that phylum all my own? And my wings. What about my wings?

Alex (changing the subject): Wing's? What about the bottle Gracie.(Alex holds up the bottle of gin with a cork screw)

Gracie (struglinked to just a jiffy's juke box): Onthale's whate'ers on the'swings into indeed my dear dumpt darling..... beconsequenced to self-proceed.....(trying to break away)

Alex(desperate): Gracie, I will, I will, I will ont I'make studied justajiffffffy juke boxsinging's jargon iffffffffff(.)ffffffffffffffffff

Gracie (Almost tempted): Iffffffffff......Tell you what, *IFFFFFFFFFF(.)FFFFFFFFFALL GOESWELL,* I'll meet you at the bridge. Meanwhile I need my metaphysics to solve whatever's wholegggraileft over. Bye bye my favorite dear dumped darling, bye bye for NOW. I really have to hurry for my appointment....

As the music begins again, Gracie starts up the mountain.

Alex: With what egggracie?

Gracie: With my wings. I just know they're must be'd waiting for me.

Alex: Where?

GRACIE'S LAST PHYZZLED LECTURE OF THE OPERA

Gracie: It's when Alex, like whenever…..

Gracie's middle ontrigger finger draws a d'iffffferontical ont I'm'equation into the wind. The storm is brewing now and she finally gives up onthreads of whatever it was ont I'm'equations wanted posters wanted to be said.

This is the equation for presentable tense plus tense presented which egggracie attempts to write into the storm…..of onthin e'er:

$$E = PT + tp + + + + + (\ )++++++++$$

Gracie: ………..Oh never mind.

But Alex is following from below.

Alex: I brought the bottle Gracie!

Gracie turns around to scream upwind into the teeth of the storm.

Gracie: My dear dumped darling. I need someone who's got sum could be's can opener…..

Alex: I think a corkscrew will do it Gracie.

Gracie (Gracie thinks): No. You can't open e'er without a can opener Alex. Your universe should have told you that.

The storm brings Gracie to the top of the mountain with Alex underneath and just behind.

Alex (yodeling his first notes of the opera): Gracie!!!! I brought the bottle!!!

All at once the storm recedes as Gracie's spirit faces the setting's sunny day.

Alex (yodeling desperately) GRACIE! I BROUGHT THE BOTTLE!!!!!!

Having searched for her wings in mid e'er Gracie turns to Alex as she sings her final aria of the opera:

OF COURSE..OF COURSE…NOT…NOT…….

OF COURSE..OF COURSE…NOT NOT

(spoken) oh yea, like ….like……..like….I keep forgetting……

OF COURSE, OF COURSE NOT NOT TO BE!!!!

With the final cadence Gracie reaches past the bottle to Alex's clean hand that is waiting to drag her away from the could be cliff's e'erprecipice and back into the shadows hiding from the setting sunny day's bigstar.

THE SCREEN PLAY ENDS HERE.

8. SO LIKE WHAT HAPPENED IN THIS PLAY?

Well after the overture of 1.2 billion years of music we find such a thing as egggracie, dreame'ergentrified just standing on sum's could be cliff that overlooks to be. Ifffreaked out as she is at having won the Miss Eternity Pageant over runnerup reality, begetting way too pretty way too fast for the speed of enlightenment to be keep up. Asiffffffreaked out as such, she precipitates the Girl War. Eggguilty and alibless as a result of the war, she can't be alive but she doesn't want to be dead either. So that's how Alex finds her always dying to be dying and meanwhile uncovering egggracie's spine ontingling workouts out of meaty physics onto ont I'metaphysic's onthin e'er. Alex, in his observatory, has spotted her with his becombination teleoscope and telescope. She is on the bridge over the river and Alex runs right over to be the hero that saves the girl. But the timing's bad.....just when it's way too embarrassing for her to be saved. So instead egggracie explains her metaphysics to both Alex and his telescope((hat reads lips) and then takes Alex on e'erides in the carnival, e'erides that are just dying to be dying(but meanwhile not be dead). Of special note, it should be mentioned here that, suspended with Alex for a moment's silhouette atop the Ferris Wheel, Gracie's hairdo explodes into a rainbotique display. Once the carnival rides are over Gracie disappears. Alex stalks her to the saloon where Alex learns that 1. Gracie drinks gin. 2. Gracie really did win the Miss Eternity Pageant over runnerup reality. So Alex heads for the cathedral where the chimes announce that Gracie's in the building. Alex finds Egggracie admiring herself(taking selfies) on the cross. As the music shifts from 1500 to 1750 to 1955 Alex sees Gracie climbing down off the cross to perform her usual sway dance routine plus singing as soloist with the Mesozoic chorus. Once Gracie's lost in the final traffic jam out of the building, Alex's heroic journey disappears for a few scenes as Mobible, the former kitchen applicance(can opener) is scened out and about soliciting for votes for Felix to be voted back as pope. But things get metaphysically s'e'erious when we find that Felix plans on being elected pope, to include, this time e'eround, as poped out, becoming sumassortmentions egggod. Things get theologically messy when the general(ont I'militarily) drags Mobible out to the beach where the investimented Felix voters are landing at the beach head. Mobible does succeed in turning the invasion party around. Accomplishing this maneuver, Mobible's can opene'er ontentelligence has second thoughts about Felix as pope becoming somegggod. Deciding that Gracie should be pope instead, the general and Mobible leave the beach. Meanwhile Bishop Speck arrives at Gracie's motel cemetary where Gracie is the Janitor having been responsible for the Girl War that was accredited for all of's Girl War dead that counted. Well, Bishop Speck brings the apple that reminds Gracie just how dead or extinct or impossible Speck expects her to be. It becomes pretty obvious by the body language as sphinctered to the tongues that there's a long history between these two egggoing back to kindergarden....which Bishop Speck still won't let Gracie egggraduate out of. With the battle for the holocaust competition lost and eternity taken, the scene ends with Gracie not sure if she can pull off her eternity test site experiment(I'll explain later). Meanwhile Alex, searching for Gracie, finds the abandoned holocaust where Egggracie's haploid ont I'm'e'erelation works as janitor. Learning the janitorial history of the Girl War Alex heads across the country club for Gracie's motel back lot cinematic kept under the lights in the dark rooms.. Meeting again, Gracie and Alex discuss the battlegrounds of what this opera's all about. When it comes to Gracie, Alex decides once and for all 1. To salvage egggracie from her eggguilt for the Girl Wars. 2. To critique egggracie's ontrophickly presentable metaphysics with his cosmic equations backed up by lenses. Well, all hell breaks loose with Gracie doing her broom dance and eventually showing off the kissing coffin where Gracie used to work the Mesozoic selling kisses. Sure enough it's in the kissing coffin where Alex finally gets his haploid kiss with egggracie's haploidolled up just a jifffy's ont I'm'egggirlipse'ervice. Just then Mobible arrives with his new sign promoterizing votes for Gracie to be pope. This event precipitates a whole new testament for the opera'script. Alex and Gracie plan to head back to the cathedral to attend the night's election rally for Felix with Gracie back up on the cross. We see Egggracie rummaging in her ontool toy box to take out her trusted pompom power tools. As Alex leaves the scenery Gracie can be seen practicing her pompom cheerleader routine. That night….. flood lights are on the cathedral entrance as Alex and Gracie arrive. Lara, a reporter, interviews Gracie as a confrontation ensues with some down and outer Gracie fans. Once Gracie dishevels and get's waltzed allove'er's place by Alex, a moment of silence is observed to clock the cosmos in just what may be this particular song and dance's dud eternity. Up on the cross we find Gracie rejecting her usual role as front man for Felix and taking off on her own with a light show announcing once and for all time that it's Gracie, not Felix, that is the light bulb of the world. After a few eggglitches in the light show, egggracie's audition to be pope achieves self-evident success. So much so that when Gracie leaves the cathedral the kiss she throws to the traffic jam is ontenteasily iffffe'ereceived by every cheek in the building. With everyone beholding to their cheek, Egggracie steps out the cathedral door in what can only be described, at least for the moment, as ont I'metaphysical ontriumph. The next morning not never's news announces Gracie as pope. Noone knows just how she won but……..well actually Mobible does know how she won. As the new pope, Gracie makes requests to the general and to Alex and has them leave so she can make a business deal with Mobible. Mobible's plan is to start up a new egggift shoppe e'ereligion with Egggracie's tale served as the head of it. Next thing you know, we see Gracie looking demurely over her dark glasses as she climbs with Alex back into the same olde carnival as when they met some scenes before. But this time on the , the asifffffffun rides……they end up at the top of the Ferris Wheel. What happens is just this. Gracie overdoes her halo's light display as rainbow'down to puddles swamped all over the carnival for janitors to mop up. Never was heaventilation's rainbowedown so egggutterly humiliated. Later that evening on the terrace, sipping gin just like champagne, gracie admits her all cringed out plans for her eternity test site experiment ever since she's now the pope. It is on this terrace half way between the toilet and the sky that Alex finally pops the question….for the first but not the last time. Making sure Alex absolutely adores her, Egggracie heads for the final scene at the eternity test site. Egge'er'd up as the abandoned holocaust bunker is, it's pretty obvious that a new level of ontechnical sophistication has been achieved. Pretty soon we see gracie on stage, engaged in crowd control 1. Just wondering why anybody ever bothers with universes 2. Iffffe'ereciting e'eresurrection of a city of angels. What happens is there's this count down from iffffe'er's ifffffffinity to e'eright now's zero'd in on just presented tense....heaventilating hope for...for...like iffffe'eresurrected e'eresults. Once nothing happens; no one's resurrection resurrects egggracie's doubts about her metaphysics, the wholegggrailaunch'd iffffe'erocket show ontentail spins to a head that exits Gracie(now Saint Grace) from the crowded scene to find egggracie outside 'iffffonthin e'er' egggroveling in the dirt. As Gracie contemplates revisions in her metaphysics, Alex pops the question once again. " I'm heading back to the universe egggracie and I want to take you with me." Well all this time egggracie has been harboring two cringed secret hopes. 1. To have a phylum all her own. 2. To have some wings to match her hairdo. Well with her brand new metaphysics now iffffffffledging(just ont I'moments olde) egggracie all at once just now's egggressive to begetting onto the ont I'm'at e'er'd horn part where all of this play's playground's been just kidding to be kidding. Never doubting that, for all her iffffffailed big time magic tricks, that like eternity just still must be, after all is sad undone, uploadable for whate'er iffffont I'm'egggrabs. Iffffledged as egggrace just ajifffly ont I'musual is, Egggracie's off to climb the clouds into the could be clearing where, of course, of course not not, she onticipates that whene'er's wings just must be waiting. Well, sceptical as usual's calculuste'er'd Alex….. does follow her up the mountain and at the summit just before she ontakes her last I'dives, he offers her a cork screw'd bottle full of gin. Egggracie turns and reaches past the bottle to the hand that Alex has been saving to pull Grace back into the universe just after Gracie's final lyrics have been screamed; OF COURSE, OF COURSE, NOT NOT TO BE!!!!!!! Well whether eternity's up for iffffe'eregggrabs or not, that's about as much as this story board can ont I'must e'er. Meanwhile that's about as little that can be said about this opera without just under onte'erestimating it in as iffffffffffffff(.)ffffffffffffonthin e'er.

END OF THE COULD BE CARTOON OF THIS BOOK TO PLAY WITH MUSIC. Ontake you're pick just what to read. But hey! FOR ALL OF'S JUST ONTOO MUCH THAT YOU'VE READ without the music……The music tells the story without being not not bothe'er'd by the words.

343